PR441 PAU.

Breaking and Remaking

Breaking
and
Remaking

Aesthetic Practice in England, 1700–1820

Ronald Paulson

RUTGERS UNIVERSITY PRESS

New Brunswick and London

Publication of this book has been supported, in part, by a grant from the National Endowment for the Humanities, a federally funded agency.

Library of Congress Cataloging-in-Publication Data
Paulson, Ronald.
   Breaking and remaking : aesthetic practice in England, 1700–1820 /
Ronald Paulson.
     p. cm.
   Bibliography: p.
   Includes index.
   ISBN 0-8135-1439-8 (cloth)   ISBN 0-8135-1440-1 (pbk.)
   1. Arts—England—History—18th century. 2. Arts—England—
History—19th century. 3. Aesthetics, British—18th century.
4. Aesthetics, British—19th century. I. Title.
BH221.G72P38   1989
700′.1—dc19   89-30375
                                                  CIP

British Cataloging-in-Publication information available

NYMPHA SACRI REGINA LACUS

Contents

LIST OF ILLUSTRATIONS   ix

ACKNOWLEDGMENTS   xiii

PART I

1. THE AESTHETICS OF ICONOCLASM: SWIFT AND GRAY   1
   Introduction: The Aesthetics of Making   1
   English Iconoclasm   14
   "Suppose me dead": Swift's Verses *and Gray's* Elegy   35

2. THE AESTHETICS OF GEORGIC RENEWAL: POPE   48
   Georgic Farming and Ovidian Metamorphosis   48
   The Unabused Image of Memory   66
   Aestheticizing the Stigma   76
   The Popean Other   87

3. THE AESTHETICS OF REVOLUTION/RESTORATION: BYRON AND
   WORDSWORTH   94
   The Body Politic of Lords Rochester and Byron   94
   The Aesthetics of Gleaning in Don Juan   114
   Wordsworthian Restoration   134

PART II

4. THE AESTHETICS OF MODERNITY: HOGARTH   149
   The Sleeping Congregation   149
   Remaking the Classical Canon   156

Feminizing the Hero   168
The "Love of Pursuit"   192

5. THE AESTHETICS OF MOURNING: WRIGHT AND ROUBILIAC   203
   The Empty Tomb   203
   The Woman on the Tombstone   230

6. THE AESTHETICS OF POSSESSION: REYNOLDS, STUBBS,
   CONSTABLE, AND OTHERS   246
   Labor Aestheticized—Painting Possessed   246
   Portrait and Landscape: Zoffany and Gainsborough   259
   Reynolds's Mrs. Abington as Miss Prue   277
   Stubbs's Hambletonian   297
   Constable's White Horse   317

NOTES   331

INDEX   357

List of Illustrations

1. Richard Bentley, Jr., Illustration for Gray's *Elegy*, engraved by Charles Grignion, from *The Poems of Thomas Gray* (Strawberry Hill, 1753).   21
2. William Hogarth, *The Sleeping Congregation* (1736), engraving.   150
3. Hogarth, *The Analysis of Beauty*, Plate 1 (1753), engraving.   157
4. Hogarth, *The Analysis of Beauty*, Plate 2 (1753), engraving.   164
5. Hogarth, *Strolling Actresses Dressing in a Barn* (1738), engraving.   166
6. Hogarth, *The Great Seal of England* (1728), engraving on silver. Salver, London, Victoria and Albert Museum; print, private collection.   171
7. Paulo de Mattheis, *The Judgment of Hercules*, title page of Shaftesbury's *Notion of the . . . Judgment of Hercules* (London, 1713).   173
8. Hogarth, *A Harlot's Progress* (1732), Plate 1, engraving.   174
9. Hogarth, *The Beggar's Opera* (1728), painting. Farmington, Connecticut, Lewis-Walpole Library, Yale University.   176
10. Hogarth, *The Beggar's Opera* (1729), painting. New Haven, Yale Center for British Art, Paul Mellon Fund.   177
11. Hogarth, *A Harlot's Progress* (1732), Plate 3, engraving.   178

12. Albrecht Dürer, *The Visitation,* woodcut from the *Life of the Virgin* (1511). New York, Metropolitan Museum of Art, Rogers Fund, 1918 (18.65.15).   179
13. Dürer, *The Annunciation,* woodcut from the *Life of the Virgin* (1511). New York, Metropolitan Museum of Art, Rogers Fund, 1918 (18.65.16).   180
14. Hogarth, *Boys Peeping at Nature* (1731), engraving.   181
15. Hogarth, *A Rake's Progress* (1735), Plate 2, engraving.   182
16. Hogarth, *A Rake's Progress* (1735), Plate 4, engraving.   183
17. Hogarth, *Scene from Shakespeare's 'The Tempest'* (c. 1736), painting. Reproduced by permission of Lord St. Oswald and the National Trust.   185
18. Hogarth, *The Distrest Poet* (1736), engraving.   186
19. Hogarth, *The Enraged Musician* (1741), engraving.   187
20. Hogarth, *Satan, Sin, and Death* (c. 1736), painting. London, Tate Gallery.   189
21. Joseph Wright of Derby, *The Blacksmith's Forge* (1771), painting. New Haven, Yale Center for British Art, Paul Mellon Fund.   204
22. Wright, *Brooke Boothby* (1780–81), painting. London, Tate Gallery.   207
23. Wright, *Miravan Opening the Tomb of His Ancestors* (1771), painting. City of Derby Art Gallery.   209
24. Hogarth, *Tailpiece, or The Bathos* (1764), engraving.   213
25. Wright, *An Experiment with an Air Pump* (1767–68), painting. London, National Gallery.   223
26. Wright, *An Academy by Lamplight* (1768–69), painting. New Haven, Yale Center for British Art, Paul Mellon Fund.   225
27. Angelica Kauffmann, *Cleopatra Decorating the Tomb of Mark Antony* (R.A. 1770), painting. Burghley House Collection. Photo, Courtauld Institute of Art.   228
28. Peter Scheemakers, Monument to Shakespeare (1740), sculpture. London, Westminster Abbey. Photo © Warburg Institute.   232
29. Louis-François Roubiliac, Monument to Lady Elizabeth Nightingale (1761), sculpture. London, Westminster Abbey. Photo © Warburg Institute.   234
30. Roubiliac, Monument to John, Duke of Argyle (1745–49), sculpture. London, Westminster Abbey. Photo © Warburg Institute.   236

31. Roubiliac, Monument to George Lynn (1758), sculpture. Southwick, Northants. Photo, Courtauld Institute of Art.   241

32. Roubiliac, Monument to Richard Boyle, Viscount Shannon (after 1755), sculpture. Walton-on-Thames. Photo, Courtauld Institute of Art.   242

33. Roubiliac, Hargrave Monument (1757), sculpture. Westminster Abbey. Photo © Warburg Institute.   243

34. Thomas Rowlandson, *A Statuary Yard* (1780s), drawing. Oxford, Ashmolean Museum.   262

35. Johann Zoffany, *The Sharp Family* (1779–81), painting. London, National Portrait Gallery. Reproduced courtesy of C.G.M. Lloyd-Baker, Esq.   264

36. Thomas Gainsborough, *The Harvest Wagon* (1767), painting. Barber Institute of Fine Arts, University of Birmingham.   272

37. Gainsborough, Copy of Rubens's *Deposition*, painting. Private collection, presently on loan to the Ashmolean Museum.   273

38. Gainsborough, *Classical Landscape* (1780s), painting. Philadelphia Museum of Art, John Howard McFadden Collection.   277

39. Sir Joshua Reynolds, *Mrs. Abington as Miss Prue* (1771), painting. New Haven, Yale Center for British Art, Paul Mellon Fund.   280

40. Reynolds, *Theophila Palmer Reading* (1771), painting. Private collection.   282

41. Reynolds, *Mrs. Abington as the Comic Muse* (1768; rev. 1773), painting. National Trust, Waddesden Manor, Buckinghamshire. Photo, Courtauld Institute of Art.   284

42. George Stubbs, *Hambletonian, Rubbing Down* (1808), painting. National Trust, Mount Stewart. Photo, Tate Gallery, London.   297

43. Stubbs, *Gimcrack* (c. 1765), painting. Newmarket, the Stewards of the Jockey Club.   300

44. Stubbs, *A Lion Attacking a Horse* (1762), painting. New Haven, Yale Center for British Art, Paul Mellon Fund.   304

45. Stubbs, *John and Sophia Musters Riding at Colwick Hall* (1777), painting. Private collection. Photo, Tate Gallery, London.   310

46. Stubbs, *Soldiers of the 10th Light Dragoons* (1793),
     painting. Reproduced by gracious permission of Her
     Majesty the Queen. Photo, Tate Gallery, London.   311
47. Stubbs, *The Reapers* (1795), enamel on Wedgwood
     biscuit. New Haven, Yale Center for British Art,
     Paul Mellon Fund.   314
48. John Constable, *The White Horse* (1819), painting. Photo
     © The Frick Collection, New York.   318
49. Constable, *The Leaping Horse* (1827), painting. London,
     Royal Academy of Arts.   321

Acknowledgments

To describe the aims of this book is to explain its origins. In particular it grew out of a lecture called "The Aesthetics of Mourning" which I delivered for Ralph Cohen's series on Aesthetic Principles in Eighteenth-Century England at the William Andrews Clark Memorial Library in 1982 (published in Cohen's *Studies in Eighteenth-Century British Art and Aesthetics,* Berkeley and Los Angeles, 1985, pp. 148–81). In another sense it picks up the thread from my earlier books *Popular and Polite Art in the Age of Hogarth and Fielding* (Notre Dame, 1979) and *Representations of Revolution* (New Haven, 1983) which addressed the question of how unacceptable materials are dealt with by polite writers and artists.

Besides "The Aesthetics of Mourning," other parts of this book were previously published in a different form. The Pope chapter goes back the furthest in time, to an essay called "Satire, Poetry, and Pope," in *English Satire* by Leland H. Carlson and Ronald Paulson (Los Angeles, 1972). The material has been largely reworked, but the basic thesis about Pope has not changed. The "English Iconoclasm" section (the second part of my first chapter) first appeared as "English Iconoclasm in the Eighteenth Century," in *Space, Time, Image, Sign,* ed. James A. W. Heffernan (New York, 1987), pp. 41–56; "Stubbs's Hambletonian" section (Chapter 6) as "*Hambletonian, Rubbing Down:* George Stubbs and English Society," *Raritan,* 4 (1982), 22–43; and part of the last section of Chapter 6 as "From White Horse to Leaping Horse: The Landscapes of Constable and Ruisdael," *Bennington Review,* 14 (1982), 67–75.

It is a pleasure to name a few of the works that set me thinking along the lines taken in this book and that particularly helped me as I wrote it: Carole Fabricant's *Swift's Landscape* (Baltimore, 1982); Frances Ferguson's essay, "The Rhetoric of Entitlement and the Politics of the Sublime," and other parts of her forthcoming book, *Solitude and the Sublime: The Aesthetics of Individualism;* Ann Kibbey, *The Interpretation of Material Shapes in Puritanism: A Study of Rhetoric, Prejudice, and Violence* (Cambridge, 1986); Peter Sacks, *The English Elegy: Studies in the Genre from Spenser to Yeats* (Baltimore, 1985); and Elaine Scarry, *The Body in Pain: The Making and Unmaking of the World* (New York, 1985). My student Joshua Scodel's Yale University dissertation, "Lapidary Texts: The English Poetic Epitaph from Jonson to Pope" (1985), on the epitaphic tradition, made it unnecessary to say very much on that subject. My particular thanks are to Ralph Cohen and Frances Ferguson, who read the whole manuscript and offered valuable suggestions that are, I hope, reflected in the final product; and to Brian Allen, without whom the photographs in this volume would never have been gathered.

Finally, I wish to thank the John Simon Guggenheim Foundation for a fellowship for 1986–87 which freed me from teaching; the Rockefeller Foundation for a study fellowship at the Villa Serbelloni, summer 1987, to complete the manuscript; and The Johns Hopkins University for supporting a sabbatical in that year.

Part I

Chapter 1

The Aesthetics of Iconoclasm: Swift and Gray

INTRODUCTION: THE AESTHETICS OF MAKING

The branch of philosophy called aesthetics asks such questions as: What is the beautiful?[1] How does the beautiful relate to other areas such as morality, permanence or flux, or to its antitheses the ugly, grotesque, and deformed? How does the beautiful in art relate to— compare with—the beautiful in nature? English aesthetics in the eighteenth century consisted of a succession of theories promulgated by the third Earl of Shaftesbury, Joseph Addison, William Hogarth, Edmund Burke, Richard Payne Knight, and Uvedale Price which focused on the response of a spectator; all, even with qualifications Hogarth, celebrated nature as the primary object of this response, the art object as secondary. The problem they addressed was how to extend the sense of the beautiful to certain natural objects that were not ordinarily considered beautiful—indeed, how to explain as aesthetic those experiences and objects that deviated from the beautiful. One way was to apply a second term, the great (or later sublime); and then, to explain phenomena that fitted neither category, Addison added a third term, the uncommon or novel (which later came to be called the picturesque). In these terms, the spectator feels beauty looking at a hill or stream, sublimity standing before a mountain or ocean, and the picturesque standing before a cottage overrun with untended vines. Art in a poem or painting tries to copy nature, the stimulus to this experience, but necessarily remains secondary.

If one line of affective theory sought to find names for aesthetic qualities inferred from their impact on the spectator, another sought to explain and understand the nature of critical judgment, the special faculty of aesthetic apprehension called taste, which was capable of appreciating the phenomenon. One reified a spectator, the other a critic or connoisseur who—as Jonathan Swift noted in the "Digression on Critics" in *A Tale of a Tub* (1704)—by either pointing out beauties or censuring faults in the art object, shows the ordinary spectator that a hill is beautiful, a mountain sublime, and a vine-covered cottage picturesque.

For Addison in his *Spectator* papers on the "Pleasures of the Imagination" (1712), taste was simply the capacity to discern these qualities, but for Shaftesbury (writing in his *Characteristics* of 1709) the capacity for "good taste" was to be found only in certain men. Taste was an aristocratic faculty, dominated by judgment, which made distinctions; the plebeian fancy made random connections and unwarranted leaps—it blurred differences. Taste required the disinterestedness gained by distance, conferred by retirement in the country surrounded by ancient texts, and authorized by ownership of landed property: the same criteria Shaftesbury required for the classical republican (or civic humanist) ideal of service to the state.[2]

Various consequences follow from Shaftesbury's "country" position (versus Addison's "city"): Shaftesbury is describing a patron (who is also a connoisseur and civic leader) and an elitist notion of the artistic transaction. If aristocratic disinterestedness emerges as the characteristic of the aesthetic attitude, beauty comes to equal order, which equals virtue, and the ability to discern this order equals a "moral sense" in the "inward eye" of the aristocratic gentleman who is capable of having an eye that can perceive harmony in both aesthetic and moral forms. "Taste," says Shaftesbury, "is a judgment of what is harmonious and proportionable" and therefore "agreeable and good."[3] A concealed agenda of Shaftesbury's theory, a politics masquerading as an aesthetics, was the expression of an ideal social order, a Whiggish one, in both form and content. The area of chaos and uncontrol which came to be called the sublime, let alone the playful and subversive picturesque, lacked the disinterest, which we may interpret as framing, required of the aesthetic experience.

My intention is to complement the general thrust of aesthetic theory in the eighteenth century in two ways: first by looking less at the theory of aesthetics than at the principles embodied in the practice of selected writers and graphic artists, and so to analyze the artist rather than the patron or connoisseur. Second by supplementing the spectator-oriented categories of this theory—sublime, beautiful, and picturesque—with categories oriented toward the artist and the object of his making. My emphasis is on making, for I deviate also from Shaftesbury and the main tradition of Renaissance art by stressing the labor of the so-called mechanic process of making as opposed to the clean-handed detachment of the artist who invents the idea, outlines the *disegno,* and leaves the sweaty execution to an assistant—as Shaftesbury "invented" his design for the "Judgment of Hercules," intended for the frontispiece of his treatise on history painting, and left its execution in paint to Paulo de Mattheis and in engraving to Simon Gribelin.[4]

What characterized the tradition of civic humanist aesthetics was the absence of material art objects. The position of the actually made object was usurped in this utopian theory by ideal hypotheses such as the Shaftesburyian Judgment of Hercules. In the case of Jonathan Richardson, monochrome engravings of Italian Renaissance paintings served as the basis for his influential post-Shaftesburyian theorizing. The primary qualities of the originals reached him only through the reports of his son Jonathan Jr., who actually visited Italy. Hogarth—who stands apart from this tradition—satirized George Turnbull's *Treatise upon Ancient Painting* (1740), a book that based its generalizations on paintings that had not survived antiquity except in verbal descriptions by ancient writers.[5] Theory from the founding of the Royal Academy (1768) was by theorist-painters: Sir Joshua Reynolds (the first P.R.A.), James Barry, Henry Fuseli, and Benjamin Robert Haydon. Their theories are fascinating to read because they are largely based on Idea and Ideal, which in practice meant memories of past glories. For all these theorists surviving antique sculptures, often fragments or copies, served as substitutes for paintings, significantly without the primary characteristics of paintings.

The paintings of Reynolds, Barry, and Fuseli were at best interesting violations of the principles laid down in their writings, at worst travesties of those principles. The contemporary paintings influenced by their theories were the heroic figure compositions, the so-called history paintings, of Benjamin West, James Northcote, George Romney, and the artists of Boydell's Shakespeare Gallery. But the English paintings of the period which we value are the theoretically humble portraits (of Reynolds and Thomas Gainsborough) and landscapes (of Gainsborough, J. M. W. Turner, and John Constable). In short, these theoretical writings amounted to an attempt to control the direction of English art and turn it into a tradition dominated by ideas, words, and Whig patriotism which in practice represented the ruling elite and which eked out its most enduring graphic progeny in sculpture, in the grotesque Westminster Abbey tombs of James Wolfe, Charles James Fox, and William Pitt the Younger.

A great deal of theory, often brilliant, has been written in the last fifteen years on the sublime (by Bloom, Weiskel, Hertz, Ferguson).[6] I have worked out a complementary vocabulary, one based on practice rather than theory (or the poet's lip service to theory) and seen from the perspective of the maker rather than the spectator, but hardly excluding the latter, who of course remains a necessary part of the transaction.

I also propose to deviate from the current practice of regarding the figures of this period from the perspective of the next generation in France or Germany. Thus, whereas it is illuminating in certain important ways to see Burke essentially through the works of Kant, I see him from the other direction, as responding to the positions of his precursors, Addison, Shaftesbury, and (in particular) Hogarth. In the same way, I regard William Collins and Thomas Gray from the direction of Pope and Swift rather than in retrospect from William Wordsworth, or even (the central figure from which many post-Derrida, post-de Man critics now regard the eighteenth century), Rousseau.

I begin with the plight of the artist who is aware of his own secondariness in relation to the beauty or sublimity of nature and must nevertheless produce *art* objects. The first question, in England at least, is how to make an art object when the unmade, the natural object is to be preferred. Another question is how to keep the object from being too much "made."

We must take care to distinguish an aesthetics from aestheticizing. Both of these are my subject. I refer to an *aesthetics* of regeneration (or renewal) or of iconoclasm, but to the *aestheticizing* of some unlikely object, hitherto off limits to the artist. A mountain is just an impassable rocky obstacle until it is aestheticized, made an aesthetic object, by calling it great or sublime. It is transformed by practice and by theory (not necessarily in that order) and then by custom. In short, something can be aestheticized by *calling* it sublime, as well as by calling it beautiful. The aim of Hogarth's aesthetics (in his *Analysis of Beauty*, 1753) was to extend the "beautiful" to include such contemporary human-produced objects as candlesticks and corsets, or (implicitly) one of his own mass-produced engravings.

But what if the object is merely ugly? The cases I shall be concerned with include not only stigmas such as ugliness or deformity but also dubious or liminal categories such as politics and property. The last serves in both capacities: It is the property aspect of something (its utility) which, according to aestheticians from Shaftesbury to Kant, has to be elided before the spectator can become disinterested, before the object or phenomenon can be aesthetic; and so dispossession becomes a procedure for aestheticizing any object, including the art work itself. (The Shaftesburyian man of good taste, however, is rendered capable of having taste by the ownership of property that, by precluding the need for labor, confers on him disinterestedness.)

The procedure that is employed to bring about this transformation of the stigmatic can be called an aesthetics, for example of farming, which is itself aestheticized into gardening by removing *use*. The principle is to work, cultivate, enclose, and improve on *what is there,* as if it were fallen nature—in Locke's terms in his *Second Treatise on Government* a waste or common area.

I focus on a specific time and place, England from the Restoration to the aftermath of the French Revolution. The historical fact that determined the aims and practice of the poets at the beginning of this period, Swift and Alexander Pope, and the painter Hogarth, was restoration after civil war; and at the other end of the century, with Lord Byron and Wordsworth, revolution followed by disillusionment and counterrevolution: a sequence from restoration to revolution to restoration again, celebrated as a series of aesthetic experiences. The terms revolution and restoration of the third chapter replay the iconoclasm and renewal of the first two chapters.

I present this as a series of mutations, one aesthetic practice growing out of another. Iconoclasm is a breaking that either leaves the idol broken or reconstitutes it as a common utensil: the statue of George III is broken by the American revolutionaries and melted down into ammunition with which to fight the British. But the utensil, becoming as a result of the iconoclastic process estranged from its original purpose, is more symbolically than morally useful: it has had a kind of disinterestedness conferred upon it.[7]

Georgic regeneration, in plain words an aesthetics of farming, is Pope's way of dealing with the shards, the low and commonplace, the seat cushions and pig troughs, when, as a Roman Catholic in England, he obviously cannot write about the vestments and triptychs out of which they were hammered. Making use of what is, and making something consciously artful out of it, is the georgic way.

But already in Pope's later work the satiric mode has turned mock-elegiac—for the idol that was broken, for the vestments and triptychs before they became shards and debris, or worse were turned into duncical reconstructions. In the next generation satire has turned genuinely elegiac, but no longer for the Roman Catholic idolatry but for absence as absence. The nostalgic continental, classical heroic imagery—the spiritual world—is now a ghost world, specifically populated by the (English) dead, and indicating only loss. If the first stage is breaking, the next is mourning the absence left behind, or literally taking the form that was *not* iconoclasted, for example funerary sculpture, and making it a model for a poetry and art of memory.

Thus the poet or painter fills the emptiness, loss, and death with possession: the possession of memory, the possessions of various sorts that fill the gap, the property that is made up of landscape and other people. Possession, in short, is one way of coping with loss-by-breakage: we possess a simulacrum of the lost, of antique statues or "old master" paintings—above all, portraits of a lost loved one, a lost self, or an elusive desired object. Another way is by what I call the aesthetics of modernity, which takes off from the quarrel of the Ancients and Moderns, employing as areas of concern the contingent and contemporary (those candlesticks and corsets), including possession, which both problematizes property itself and deals with other objects as if they were possessions.

With the French Revolution at the end of the century we come full circle, back to iconoclasm by way of property, primogeniture, and the idols of church and state. There are so many ways of regarding this historical phase in England (and I have written a book that deals with the subject from the direction of such conventional aesthetic categories as the sublime)[8] that I can select only an early stage, Wordsworth's *Lyrical Ballads,* and the final stage, post-1793 (post-1815, for Byron and Wordsworth), of seeking ways to restore the loss once again. Wordsworth first strips down poetry to the broken, low, commonplace ("break" and "level" being key words)—idiot boys, leech-gatherers, Michael's ruined sheepfold—but then has to do secondary revision on this thing, adding (one by one) a poetic consciousness, superstition, and imagination to accomplish an act of recovery or (to use his own words) "restoration" or "recompense," until he has repressed the original, inherent meaning of the person or the "spot of time." By the writing of *The Prelude*—let alone *The Excursion*—he has shifted to another mode of poetry, one devoted to restoration rather than revolution, that is, parallel with the political disillusionment and counterrevolution.

We might say that the period was one in which Greco-Roman male and female bodies (carried straight down from classical art through the Renaissance) were being replaced as the ideal of beauty by various other objects: by nature, for a start, sublime and picturesque landscapes; but also by ugly and stigmatized objects, and modern, contemporary, and plebeian (or subculture) ones as well. Any period, of course, to a lesser or greater degree requires "secularization," "demythologizing," and the absorption of unassimilated materials. Transgression, iconoclasm, property, and subculture are by no means new terms. Part of my approach is to test these terms against their historical and literary referents: iconoclasm and property were extant categories in the eighteenth century, the first vestigial and the second on the rise—and the popularly held assumptions of the Englishman Locke complement the traditional school-taught literary assumptions of the Roman Virgil or Horace. The thing corresponding to the modern terms of transgression and subculture, if not the word itself, existed in the most immediate way.

As my proposed categories suggest, I believe that the modes of making respond to the facts of history or seek out literary, largely classical but also Christian, prototypes that represent history. Thus one of the central issues of the practical aesthetics of this period is how to cope with past disaster and the possible return of disaster—a feared instability, a mentality of iconoclasm and the empty spaces and deterrants to painting it fostered. Another is how to cope with the "ugly" or the transgressive, the uncomfortable materials thrown up by that bad time: not only rebellion itself (overturning, radical change, and debasement of authority), but regicide, iconoclasm, and too much religious enthusiasm; an excess of freedom as well as other "monstrosities"—plebeian shapes and apocalyptic fantasies, including shoddy hack writing, popular fairs and theatricals, and the so-called crowd rituals that parodied and displaced the official structures of the dominant culture.

The artists coped by concealing, absorbing, containing, metamorphosing, and/or utilizing the transgressive materials. But always in the name of aestheticizing. There was no attempt to denigrate the aesthetic, only to extend or revise its range. There is no indication that any of these poets or painters was willing to paint an ugly picture or (with the notable exception of Swift) write an ugly poem. But it was possible to make use of ugly or unsuitable materials—almost as a challenge—in a "beautiful" poem, even in one that, if not ugly, is at least loose, conversational, casual, and occasional.

THE two elements, of making and of utilizing transgressive materials, connect in the crucial issue—most firmly articulated on opposite sides by Shaftesbury and Hogarth—of whether the highest art deals only with the true, beautiful, and good, that is, with the ideal, or whether it includes contingency; and whether art is *created* by a clean-handed genius as an Idea, a form that can be executed by subsidiary craftsmen, as Raphael's studio executed paintings after his designs; or whether it is secondarily *made* (as Shaftesbury believes) by a low mechanic, a laborious Dutch craftsman. Shaftesbury's very different version of the artist is as "a second *Maker;* a just Promethean under Jove," and so something like the gnostic demiurge.[9]

The analogy is with the laborer and his product, and the most powerful expression of this plebeian view appears in Daniel Defoe's *Robinson Crusoe,* but the myth of mechanic labor it expresses—that the beauty is in the making itself—derives in the eighteenth century from two ancient sources, the Christian *felix culpa* and the classical (Virgilian) georgic.[10] The Fortunate Fall left Adam with the need to reconstruct the lost Eden out of whatever materials were at hand—a simulacrum of it, or possibly something even better, given the freedom of the remaking itself. The Virgilian georgic postulated the farmer, survivor of the fallen world after the pastoral Golden Age (historically, after the ruinous civil wars), who must teach us to utilize the seasons and the different weathers in order to bring out of the earth the means of survival. Ultimately, in the fourth *Georgic,* regeneration takes place in the decaying carcasses of cattle. This tradition invokes a terminology of change which asks the poet to be not a poet, a pastoral or epic figure, but a farmer, one who simply utilizes what is already there. The Christian version is a story about Everyman, every Adam and Eve; but in the classical georgic the farmer becomes a trope for poetic as well as political work that accommodates disastrous reality following civil war.

The Defoe hero—a useful paradigm to keep in mind as we approach those apparently antithetical, elitist writers Swift and Pope—is a child in London without money, a man on a savage island or crossing the African continent, or a widow without any money and only her (fading) good looks, or even a Londoner in the middle of a plague-stricken city. The pilgrimage of the hero toward a conversion experience no doubt pleased Defoe's more pious readers, but what gave him the extraordinarily large public he enjoyed then and has enjoyed ever since, was probably the how-to-do-it plot of building a house with salvaged materials on a remote island, or scrabbling for money if you are a female alone in the metropolis, or even getting from St. Bartholomew's Close up to St. John's Street and away down Holborn with the money you have just stolen. The Adam who is cast out of Eden is for Defoe someone who tries to rebuild this lost world— whether it is gentlewomanliness or a middle-class business—out of the fragments at hand. The essential part of the myth that Defoe created, it has always been apparent, is not the fall of man but his isolation after the fall and his attempt to bring order out of unfamiliar and minimal materials, often unpromising and seamy materials. The desire for religious redemption or gentility is the obbligato of the endeavor, the conscious or unconscious formulation that tries to raise the making above mere survival.

The paradigm, as Defoe's case attests, is most plainly carried out in that makeshift genre, itself a Crusoe's island of need and reconstitution, the novel (which recalls Addison's intermediate term between the beautiful and great). Samuel Richardson's Pamela, like Crusoe, is trying to defend her integrity in a narrow place and at the same time rebuild some kind of a society for herself in place of her lost home (her father's) and her dead mistress's house, now taken over by the lecherous believer in the *droit du seigneur,* Mr. B. She does so, of course, through her own writing, in her letters and journals, and then in the passing around of these documents that record the process of her rebuilding. At stake is the creation of an inner space, one where she will be safe: ultimately her closet, and within that the clothes she wears on her body, in which she conceals her letters, the inmost dwelling place of her identity. But at the same time, of course, she is metaphorically—with her letters as well as the behavior she chronicles in her letters—creating a larger space which is a social reconstruction she prepares to occupy as the wife of Mr. B.

As a close reading of Pamela's letters by Henry Fielding, as well as by later critics, has shown, the sort of "making" we are discussing invites psychoanalytic modes of interpretation, whether Freudian or Jungian:

> The delusional formation, which we take to be the pathological prod-
> uct, is in reality an attempt at recovery, a process of reconstruction.[11]

> Closer study of Schreber's or any similar case will show that these
> patients are consumed by a desire to create a new world system, or
> what we call a *Weltanschauung,* often of the most bizarre kind.[12]

Swift wrote, indeed *represented,* these bizarre world systems in his *Tale
of a Tub* (1704). But even Fielding's Tom Jones, once cast out of Paradise Hall, sets about reconstructing a simulacrum of his own, which
in his case means a world in which he can earn Sophia on his own
terms. And, as Fielding demonstrates most strikingly in *Tom Jones,*
this reconstruction by the protagonist is analogous to the process of
making-anew by the writer, whether the old Crusoe who reconstructs
young Robinson's existential experience within a providential order,
or (closer to Swift's Grub Street Hack) the old Tristram Shandy whose
writing is his obsessive reconstruction of his own origins in order to
demonstrate the etiology of a wound. The narrative itself is a demonstration, following from the function of the Puritan diary and spiritual autobiography, first to the narrator himself and then to his
reader, of his power to remake—literally in his case out of the shards
of experience as well as the moribund genres of epic, georgic, and
satire.

There is also a sense in these writings that Robinson, Tom, Tristram, and even perhaps Pamela express for the author the Flauber-
tian "C'est moi." Defoe spoke for the rest when he claimed that
Robinson Crusoe was the true history (i.e., the allegory) of his own life.
He was a tradesman who lived, not as a divine, let alone a soldier, but
as a projector, stockjobber, and speculator in civet cats and the raising of sunken treasure ships, dependent on seasons and weather,
while at the same time, often to the detriment of his business enter-
prises, he wrote political, social, and theological tracts. It is not surprising that, not satisfied with an ordinary stable trade, he embodied
in his works of fiction the double mind of an entrepreneur and a
writer—the double act of doing and making, both in chancy, often
marginal causes. And so the "allegory" of Crusoe represents the
bankruptcy, disgrace, and imprisonment of Defoe the author followed by his attempt to rebuild his world, specifically through the act
of writing.

How, then, can Crusoe's or the georgic farmer's labor or making be
said to be aestheticized? In various ways: when farming is turned into

gardening, or into poetry; or when it serves as part of an analogy with poetic making, as in Virgil's *Georgics* or Pope's *Windsor Forest;* or when (as in the same works) it is part of an analogy with other less already aestheticized matters such as politics, thus problematizing the historico-political situation. Of Crusoe's work—the making of his "world"—we can say that the distancing of the representation itself (i.e., we are not working alongside him) aestheticizes the labor. But also his own sacralizing of his work, superimposing upon it the conversion story, in the sense of both distancing and problematizing, aestheticizes it.

As these remarks suggest, the Shaftesbury tradition in which idea is regarded as superior to mechanic labor is complemented by the tradition that stems from Locke's *Second Treatise* (pub. 1704), Chapter 5 on property. "Property" for Locke begins with one's "own *Person*," and then proceeds to the "*Labour* of his Body, and the *Work* of his Hands, [which] we may say, are properly his":

> Whatsoever then he removes out of the State that Nature hath provided, and left it in, he hath mixed his *Labour* with, and joyned to it something that is his own, and thereby makes it his *Property*.[13]

I shall discuss the aestheticizing of property in Chapter 6, but the immediate point to notice is that the labor of classical georgic and biblical *felix culpa* are supported by, and linked to, Locke's modern identification of the individual with the ownership of property. Crusoe's making of his island also turns it into his property, which he later staffs with servants and subjects.

Given the assumption that the title to property is labor, what is projected in Locke's *Second Treatise* is a conflict between the natural title of the worker and the legal title of the owner (or patron)—with reference to the artist, to the picture itself, but also to the "possessions" represented within the picture. Much practical and intellectual play by Hogarth and his followers was given to the relationship between the artist's labor and the physical possession (someone else's) on which the labor has been expended. This will be seen to apply in one way to Reynolds, in another to George Stubbs—and in a more generally aesthetic sense to Gainsborough and Constable. The "affect" on a spectator meant not only his/her experience but the state of possession—by the landscape of the spectator or equally possession by the spectator of the landscape.

ALTHOUGH I make passing remarks on the novel (primarily *Tristram Shandy*), I am concerned primarily with poets and painters who, more than the novelist, needed to retain dignity, appearing to be polite and (as John Caryll advised Pope) "correct," but who, as much as the novelists, used certain *infra dig* materials to revivify high art at a time when it seemed to be languishing. This is a period in which the term "high art" or the canonical was put seriously into question: a period noted for the emergence of new genres (the most obvious being the novel) in both literature and art based on materials hitherto considered unsuitable for the serious poet or painter.

I have in fact excluded the novel from this study. It has so often been written of as the "modern" genre, the genre of contemporaneity, the form that like satire (I have argued myself) lives parodically, incorporating poetic or romance elements of the high genres, as well as low and forbidden elements and discourses (and ultimately, as it refines this process into what Mikhail Bakhtin calls a poly- or heteroglossia, incorporating all genres, all discourses), that it has virtually come to stand for the process.[14] It is worth indicating how the genre of the novel described by Bakhtin with its valorization of the low, contingent, and contemporary differs from the across-the-genres progression I describe. Bakhtin's argument, that the novel arose by absorbing or parodying the older, especially the high, official, and privileged genres (epic, tragedy, lyric), may be only another way of saying that opera, Walpole, and military heroism are iconoclasted in the 1720s, with georgic, a high genre, as an alternative, somewhat broader model of accommodation, one that may include Bakhtin's novel. But I am interested in showing how not the genres but specific poets and painters (and here Bakhtin would thoroughly disagree) absorb these and other transgressive materials, including the stigmatic, *without* writing the novel.

Perhaps Bakhtin would regard these as merely novelizing poems and paintings. Perhaps "novelizing" is another word for what I describe as the aesthetics of the modern. But I wish at least to offer an alternative explanation: For Bakhtin's myth is, first, of a "truly historical struggle of genres," with the Novel standing in for the New Class that absorbs the old, aristocratic class (it "exposes the conventionality of . . . forms and languages"); second, of the reassertion of the People—of all the popular forces that have been reduced by the monoglossia of Greek, Latin, and the vernaculars—; third, of the manifestation of this assertion as laughter.

It will be apparent (as I see now that I am finished) that I describe a phenomenon very similar to the one Bakhtin envisions as a transformation of the high genres (with their "absolute past" and "absolute epic distance") "through the intermediate stages of familiarization" (p. 15); for the Romantic Bakhtin the agent of familiarization is "laughter," by which he means popular laughter which (theoretically in his myth) "demolishes fear and piety before an object, before a world, making of it an object of familiar contact and thus clearing the ground for an absolutely free investigation of it" (p. 23). The epic past, characterized by "defamiliarization," much as Burke and Kant described aesthetic experience by distancing, is thus familiarized. But where Bakhtin uses the archetypal term laughter (though in many cases the generic term satire is more accurate), I use the historically English, Protestant term iconoclasm, the classical generic term georgic, and so on. Bakhtin is concerned with one genre—I with many types, words, and artists. For above all, his myth of the struggle of genres, a supraindividual agon, is proposed to replace the more common struggle of writers (with their precursors and contemporaries) and of "schools" and "trends."

In short, if this book began as an attempt to supplement spectator- and nature-oriented theories of aesthetics, it ended as a supplement to Bakhtin's myth of class-generic warfare and (another brilliant approach to the subject of the novel) Michael McKeon's myth of a dialectic progression (that revises Ian Watt's "rise of the novel/middle class") from aristocratic/romance to progressive/skepticism to conservative/extreme skepticism.[15] This study substitutes for their focus on external forces the individual worker within a tradition based on assumptions, conventions, and myths of making (and its opposite breaking), as well as within a specific politico-historical situation.

This is not, however, as the reader may have begun to fear, a book with a close and continuing argument. Rather it poses a thesis—or, perhaps more accurately, another myth—and explores various aspects of it with examples that both illustrate and exceed the thesis. The thesis outlined in these pages should be regarded as an occasion for a series of essays on some major works of poetry and painting. But I am inevitably concerned at bottom with the question of art itself and whether to aestheticize necessarily means only to distance and depoliticize. It is fashionable to see the most subversive potentials of an artist as finally contained—self-contained by an artist who (possibly without even knowing it) has sold out to the establishment because he is an artist. This view does not so much show realistic skepticism as bourgeois contempt for art. Even those artists I discuss as restorers—even Byron's "Wordsworth"—are turning up meanings repressed by the various impositions of order and meaning of their time. When they write or paint they stand outside the political and all other orders; and they are, I believe, major artists because they write or paint in this way.

ENGLISH ICONOCLASM

Iconoclasm is a historically grounded term with a long doctrinal and polemical history, a term that was in common currency during the eighteenth century.[16] An iconoclast, in Johnson's *Dictionary* (1755), is simply one who breaks images. The best-known form of active iconoclasm in the century was, of course, the French Revolution. The process required a given, extant Christian or royal art of the *ancien régime,* and then proceeded as follows (I quote from the minutes of one of the Jacobin Clubs):

> Destroy these signs of slavery and idolatry which only serve to perpetu-
> ate ignorance and superstition. Replace them with images of Rousseau,
> Franklin and all the other great men, ancient and modern, which will
> fill the people with a noble enthusiasm for liberty.[17]

"Destroy" is followed by "replace": destroy the cult of kings and saints and replace it with a cult of "great men." In the first phase the cathedral of Notre Dame was renamed the Temple of Reason; in the second phase the renaming progressed from the Enlightenment terms of Nature, Reason, and Republican Rome to a more popular sansculotte vocabulary based on the old "superstitions" of the Catholic Church. Jean-Paul Marat was substituted for Christ and other revolutionary heroes for martyrs of the Church. This form of iconoclasm could be interpreted as involving either (the counterrevolutionary interpretation) raising the leprous, unpresentable Marat by means of the parallel with Christ, or destroying the idol Christ and replacing him with the living contemporary national hero. The question is whether the emphasis falls on the glorification of Marat or on the destruction of Christ—or on the act of replacement itself. In the polemics of the time it falls on all three. The idea of iconoclasm as replacement always poses the possibility, even likelihood, that glorification (a new idolatry) may usurp the iconoclastic aspect of the act.

This is the pragmatic iconoclasm that has to take place in a practical revolutionary situation. The artists of the French Revolution were brought up in a Roman Catholic world; they could therefore continue to think only in terms of Catholic forms, saints, liturgy, and catechism. To an English observer they seemed to be replacing one superstition with another.

But there was also a more popular, direct, and unmediated iconoclasm at work which turned a church into a stable, theater, barracks, or workshop; a palace like the Petit Trianon became a tavern. The utilitarian aspect of iconoclasm was already present in the American Revolution when the colonists in 1776 pulled down the bronze statue of George III in New York City and melted it into bullets for the American armies. Thus the French in the 1790s decreed that "the seals of royalty, the scepter, and the crown all be broken into pieces, transported to the mint, and melted down into republican coins." The base of the statue of Hercules proposed by Jacques-Louis David was to be "made up of the debris from the statues of kings knocked off the porticoes of Notre Dame." [18]

Ultimately there is also a purer, or more rigorous, iconoclasm that simply levels the church. It intends to question if not destroy *any* image, any idol (or anything it designates as an idol) without a replacement. The revolutionary who is also a true iconoclast seldom reaches the final revolutionary phase of stability; in fact, he cannot reach this stage of rest but must insist on the continuing, the permanent revolution.

The case in England had been very different from that in France: England entered its phase of iconoclasm nearly three hundred years earlier, and with the sanction, indeed the encouragement, of its monarch. The icons destroyed were originally replaced by a lateral transference from God, Church, saints, and pope to the English monarch and his family. The iconoclasm that spread from this center to all corners of the kingdom was carried out under the direction of the crown itself, in the case of Henry VIII as part of his very practical dissolution of the monasteries, less as a sign of theology, certainly not of revolution, than as part of a process of consolidating royal (and national) power. England was the only country of any size where iconoclasm—as an important part of the Protestant Reformation—was carried out as a government policy with a fair amount of consistency and so produced a mind-set that was national rather than factional or local and continuing rather than sporadic.

Some strains, of course, were more intense than others; and the succeeding phases—the Henrician, the Edwardian, and the Puritan

Parliamentarian of the 1640s—increased in intensity, until any image in a church, of deity or of the dead on funerary monuments, was destroyed, and the destruction reached even to royal images and (in 1649) to the king's body. Stephen Gardiner had warned at the outset (as John Phillips, the chronicler of English iconoclasm, says) that "if religious images were to be destroyed, . . . the political order of society would be disrupted and men would come to attack even the badges and symbols of government and nobility": "the ambiguity over what constituted acceptable images, coupled with the indiscriminate popular destruction of them," opened the gates to a larger and more pervasive sense of iconoclasm—certainly than was to appear in France.[19]

There were two kinds of images: one was an image as a "sensible" or material reflection, that is, a "reminder," of a spiritual truth. Such images were called "unabused images." The other kind of image, which actually attempted to represent spiritual truths (or figures of deity), was liable to idolatry. These were "abused" images. The problem was where to draw the line between images of memory and images of worship.

Memory was the essential criterion for the "unabused" image: the visual image permitted recall of the absent reality, whether the referent was material or spiritual, but (with printing) words could do the job better. This sense of memory makes a strong link with the Homeric and classical function of poetry to preserve and instruct (as opposed to the Longinian to create anew and move or elevate). The muses, according to Hesiod's *Hymn to the Muses,* are the daughters of Mnemosyne, signifying memory, recall, record, and memorization. As Eric A. Havelock has written, "They are not the daughters of inspiration or invention, but basically of memorisation. Their central role is not to create but to preserve."[20] But at what point, it was asked, does remembrance turn into worship? Does one pretend to remember but actually worship? Is memory merely a disguise for worship? Or is memory too secondary—too far removed from the absent object? In practice the Puritan reformers turned from using images as an aid to memory to memorizing printed texts: "Instead of the vanished and banished images, the 'laymen's books,' the literate layman can now, presumably, read and memorize a written text" such as the Bible.[21]

The essence of English iconoclasm was the substitution—on the walls of churches as well as in books—of words for visual images. Words—whether seen, spoken, or imagined—were privileged, while visual images were marginalized and discredited. English culture has the reputation of being centrally verbal: Its masterpieces are the works of Shakespeare, Milton, Pope, and Wordsworth; the tradition of painting and sculpture is sporadic by comparison with the great traditions of Italy, France, and the countries of Northern Europe.

One paradigm for English iconoclasm then was the replacement of visual images with words. But words too could be raised to the dangerous status of the image. Beyond the destruction of the visual images, Puritan iconoclasm included in its range of attack all "custom" and "legalism," as in those "set forms" of liturgy and other rituals, including the *Book of Common Prayer*. As the holy altar was supposedly replaced by the desanctified pulpit (as *Hoc est corpus meum* was replaced by *Hoc est verbum meum*), there was always the clear danger that the pulpit might also become "holy" and so an idol.

Idolatry for the Puritan divine William Perkins occurred whenever "something that is not God is set up in the roome of God."[22] Perkins is in effect saying that anything is an idol "that is allowed to come between ourselves and God. Anything that is *instead of*."[23] For a pure iconoclast we must posit a general hostility to any replacement, whether by word or gesture, not only of God but of any absolute whether of nature or of selfhood. The icono*clastic* sensibility, as opposed to the icono*phobic* mind of the Jew or Moslem, was that of the Protestant who had been an idolator and probably in his heart feared that he remained one—and so joined a strong inner attraction to an even stronger public manifestation of rejection. The act of desecration without replacement expresses the English iconoclast's constant fear of raising up another idol in the place of the old one. His worst scorn is reserved for the political "iconoclast" who only replaces God with a king or a king with a prophet (Christ with Marat or, later, with Lenin).

Yet distinctions were possible. The pulpit was preferable to the painted or printed words as the living was to the dead because the preacher's words were spoken and included the immediate, unmediated, though still visual, elements of gestures, facial expression, and stance. William Perkins's position, used by Archbishop Laud's opponents in the 1630s, was that "knowledge of Christ's agony and crucifixion was to be transmitted not through dead art but through living words, gestures and [most important, beyond these,] actions."[24]

The idol was traditionally distinguished from the true god as dead from living. The crux was Psalm 115, where idols, as opposed to the Jewish God, "have mouths, but they speak not: eyes have they, but they see not: they have ears, but they hear not," and so on—that is, they are inanimate images void of voice, sight, or breath, to be distinguished from life lived.[25]

Many English examples could be cited of this model of iconoclastic sensibility—from Hogarth's formulation, "Who but a bigot, even to the antiques, will say that he has not seen faces and necks, hands and arms in living women, that even the Grecian Venus doth but coarsely imitate?"[26] to Byron's:

> she was one
> Fit for a model of a statuary,
>   (A race of mere imposters, when all's done—
> I've seen much finer women, ripe and real,
> Than all the nonsense of their stone ideal.)[27]

The iconoclast can also be said to replace the symbol with the reality, the stone image with the human flesh or human action.

If one paradigm for English iconoclasm was the replacement of the dead image with a word, and a second was its replacement with the living human voice or gesture, then a third, related paradigm— one more immediately capable of implementation—was the destruction of the intervening medium. To remove the stained glass images that mediate between you and the natural world is to see more clearly God's work. It is folly to look at the works of man when by removing them you can see directly, unimpeded, the works of God. The world "seen by one's own eyes" (Calvin's words) takes on a profound importance, set against the world of idols and "phantoms."[28] Whether in images or set forms or even words, the temptation is to accept formula and artifice, a Bower of Bliss without natural leaf or flower, a face plastered with cosmetics, cut off from the unmediated work of God in nature.

A fourth model for English iconoclasm emphasized an act of violence. The Biblical texts authorized the breaking down of idols, not simply the intellectual turning away from them: "Ye shall destroy their altars, break their images, and cut down their groves" (Exod. 34.13). Johnson's definition, earlier cited, was simply the breaking of images. One important aspect of the practice in England was the peculiar violence with which it was carried out. The image was broken, ground into dust, and cast into a river.

Equally characteristic of the English Calvinists, however, was the remaking of the image, either by recasting the pulverized materials or by other modifications, into a substance that could not by any stretch of the imagination be worshiped. A triptych was remade into a pig trough, a basin of holy water into a trough for salting beef, priestly vestments into seat cushions, a chapel into a dining room, an icon into a child's doll; or an icon was melted down into plates to eat from or into coins of the realm.[29]

The idol was transformed downward into a secular object, into a vulgar, commonplace equivalent. But the original memory was not quite lost. We might say there was a kind of exorcism but also a secular or commonsense irony in the practice of the iconoclast. The main aim was to take away all of the old mystifications or to replace significance with utility, to bring down the abstract or spiritual to the commonplace and particular, which we might also call the immediate and lived.[30] The classical source was something like the Roman mob's breaking up and melting down the statues of Sejanus into (in Juvenal's words) "wine jars, frying pans, basins, and platters, and piss pots," the sort of transvaluation which also recalls within England sub-culture parodies of the ruling-class forms in the so-called crowd ritual.[31]

But the iconoclastic process also involved a *re*-enlivening of dead matter. The idol was traditionally distinguished from the true god in that it was dead, and Calvin attacked the related notion that an image of a deity could be fashioned from "any dead matter." Puritans constantly referred to the crude materials out of which the god had been made, a piece of wood, for example, the other half of which the idolator might use to cook his meat over. Thus the iconoclast's reduction of the image to its basic crude physicality or utility also returned it to a living function.

The basic idol feared and attacked by Calvin, and so the basic subject for iconoclasm, was the sacrament of the Eucharist: Calvin denied the actual miraculous presence of Christ's blood and body— both the notion and the image, the wafer of the Mass which stands for it—and replaced them with the common bread people ate in their daily lives.[32] This was the "sacramental realism" expressed in the Puritan's act of not only refusing to wear the surplice but using it for a seat cushion—transforming the mystified object into (or re-turning it to) its original, material, common form, its living use. If one side of the Puritan distrust of mediation was to invest common objects with spiritual value, the other was to desacralize idols by destroying their religious forms and returning them to their material substance—by returning them to everyday life. This reconstruction was distinct from simple renaming, which retains the substance and changes the name; here, in a scene of literal (not metaphorical) iconoclasm, one based on the model of the Eucharist itself, a reconstitution of substance was required.

We must therefore add to the pragmatic iconoclasm in which the contemporary living leader replaces the dead idol, and the pure iconoclasm in which there *is* no replacement, the transmutation of the idol into a contemporary commonplace utensil for living.

But if one form taken by iconoclasm is the church window, its stained glass removed to reveal the natural world outside, another is the incongruous sight of a cathedral with rows of headless statues and huge perpendicular traceries filled with clear (indeed, in practice often opaque) glass. This was, in Horace Walpole's words, describing Richard Bentley's 1753 illustration for Gray's *Elegy in a Country Churchyard* (fig. 1): "a church-yard and a village-church built out of the remains of an abbey." The result was a surviving iconoclasm that played into—provided subject matter for, helped to create—the mode of art known as the picturesque: the church with the traces of the abbey absurdly showing; the wheel for the bell rope in the new, tiny tower intersecting the gigantic wheel of the abbey's rose window, juxtaposing practical and ornamental, present and past; the archway, itself constructed from the old, with "emblems of the nobility" on one side and of the poor on the other.

The inset, with the story of Gray's elegist, with its allusion to Poussin's painting and the *Et in Arcadia Ego* motif, is enclosed as if in a tomb. The shadow of the meditator on the grave is cast over the grave so that it lies precisely in the position of the dead body, becoming a *vanitas* image, a *memento mori,* but also summing up the function of the relationship of the spectator to the epitaph (see below, Chap. 5).

This mixed mode sums up not only the picturesque but the alternative to Swift's broken objects in an art of the patched-together and composite. It will explain some of the comic effect of Hogarth's *Sleeping Congregation* (fig. 2) as well as the more solemn effect of Wright of Derby's *Blacksmith's Forge,* a utilitarian shop constructed out of a ruined abbey (fig. 21).

THE central insight of the secular branch of English iconoclasts, the empirical philosophers beginning with Francis Bacon, was that words were no different from visual images as idols—and perhaps worse because images could at least *represent* "that seen by one's own eyes." If the first Lockean insight was that all experience enters through the

1. Richard Bentley, Jr., Illustration for Gray's Elegy, *engraved by Charles Grignion, from* The Poems of Thomas Gray *(Strawberry Hill, 1753).*

senses, the second was that words are not, as the iconoclast may have supposed, any more transparent than images, that both words and images are only conventional signs for reality. For Locke the idols are the "innate ideas" of Scholastic philosophy and the true images are the direct impressions of the senses (whereas for the Platonist the idols are the false images of sensory appearance, and the true are the abstract, ideal forms of mathematics).[33] The dichotomy was between mental constructs of all sorts, visual as well as verbal "phantoms," and those living "gestures and actions" or experiences of the senses—the phenomena of the so-called real world—that were the true foundation for the formulation of hypotheses. The danger appears at just the point where words are used to represent, interpret, or communicate the results of the senses—in short, where words are used to intervene between ourselves and nature (or God) and take its place, thus becoming "idols." In this context we can see the problem as a fear of turning objects of the senses into false hypotheses, and this is done by the use of verbal structures applied to what is immediately seen or felt.

The great theme of much English philosophy, literature, and art has been nature versus art and empirical observation versus apriori theory, with the first term usually privileged. The prototypical English iconoclast may be the philosopher who distrusts innate ideas and goes the way of stripping away all illusions until (like Hume) he can only return to belief and feeling based on convention, common-sense replacements for either authority or reason. Or it may be the English satirist who questions and ridicules until no artifice or artifact whatever remains intact—no value whatever is to be found in art or authority. Both of these phenomena, philosophical and literary, reached a high point of fruition in the eighteenth century.

In a letter of 1729 to Viscount Bolingbroke, Swift tells of having a wall built around his Dublin garden:

> I built a wall five years ago, and when the masons played the knaves, nothing delighted me so much as to stand by while my servants threw down what was amiss. I have likewise seen a Monkey overthrow all the dishes and plates in a kitchen, merely for the pleasure of seeing them tumble and hearing the clatter they made in their fall. I wish you would invite me to such another entertainment.[34]

The last clause suggests that Swift would like Bolingbroke, back in London, to extend the "entertainment" to the political realm with the prime minister Sir Robert Walpole its object. Swift's biographer Irvin Ehrenpreis uses this passage to show the care Swift took to make sure his garden had a well-built wall (and "the delight that gardening . . . gave him").[35] I am sure this is true biographically, but it overlooks the way Swift in Ireland tells the story to Bolingbroke in England five years later, to emphasize his glee at the destruction of knavish work, in a passage that ends with the famous words about Swift's refusing to die "here in a rage, like a poisoned rat in a hole." The hole, of course, is Ireland, and the enclosure of the garden is both politically and aesthetically inimical. The man Swift probably did delight in gardening; but the Irish dean (itself a metaphor for not-bishop) delighted equally in making tropes of the "rotten stones" and the knocking down of "what was amiss"—by extension of that "pagod" or "idol" Walpole (as the "prime" minister of England was called)—but perhaps of *any* wall, in the manner of Robert Frost's "Something there is that doesn't love a wall."

Swift opened his sermon *Upon the Martyrdom of King Charles I* (1726), with the Genesis text,

> Simon and Levi are brethren . . . in their anger they slew a man, and in their self-will they digged down a wall. Cursed be their anger. . . . I will divide in David, and scatter them in Israel.

The sermon itself attacks Puritan iconoclasm, applying "digged down a wall" to Anglican churches:

> They spared neither the statues of saints, or antient prelates, or kings, or benefacators; broke down the tombs and monuments of men famous in their generations, seized the vessels of silver set apart for the holiest use, tore down the most innocent ornaments both within and without, made the houses of prayer dens of thieves, or stables for cattle.[36]

Puritan iconoclasm supports Swift's main attack on their interpretations of scripture as demands for a "thorough reformation" that will destroy and deface the "most innocent ornaments" of the Church and inevitably end again in regicide. The self-fragmenting of the Puritans, who agree on nothing, changing "every day from schism to schism, from heresy to heresy, and from one faction to another," reflects their destruction of the Church against which they inveigh.

The Genesis passage sums up Swift's own practice: the force of his satire is on those who break down walls, but his own response is to "divide and scatter them." He reacts to an act of breaking with a more comprehensive one, in a characteristic Swiftean manner mimetic of their own ethos.

The Swift we see here is sometimes discerned from the vantage of his literary descendant Samuel Beckett and credited with the same aesthetic, based on the destruction of old forms, which loves to dash things to pieces or which loves things that are dashed to pieces—and prefers the consequent fact of detritus to a reconstruction. We are now seeing the same Swift from another direction, from the tradition of Protestant and English iconoclasm of the extreme sort which hates anything that intervenes between us and nature.

Swift, the Anglo-Irish Protestant, with ancestors on both sides of the Civil War, had a strong sense of the iconoclastic tradition. He came only a generation after that "last and most severe and most systematically destructive outbreak of iconoclasm in England," which had extended iconoclasm to the monarch himself.[37] We can, in this regard, contrast him with his friend Pope, who came from the Counterreformation tradition of the opposing religion, Roman Catholicism. Pope might have seen an analogy between his own art and the miraculous image such as the swaying crucifix of the Abbey of Boxley which, when examined by the iconoclasts, proved to contain a mechanism that produced the movement: simply an example of art, like the poet's feigning. Pope always makes a case for art, and if his forms draw on iconoclasm it is never to destroy, let alone destroy and replace, but to construct with his own powerful art, turning even the muck (or debris) of his enemies, which they attempt to idolize, into the brick and mortar of a true garden, the *hortus conclusus* Swift despaired of having built.

One need only contrast Pope's Belinda at her toilette, where her cosmetics "awaken" the beauties and bring out "purer blushes" in her cheeks, with Swift's Celia who uses art to patch holes where her eyes and lips and nose had once been. In Swift's poetry art is only an affectation, however well intended, which amounts to idolatry. Idolatry is the worshiping of a fabricated female ideal, which men in fact impose on the woman herself, who is forced into the aesthetic subterfuges of Celia. And iconoclasm in Swift's poetry, beginning with the physical "killing" of the astrologer Partridge, reaches eventually as far as the self-destruction of the poet himself in *Verses on the Death of Dr. Swift*. But its primary idol is woman, whether rotting Celia or naturally aging Stella.

The iconoclast is defined by the images he breaks, or tries to break. Swift breaks the idol woman—into teeth, eyes, nose, bits and pieces of flesh, and cosmetics—in order to disperse the totalizing quality, disturb the unity, obviously with the purpose of exorcism—though of exactly what we will not take time to consider here. But it is also clear that he extends the iconoclasm to include even himself, as in the *Verses*, as a scapegoat for the notions of friendship, fame for the de-

serving, and all the rest he held dear but could only approach indi-
rectly—disinterestedly—by means of his famous praise-by-blame
irony, carried out with such consistency as to become an ontology. It
is also clear that he distinguishes between kinds of breakage, as when
he also allows Time to erode his dear Stella in order to prove to himself that there are noniconoclastic dispersals.

Swift derives from a satiric tradition that goes back to the Romans
but carried also the authority of such Church Fathers (with Pauline
sympathies) as Jerome, Cyprian, and Tertullian. A chief object of satire shared by the Romans and the Church Fathers was woman, the
fallen Eve. As Felicity Nussbaum has noted in her study of anti-
feminist satire, the "Dressing Room Poems" take their departure
from the Juvenal of *Satire 6* who urges love-sick men to "but, look
behind, / And then she dwindles to the Pigmy kind" (ll. 647–48), in
other words to get into the woman's dressing room and discover her
cosmetic disguises.[38] The mode is travesty/iconoclastic: regard her as
idol and break her in order to reveal her material reality. For Ovid it
is the awareness of cosmetics, not the sweat and dirt of her body,
which directs the wise man to keep passion out of the act of love: "Go
take a look some time when she's smearing her face with cosmetics—"
he writes in his *Remedies for Love.*[39] Swift takes off from these love
poems and their anti-Petrarchan descendants, especially as they flour-
ished in the Restoration, producing a yet more earthy catalogue of
antithetical attributes.

But the woman happens also to have been the prime example for
writers who, like Swift, focus on the opposition of art and nature.
Two senses of "art" were available in the last quarter of the seventeenth century. One, which Pope followed, held that art is close to
being one with nature, "nature to advantage dressed," revealing
rather than concealing her. In Dale Underwood's words, "Its end was
not aggression and conquest but the maintenance of order, balance,
harmony. It therefore served individual fulfillment by the keeping of
degree and measure, by conformity and restraint."[40] The second
sense of "art" was as a disguise, the opposite of nature; and its function was deception and conquest. Although the first was the orthodox Christian view, the second represented a powerful and persistent
theme of the Church Fathers. The first emphasis would have seemed
more Roman Catholic, the second more Pauline and Augustinian, or
more iconoclastically Protestant.

"There is a dress proper to everyone," says Tertullian, "as well for
daily use as for office and dignity." This dress helps to define the

man, as a judge wears one dress, a senator another. The trouble comes when a person wears a dress that either does not fit his office or serves no useful purpose, and is therefore purely decorative. Tertullian is talking about women: thus the wearing of ornament or inappropriate dress is the woman's attempt to make herself what she is not, by altering the exterior to suggest an equivalent inner change. The example he gives is the fallen angels who, by wearing ornaments, tried to alter their hierarchical position in heaven. To this Cyprian adds: "[The apostate angels] taught [women] also to paint the eyes with blackness drawn round them in a circle, and to change the hair with false colours, and to drive out all truth, both of face and head, by the assault of their own corruption."[41]

Closely connected, but with a slightly different focus, is the idea that by applying paint and altering her reality woman is committing blasphemy because she is altering the face God gave her. The full force of God's own name is brought against this particular sin, blurring the original distinction between what is appropriate and what is excess. Now Tertullian is saying that *any* decoration is evil:

> For they who rub their skin with medicaments, stain their cheeks with rouge, make their eyes prominent with antimony, sin against HIM. To them, I suppose, the plastic skill of God is displeasing! In their own persons, I suppose, they correct, they censure, the Artificer of all things! For censure they do when they amend, when they add to, (His work;) taking these their additions, of course, from the adversary artificer.

He concludes: "Whatever is *born* is the work of God. Whatever, then, is *plastered on* (that), is the devil's work."[42] And from this strain enters another, hitherto hidden: the particular weakness of woman. Besides (or as a result of) wishing to alter her status, Tertullian adds, she sets out to seduce men.

This is the point at which the theme of the prostitute enters. It lends its special force as part of the complex of ideas surrounding cosmetics, and as such it informs Swift's *Progress of Beauty* and *Beautiful Young Nymph Going to Bed* (1714 and 1734). Jerome sums up:

> The harlot in the Gospel found salvation, baptized in her own tears and wiping the Lord's feet with the hair which had before lured many a lover. She wore no waving head-dress, no creaking shoes, nor did she darken her eyes with antimony: the more squalid she was, the more lovely she seemed. What have rouge and white lead to do on a Christian woman's face? The one simulates the natural red of cheeks and

lips, the other the whiteness of the face and neck. They are fires to inflame young men, stimulants of lustful desire, plain evidence of an unchaste mind.[43]

The other side of the "rouge and white lead" is therefore: "the more squalid she was, the more lovely she seemed." Swift's purpose is, on the one hand (quoting Nussbaum), "to release men from passion and its attendant madness," that is, from idolatry. The evil, as Swift explores it, is reciprocal: "If women create myths for themselves, as they do at the dressing table, they also are subject to the myths men create for them";[44] and that makes the idolator the creator of his own idol.

But in the second place, the cure is to make the woman "more squalid" than she is, therefore with equal wisdom to make one's own writing "more squalid." It should certainly eschew "rouge and white lead," but of course Swift's iconoclasm involves the poet's reconstruction of the harlot's making or unmaking of her face. The forbidden materials crowd to the center of the work, however disgusting their details, and become part of the squalid reduction that is the truth of both the woman's appearance and the poet's text. In the case of the "Beautiful Young Nymph," this takes the form of not only an aging reality but a "batter'd" one (she is a "batter'd strolling Toast") racked by disease and dreams of confinement and beatings in prison, embodied in the unmediated language of Swift's squalid poem.

But there is another side to Swift's breaking and remaking, most evident in his celebrations of Stella's clean, unornamented face, and his summation of the plight of Strephon and Chloe in the metaphor (one he also applies to Stella) of building, disassembling, and reconstructing:

> A prudent builder should forecast
> How long the stuff is like to last;
> And, carefully observe the ground,
> To build on some foundation sound;
> What house, when its materials crumble,
> Must not inevitably tumble?[45]

By contrast, in *The Lady's Dressing Room* he uses the organic metaphor, giving it a specifically georgic twist:

> When *Celia* in her Glory shows,
> If *Strephon* would but stop his Nose . . .
> He soon would learn to think like me,

And bless his ravisht Eyes to see
Such Order from Confusion sprung,
Such gaudy Tulips rais'd from Dung.   [ll. 133–34, 139–42]

The difference between this passage and Pope's description of
Belinda's face is merely between "purer blushes" and "gaudy Tulips
rais'd from Dung"; the latter is an earthy equivalent, what we would
expect of the more straightforward Swift, the plain georgic farmer
rather than gardener. One could argue that the message of *Strephon
and Chloe* (if not of *The Progress of Beauty* and *A Beautiful Young Nymph
Going to Bed*) is for the young woman to husband her resources, to be
like the prudent farmer who adjusts to the realities of the seasons.
But the iconoclastic mode remains operative in the spirit-matter relationship that continually reminds that what pretends to be spirit always resolves into matter, a Eucharist into a hearty dinner.

Swift's georgic is of course an antigeorgic because it refuses to acknowledge the generative stage. As in *A Description of a City Shower,*
the georgic order is reversed and the prognostics (how to avoid the
Deluge that is coming) are moved from the end, where they appeared in Virgil's first *Georgic,* to the beginning. It is the purgation,
the crime and filth spewed into the Thames, which ends the poem.
Indeed, we might say that if Pope absorbs such filth, Swift expels it.

But if Swift occasionally implies a metaphor of farming, he more
often uses one of house building. As a primary metaphor for his
own act of writing, building always takes place in the context of Ben
Jonson's simile of fitting stones so perfectly that no mortar is needed:
"The congruent, and harmonious fitting of parts in a sentence, hath
almost the fastning, and force of knitting, and connexion: As in
stones well squar'd, which will rise strong a great way without mortar."[46] Swift's own version has "the right words in the right places,"
a succinct description of his prose. His poetry, however, with its
Hudibrastic rhythms and rhymes, can only be said to put the wrong
words in the wrong places and *therefore* becomes not prose but "poetry." This Swift, who is against gardens and Palladian structures,
who is antiart and delights in disorder, has been brilliantly described
by Carole Fabricant.[47] My purpose is simply to set out, as against
Pope's metaphor, Swift's assumptions about "building" poems laid
out in his early pre-Pope poems—the poems that still reflect and re-
formulate the incredible, destructive energy of *A Tale of a Tub.*

The poem that most cogently pulls together the strands scattered
in other poems of the 1703–14 period is called *Vanbrugh's House Built*

from the Ruins of White-Hall that was burnt, which survives in two versions, a manuscript of around 1703 and a printed text of 1709. Characteristically, Swift starts with a historical fact or series of facts: Sir
John Vanbrugh was a successful playwright of comedies, in particular
The Relapse, written as a sequel and reaction to Colley Cibber's popular sentimental comedy *Love's Last Shift;* he had secured for himself
the office of Carlisle Herald; and he was also an aspiring architect
who built himself a very small house out of the ruins of Whitehall
Palace, destroyed by fire in 1699.

Therefore Swift activates an analogy between Vanbrugh the writer
and Amphion, whose singing built cities. The difference between
Amphion's cities and Vanbrugh's tiny residence suggests the fatal discrepancy between public and private, ancient and modern. And with
this in the background is the knowledge that Vanbrugh's house was
made from the ruins of a royal palace. Because in *ancient* times,

> A verse could draw a stone or beam
> That now would overload a team;
> Lead 'em a dance of many a mile,
> Then rear 'em to a goodly pile.   [ll. 3–6]

Epic poetry "could build" a tower, for example, while sonnets and
elegies could "raise" a two-story house, and so on down to odes slat-
ing and epigraphs thatching roofs. But now, in modern England, ar-
chitects construct buildings for the rich, and poor poets are left "to
build Castles" in "the spatious Air," which, of course, refers to their
residence in garrets.

So far the tropes are extensions of those in the *Tale of a Tub*—the
house or container, the airy castles and the shabby garret life to
which these imaginative constructs correspond and at the same time
condemn the poet. In the manuscript draft (Pierpont Morgan Library) the silk worm who "consumes it self to weave a Cell" derives
from the self-generating spider (in *The Battle of the Books*), and itself
self-generates a series of analogies: worm, silkworm, chrysallis, butter-
fly, and the "Insect of the Age" (what a bad poet is called) who, like
the silkworm, "feeds upon imagin'd Bays" and produces "an ill-spun
Play" which "gives him lodging," and so on.

These metamorphic changes project the question of whether the
poem itself (i.e., Swift's poem) is constructed in the old way by stones
and mortar and slate on the model of a house, or in the "modern"
way by webs woven out of the poet's own bowels in flimsy struc-

tures—or (returning now to the facts of Vanbrugh, and to the various puns on "house") by the herald who "repair[ed] a House gone to decay," the poet who built a play and "brought forth a House," constructed of the ruins of larger, more venerable and sturdy structures, whether a royal palace or someone else's play ("A Type of Modern Wit and Style, / The Rubbish of an Antient Pile"). In both the draft and the published version the organic and architectural metaphors merge at the end:

> As animals of largest size
> Corrupt to maggots, worms and flies.

And:

> So modern rhymers wisely blast
> The poetry of ages past,
> Which after they have overthrown,
> They from its Ruins build their own.   [ll. 123–24, 131–34]

The published version differs from the manuscript in that it removes the organic metaphor from the middle and replaces it with a development of the architectural metaphor (as if Addison had perhaps persuaded Swift of the need for harmony). The metaphor is now consistently developed until the last few lines, where Swift returns to the *Tale of a Tub* metaphor of a body degenerating into maggots while retaining, momentarily at least, its original human shape. The middle of the published poem simply compares the building of a play and a house (acts equal rooms), with the meagerness of the play emerging in the physical slightness of the house, for which indeed the poet—as in that other passage in the *Tale* describing the disappearance of modern writings virtually upon publication—"Lookt high and low, walkt often round, / But no such House was to be found." The modern's spiderlike unity of author and work remains in the form of a snail: Vanbrugh "may trail / [His] house about [him] like a Snail."

The first version, with its organic-metamorphoric phantasmagoria, looks back to the *Tale*, the second with its consistently developed building trope, looks ahead. The first is probably closer to the mode Pope was to develop, based on organic transformations that are resident in nature or drawn out of nature by the power of the poet. The organic ought to be valued as against the mechanical, but it is not. Both are devalued by Swift. But the simple trope of building, especially in the last lines about blast and ruin, looks ahead (surviving in the "repair" of Belinda's face) to the iconoclastic mode of Swift's mature writing, where everything is a matter of unstable building units.

In virtually all the poems of this period Swift starts by reducing the poetry of such poetasters as Vanbrugh to a mechanical (and mechanic) process. But then he also presents his own poetry in the same way, emphasized here by the "mechanical" development of the building trope that replaces the shifting architectural-organic figures of the earlier draft. It is not Swift but the modern poet who is the iconoclast in this scenario: he "blasts" the poetry of the past in order to build his own out of its ruins. Modern poetry is "built" of the rubbish—made by the modern poet's destruction—of ancient poetry. But how is this different from Swift's own procedure? Does he borrow his metaphor from the shabby modern, in some sense acknowledging either that there is no more now to work with or that, following Tertullian, the poet should flaunt his squalor?

For one thing, Swift might have cited the pseudo-Clement's description of St. Paul as a celibate who by "treading down and subjugating the body" made of himself a beautiful example and pattern to believers." As in the practice of iconoclasm, the ascetic's contempt for the "body" of writing and the written text was contrasted with the "soul" of the spoken word.[48] But Swift would also have argued that his mode is intimate and conversational, in that sense itself organic and antithetical to the mechanical demolishing and rebuilding he associates with the modern poet. But in his first, clearest model, the story of the spider and bee (in *The Battle of the Books*), the spider spins his art out of his own excrement, itself derived from the reinfunding of his previous excrement, whereas the bee flies about gathering pollen from the flowers of the ancients, which he makes into the "sweetness and light" of honey. The second (we might say organic) version is a positive model for the poet to follow, but it is not Swift's, at least in his poetry. His own subject, wherein he finds poetic substance, is the spider's procedure of making and therefore the weird airy castles that result. And the only way he can produce something out of this is to treat it in precisely the way Vanbrugh treats Whitehall Palace in the building metaphor: except that *he* can halt his mimesis at the stage of destruction and display the broken pieces. He can chart the process and attribute it to the modern poet, as in the later letter to Bolingbroke he attributed it to his workmen (who, however, took instructions from him) and to a monkey.

But by doing so he produces an edifice of his own, one that can be described as built from the ruins of some other house; that also, it must be added, is built on the metamorphic analogy of his own body. It is in the body, a parody house, that the organic metaphor returns, joining the mechanical-architectural, pointing toward the alternative endings of *The Lady's Dressing Room* with the gaudy tulip sprung from dung and *Strephon and Chloe* with the futile advice to "build on some foundation sound." The fact is that the poem, the body, and (as Fabricant has shown) the buildings Swift describes are all—as opposed to Pope's gardens and Palladian villas—conscious ruins, brought about by the laws of gravity, aging, and poor construction. He does not claim, or demonstrate, that he is rebuilding the iconoclasted ruins into a firm Palladian edifice, as Pope does. The result is more like a folly, a consciously constructed imitation of a ruin.

If Pope presents himself as "Poet," defined by employing great themes, grand models, and a finished, crafted, "correct" poem, Swift defines himself as a casual versifier of throw-away, absolutely occasional poems. This is not exactly the pose of the aristocratic amateur who only dashes off occasional poems for his friends (although Swift sometimes invokes the pose). On the contrary, these poems are presented as consciously un-Popean, as earlier, before he was aware of Pope and what he represented, they were un-Cowleyan, un-Drydenian, indeed antipoetic poems.

THE term iconoclasm then may designate a particular frame of mind, with a broad spectrum of origins running from Anglican to the radical fringe, which might help to explain certain characteristics of English literature and art as late as—perhaps particularly in—the eighteenth century. As I have said, what primarily distinguished English iconoclasm from its continental equivalents was its intensity, continuity, and duration. In a new world of business, paper credit, and upward mobility (what McKeon has called a "progressive" phase) in which people still held onto their religious memories, those memories in some cases expressed themselves in the form of iconoclasm. We may also add a nationalistic John Bullish iconoclasm, especially emphatic in a period of self-definition like the middle of the eighteenth century. A legitimate English yet Roman Catholic monarch lived abroad, a remote relative born in Germany and able to speak little or no English was *de facto* monarch, and a government and Opposition agreed on little more (including who should be king) than their opposition to Roman Catholicism.

This was the moment when in both literary and graphic traditions the models of the High Renaissance seemed to be petering out in academic formulae and stale imitations. We might say that, with the rise of the new science and the so-called English Enlightenment, the embedded mode of iconoclasm provided a particularly stringent way of going at accepted hypotheses; as in art, new, supposedly more "alive" images were made out of old stereotypes regarded specifically as idols, objects intervening between a man and the reality of God or nature, which usurped the experience of those realities.

If the basic assumption of the iconoclast was the absence of mediation between man and God—no idol, no priest, no set forms, and so in philosophy no hypotheses and in politics no king—then for the artist this meant no prescribed models. What follows is a break with art or literature of the past in order to reconstitute an English art of the contemporary (by which was meant business, credit, and upward mobility, among other things). As both Swift and Hogarth show—and even more powerfully the emergent novelists Fielding and Sterne—the images to break include literary and artistic precursors, or at least the canonical ones idolized by society's connoisseurs and critics. Swift cuts himself off from the past as strikingly as does Hogarth; he discredits his muse, replacing her with his immediate, contemporary, sometimes plebeian friends and neighbors. The poetic power derived from a muse, divine afflatus, or the past in general is replaced by a deep and abiding dissatisfaction with literary form let alone formalism.

The works in the tradition of iconoclasm are written at and for a lower level of audience than say Pope's or Collins's, which were always directed to a small educated elite. Whether addressing intimate friends or the Drapier's Irish "mob," and in particular in his elaborate hoaxes, Swift is practicing a popular mode related to Charivaris and Skimmingtons, those crowd rituals in which the subculture mimes and corrects the dominant culture. The muffled ringing of St. Patrick's bells in the 1720s following the latest English depredation against the Irish was both a Swiftean hoax and a subculture adaptation of the ruling class ritual of state mourning.

The relevant formulation of iconoclasm in this case would be the destruction of an idol of the ruling culture and its replacement by, or revelation of, a subculture equivalent. The subculture process itself is often "iconoclastic," though it is not thought of as revolutionary, rather reaching back in a reactionary way to a former, more stable time.

Idolatry was originally, in the context of the Old Testament and English history, a deviation, a backsliding from orthodoxy within the society. But by the seventeenth century (from James I and Charles I onward) the iconoclasts were at least some of the time a minority and deviant group within a dominantly High Church society, which to the Puritans was not iconoclastic but idolatrous (of king, sacraments, graphic art). It was this vein of thought or feeling which challenged what increasingly became the hegemonic view. What may have thought itself still iconoclastic appeared to be, or was labeled, idolatrous.

In the eighteenth century iconoclasm comes to speak for not only Protestantism—at least radical Protestantism—but scepticism and subversion, depending on whether the mode is philosophical or political; whereas iconolatry becomes associated with institutional authority or religion in general. As Archbishop Laud had been attacked as an idolator in the 1640s, so in the 1720s the idolator was any supporter of an idol in the present, whether a Walpole as prime minister, or a Cibber as poet laureate. But it could also (we shall see in Chapter 2) be construed as the poet like Pope who believed in an idol in the past, something that can still be worshiped, whether it is a god or a Greek statue, in contrast to the "modern."

Idolatry retained a more general significance in art—in particular graphic art (see Chapter 4)—as a designation that extended from a lady's cosmetics to an old master painting or a canonical sculpture. Idolatry at this time was coming to be connected with the "ancient": equally with Old Testament stories of vengeance and murder, with antique "paganism" and the erotic myths and with "old master" paintings. These were programmatically ridiculed by the *Spectator* (c. 1711–12) and replaced, in a radical reformulation, by stories of Christ and St. Paul, or (*faute de mieux*) of contemporary London life. The second term of denigration was "foreign." Mr. Spectator applied "foreign" to both the Roman Catholic religion and Italo-French paintings of Old Testament or classical subjects, to both castrati divas and the operas they sang in (Italian). As Mr. Spectator never tired of reminding his readers (and both Hogarth and, more moderately, Pope followed suit), these idols, worshiped by Londoners, elided the real flesh and blood of English men and women.

In short, the first quarter or third of the eighteenth century in England was a period regarded by both Whig and Tory as characterized by the worship of "false idols." Around 1710 this was the idolatry of Italian opera, foreign entertainments, and foreign art. In the 1720s and 1730s it was the idol of a prime minister who appeared to over-shadow both monarch and parliament. These and other "idols" were responded to in different ways by the Addison-Steele group, by Swift and by Pope (Defoe deplores making "an Idol" of noblemen),[49] while joining the fray in the 1720s was the young Hogarth who would work out his own reformulation of the issues in the next quarter of the century.

It is worth asking whether iconoclasm has a monopoly on violence or destruction, which was also, it is well known, a convention of the master genre of the period, satire, going back to the Renaissance and indeed back to St. Jerome and Tertullian and the early Church Fathers. The intensity of Swift's metaphoric dissection of Lord Allen or Sir Richard Tighe might be explained in terms of medical and punitive tropes of satire as well as in terms of the iconoclastic tradition.

But the iconoclastic term explains something the other does not. The difference is that iconoclasm, unlike satire with its convention of extralegalism, involves a toppling or overthrow. Because of England's ambiguous history the artist feels the right to challenge authority specifically as "idolatry" (and make this a theme of his satire). Perhaps this is only another way of saying what has often been said: that the Calvinist mind carried within it the seeds of civil rebellion. And perhaps we are dealing with people who directed their iconoclasm with such intensity at literary and artistic idols because they did not dare direct it higher. I suspect that the strength of the trope for these artists of mixed political and religious allegiances originated at least symbolically as a response on one side to the greatest of all English acts of iconoclasm, the beheading of the king, and on the other to the substitute idol of the "saints," the regicides who seemingly professed to false virtues. Perhaps in this period iconoclasm served as a uniquely ambiguous weapon, one that carried still an official and a religious sanction of a sort but could always be counted on to cut deeper than was called for and reach further than the immediate idol.

"SUPPOSE ME DEAD": SWIFT'S *VERSES* AND GRAY'S *ELEGY*

Two of Swift's most powerful symbols are the political hack writer who claims that he is unrewarded and shabby, his body battered with poxes and beatings, and the writer whose work is unread, unpreserved, and simply absent—whose own identity and existence themselves are therefore in jeopardy. The first returns in the poems about

Swift himself and his close friends; the second in the *Verses on the Death of Dr. Swift* (written in the 1730s), where both body and writings deteriorate to the point of demise, in a grim recapitulation of the passage in *A Tale of a Tub* about the fruitless posting of modern writings:

> The Originals were posted fresh upon all Gates and Corners of Streets; but returning in a very few Hours to take a Review, they were all torn down, and fresh ones in their Places: I enquired after them among Readers and Booksellers, but I enquired in vain, the *Memorial of them was lost among Men, their Place was no more to be found.*[50]

In the *Verses* this becomes the scene following Swift's death:

> Some country squire to Lintot goes,
> Inquires for Swift in verse and prose:
> Says Lintot, 'I have heard the name:
> He died a year ago.' The same.
> He searcheth all his shop in vain;
> 'Sir, you may find them in Duck Lane:
> I sent them with a load of books,
> Last Monday to the pastry-cook's.
> To fancy they could live a year!
> I find you're but a stranger here.   [ll. 253–62]

Each writer ends in the transient contingency of jakes, pie pans, and lanterns, and is (in the words of the *Verses*) "no more . . . missed, / Than if he never did exist." The emotional power of the two passages, from the beginning and the end of Swift's career, is equal: in the second he can be seen, having broken all the other idols, to have iconoclasted himself. He has proved himself the iconoclast (as every Protestant knew, only the most susceptible idolator) who first destroys external idols and at last the internal idol that may have served as point of origin for all the others.

Thus if goddesses and shepherdesses are reduced in Swift's poems (*A Description of the Morning*) to shabby London housemaids and prostitutes, and the Irish Parliament degenerates into a madhouse (as in *The Legion Club*), the figure of the poet himself, Swift or the Patriot-Drapier-Dean-Hero of the Irish, is treated no better.

This battered Swift has already emerged by 1713, even before the fall of the Tory Ministry, as the protagonist of his poems.[51] He is characterized as Dean (i.e., not-Bishop), penurious, deaf, vertiginous, aging, and all too conscious of his deteriorating body.

In his imitation of Horace's *Epistle* I.vii (1713) Horace, Augustus, and Maecenas become Swift, Queen Anne, and Harley in a relation-ship quite different from the one Pope would employ in the 1730s: they are all, and Swift in particular, sad reminders, shabby modern equivalents of the great Augustans. He is "Poor Swift, with all his Losses vext," "Above a Thousand Pounds in debt," "so dirty, pale and thin," "so lean," and when he is asked why "neglect your Self"? he replies, not for "Pelf," but also not for selfless service, but simply be-cause he has been put in such a difficult position—to be a dean in Dublin—that his only recourse is to concoct a classical parallel like this one, add rhyme, and make a poem out of his experience.

The message of the poem is that he has been taken from his true station in life, lifted up, in effect "idolized" by the Tory ministers, and thereby loaded with troubles, as if for Harley's "Jest" (anticipating the God of his *Day of Judgement* who says, "Go, go, you're bit"): "And since you now have done your worst, / Pray leave me where you found me first," that is, back on the streets of London.

This poor lean ragged figure recalls not only the Grub Street Hack of the *Tale of a Tub* but the poet-goose of *The Progress of Poetry* (1720), whose "cackle" is poetry, and whose poetic cackle is elicited only when he is hungry. As in *The Dunciad,* poetry, poverty, and hunger are directly related, but Swift leaves us not only with a comic paradox but with no alternative. There is no suggestion in these poems of the way another, supposedly better kind of poetry is to be made, or what it would consist of. Neither the ancient classical building nor the rea-sonably well-fed goose will serve. Poetry can be made now only from the representation of this paradox or from the imitation of the "lank and spare" goose's cackle. It is obvious that, being a satirist, Swift chooses the latter: to ridicule and destroy the cackle, but thereby in-corporate it into his own mode. And the ruinous modern poem is directly represented, or reflected or echoed, in the poems by Swift's own "lank and spare" deteriorating body. What is produced with this "cackle"? In the case of the hungry goose,

> Her Body light, she tries her Wings,
> And scorns the Ground, and upward springs,
> While all the Parish, as she flies,
> Hear Sounds harmonious from the Skies.

And in the case of the hungry poet,

> He singing flies, and flying sings,
> While from below all Grub-street sings.

In the same mode as Pope's later description of a poor poet in the *Epistle to Dr. Arbuthnot* ("high in Drury Lane / Lull'd by soft Zephyrs thro' the broken Pane"), these lines happen to be the most "beautiful" Swift allows himself in his poetry. "Beauty" equals poetic, flatulent verse.

In terms of the iconoclastic trope we can try another phrasing: Swift breaks and empties the idol and then climbs (or suspects that he climbs) inside the shell himself, becoming what he has broken now that it is clearly broken and no longer idolizable. What is, of course, unsettling about this proceeding is that Swift is made to fit precisely the image of the decrepit house or lantern in which the religious enthusiasts of the *Tale of a Tub* tried to manifest their spirit. In this as in other ways, Swift becomes his own Grub Street Hack. Ultimately, in the *Verses on the Death of Dr. Swift*, he is dead, his writings forgotten. But he cannot let go, and so (although Pope objected and made cuts in the London edition) he retains the memory of himself, as the form taken by his spiritual part. His deteriorating body is theoretically justified (as in the related case of his friend Stella's) by the elevation of mind or spirit, whatever transcends body; but this body comes very close to the sooty lantern of the enthusiast or the airy castle of the poetaster.

When all is broken and destroyed, what remains?—the spirit, though we are aware only of the materiality of the ruins in which it supposedly dwells, or from which it has been released, or around which hovers memory, or its external version, fame. Swift's *Verses* can be taken as a model for the transition from idol to tomb, from an iconoclastic to a memorial mode.

How is the tomb of the *Verses* arrived at? As one result of the famous Swiftean "irony," entombment is the logical outcome of a procedure of praise-by-blame (Stella is mean, cranky, and self-centered) which is the other half of blame-by-praise, the more viable, satiric half of irony. In other words, Swift's ironic and self-destructive blame (i.e., praise) embodies the imaginative truth of his ironic writing. Swift's works, his body, and his being are blamed (said to be self-centered, trivial, and ephemeral) and, in the end, are rendered nonexistent—by his friends, his enemies, himself. And by making them so, Swift acknowledges in the most poignant way that he is himself part of all that he has iconoclasted as Other—the world of the Grub Street Hack, which is in fact *our* world. But at the same time, as a function of praise-by-blame, he is actually all the opposites—heroic, immortal, and the only true friend, as at the end of the

Verses he allows the "impartial voice" (to some readers' confusion) to verbalize.

The purpose of the "impartial" Man at the Rose is to refill the empty space of Swift's identity created by the almost infinite division of opinions that eventuated in dissolution. Likewise all those different interpretations of the *Verses* (one of the cruces of eighteenth-century scholarship) imply a dispersal of meaning and of self which is Swift's primary intention within the text itself. The self-ironies and contradictions pointed out by Barry Slepian and others are only a part of this dispersal, in the form of safety nets.[52] When Swift gives us once again the official story of "Dean Swift" which he has been re-writing in poems ever since 1713–14, he must put it in the mouth of one ironically referred to as "quite indifferent in the cause," who tends, for example, to praise Swift's originality in lines lifted from Denham and his public role in Ireland (genuinely heroic) in the jingling verses beginning "Fair Liberty was all his cry" which Swift himself would have spurned.

The point is that Swift's body is completely gone, and his works as well. What survives is his memory—what I once referred to as a platonic spirit but now see is more accurately summed up in Pope's terms "fame" or "character" or opinion.[53] The ironies thus demonstrate the instability of Swift's identity even here, or perhaps of all places here, in his "fame." In terms of the iconoclastic structure, his body has been destroyed and remade into something utilizable—an "example," no more real than the original, and indeed capable (as Swift's profoundest irony shows) of itself being turned into as much of an idol as the old broken one (or as the one Pope was laboriously constructing for himself on the other side of the Irish Sea out of his correspondence and portraits).

Swift's point, as throughout his poetic oeuvre, is that one must destroy in order to make: kill the body, destroy the (his own) literary works in order to replace the potential, the dead idol himself (to others, to himself, *like* Walpole an idol) with the living reality. This means replacing the abused, that is, worshiped icon with the unabused image of his memory expressed in the words of an "impartial voice." So the broken idol is replaced by memory and the poem becomes the funerary monument that expresses or represents the lifeless body as well as the memorial apotheosis. Or (as in Hogarth's procedure in *The Analysis of Beauty* Plate 1, fig. 3), you take Dean Swift, literally kill him, that is, empty the sign of its conventional iconographical meaning, and put it, now dead and empty, in another, an existential context—and so give it a different, and therefore a reenlivening meaning.

In much the same way in his *Elegy Written in a Country Churchyard* (1750) Gray regards the great funerary monuments within the country church, shows them to be empty, moves outside to the humble epitaphs in the churchyard, and attaches such an epitaph to an unknown, unknowable figure, without even a name, but who is designated as the Poet and appears to be as much Gray as "the Dean" was Swift.

THE basic assumption established in Addison's essay on georgic (1697) was that while the pastoral voices are those of shepherds, the georgic is spoken not by the farmer but by the poet, who gives his voice to the homely formulations. Addison contrasted Virgil's precursor Hesiod the farmer (of the *Works and Days*) with Virgil the poet, who in his *Georgics*

> has so raised the natural rudeness and simplicity of his subject with such a significancy of expression, such a pomp of verse, such variety of transitions, and such a solemn air in his reflection . . . [that] He delivers the meanest of his precepts with a kind of grandeur. . . . He breaks the clods, and tosses the dung about, with an air of gracefulness.[54]

Thus the georgic bequeathed to the age of Pope and Swift was one in which the juxtaposition of style and content was built in, and with it a way of handling dung and other unsatisfactory materials by means of art. It also indicated a distinct tendency (the crux for which was Virgil's account of the bees in his fourth *Georgic*) toward the mock-heroic contrast, the playing of subject against tone, which will problematize one or both. Given the georgic assumptions, the high poetic style might confer pathos on the discrepancy between the high incantatory, ceremonial voice and the reality, both in the regularity of the seasons that can be utilized and in the storms and earthquakes, plagues and wars that are not controllable by the human voice; as it might also, as in John Gay's *Shepherd's Week*, complicate both character and spectator response.

Gray's *Elegy* represents the interface of georgic and iconoclasm, and then of iconoclasm and mourning. In so far as the *Elegy* identifies with the life of rustic farmers, yet speaks in the clear voice of a learned poet (whose every line echoes earlier poets), Gray is writing in the georgic tradition as prescribed by Addison. But he hyperbolizes and thematizes these facts into a meditation on the contradictions implicit in this idea of georgic poetry. The opening starkly opposes the world of "the ploughman" to "darkness and to me." The georgic ploughman has to go home from his labor, into his cottage and out of sight, in order for the georgic poet to emerge to write his poem.

It is the ploughmen who are buried in the graveyard; indeed buried in georgic fashion like seed pods (l. 16), promising crop and harvest. Their obscure life of "useful toil" is contrasted by the poet to the public-poetic fame consequent on ambition, as their burial, like one of their own crops under the ground of the churchyard, is contrasted to the heraldic designs and allegorical figures (such as Ambition) inside the church. In short, the ploughman is given by the poet (that is, by the power of Ambition itself) the potentiality of a Hampden, Milton, or Cromwell, one of the other figures of Ambition within the church. But it is clear that outside in the churchyard the ploughman will only produce more crops. It is one of the rustics, not the poet, who inscribes his halting verses on the ploughman's tombstone. The *Elegy* is about the interplay of the rustic's and the poet's poem and Gray-the-poet's attempt to reconcile them. But the poet himself also ends his life in the churchyard with words on *his* tombstone which associate him with the rustics rather than the poet of the poem. In fact, it is not altogether certain whether the inscription on his tombstone was written by himself or by the "hoary-headed swain" (whose designation suggests the conflation of hoary, grey, and Gray). Whoever its author, however, the physical labor of the inscribing was certainly carried out by a rustic hand.

What Gray himself does in the opening lines of the *Elegy,* as the author of the poem, is to wipe out the lowing herd, the ploughman, and all human figures (they all "part"), along with the fading landscape. Leaving "the world to darkness and to me" is to clear a page on which to write. What remains are faint sounds, the "droning flight" of the beetle and the "drowsy tinklings" of the distant departing herds, which are being replaced by the inscriptions of the survivor-poet. The poet who experiences this scene is the epitaphic survivor, who draws the analogy between this darkening landscape and the graveyard with its "narrow cells." Because he is writing a poem, the link also seems pertinent between the lines of his poem and the uncouth rhymes and shapeless sculptures with which the simple tombstones of the poor in the churchyard are decked.

But having in fact cleared away the living, the poet turns to the dead, "Each in his narrow cell for ever laid, / The rude forefathers of the hamlet sleep." "No more" is the refrain that removes them from the empty landscape. It is this process of emptying that corresponds to the action of Swift's *Verses* on his own death. But it is the "mute inglorious Miltons," extended to the village-Hampdens and guiltless Cromwells, about whom he writes the poem. Their death, plus their obscurity in this country churchyard (as opposed to inside the church with its storied urns), is Gray's supposed subject. Death here is a kind of leveling for Gray the poet, putting himself out of the poetic competition as he links himself with those "mute inglorious Miltons," but also a specific act against the older poet, rendering Milton himself (albeit through displacement) dead, mute, and inglorious. It is a poem which removes, renders dead or mute and inglorious the poetic precursors whose words in fact, line by line, dominate the poem: it bulges with the words of other poets (including Milton, including cases in which the murdered precursor himself is shown doing the same to *his* precursor, for example Milton to Virgil).

The *Elegy* then begins with the poet emptying a scene or landscape into absence and loss, and proceeds to the removal of the poet himself. Gray's point is his own "obscurity," "to future and to fame unknown." The epitaph is the sort Samuel Johnson believed to be a contradiction in terms, for an *un*known person; yet also obviously for the poet of *this* poem we are reading (like the epitaph that concludes *The Dunciad*). "Approach and read (for thou can'st read)" refers to the reader's reading of this poem by the same poet. The *Elegy* is built on the dual paradoxes of fame/obscurity and presence/absence: the poet who is dead but not dead, surviving not just in this imaginary epitaph but in the poem that creates this imaginary death as it projects the imaginary epitaph, all of which begins for us with the final *Dunciad*.

The poet's epitaph, with which the poem ends, is in the third person and employs another survivor, the "hoary-headed swain," who describes in effect the poet of the earlier part of the poem: Gray allows himself to have his cake and eat it, giving us both the deceased and the survivor, himself and his other self, commenting on each other, in the manner of the conventional epitaph of the time and, of course, the epitaph of Swift's *Verses*.

BEN Jonson (who served as a context for Swift's metaphor of writing/building) provides an epitaphic context for these tomblike poems. I quote his epitaph, *Charles Cavendish to His Posteritie* (c. 1619):

Sonnes, seeke not me amonge these polish'd stones:
These only hide part of my flesh, and bones:
Which, did they ne're so neate, or proudly dwell,
Will all turne dust, and may not make me swell.
Let such as justly have out-liv'd all prayse,
Trust in thy tombes, their care-full freinds do rayse;
I made my lyfe my monument, and yours:
To which there's no materiall that endures;
Not yet inscription like it. Write but that;
And teach your nephewes it to aemulate:
It will be matter lowd inoughe to tell
Not when I died, but how I livd. Farewell.[55]

Swift's *Verses* derive from the tradition expressed in the second qua-train of Jonson's epitaph. The monument itself, the stone marker, the icon, is repudiated; "tombs" are canceled by "prayse," for Cavendish says "I made my lyfe my monument"—and, extending the reference, his offspring's ("yours"). The essential survival of Cavendish is in his actions, not in the monument, and in his unverbalized actions, since the fact of them alone is indicated. The iconoclastic series is implicit here: the image goes first, then the verbalization of an action, leaving the action itself—which, of course, in practice, is memory—but memory not materialized, actions not specified.

Nevertheless, in Swift's case the deeds *are* specified in the words of the "One quite indiff'rent in the Cause," as they are also in the case of Gray's epitaph by the "hoary-headed swain": as if the sons do carry out Cavendish's instructions to "write but that. . . ." The function of a visual monument in these poems, and quite consciously in the icono-clastic tenor of Gray's description of his graveyard, is canceled by a linguistic monument.

The other mode of survival—the soul in heaven—is not men-tioned. The protagonist does and does not identify himself, now dead, with his soul: because the soul, as in the climactic passage of the *Verses*, proves to be memory, the unabused image of Fame. As John Davies of Hereford wrote, in *An Epitaph upon . . . Sir Thomas Gorge,*

Then though the Earth his corps hath in her gorge,
Men keepe the fame and God the soule of Gorge.

That is, the grave, earth's "gorge," is opposed to the transcendence of "men/fame" and "God/soul", the two modes that are equally stressed in this epitaph.

It must be said that in Swift's poem the humanist ideal of fame (as still centrally celebrated by Pope) is combined uneasily and paradoxically with *contemptus mundi*. Exactly where one expects the assertion of Christian transcendence—when the body has been destroyed, and the writings and even, according to the examples of the deceased's best friends, memory—we are given the long circumstantial account of actions, the equivalent of humanist fame. Swift asks us to give him both spiritual transcendence and earthly fame by combining them. Coming a few years later, Gray's poem, with its vagueness as to who even is the deceased, let alone as to any positive acts, even writings, that can be attributed to him, points to a spiritual negativity. Where one expects an expression of spirit, there is nothing but the memory engendered by the poem itself.

In the epitaphic tradition, a stone comes to stand for the dead and absent person. It marks or contains the spot of burial. But the content is radically ambiguous: the deceased is both absent and present, alive and dead, the ashes and the soul, under or within the monument. The monument is both a facade and a hollow container: indeed, both filled and hollow, with the body and without life, with the spirit and without the body, and so on, one paradox after another. The literary epitaph merely simulates this situation on paper, taking the reader to one remove from the physical encounter of a passerby (whether bereaved or stranger) and the symbol of the dead. The epitaph on a gravestone is only a more compact form of the plot of Swift's *Verses* and Gray's *Elegy*.

What we have is another version of the sacramental realism of iconoclasm, the knowledge passed on from beyond the grave, though in fact from a human projection based on observation, common-sense, and/or faith, that the spiritual and bodily coexist most significantly here. That the body dies and deteriorates as the soul expands and rises is the horrid insight that Swift was exorcising in his attack on the gnostic heresy in the *Tale of a Tub*. But this heresy, as he knew and showed in the *Verses* on his own death, is the ugly reality of what happens under or within the funerary monument, when corpse gas expands and breaks out of the bodily container.

But the process is the opposite of iconoclasm in that the spiritual representation is not replaced by a commonplace material equivalent but the physical body breaks in order to be replaced by spirit. The paradox of the grave is that the physical, bodily gasses released are to the soul as common bread is to the Body of Christ. And yet the assumption is that the tomb holds one and releases the other, is an enclosure as well as an exit; that the home and the tomb are one, as Thomas Randolph wrote in his *Epitaph upon His Honoured Friend, Master Warre* (ll. 15–16):

> Learn (Reader) here to what our glories come;
> Here's no distinction 'twixt the House and Tomb.

I shall quote a series of points made by Joshua Scodel in his study of the epitaphic tradition, focused on (his example) the Cavendish epitaph by Ben Jonson quoted above: the central paradox, in Scodel's words, is that "the voice of Cavendish is represented as emanating from the tomb in order to deny that he is in any important sense to be found there." Thus "contact at the tomb between the living and the dead is both denied and affirmed: the dead are no longer present except as ash, but they communicate through the pessimistic message they somehow manage to deliver to the living." Except of course, as we have seen, the commonsense eighteenth-century epitaph writer knew the dead was not speaking. Swift and Gray had to invent fictions to convey the message of death to the living.

Scodel notes that in the verses on Cavendish "the emphasis upon the act of *transmitting* the message suggests the transcendence of time and place through continued human communication"—and indeed it suggests the basic tension in any epitaph between the constraints of time, place, and tomb and "the space- and time-defying message" conveyed by the epitaph. This amounts to the "much in little" (or house/tomb) motif of the epitaphic tradition, "the wondrous containment of the great within the small." Whether the "great" is the remains of a great man, any man, any absent one, or the spiritual survival, the "great" is opposed to "the ironic contraction of all aspiration to greatness" which is represented by the ashes or bones in the urn or sarcophagus—as well as the small space in which the epitaph itself allows us to speak of the dead. The epitaphic tradition dwells upon these paradoxes and relationships, embodying them in the topos of inexpressibility: nobody could praise X adequately, or (if X is a poet) nobody now that X himself is dead can praise him adequately.

At the center of memorial art is the acknowledgment of—or play upon—the impossibility of expressing the dead or the poet's sense of the dead or of grief. There is therefore a blank at the middle—the emptiness/fullness of the actual space within the sarcophagus or urn—which we shall see Wright of Derby leaving as a consciously ambiguous area (Chapter 5).

But for the sculptor and the mason the paradox of the absence-presence of the dead cannot be resolved in a poem printed on paper. A more concrete and moving drama is inevitable in the actual spot where the burial has taken place, in front of the monument itself. Memorial sculpture and iconoclasm meet in the inefficacy of the monumental icon, its inability to express the great soul or the life-as-monument of the deceased. Every tomb is a type of Christ's empty tomb visited by the Marys, and most epitaphs (including both Swift's and Gray's) emphasize the failure of words as well.[56]

Scodel has shown that beginning with royalist epitaphs in the Civil War and increasing in the disillusionment of the Restoration, the literary epitaph adopts an adversarial relation to the age, reflecting on those others the survivors and suggesting that they help to bring about the end of the epitaph's subject. A simple example Scodel cites is Charles Cotton's *Epitaph for His Uncle Robert Port:*

> Here lies he, whom the Tyrant's rage
> Snatch't in a venerable age;
> And here with him, entomb'd do lie
> Honour, and hospitality.

As Scodel says, it "mingles the praise of a past ideal with an attack on the present and enunciates, within its little compass, a pessimistic view of current history." In other words, epitaphic poetry has become—in this period of satiric efflorescence—a satiric mode. The example offered by the epitaph is dead, an inimitable ideal in these fallen times, and, moreover, his death is the result of the prudential maneuvering of successful survivors. Pope's mode is in fact epitaphic in the sense that he presents himself as a survivor and the poem, with the authority of the last, the final word, as a kind of epitaph.[57] Elegy and satire show their common subject of loss and grief, including a certain resentment of the surviving multitude, those who (according to the old saw) were "not good enough" to die. In the 1740s then the panegyric mode changes decisively from addresses to the living (as in the tradition of the love lyric as well as the political panegyric) to addresses to the dead. This is an address not spoken by the dead but to and about the dead, or more often the absent—and thus an invocation, an apostrophe, an enlivening of a dead or inanimate object.

We can now project a narrative of the iconoclastic sequence: myth and idolatry are broken by Reformation iconoclasm, and a skeptical, rationalist, and nationalist cast is given English poetry and art. A poet like Pope, to whom we now turn, farms and gardens among the ruins—building on what is *there,* making *useful* (joining iconoclasm and georgic) objects from the remains. But the next generation, returning to the moment of Reformation when the idols were broken, seeks restitution—new idols, a spirit that can be instilled into the broken shells—and makes *this* the subject of its poems and paintings.

Chapter 2

The Aesthetics of Georgic Renewal: Pope

> *Pope* . . . chose rather, with his namesake of *Greece,* to triumph in the old world, than to look out for a new. His taste partook the error of his Religion; it denied not worship to Saints and Angels; that is, to writers, who, canonized for ages, have received their apotheosis from established and universal fame. True Poesy, like true Religion, abhors idolatry . . .—Edward Young, *Conjectures on Original Composition,* 1759.

GEORGIC FARMING AND OVIDIAN METAMORPHOSIS

This chapter approaches Pope the Roman Catholic who had to write within the gap—literally the "yawn"—left by iconoclasm, the iconoclasm of "others," and claimed to do so by way of the georgic cultivation of broken, fallen, season-governed acreage. As far as Pope was concerned, what the Civil War and the Glorious Revolution (and above all, William III, and then George I and II) stood for was iconoclasm. But writing from the position of the iconoclasted, Pope at the same time required an idol of his own in the form of an "Other" against which to react in his own iconoclastic fashion. Perhaps it was impossible to write in England without in one way or another partaking of the iconoclastic tradition.

The central question of *The Dunciad* (1728) is how does a poet make use of iconoclasted materials, by which we mean both the ancient gods iconoclasted by the moderns and the new gods set up by the iconoclasts which are being broken and dispersed by the poet Pope. The answer comes on many levels: as georgic farmer he grows food and flowers from the compost, as Ovidian poet he transforms these intransigent materials (metamorphoses them) into art, and as the Miltonic poet of *Paradise Lost* (conflating the poet and the Son of God) he redeems the fallen world. We would be misunderstanding Pope's sense of his own poetry if we overemphasized one of these models at the expense of the others. Satire, the fourth term, the one most frequently applied to Pope, is simply the fallen, rather secondary genre (Pope like Horace apologizes for using it) that is at hand for practical use by the georgic farmer who must till, sow, and reap in the fallen world. The fallen world, we must emphasize, includes both the consequences of modern iconoclasm and of the poet's need to wreak his own havoc.

The poor hacks and their shabby poetry Pope loathes and wishes to obliterate. But he also knows that these dregs are, in one of its aspects, nature—though he would say unredeemed nature, a perversion of nature, or fallen nature plastered over by false art, made into an idol. And for various reasons he is drawn to this subject, perhaps as more interesting, certainly as more viable, more probable, more threatening in the 1700s than, say, the poet's conventional, classical canonical subjects of Hercules, Achilles, and Hector—or (the chief immediate subject of most seventeenth-century poets) the monarch. In the same way, but at a higher level, the world of Belinda, Clarissa, and the Baron in *The Rape of the Lock* is more local and national, as well as trivial, than that of Sarpedon and Glaucos in the *Iliad*. In both *The Rape of the Lock* and *The Dunciad* Pope demonstrates his duty but also his prowess as a poet by absorbing these local, particular, ephemeral, and often ugly materials into the beautiful world of classical learning and art.

The principle of accommodation most clearly enunciated in Pope's poetry is Virgilian georgic, supported of course by its Christian analogues in *Paradise Lost* (and in the Church Fathers' interpretations of Virgil's "Pollio" eclogue). The georgic statements are scattered throughout Pope's poetry. In the *Epistle to Burlington* (1731) he bases the process of landscape gardening on the need to "consult the Genius of the Place in all."[1] This involves first a knowledge of the capabilities of the terrain, that is, its climate as well as soil, from which its beauty and utility can be drawn out by the skillful gardener. It is, in this sense, the genius of the place "That tells the Waters or to rise, or fall, / Or helps th' ambitious Hill the heav'n to scale": It "tells" and "helps," and as the passage continues, it "scoops" the vale and "calls in the Country, catches opening glades, / Joins willing woods, and varies shades from shades." But its relationship with the patron-architect Burlington, to whom the poem is addressed, is reciprocal: "Now [it] *breaks* and now *directs,* th' intending lines; / Paints as *you* plant, and as *you* work, designs" (ll. 57–64, emphasis added). In the course of the poem Pope sets up the addressee and the poet, Burlington and himself, as parallel figures, and the making of a garden and a poem (*this* poem) as analogous acts. Both involve the human inability to create out of whole cloth, by means of either mathematical ratios or the unaided imagination. This collaboration of the gardener with his land and the poet with his indigenous subject matter is couched in the discourse of the georgic farmer.

The analogy was implicit in Virgil's *Georgics* (especially the fourth, between Aristaeus and Orpheus) and emphasized in Addison's essay on georgic and Dryden's authoritative English translation (both, 1697), where Dryden renders Virgil's line, "ignarosque viae mecum miseratus agrestis," literally "pitying *with me* the rustics who know not their way," as "Pity the poet's and the ploughman's cares."

Of course, Pope and Burlington can expect to learn that their "Just," their "Noble Rules" for drawing art out of nature, for fixing the transient in nature by art, will "fill half the land with Imitating Fools" (l. 26). Both poet and Man of Magnificence (or true patron) therefore "make falling Arts [their] care, / Erect new wonders, and the old repair" (ll. 191–92), with the same ironic glance at the duncical distortions and recreations of Timon and the monarch, whose failure of patronage makes necessary the work of the restorers Burlington and Pope.

As the *Epistle to Burlington* suggests, although "farming" carries the bluntness of the georgic intention, "gardening" is the more precise term for Pope. Gardening was more aristocratic by association and implied the remaking of the Garden of Eden with another garden, not some corn or wheat field. Pope's examples are lordly estates and landscape gardens, and they carry a nostalgia for both the Christian and classical pastoral garden. However "natural" an English landscape garden was to become, at least as late as the work of Capability Brown, its "art" in fact predominated.

In the complementary epistle, *To Bathurst* (1733), the Virgilian view of man in *Burlington* is qualified by the Christian, Bathurst's classical ethos with the Man of Ross's *Imitatio Christi.*[2] Bathurst is not a creative restorer like Burlington but a great man who understands the classical virtue of the middle way: "That secret rare, between th' extremes to move / Of mad Good-nature, and of mean Self-love" (ll. 227–28). The Man of Ross, like Burlington but with only limited means, "*hung* with woods yon mountain's sultry brow," "*bade* the waters flow" from dry rocks, not for purposes of grandeur but for "health to the sick, and solace to the swain." He put up seats for the weary traveler, and "taught" a church spire to rise.[3] The language parallels the description in *Burlington* of how the architect-gardener brings out the genius of the place, but added now are Christ echoes that become more insistent as the Man of Ross "divides the weekly bread," feeds the poor, "relieves, / Prescribes, attends the med'cine makes, and gives" to the sick, and moreover drives out "Despairing Quacks" and "vile Attornies" from the temple (ll. 253–74).

The ideal of the poem emerges in the obscure, hitherto unsung Man of Ross, a private man whose fame the poet (as part of *his* function) draws out, as Burlington drew out the potentialities of a landscape. At the same time Pope the poet is consulting the genius of this obscure man (who died in 1724, "his name almost unknown"), drawing attention to his Christian life, and giving him the "monument, inscription, stone" he lacks: producing in effect a prospective epitaph. He does the same for the antithetical figures of the poem, the Blunts and Sir Balaams, whom he polarizes in his satiric mode as pseudo-Noahs and pseudo-Jobs (and, on the classical side, pseudo-Danaës). But the point to notice is that Pope has associated himself with the Man of Ross, in a subtle way capping the patron of the poem, Bathurst. Three figures play in Pope's georgic drama—the same three as in Virgil's: the poet, the farmer, and the patron. The presentation of this uneasy trio always turns the patron into something of the Other (as we shall see, Pope even turns Horace into a slightly alien Other).

The Christian-classical parallel/antithesis appears at its most striking in the description of Belinda's toilette in Canto 1 of *The Rape of the Lock* (1712–14). Belinda, carrying (ll. 35 ff.) overtones of Eve before the Fall, is shown looking at herself in the mirror, regarding her own image as Eve lost herself in her reflection in the pool. Pope combines by way of the mirror Belinda's functions as both idol and chief priestess, worshiped and worshiper. In this context, the donning of makeup assumes an Eve already fallen.

First, "awful Beauty *puts on* all its Arms," as Achilles "puts on" his suit of armor. Second, "The Fair each moment *rises* in her Charms"—Beauty "*repairs* her Smiles, *awakens* ev'ry Grace, / And *calls forth* all the Wonders of her Face." The carpenterlike word "repairs" is qualified by the more positively georgic (and organic) "awakens" and "calls forth": that is, from what is already present in the genius of Belinda's face. But the last couplet is the most precisely Christian. Beauty, Pope concludes,

Sees by Degrees a *purer* Blush *arise*,
And *keener* Lightnings *quicken* in her Eyes.   [ll. 139–44, emphasis added]

The "purer" blush is, of course, the "blush" made by cosmetics, which replace, augment, and fix the color at a point where an impure thought could produce a *natural* blush that is in fact less pure than one created by art: but art requires the basis of fact, Belinda's natural beauty, though fallen and so in need of "correcting" by art.[4] (In Belinda's case a blush would only give her away, revealing the crucial fact that she is in love and with whom. Love, we shall see, is in this case the crux.)

POPE wrote his georgic *Windsor Forest* (1713) in the context of his quarrel with Addison, Ambrose Philips, and Thomas Tickell over the way pastorals should be written. The Addison–Philips–Tickell theory of the pastoral recommended a program based not on the international, classical tradition of Virgil but instead on native English poetry and life; not on "heathen" "Fauns, Nymphs and Satyrs," but local superstitions, the "tales of Goblins and Fairies," and proverbial sayings;[5] not on the habits of the court and city but the customs of the specifically English countryside. (This is the same contrast outlined by Addison and Steele in the *Spectator* essays on history painting, which they argue should avoid the continental, classical, and antique stories of gods and heroes, replacing these with stories from the Bible and contemporary life.[6])

The Pope–Philips alternative versions of pastoral present essentially different aesthetic modes: Pope's emphasizes art, offering in his "Spring" pastoral both lamb and engraved bowl but clearly seeing his poem as analogous to the bowl that imitates nature in its own decoration, moreover with sky framed by the zodiac and the seasons by emblematic human figures called Seasons. The Addisonian tradition (in this particular respect) wants to emphasize the discontinuities with the past, with the classics, and give us a local, indigenous "art" for the 1700s.

The basic assumption, already established in Addison's essay on georgic, is that the pastoral voices are those of shepherds, whereas in the georgic not the farmer but the poet gives his voice to the homely formulations. The innocence and simplicity of pastoral, according to Tickell, should derive from the "Character of Shepherds":

> Their Minds must be supposed so rude and uncultivated, that nothing but what is plain and unaffected can come from them. . . . Those who have little Experience, or cannot abstract, deliver their Sentiments in plain descriptions, by Circumstances, and those Observations, which either strike upon the Senses, or are the first Motions of the Mind. [*Guardian* No. 23, pp. 107–08]

Tickell's examples juxtapose the poetic diction of a "courtly lover" with the simple, proto-Wordsworthian words of Philips's shepherd, to the advantage of the latter:

> Come Rosalind, Oh! come, for without thee
> What Pleasure can the Country have for me?

Whereas it is precisely the elevated diction that Addison–Tickell find appropriate for the georgic mode.

Pope's *Pastorals* (pub. 1709) might at first appear to be Addisonian georgic poems. But neither georgic nor the Virgilian imitation Tickell felt he wrote defines the *Pastorals*. Though Pope employs the strain of dispossession and postpastoral malaise he found in some of Virgil's *Eclogues*, the mode is satiric, the first genre one associates with Pope, inherited from Dryden and sanctioned by parts of Milton's *Paradise Lost*.[7]

The young Pope followed Spenser in making his *Pastorals* seasonal, indeed simplifying twelve months into four seasons. But when he divides his pastorals into four seasons, and begins with spring, he is limiting the unfallen world (the pastoral world) to spring; each of the succeeding eclogues portrays a stage of decline. *Spring,* therefore, with its harmonious conjunction of art and nature, of contesting poets, their loves, alternating songs, and shared prizes, is the only true pastoral of Pope's *Pastorals*.[8] The other three offer indications of representative satiric modes, or at least of elegiac modes on the way to the fallen world of georgic in *Windsor Forest*.[9]

Summer, though a conventional pastoral complaint, already approaches, with its oppressive heat and paranoia, Pope's more characteristic mode. The speaker Alexis, associated by name with Alexander Pope, is the young poet trying to write poetry to his beloved in a world from which the muses have fled (to the fashionable poets of Oxford and Cambridge). The beloved is not to be found, and the

only harmony that remains is between the poet and his own rural setting. The dedication is to Sir Samuel Garth, the satiric poet and
translator of Ovid, but Garth is invoked as a physician, a body-doctor
(as Dr. Arbuthnot will be in Pope's mature *Epistle* to him), yet one
who cannot cure the "disease" of love. And mingled with the address
to him are the references to the "You" of the ideal that is unattainable
in this Miltonic garden in which love is now a "Serpent." Only in the
poet's love complaint itself is there an art, already prefigured in the
bowl inscribed with the Four Seasons in *Spring*, which cures in a way
that Garth's medicine cannot. The present but inefficacious Garth,
the absent but longed-for ideal, and the busy poets of the universities
will reappear in modified form in the satires of the 1730s.

The most obviously satiric is the third pastoral, *Autumn*, dedicated to William Wycherley, the satirist of *The Country Wife* and *The
Plain Dealer*. Here Pope simply sets up a dramatic situation in which
Hylas and Aegon, two foolish shepherds, whose loves are absent and
unfaithful respectively, maunder on about themselves and project
equally delusive visions of happiness and suicide. The poet returns
only at the end to note that they sang this way "till th' Approach of
Night" and then went to bed without having recovered the mistress
or accomplished the suicide. This is a rehearsal for a satiric mode,
but not, as it happens, for Pope's. It acknowledges Wycherley's satiric
drama and may recall Swift's straight-faced reporting of incriminat-
ing documents or voices. Pope, however, except in some of his (un-
signed) prose satires, never allows the reader to believe he is merely
overhearing the words of a Hylas or Aegon. In his poetic satires we
are always aware of the voice and presence of a, or rather *the*, poet.
The poet may have many and shifting tones, or be accompanied by
other voices or felt presences, but the voice remains normative, encompassing the dramatic scene. Indeed, even the "delusive vision of
happiness and suicide" that is projected in Pope's mature poems is
made in his own voice.[10]

Winter, Pope's pastoral elegy, is a lament for what was; the "You" of
Summer is no longer missing but declared dead, with a possible apotheosis in the afterlife but no hope of restitution in this world. *Winter*
ends evoking a world in which not Love but "Time conquers All, and
We must Time obey," and Thyrsis bids the shepherds "arise" and
withdraw. The combination of complaint—or the sense of loss—with
the lone counterefficacy of the poem itself will also inform Pope's satiric writings, where the lost loved one has become Astraea.

The crucial eclogue, however, is the *Messiah* (1712), based on Virgil's fourth, "Pollio" eclogue, which furnishes the answer not vouchsafed by the *Pastorals*. The presence of the Messiah projects the pastoral Golden Age into the future—but in the Christian terms of redemption and rebirth. There the disjunctions of the fallen world will be banished and the contraries, including lions and lambs as well as separated lovers, will be reunited.

Pope had a genius for such visionary passages, where the action is a slow unfolding of apotheosis or apocalypse, and the real action takes place in the smallest units of meaning—the words, half-lines, lines, couplets, and their interactions. The Messiah's miraculous act of correction seems to have intrigued Pope almost above all else in the poetic range. It permits the figure *adynaton* ("impossibility") in its commonest "world turned upside down" form of mountains sinking and valleys rising and lions lying down with lambs (summed up in "*Hear* him ye *Deaf,* and all ye *Blind behold*"). But a similar use of *adynaton* will herald the approach of Dulness:

> How Time himself stands still at her command,
> Realms shift their place, and Ocean turns to land. . . .
> In cold December fragrant chaplets blow,
> And heavy harvests nod beneath the snow.   [*Dunciad,* 1.69–76]

> The forests dance, the rivers upward rise,
> Whales sport in woods, and dolphins in the skies . . .   [3.244–45]

This sort of poetry, whose fancy is at the expense of judgment, began for Pope with Ambrose Philips's "natural English" pastorals in which (as he acerbically noted in *Guardian* No. 40) "Roses, Lillies and Daffodils blow in the same Season."

This poetic solecism takes many forms, going back to the hyperbole of Tityrus's claim in Virgil's first *Eclogue* that before he can forget the generous acts of his patron, "stags must take wing and feed in the upper air; the sea roll back and leave her fishes high and dry," and so on.[11] But as Swift's poems repeat the Modern process of breaking and remaking, Pope's repeat the dunces' own fantasticating process—the evil of which Pope is careful to stigmatize—as one of creating graven images out of rubble. And yet Pope seems to acknowledge, in *Windsor Forest*, that poetry inherently depends upon some such trope when he describes the transformation of Lodona, the warlike nymph, into a still mirror of nature consisting of

> The headlong Mountains and the downward Skies,
> The watery Landskip of the pendant Woods;
> And absent Trees that tremble in the Floods;
> In the clear azure Gleam the Flocks are seen,
> And floating Forests paint the Waves with Green.   [ll. 212–16]

An inverted or pseudo Pollio vision is the chief, the best-known mode of his satire from *The Dunciad* to Vice's triumphal procession at the end of the first dialogue of *One Thousand Seven Hundred and Thirty-Eight* (the *Epilogue to the Satires*). There is always the temptation in Pope's grander moments to slip into a messianic pose, but this (we shall see) is accomplished by way of Milton's melding of Son and Poet. In general the Pollio's Messiah becomes an inversion at the hands of dunces, and it is the georgic to which Pope turns for his authority, with the georgic farmer serving as the model for the poet. The poet does not create afresh, like the Messiah; he lets his art draw out the inherent potential, whether in a landscape, in the subject matter of the satirist, or in the texts of his great predecessors Homer and Horace.

Two relevant quotations are, first, Pope's statement in the *Epistle to Burlington* about the "imitating Fools"

> Who random drawings from your sheets shall take,
> And of one beauty many blunders make. . . .   [ll. 27–28]

and second, Swift's remark to Pope in a letter: "You turn a blunder into a beauty."[12]

For Pope the poetic project was to make a garden out of his tiny estate in Twickenham which was divided by a highway, or to make poetry out of dullness—or even out of his own physical deformity. Only the second is a satiric transformation, and I suggest that Ovidian metamorphosis may be a term that subsumes satire as one of many forms of transformation. All have in common the transformation of a "blunder" into something that is specifically "art." This is an ordering that transcends farming, though it remains closely related to gardening with its vocabulary of sculptures, temples, and poetic allusions and inscriptions.

There was a satiric dimension in Ovidian metamorphosis, which originated as a reaction to the official Virgilian image of Rome and Augustus in the *Aeneid* as well as to the earlier, less imperialist, more pragmatic response to the Civil War in the *Georgics*. It indicated (as

Augustus saw) a refusal to serve the state or honor the Augustan principle of utility.[13] Ovid was, compared to Virgil and Homer, even Horace, slightly subversive, and remained (however popular) slightly off the map for Pope's contemporaries. Virgil wrote the official epic of Rome, in which duty wins out over Dido's love. Ovid wrote the *other* epic, the *Metamorphoses,* in which Rome originates in sexual dalliance. Only partly assimilated (necessarily allegorized) by the Christian commentators, Ovid retained the sense of being amusing, aesthetic, and amoral. He was known for the "truth" of his imitation of nature, especially his depiction of the passions, and in this regard he was a Latin poet to be imitated. But he was also known for his wit, cleverness, and (often) sensuality, and for these qualities he was to be avoided. The Christian allegorization of the stories of Syrinx (bk. 1) and Alpheus-Arethusa (bk. 5) amounted to little more than "virtue pursued by the soul." But when Pope imitates Ovid, it should be emphasized, he always retains the subject of sexuality as at least a blunder out of which beauty can be made.

The georgic fiction is, of course, related to a kind of metamorphosis, but one brought about by hard work in the fallen world, by a realistic appraisal of possibilities and a conscious awareness that without care we can slip back into the bloody civil war and the ploughshare can be replaced by the sword. Where the georgic speaks of truth, nature, earth, and vegetation, Ovid's *Metamorphoses* speaks of love, magic, fiction, and art. In his early poems at least, Pope endows his restorations and re-creations (and/or others' perversions) with the fiction of metamorphosis.[14]

Pope's gardener is always slipping into the Ovidian artist, the Pan who makes a flute of Daphne. It is safe to say that, while Pope may preach georgic, in practice he metamorphoses a blunder—or, in fact more often we shall see, a love/hate object (whether Colley Cibber and Lady Mary Wortley Montagu, or Teresa Blount and Arabella Fermor)—into an instrument specifically of beauty. The Ovidian metamorphoses that Pope evokes are the fables of the artist (or of art): the initial transformation is at the wish of the pursued (Lodona, Arabella Fermor, or Lord Petre), the second by the pursuer himself, who turns Daphne or Syrinx or Arabella into an instrument or product of his art.

Pope's earliest translations and imitations were of Ovid's *Metamorphoses,* and in *Windsor Forest* the georgic readjustments are posed in Ovidian terms. The central metamorphosis is of Lodona, fleeing from Pan, transformed into a river, her flight into a smooth-flowing, contemplative "mirror of nature," in other words poetry, as war is transformed into peace. As Lodona invokes Diana, her patroness, the poet invokes Queen Anne, his Diana-equivalent, to change war (with France, but with memories of the English Civil War, as the Roman Civil War was recalled by both Virgil and Ovid) into peace.[15] And, as author of this poem, the poet invokes his muse to change nature (politics, chaos, and contingency) into art.

The Lodona episode, which compacts the three levels of politics, art, and nature,[16] starts as georgic and ends as Ovidian metamorphosis. The climax of the passage is the upside-down poetic world that results from the metamorphosis of Lodona. Although the poem goes on to represent the political metamorphosis of war into commerce in the speech of Father Thames, it nevertheless returns at the end to the poet: to "my humble Muse," who "paints the green Forests and the flow'ry Plains," and the poet himself, who with the Peace of Utrecht can "more sweetly pass my careless Days," as both beneficiary, the subject of "empty Praise," and—manifest in the text before us—author of the transformation that has subsumed all of these elements. (He asks his dedicatee Granville to write the heroic; he will write the humble version.)

Metamorphosis involves the substitution, or the dissolution (as with *adynaton*), of categories or essences. Boundaries and limits are broken and reformed—not only of territories but those between hunter and hunted, art and nature, and victor and vanquished—in the ultimate breakdown of rational boundaries in death: "The grave unites; where ev'n the great find Rest, / And blended lie th' Oppressor and th' Opprest" (ll. 317–18).

The sequence leading up to the Lodona episode makes it clear that the hunt that is the sublimation of Williamite chaos nevertheless evokes the pursuit of innocent creatures, the cannibalism of fish, and ("if small Things we may with great compare") military conquest. The hunt is seen through the eyes of the hunted prey, but they are not finally permitted to be innocent. The pheasant "mounts *exulting* on *triumphant* Wings"; his "glossie, varying dyes, / His Purple Crest" and "shining Plumes" make him a symbol of pride and its consequent fall, of vanitas and pathetic loss—in short, an anticipation of the nymph Lodona.

The first two-canto version of *The Rape of the Lock* (1712), written at about the same time as *Windsor Forest*, repeats the form of metamorphosis with Belinda, another Lodona who goes too far, also pursued, her flight merely exciting her pursuer the more. When she loses her symbolic lock it is transformed by the poetic muse into a star. The Baron replaces Pan in the story and, by implication, Belinda's "honor" replaces Lodona's vow to Diana. When she defeats her suitor at cards her "exulting fills with shouts the Sky"; and, as with the "exulting" pheasant, the poet admonishes her pride ("Oh thoughtless Mortals"), followed shortly by Clarissa's shears and the Baron's rude act. The whole poem, it is clear from his Preface, Pope regarded as his own poetic metamorphosis of the Petre–Fermor squabble into peace, of anger into comedy and good feeling, of chaotic reality into art.

The source of Lodona's disaster recalls the love-lust described in Virgil's third *Georgic*, but primarily the love-lust that distinguishes the flawed past of *Georgic* 4 (Aristaeus's sin and the similar sin that led to the fall of Antony, to the Trojan War, and so on), which is redeemed in the butchery and maggoty rebirth of the hive.

The similarity between georgic and metamorphosis should now be obvious. If the *Metamorphoses* is filled with surrogate poets, the *Georgics,* as Addison emphasized, are spoken by a poet, not a farmer.[17] Both forms share the subject of the relationship between a rustic and the poet, summed up by Ovid in his combining in the person of Pan both nature and art, attacker and artist. It is a natural urge (often embodied in a natural creature, a satyr, though sometimes a slumming deity) which precipitates the metamorphosis. This metamorphosis is carried out by a supernatural force (a god, muse, monarch, or patron) as a transformation of living flesh into organic nature, and this transformation is recouped—in an almost georgic fashion—by the original perpetrator, who fashions and symbolizes the now inhuman substance into something no longer living but, by art's craft, immortal. The poet-satyr is the important and ambiguous figure at the center of Pope's fiction of poetic making.

In the fourth *Georgic* the farmer and the poet are divided, drawn apart in the would-be rapist Aristaeus and the bereaved Orpheus. Aristaeus has learned why he is being punished—how his satyrish pursuit of Eurydice caused her death and Orpheus's curse, which killed his bees. But the story continues with Orpheus's pursuit of Eurydice to Hades and his loss of her on their return, and then after his murder by the Bacchantes his severed head continues, even now, to lament his loss, calling Eurydice's name. In this ultimate georgic, farming and poetry have been divorced; or at any rate the poet has been shown to be the lamenter of loss, as distinct from the beekeeper who has learned how to recover his hive.

Pope echoes Orpheus's lament directly in his "Ode to St. Cecilia," but ultimately in *The Dunciad* he carries the story one step further than Virgil by picking up Ovid's account of Orpheus's yet-declaiming head which, floating down the stream, comes to rest on a shore where it is threatened by a serpent with widespread jaws—until Orpheus's patron Apollo freezes the jaws in their open, yawning, devouring gesture into immortal sculpture. This is the epigraph Pope attaches to the final version of *The Dunciad* (1743), thereby turning himself into Orpheus, murdered but, even in the act of devourment by the yawning jaws of Dulness, surviving as a poetic voice—while his muse has frozen into the immortality of literature the dunces, hacks, and politicians who have overwhelmed him with personal abuse. This final overview does not cancel the more general sense of *The Dunciad* as a georgic ritual by which life is engendered by the farmer from the maggoty corpse of the bullock or heifer, while the desolate poet (with a dead love in his past) laments his own personal loss.

The large action of Pope's satires takes two general forms. One is the emblematic, allegorical, allusive anti-Pollio vision of chaos and disorder, or of delusion and abject fantasy. The second action concludes with the Horatian sermo in which "Pope" converses with somebody. But it begins with the love lament of an Alexis or Orpheus, whose tone is never quite lost, supporting the strong tendency toward apologia, in which the satirist defends himself and at the same time produces satire on his maligners. One action is visionary, the other a dialogic interaction between two or more people. And yet they usually join; the latter is often a frame action for the vision, an "occasion" created for projecting visions of false creation. Pope's career as a satirist begins and ends with fictions of a lone poet complaining of the discontinuities of the world, the victory of Time over love, and projecting a vision of decline—his own and his society's—expressed, however, in the form of something beautiful and lasting which contradicts the pessimistic conclusion of the vision itself. The poetic act, following both georgic and Ovidian modes, is concerned with loss and the healing of that loss through art.

IT is necessary now to say something more about the types of transgressive materials transformed by this poet. One is the literary and moral dreck that is farmed or metamorphosed into the beautiful garden of classical art. But another is the satirist's rage itself, an excess not allowed to the "correct" poet (which Caryll advised Pope to become). The rage is directed against those who malign him and, equally, against what they malign in him. As the contemporary attacks (which he collected, listed, and in part quoted in *The Dunciad Variorum*) show, there was obviously a place in the English demonology of that unstable time for his Roman Catholicism (and so the suspicion of Jacobitism), his shortness and bent back, and his too-great brilliance ("wit to madness near allied"). From the first onslaught of John Dennis through the attacks of Lord Hervey and Lady Mary Wortley Montagu, and almost to our own day, these stigmas were represented by images of toad, spider, wasp, and monkey, easily grafted onto the emblem of malicious deformity—a Thersites or Richard III. Even his name allowed him to be called Pope for his religion and Ape (A.P—e) for his poetry. These names must have caused Pope to reconsider seriously the aesthetic that equated beauty and goodness, ugliness and evil. How does a grotesque hunchbacked body—as well as the rage it utters, the satiric venom it produces (one had almost said, adopting the satiric metaphor, excretes)—relate to the classical ideal of order and harmony? Marjorie Nicolson remarks on the growing admiration in these years for mountainous prospects including craggy mountains previously condemned as "hook-shoulder'd" deformities: Pope's shape also called for a new aesthetics or at least an aesthetic accommodation.[18]

Pope's earliest attempt at translation is of Ovid's *Acis and Galatea*, in which the theme of unrequited love in the "Summer" pastoral has been slightly complicated by the addition of a third party. Acis and Galatea love each other, and are not (like pastoral lovers) separated; but the story Pope translates is about Polyphemus the monstrous cyclops, who also loves Galatea, and, seeing the lovers embrace, "Frantick with his pain, / Roar'd out for Rage" and crushed Galatea's Acis, who is then metamorphosed into a fountain.[19]

If *Acis and Galatea* introduces a metamorphosis that is separate from the protagonist, it also introduces rage and the disproportionate body, which are other major elements of *The Rape of the Lock*. The rage of course came as part of Pope's donnée, but both Belinda and the Baron are invested with Polyphemus's fury—Belinda with his "Rage, Resentment, and Despair" and the Baron with his violent action. Belinda's beauty and aloofness, and her "exultant" victory cry, plus a drink of coffee which stimulates "New Strategems, the radiant Lock to gain," lead the Baron to commit the Polyphemus-like act of cutting the lock. If his response is excessive, however, Belinda's too is closer to Polyphemus's than to Galatea's. At first she does not know what to do. Thalestris's speech of poor advice is necessary to get her started, and this is supplemented by Sir Plume's expostulation, most unheroic by comparison, which serves to provoke the Baron to a further refusal to return the lock. And with this chain of provocation Belinda initiates the battle of the sexes, and "all the Prize is lost."

Pope's epic invocation asks the questions of how "dire Offense" can follow from "amorous Causes," "might Contests" from "trivial Things," great "Praise" from a "slight . . . subject," "Tasks so bold" from "Little Men," and finally, but above all, "such mighty Rage" from "soft Bosoms." The last two oxymorons closely relate to the Polyphemus story, but that was only one of a series of significant translations, including Chaucer's January and May and Ovid's Sappho and Phaon, which dramatize various kinds of disproportion between a lover and the object of his/her love, and in which the human relationship, ending in failure, nevertheless engenders poetry. In the cases of Polyphemus and Sappho, Pope is working with a story of the way in which poetry gets written, that is, out of loss, frustration and absence of the loved one—plus an act of uncontrolled violence. Polyphemus sings out of longing, but when he sees Acis with Galatea he can only respond with physical violence. And Sappho's story ends with her leap—and Orpheus's, of course, with his violent death at the hands of the Bacchantes (and Achilles' wrath).

Let us begin with "little men," not great heroes but tiny and diminutive, even feminine creatures. *Sappho to Phaon* is Ovid's only heroic epistle from a poet, and in particular a poetess (obsessed with a lover whose young body contains an aged heart), who writes in Pope's version, "Tho' short my Stature, yet my Name extends / To Heav'n it self, and Earth's remotest ends." The Baron is a "little man"; but Pope was also a little man, and the emphasis on the words in the *Rape* should be compared with Pope's papers on the "Club of Little Men" in the *Guardian* of June 1713 (Nos. 91, 92).[20] No. 91 announces:

> I question not but it will be pleasing to you to hear, that a Sett of us have formed a Society, who are sworn to *Dare to be Short*, and boldly bear out the Dignity of Littleness under the Noses of those Enormous Engrossers of Manhood, those Hyperbolical Monsters of Manhood, Monsters of the Species, the tall Fellows that overlook us.   [p. 325]

The "most eminent" members are a little poet, lover, politician, and hero. The poet, Dick Distick, has

> been elected President, not only as he is the shortest of us all, but because he has entertain'd so just a Sense of the Stature, as to go generally

in Black that he may appear yet Less. Nay, to that Perfection is he arrived, that he *stoops* as he walks. The Figure of the Man is odd enough; he is a lively little Creature, with long Arms and Legs; a Spider is no ill Emblem of him. He has been taken at a Distance for a *small Windmill*. . . . He hath promised to undertake a long Work in *short Verse* to celebrate the Heroes of our Size.   [p. 328]

And this, of course, was called *The Rape of the Lock*.

Interestingly, the poet is linked contiguously with the lover Tom Tiptoe, who goes to bed with a woman who, however, keeps the affair platonic by tying his toe to hers. Maynard Mack has documented the "gay-doggishness" of Pope's early London years, which took the form of the gallantry that defended Arabella Fermor by writing *The Rape of the Lock*—as later Lady Mary Wortley Montagu against Edmund Curll by administering an emetic to the bookseller and writing a pamphlet about it.[21] Even his initial attack on John Dennis in *An Essay on Criticism*, which elicited the first of the horrific personal attacks, must be attributed less to malice than to a sort of self-assertion parallel to his jokes about taking on London "women," which derived from the need to prove himself courageous and "manly" beyond his size and physical capabilities.

Pope also refers to the Little Poet as spiderlike and "stooping," and his translation of Homer's description of Thersites is another case of his dwelling on a figure, here combining deformity and satire, which must—to himself and to his readers—recall his own. Back in the "Summer" pastoral he named the poet Alexis, a conventional name but close to Pope's own. He gave Alexis a hopeless love, and one reason for its hopelessness was said to be his lack of university education (the muses wander beside the Isis and Cam). The reason that Pope could not attend Oxbridge was not financial but political: his Roman Catholicism. Just as the reason that, like the fictional Alexis, he was remote from a love object, was not his lack of university education but of a strong body.

In his reply to Tickell's *Guardian* essays on "English Pastoral," in which he polarizes and exaggerates his own Virgilianism against Philips's Spenserian pastoral, Pope makes two remarkable statements that introduce the personal. The first is when he characterizes himself as one who "takes the greatest Care of his Works before they are published, and has the least Concern for them afterwards." Everything we observe about his career gives the lie to the second clause; in fact, Pope devoted at least as much attention to his works "afterwards" as before publication. The second is when he writes that he "has imitated some single Thoughts of the Ancients well enough, if we consider he had not the happiness of an University Education."[22]

Returning to *The Rape of the Lock*, the "mighty Rage" also calls for some discussion. Although Pope does not always seek out causes, the situation and, more, the effect of the "mighty Rage" are subjects of concern for him: what are the causes of passion and indignant outburst? In this instance they are satirized as excessive all around. But a basic pattern of Pope's satire is established, a pattern not so much of cause and effect as of action and response, provocation and over-response. Somewhere within the Baron and Belinda and their over-reactions is the later obsessive question: what could make an innocent well-brought up poet, indeed one who has his own soul to think about, attack such powerful men as Hervey, Walpole, and even the king? This question is sometimes posed by enemies, sometimes by friends, and sometimes by the poet himself. However different in evaluation, the outbursts of Belinda and the Baron share with the poetic indignation of Pope's satires the apparently spontaneous emotion that has no place in the world of Augustan society and art. While Pope's preparations for his satiric outbursts are always carefully constructed, the construction is based on that of *The Rape of the Lock* and is both a way of getting himself into the position of uttering a Pollio vision and perhaps the only way of creating a poetic effect of an intensity that recalls the great poetry of preceding centuries.

The pattern is considerably clarified in the five-canto version of the *Rape* published in 1714, which adds explanations or motives for the "mighty rages." This version also attempts to distinguish Belinda's rage from the Baron's, making it plain that her rage reflects fear for reputation and appearances ("Hairs less in sight, or any Hairs but these!"), while his can be taken to represent a touch of the real world which Belinda the coquette needs—but which she rejects by simply going over from the sylphs to the gnomes.

The addition of Ariel and the sylphs sets up a third agency which explains the way "a gentle Belle" could "reject a Lord," and "dire offenses" can be related to "amorous causes," "mighty contests" to "trivial things." Within this contrast of opposing worlds an action of a different sort takes place, beginning with the vision vouchsafed Belinda in which her guardian sylph Ariel persuades her of (or supports her belief in) her personal sanctity and ideality above "dire" reality. *The Rape of the Lock* begins with these contrasting worlds, or at least ways of interpreting the real world, and a student and her mentor who urges upon her the false interpretation. The sylphs, whether we take them as a level of Belinda's consciousness or a social paradigm of honor, make the essential mediating link between Belinda and her imagined inviolability. Ariel's speeches project a lovely, artificial play world which is meant to replace the real world of marriage and deflowering—a world with its own laws and games that Belinda must obey or be abandoned. They also carry overtones of the temptation of a deluded Eve into seeing herself as godlike when she is a human in a humanly limited situation of courtship, and this temptation is followed by a parody Mass with Belinda officiating before a mirror altar at the "sacred Rites of Pride."[23]

A result of making Belinda a tempted and fallen human being—fallen through pride—is to elicit the exulting hubris of her victory speech, which is the direct stimulus to the Baron's overresponse (prompted only by coffee dreams in the earlier version) of breaking the rules of the game and cutting the lock. The response of Belinda then is hysteria, followed by the Baron's own exulting speech, which in the new context, though excessive, serves a corrective function. Because he has cut the lock, his "Honour, Name, and Praise shall live." Echoing Catullus's "Berenice" and its context of married love, he apostrophizes his sword—his "steel"—which "strike[s] to Dust th' Imperial Tow'rs of Troy," confounds "the works of mortal Pride," and hews "Triumphal Arches to the Ground." In the first version this was empty mock-heroic exulting; now in 1714 with the provocation of Belinda's pride and her own exultant speech, it sounds more like a forerunner of Pope's own vaunt, twenty years later in the *Epilogue to the Satires*: "O sacred Weapon! left for Truth's defence, / Sole Dread of Folly, Vice, and Insolence!" But even in the first version Pope has indicated the odds that are against the Baron, distinguishing between "soon to obtain" and "long possess the Prize"—words that recall the presence of the conqueror Time, with *his* "steel," as well as the power of reputation.[24]

A final addition, made in the 1717 revision of the *Rape*, is the speech of Clarissa, which balances Thalestris's angry outburst with counsels of commonsense and moderation. She is the unheroic and commonsense antithesis of Sarpedon, the hero who goes off to his death. Given the same assumptions about a world dominated by Time in which "frail Beauty must decay," he responds with "great Acts" and "Valour," she with "good Sense" and "Virtue." Clarissa speaks for the acceptance of truth, nature, and reality. Her handing the scissors to the Baron, already present in the first version, represented the same values, though with a militance that is lacking in her 1717 speech. As Pope observed, the latter was introduced to materialize the moral of the poem, but in her realism there is also the germ of a plea for the status quo. If only, the echoes of the *Iliad* seem to say, there were room for a Sarpedon in our world. Even poor Belinda and the Baron are at least fighting for their beliefs, however mistaken, in a losing battle with Time.

At any rate, Clarissa's counsel of moderation, even more than Thalestris's of rage, only serves to provoke Belinda to attack, and the battle of the sexes ensues. She rounds off a fiction of a passionate person who brings down the paragon of pride and affectation, even if it means disrupting the structure around her, violating the laws of politeness, and precipitating a battle. In time, in the age of Walpole, it will become necessary to rethink the alternatives of Thalestris and Clarissa, Clarissa and Sarpedon. The fiction develops through two phases for Pope, first the justification for that "mighty rage," and second the questioning of it as a way of life.

The most obvious, most public transgression of all has not been mentioned: Pope's Roman Catholicism. The anti-Williamite content of *Windsor Forest* is well known. Howard Erskine-Hill has convincingly drawn attention to the Jacobite content of *The Rape of the Lock*, beginning with the game of ombre as itself a metaphor in the 1700s for political affairs. There was a sense (emphasized in *The Key to the Lock*) in which the whole poem was a political allegory: the "rape" also applies to the "rape of a kingdom" by "Foreign Tyrants" that (in Erskine-Hill's words) "yield to what the Jacobites alleged James II's England had yielded to," that is, "The conqu'ring Force of unresisted Steel" (3. 179). In this context, Clarissa's speech is added in the aftermath of the Jacobite failure and Hanoverian triumph of 1714 to advocate "the heroism of submission."[25] The Jacobite cause was only more overtly unspeakable material than the personal issues of Pope's body and voice, for which perhaps his Roman Catholicism stood as emblem.

THE UNABUSED IMAGE OF MEMORY

The *expression of the truth*, though possibly a euphemism for the power of metamorphosing truth (what really happened) into art, was the focus of attention in *The Rape of the Lock*. Belinda was primarily concerned with her reputation, and Pope himself with correcting rumor's distortion of the Petre–Fermor misunderstanding as an act of memorializing.

In *The Temple of Fame* (1715), an exploratory work that must have been written very close in time to the *Rape*, Fame's throne is surrounded by—held up by—the pillars of the great poets and orators, Homer, Virgil, Cicero, Aristotle. And the poet's role, Pope learns in this poem, is to keep Fame true. In Pope's dream vision the young Alexis–Pope, who like the Baron wishes that his "Honour, Name, and Praise shall live," goes out to learn about the fame he seeks as a poet and discovers that instead of his own fame it is the fame of others with which he will be concerned. He is himself young and unformed, one of those "opening Buds [that] salute the welcome Day." The world spread out before him in his dream is a *concordia discors* of mountains and oceans, rocks and wastelands, cities and forests, and of the "clear Sun [that] the shining Scene displays" and the clouds that obscure the "transient Landscape." The world is a tension of these forces, serving as a model for the tension between praise and blame at their extremes of flattery and libel (ll. 40 ff.).

Thus in the Temple of Fame the Homers and Virgils are not themselves celebrated but serve as pillars supporting the edifice of Fame. Here Pope sees those who come seeking fame and learns that his role as poet is not to seek fame for himself but to create fame for others: if he does that he earns his place with Homer and Virgil in the Temple. One band of the good and just come and receive their earned fame, but another, who "no less deserv'd a just Return of Praise" (l. 331), are slandered: "From the black Trumpet's rusty Concave broke / Sulphureous Flames, and Clouds of rolling Smoke: / The pois'nous Vapor blots the purple Skies, / And withers all before it as it flies" (ll. 338–41). The subject matter Pope will be concerned with in his satires begins to emerge here in the Temple of Fame.

The poet's duty is to bring to light those who do good by stealth, to repair the reputation of the slandered, and to bury in oblivion those who do evil, but if they are falsely praised or their wickedness made an object of emulation, his duty is to show what they really are in the strongest colors.

But the Temple of Fame is also complemented by a Temple of Rumor, where there is no longer any correlation between reality and fame or merits. From here emerge lies, or truths and falsehoods mixed. Pope learns that his own essential theme is the need to rectify the effect of the Temple of Rumor with true fame; the poet's dual task is to praise the great and good and satirize the wicked. It is to represent the good who are defamed by such slanderers as Sporus, and therefore also the Sporus who does the slandering. "Honest Fame" will only come to him because he maintains its truth in a world controlled by Time, liars, flatterers, and slanderers. His career will be spent satirizing "the guilty Bays" (the poet laureate) who soothes Folly or exalts Vice, following Fortune and pandering to the great's "Lust of Praise," and the Sporus who slanders the truly virtuous. In the alternative (but not entirely suppressed) discourse of iconoclasm, he will destroy idols and make virtuous men and women into unabused images of memory.

As any reader of Pope's mature satires must notice, vice itself is very vaguely defined; it is often given particular names, but Ward, Waters, and Chartres are virtually interchangeable. The vice they denote is only a "mean Heart that lurks beneath a Star" or a "Rich or noble Knave."[26] The danger resides in the phrases "beneath a Star" and "rich or noble," for the figure of Vice, vague in itself, is defined in terms of its fame, given or received. Pope's satire is less about Vice than about the reputation that allows it to ride in Virtue's chariot or that overpraises and awards honors to Colonel Chartres (or Charteris) and makes him an example to emulate. He finds a place in the satires not because he was a despicable old rapist but because instead of punishment for this crime he received royal favor. Pope's real subject tends to be the people who accept, flatter, and glamorize Charteris; people who, beginning with party writers and hack poets, shade off into attorneys, stockjobbers, forgers of wills, and swindlers, and rise to prime ministers and kings.

Thus the wretched, often poverty-stricken hacks of *The Dunciad*, as Pope tells us more than once, are serious subjects (for satire at least) not only because they write flattering lies about the monarch and his court, but because they have been given the seal of approval by this same monarch and his court—embodied, for example, in the Poet Laureateship. The reason Sporus is evil is that he is a liar; he is dangerous because he has the ear of a figure of power, the queen, who controls the king.[27]

Pope's analysis of fame includes equally "who gives it, or receives it," the flatterer but also the flattered. As in the *Epistle to Augustus*, they are interchangeable: Cibber the poet laureate is both, as is George Augustus, who is equally the egregiously flattered and, raising Cibber to the laureateship, one of those "Bestowers of Titles; which they [kings] are generally most profuse of, to wh—s and kn—s."[28] The only true poet is far removed from both England and the court (Jonathan Swift, exiled in Ireland); attacking rather than prais-ing the court, defending freedom and providing for the poor and ill, he and not the king brings about "a Nation's cure." Above all, his function is "Proud Vice to brand, or injur'd Worth adorn, / And stretch the Ray to Ages yet unborn." Ultimately the antagonists are the two great bestowers of fame, the king and the poet. Within the poem it is the poet Pope who can show how true praise, *his* praise of this particular king, would sound (parallel to the mock acceptance of Vice at the end of the *Epilogue to the Satires*).

The Temple of Fame shows why Pope spent so much time arguing for particular over general satire: only in the first are real, living people involved—those who appear in the Temple—as opposed to gener-alized vices and follies. It also shows that his poetry will be less con-cerned with correction of morals than with correction of falsehood, or with both exposure and praise, which *The Temple of Fame* shows must begin with the true presentation of the evil and include the overarching praise of God's creation in the beautiful poetry into which Pope metamorphoses the evil. In this way the Ovidian meta-morphosis fits into the plan of the Temple of Fame.

THE *Temple of Fame* was accompanied in the period of 1711 to 1717 by a series of poems in which the fame of someone admirable—an Eloisa, an "Unfortunate Lady," a Cleopatra—is in jeopardy, and the poet rescues it by his poetical transformation. These require our at-tention because the satires that began to appear a decade later merely shift the emphasis from the slandered to the slanderers and libelers, and the slandered figure becomes the poet himself or his friends whose fame is put in jeopardy by the lies of Sporuses, Dennises, and assorted dunces.

The *Rape* and *Eloisa to Abelard*, two of these poems, are both about the questionable passion of a young woman in a monastic community (whether of those now sexless ladies, the sylphs, or of nuns), with "an earthly Lover lurking in her Heart," and no outlet except upward into self-worship or the true (Christian) religion. Belinda, and before her Lodona, was a virgin who successfully avoided the entrance into sexuality and thereby gained eternal fame and/or transformation into art.[29] In both Belinda and Eloisa the choice between loving to the point of crime (breaking society's law) or sin (breaking a religious law) lies in the conflict between a sensuous, "earthly" love and a love of a higher sort, which is, however, associated to a large extent (as Murray Krieger has noted) with "the humanly unsatisfying, empty promises

of disembodied, airy, artful perfection" in the sylphs,[30] and with monastic repression, a nun's cell, her vow of silence, her confinement by
the order's "rule," and emasculation and sterility. On the side of the
Church and God's law are the all-too-human agents who waylaid
Abelard. (Inevitably we associate them with the marriage law of Clarissa and with her shears, but they will also become the dunces who
attack Pope.) It is hard to say how much emphasis Pope intends to
put on "Church" as opposed to God, but certainly in Eloisa's mind
the monastic world, where only the statues can weep, is a more sti-
fling equivalent of the world of bric-a-brac and game rules supervised by Ariel.

Eloisa is a much more difficult, more problematic case, however,
because she is her own speaker and because value is patently on the
side of the absolute, the immortality of her soul, as opposed to the
mortal and sensuous life of love. Rather like Galatea, who in Ovid's
Acis and Galatea was also the speaker, she is a person with two demands upon her love. And these tend to be related to the polarizing
demands of Acis and Polyphemus. Pope shows how it feels to be the
victim caught between love for one man and the jealous demands of
another (a transcendent Other). The Ovidian episode included both
the narrative of Galatea's loss and the love lament and roaring rage
of Polyphemus. The power of *Eloisa to Abelard* derives partly at least
from the embodiment of both alternative loves and alternative responses to love in one speaker.

Eloisa's dilemma is resolved in favor of withdrawal to God, the
settlement of her own salvation, but her rage is what has received the
emphasis—what is down on paper, what in effect *remains*. Writing is
an act of compensation, for if reading produces weeping, ink replaces Eloisa's tears. Her stimulus to write was, of course, the sight of
Abelard's letter and his name (ll. 15–16, 51 ff.). Response is once
again primary, from the provocation of Abelard's letter, which,
"awakening all her tenderness," makes her intensely aware of her divided allegiance, to her vacillating outbursts and subsidences. The intensity of her yearning for Abelard outweighs her final resolution.

A reader cannot help noticing that she really has no choice, for
Abelard's sexuality is only a memory now. Her withdrawal, however
painful, is inevitable. When she appears on the scene, writing her
letter, she is writing in the elegiac strain of the "Winter" pastoral
rather than the hopeful conflict of *Summer* (or *The Rape of the Lock*).
She can regret her Abelard and curse his punishers, or find a way to
live within the possible, which involves an emasculated and faraway

lover. While her choice, on one level, is between the absolute and the temporal, on another it is simply between holding out for a lost love and accepting her situation in the convent, which means making a poem of it.

Like Aristaeus Eloisa is guilty of the sin of lust, is punished, and redeems her sin by the labor of writing this letter/poem—or (perhaps more accurately) by her setting straight in her writing the "fame" of herself and Abelard. And Abelard's story is parallel. His sin is redeemed by building a monastery and becoming, in his own way, a georgic farmer. "His flock," Eloisa compares to

> Plants of thy hand, and children of thy pray'r.
> From the false world in early youth they fled,
> By thee to mountains, wilds, and deserts led.
> You rais'd these hallow'd walls; the desert smil'd,
> And Paradise was open'd in the Wild.   [ll. 129–34]

Abelard has reconstructed Paradise; the historical referent in this case is, as Pope's note tells us, the fact that "He founded the Monastery."

But Eloisa's letter does not construct anything; it is close to Polyphemus's cry and very different from the metamorphosis of Lodona. The latter returns icily to this poem in the brutal transformation of Abelard by his abductors, involving

> A cool suspense from pleasure and from pain;
> [His] life a long, dead calm of fix'd repose; . . .
> Still as the sea, ere winds were taught to blow,
> Or moving spirit bade the waters flow.   [ll. 250–52, 253–54]

This transformation is the alternative to the one projected upward by Eloisa at the poem's climax (punningly sexual as well as religious).

If the Virgilian georgic is centered on human mortality—the principle is seasonal, one of natural fertilization, only to be observed and formulated by the poet-farmer—then the Ovidian metamorphosis follows death with *immortality*, of art or of religion, depending on one's viewpoint. Thus the Christianized Ovid of the *Ovide moralisé* construes metamorphosis as the movement from finite human woes to a new infinite life with God. God rewards the good by granting them a new life of bliss after death, and metamorphosis dramatizes this situation.

There is less a congruence than a rivalry in *Eloisa to Abelard* between divine and artistic immortality, whether the latter is Eloisa writing her letter or the poet who (as in *Windsor Forest* and the *Rape*) returns at the end to enfold the religio-political fiction within his own. Eloisa may ultimately conflate Abelard and the deity, love and death, as she proposes, but the poem can only demonstrate the process of literary metamorphosis, on Eloisa's part and the poet's.

It is useful to recall Pope's translations of Ovid's *Sappho to Phaon* from the *Heroides*. Though in a sense a continuation of the complaint of unrequited love in *Summer,* it leads directly into Pope's attempt at a heroic epistle. A possible reason for translating this particular epistle is that in the story, very much like Eloisa's, Sappho falls in love with the beautiful youth Phaon, who however cannot return her love because in fact he is an ancient boatman whom Aphrodite has transformed only outwardly into a youth. But it is also the only Ovidian epistle in which the speaker is a poet, and her situation that of lover *and* poet.

In *Eloisa* the poet enters directly into the last lines as a parallel case—as the "future Bard [who] shall join / In sad similitude of griefs to mine," says Eloisa, for "He best can paint 'em, who shall feel 'em most." The poet has suffered as she has and therefore can properly memorialize her, present her as she was, and order her writing-to-the-moment into heroic couplets. It does not matter whether Lady Mary Wortley Montagu was the referent in these last lines (she was much on Pope's mind as he wrote them); the point is that he himself comes in to explain what he is doing and makes it clear that his situation as a human is parallel to Eloisa's, and even as an artist (though he keeps them, in this respect, distinct). By enclosing the poem with his own presence, joining the subjects of fame and love in his own person ("He best can paint 'em, who shall feel 'em most"), he merges the figures of Eloisa and the poet.

By the time he wrote the *Epilogue to the Satires* (1737) Pope, by refusing to listen to his "friend," who either urges him to write or not to write satire, is behaving in a way analogous to Eloisa, expressing the urgency of his human duties while acknowledging the safety of his immortal soul in the light of church doctrine. Pope has taken the aspect of church forms—of sylphish false pride—and yet not forgotten the matter of the soul. In other words, the problem of the woman and the length to which her love ought to be pursued in relation to other commitments or forms, both social and prudential, or in relation to her own (or her lover's) soul's salvation, may be reflected in the ostensibly different problem of the satirist vis-à-vis a corrupt society, his duty as an active citizen, and his duty to himself as a private man.

The poet for Pope does two things. He/she responds to loss of love with song—and with a violent action, which is either transitive (Belinda, Baron, Polyphemus, Pope himself in his satire) or intransitive (Orpheus, Abelard, Pope himself in his victimization that *leads* to his satire), the song continuing, immortalizing even this destruction. In the second place the poet establishes the "truth" or "fame" for other people, but especially himself: at first for others, though aware (as in *Eloisa*) of the analogy with his own plight; but later increasingly and unabashedly for himself.

In the *Elegy to the Memory of an Unfortunate Lady*, though the triangular relationship is the same as in the *Rape* and *Eloisa* (there is a young lady, her lover, and the force of social and divine law),[31] now there is no internal conflict; her "false guardian" is plainly repressive, separating her from her true love.[32] But it is the poet's response to her example that has now become central. As at the end of *Eloisa*, he has assumed the role outlined for him in *The Temple of Fame* and is setting the record straight. The emphasis in the title is on "the *Memory* of an Unfortunate Lady"—memory meaning that the poem will stand as a kind of monument to her, because she is now slandered or totally forgotten, "without a stone, a name." The poet's function, become at this point epitaphic, is to draw out her fame as it should be and also stigmatize the "false guardian" and those who brought about her sad fate, and this results in a passage of invective side-by-side with the elegiac celebration. Immortality therefore—which in *Eloisa* was in one sense on the side of God and the Church versus the "earthly lover" in her heart—is here on the side of a suicide, because her action, which denies her burial in sanctified ground, raises her above the usual limited responses of mortals, and because the poet is immortalizing her. The poet again takes the closing lines of the poem to himself and parallels one aspect of the Lady's fate with his own: "Ev'n he, whose soul now melts in mournful lays, / Shall shortly want the gen'rous tear he pays."

The poem ends with the Popean surmise that the poet himself, as well as the memory of the Lady, will be swept away by Time; but that the edifice of fame he has constructed—by the very fact of its existence, its being read—has granted immortality to both.

With these poems we are approaching the triangular relationship of the epitaphs and funerary monuments we shall discuss in Chapter 5 in which a female figure presides over an object of longing and loss, faced by a force of contingency (Death, Time, disorder, dissolution), and controlled by the hand of an artist who represents all three. The subject is fame, art, and survival. Pope, however, displaces the

Marian figure's function of meditation to the poet. In this regard, the difference between Pope's and Swift's use of women is instructive. Swift's mode, basically iconoclastic, sees the world as full of idols, primarily women; whereas for Pope, who recovers "idols" as images of memory, the main poetic subject is this recovery—or ensuring—of memory against, among other things, idolatry. Pope attaches his own iconophilia (if not idolatry)—however complicated and ambivalent— to the safer mediating figures of the classical tradition—Homer, Virgil, and Horace—though retaining a central place for a grieving woman; Swift, who sees the classical-imperialist mode as itself an object of idolatry, even keeps his beloved Stella safely within the category of broken idol.

Opposite the poet in these poems about women in love, sylphish advice has developed in Church Law, the repressiveness of a "false guardian," and (in the poem *Cleopatra*) the tyranny of an Octavius.[33] Clearly the constraining force has become more repressive, has increasingly brought its weight down hard on both lovers, as the subject has shifted from the protagonist's dilemma to the woman's correct choice of defiance. The poet has developed from an implicit side issue to a figure almost as important as the others: parallel with the protagonists but also able to celebrate them. From these it is only a step to the ethic epistles (ethic rather than Ovidian or heroic) which begin with the *Epistle to Burlington*.

To get a larger perspective on this series we can go back to an even earlier poem, the *Ode for Musick* of 1713, in which the poet is both the protagonist and the lover, and which is specifically about the power of music (poetry) and makes quite plain the alternatives in terms of temporality and immortality. Here Pope ascends from the music that arouses heroes to battle to the music of the poet who is in love and, finally, to the sacred music of the saint. He shows the alternatives as they were in *Eloisa*—and admits that the latter is the correct choice. But, since the poem is about "fame," perhaps we should use Pope's own words:

> Of *Orpheus* now no more let Poets tell,
> To bright *Cecilia* greater Pow'r is giv'n;
>   His Numbers rais'd a Shade from Hell,
>   Hers lift the Soul to Heav'n.

Orpheus's passion for Eurydice, which led him to descend into Hades and continue to sing her name even after his own dismemberment by the Bacchantes, is contrasted with Cecilia's renunciation of her passion for Valerian, in order to convert him to Christianity.[34] Pope knows that Cecilia is right to love God more than her human lover-husband; Orpheus is wrong to love his wife beyond reason. He also knows that Cecilia's is therefore the higher poetry. But he cannot refrain from asking if it is a crime to love too well and giving Orpheus in the most deeply felt lines of the poem—corresponding again to the passion of Eloisa's feeling for Abelard, though he goes against the grain of the poem's orthodox conclusion:

> See, wild as the Winds, o'er the desart he flies;
> Hark! *Haemus* resounds with the *Bacchanals'* cries—
>   —Ah see, he dies!
> Yet ev'n in Death *Eurydice* he sung,
> *Eurydice* still trembled on his Tongue,
>   *Eurydice* the Woods,
>   *Eurydice* the Floods,
> *Eurydice* the Rocks, and hollow Mountains rung.

One part of Pope's feelings is more fully engaged by the human Orpheus, the archetypal poet, than by the saint, Cecilia—certainly by Orpheus's hopeless, repeated cry (which Pope will refer to again in the final epigraph to *The Dunciad*).

As always, Pope is the poet of human possibilities, of Clarissa's advice and the Baron's action, and so must do his best in the ordinary world. And though he is aware of the superior virtue of St. Cecilia and of her divine song, he writes his own poetry, from the *Pastorals* onward, about the ordinary world of hopelessly separated lovers. There is the poet whose "numbers raise a Shade from Hell" and the poet whose verses "lift the soul to Heav'n." Pope knows the second is higher, but must himself choose the first and make this choice his subject. He has also set up in Orpheus the paradigm not only for his Eloisas and Unfortunate Ladies but for his poet, who is willing to descend into hell in search of the one he loved too well; and who, pursued and dismembered by Bacchantes, continues to sing about his lost love (which he will later call Virtue, Astrea, Bolingbroke, Swift) even as a bodiless head floating down the river; but who also asks himself if he should not rather be singing of God, lifting up his own or another's soul.

In a world where "Time conquers All," where time, and not human love, is supreme, one can either accept the fact and choose divine love, turning one's back on the world, or make a hopeless stand for human love against Time, the state, its church, Walpolism, liars, and slanderers.

AESTHETICIZING THE STIGMA

The transgressive materials in *The Dunciad* are primarily duncical writings. In the scatological transformations of Book 2, Lodona's clear poetic stream is turned into the cloaca where London's sewers meet, a place where diving and swimming recall Satan struggling through chaos,[35] as well as the source of writing in his own excrement for Swift's modern spider.

The passage is introduced (ll. 141 ff.) by Dulness's showing Curll the "shaggy Tap'stry" (made from Dunton's bedspread) which depicts the dunces' previous travails. The tapestry recalls the paintings of the Trojan War seen by Aeneas on his arrival in Carthage. But whereas those were the sad images of Hector and other heroes dying nobly, these modern equivalents consist of Defoe in the pillory and Curll being tossed in a blanket. The painting that moved Aeneas to tears was the central image of poetic mimesis in the *Aeneid*, the point where the epic inscribes itself and the theme of art as compensation for loss. Curll's response exactly recovers the sense of Virgil's passage:

> "In ev'ry loom our labours shall be seen,
> And the fresh vomit run for ever green!"   [ll. 155–56]

As he sees, the vomit of the moment (still "fresh") will be rendered immortal ("for ever green"): The question is by whom, by the dunces or by the poet Pope?

Their metamorphosis is, after all, of Defoe and John Tutchin into the shaggy tapestry; it is Pope who transforms this modernity into the beauty of the line "And the fresh vomit run for ever green," who renders mud as "deeper sable" and Thames sewage as "silver flood." Whether we apply his own metaphor of embalming the dead (from *Aristarchus* prefixed to the *New Dunciad*) or his later metaphor of embedding insects in Shakespearean or Miltonic amber (in *Arbuthnot*), the result is a radical divorce of form and content, sound and sense, which may be said to epitomize modernity at the same time that it absorbs it into the poet's art. In the form of Pope's poetry alone does the dirty world of the mud nymphs, into which Smedley is "suck'd," resemble the lovely abode where Hylas was ravished:

> How young Lutetia, softer than the down,
> Nigrina black, and Merdamante brown,

Vy'd for his love in jetty bow'rs below,
As Hylas fair was ravish'd long ago. [ll. 332–36]

The beauty is in the words' sound, not sense; and the dislocation—contrary to the principle enunciated in *An Essay on Criticism*—is that of Addison's description of the georgic poet as one who "breaks the clods, and tosses the dung about, with an air of gracefulness." But Smedley's visit to the mud nymphs' bower raises the issue that divided Addison and Pope: Pope reminds us with his words of the story of Hylas as a lost beauty related to what Aeneas saw on the wall in Carthage. Whereas Addison, Tickell, and Steele would have recalled Hylas only to show that in Italian opera, continental history painting, and epic poetry, the Greco-Roman myths were moribund, inappropriate, and unnatural (and unnational) in England of the 1700s: the view carried forward by Hogarth and Fielding in the years immediately following the publication of *The Dunciad Variorum*.

These are the obviously transgressive materials out of which Pope made his *Dunciad*. But the whole metamorphosis, the incorporation of these materials, had somehow to be absorbed into the canon of English poetry—not relegated to an outhouse of Parnassus where vituperation and bile were kept to themselves. And this prompts us to recall (as Pope insists that we do) how the *Dunciad* came about, returning us to the theme of "fame."

Pope's Homer is "true" to its original in the same sense that his "Eloisa" or "Unfortunate Lady" or his own "Pope" was "true" to the reality: "A fine poem, Mr. Pope," the great classical scholar Richard Bentley is supposed to have said, "but not Homer." "Truth" here meant exemplary for Pope's own times. The English *Homer* made Pope's reputation and fortune: by 1720 he was ostensibly the literary arbiter of his age and also the English Man of Letters who broke the hammerlock of personal patronage to become financially independent.

But then in the 1720s came a change of direction. Pope extended the professional Man of Letters by two new projects that brought discredit on his name. The first was his continuation of his translation of Homer in the *Odyssey*, using other translators for most of the work and not sufficiently acknowledging their help. His deception about how much of the translation was his own led to charges of mistreating his friends and of plagiarism (later carried even further when he "imitated" poems by Horace). The second was his edition of Shake-

speare and his simple incompetence and carelessness, which were re-
lentlessly exposed by Lewis Theobald in *Shakespeare Restored* (1726).
Faced with these slurs on his name and the aspects of his identity that
he held dearest, Pope altered radically the direction of his career.

There is no other explanation for the huge overkill of *The Dunciad*,
a veritable epic on the subject of Theobald and Pope's other critics,
whom he inflates into Achilles and Hectors of dullness. This poem is
the great epic-satire in English; and the remainder of Pope's career
(with the exception of *An Essay on Man*) was devoted to the writing of
satire and the pondering of its meaning. If we regard *The Dunciad* as
a whole—with its voluminous prefaces, footnotes, and appendices—
there is no way to avoid the conclusion that the majority of the space
is used to justify his own character as a true recorder of fame surrounded by all of these slanderers of *his* fame. The so-called satires
that followed the *Odyssey* and Shakespeare scandals were in fact satiric "apologias," the traditional form in which the satirist justified
himself as a moral agent. This was the literary form that Pope now
made his own.

Pope's overly emphatic program for establishing his own post-
humous fame, set in motion by the late 1730s, was only another aspect of the apologia. In his letters Pope reshaped himself for his
immediate correspondent to the point of sacrificing a central core
of identity, and then he rearranged the letters for posterity, piecing
together fragments from different times and even different ad-
dressees.[36] All this manipulation, which included attributing letters
from a lesser- to a better-known correspondent (from Caryll to Addison, the backs of whose authentic letters "paper-saving Pope" had
probably used for his translation of Homer), was aimed to reconstruct a general and exemplary truth for which material evidence did
not otherwise exist.

He arranged for an unprecedented number of portraits and busts
of himself to be distributed among his great friends and in engravings to the general public. These were exemplary in the sense that
Jonathan Richardson and others felt portraits or history paintings
should be hung on the wall where they can be seen and imitated.
They show Pope thin and intense and with no indication of a hump.
As David Piper puts it, "vanity was intensified by the need to rectify
the tragic twisted reality of his crippled body with an image worthy of
the lucid, beautifully articulated construction and spirit of his poetry—the need, very literally, to put the image straight."[37] Pope's
control of his portraits has been well established by W. K. Wimsatt,[38]

but Piper's opinion is also in line with the view that Pope absorbed the monstrous shapes of duncical writing into the beautiful, rational order of his couplets. Does Pope, we wonder, on some level associate these distorted forms with his own as material for "turning a blunder into a beauty"? Or does he merely displace *his* hump (concealed in the portraits) to the backs of the dunces? Is the difference finally a similarity, one that explains why he retains, augments, cherishes, and apotheosizes duncical deformity? All this, of course, is because he clings, despite all of his personal evidence to the contrary, to the classical ideal of beauty.

THE words addressed by the Queen of Dulness to Theobald in the first *Dunciad* (1728, 1729), "All hail! and hail again, / My Son! the promis'd land expects thy reign," are analogous to those addressed by another guardian to his charge, Ariel to Belinda, and are similarly false fame. If we seek satiric progenitors, we find in *Mac Flecknoe* and *Absalom and Achitophel* the relationship of old folly to young, of mentor to student, of king to heir. John Dryden's particular fiction was that of a succession: the evil either try to usurp the real succession, the end to which Achitophel persuades Absalom, or they build a parallel world of their own in which King Flecknoe, a parody Augustus, can appoint his own successor. In relation to the true succession of Augustus to Tiberius, of Charles II to James II, of Shakespeare to Jonson (to Dryden), indeed of Aeneas to Ascanius and John the Baptist to Christ, this is a bad copy, an idol as false and ephemeral as Satan's pseudocreation in *Paradise Lost*.

The difference lies in the fact that the *relationship* is central to Dryden's satires, intimately related in *Absalom and Achitophel* to a temptation or seduction, again layered (alluding to Satan's temptation of Christ or seduction of Eve) but basically a dramatic encounter, natural for a professional dramatist like Dryden. The succession (here Pope invokes Christ and Mary / Cibber and Dulness) is only an occasion in *The Dunciad* for the splendid vision of false, perverted creation. The Dulness–Theobald or Cibber relationship is vestigial beside the complex psychological interrelations of Absalom and Achitophel. In a perfunctory way Theobald is shown by Dulness and Settle how to carry on his self-willed, hermetic career without having to despair, and what he must do and what the future of his movement will be. But the emphasis is on the grotesque projections of Dulness's fancy. The verbal texture is much richer and more energetic in Pope, the dramatic much thinner.

The "action" of *The Dunciad,* described by Pope in Cleland's "Letter to the Publisher," is the *Aeneid's* transference of empire from Troy to Latium. What happens in the 1728 *Dunciad,* however, bears little but a fleeting relationship to the encounters with Dido and Turnus which take place in the *Aeneid* but a very precise relationship to the import of its "fable" as outlined by Le Bossu and the commentators: the education of a prince and his election to empire. Pope dramatizes in his character relations not the action or plot of the *Aeneid* but its abstract moral. This allows for the emblematic unfolding before a shadowy and passive Theobald, as the prince who is instructed, of one huge anti-Pollio vision. And against the basic inversion of the Pollio, analogous ones are piled up like the cities of Ur, with the burden less on the characters in a plot than on the polysemous activity of verbs and nouns, the "nods" and "yawns" that slip back and forth from the sublime to the soporific, and on the allusions that look in one direction back toward Christian and classical values and in another toward their perversion in present-day England. Many excellent critical studies—by Maynard Mack, Aubrey Williams, Alvin Kernan, Thomas Edwards, and others—have outlined these analogical and metaphorical equivalents for the movement backward from creation to uncreation, for the unnatural duncical metamorphosis of the values of Renaissance Christian civilization into filth and meaninglessness.[39] And this duncical metamorphosis is at the same time being reversed by the poet's patient remetamorphosis of it into a permanent and beautiful poetic edifice via his heroic couplets, his diction, and the clarity of his awareness of the nature of the dunces' bathetic metaphoric activity. This poetic metamorphosis is the central activity of the poem.

But another fiction develops around the Pollio vision of *The Dunciad* proper. This larger fiction was broached in the 1728 *Dunciad* only in its preface, which explained that "every week for these two Months past, the town has been persecuted with Pamphlets, advertisements, Letters and weekly Essays, not only against the Wit and Writings, but against the Character and Person of Mr. *Pope.*"[40] This "author" explained that the poem is a response to all the attacks on Mr. Pope, by the only person (as yet unnamed) who has stood up in his defense. But the fiction reached even further. The sequence begins with the historical referents—transformed into the pro and con comments of Martin Scriblerus's "Testimonies of Authours"—of Pope's *Odyssey* and Shakespeare scandals. Before publication, Pope had issued *Peri Bathous,* with its transparent initials making the identities of the poets satirized perfectly obvious, "as a sort of ground-bait" to draw attacks that could then be answered by—and explain the attacks in—*The Dunciad* (p. xvi). He has already begun to fit *The Dunciad* as an object into a pattern of action and response similar to that of *The Rape of the Lock* (with its additions-to-the-text). In a way this outer, larger action—which includes publication as by "Mrs. A. Dod," making it the response of a "friend," and beginning with *Peri Bathous*—is the real, meaningful action; inside *The Dunciad* is the poem itself, which is more utterance than action.

The addition of preface and notes in the 1729 *Dunciad Variorum* helps to substantiate the effect of the poem as an independent artifact. The poem itself, the act of poetic metamorphosis, once in print, is an ontological fact, a real object, and Pope employs it accordingly, making it part of a larger fiction. Like the 1714 *Rape of the Lock,* the 1729 *Dunciad Variorum* expands the explanation. Cleland's "Letter to the Publisher" replaces the 1728 preface, turning the poem's author into Pope, who has also emerged as his own defender. "Abus'd by the ignorant pretenders to Poetry," we are told, he responded with *The Dunciad,* attacking "few but who had sland'red him" (p. 18). The introductory matter presents *The Dunciad* as a personal thing, Pope's own, and the notes he added confirm this, down to clearing up personal allusions to him in the "Publisher's Note."

His emergence as protagonist is the important shift in the 1729 *Dunciad*. His "fame" and that of the dunces he has satirized are the subject of Cleland's "Letter," as, it is now clear, of *The Dunciad* itself. Dennis, Theobald, and the rest are presented in the text as dull writers, but in the context of the prefatory sections and the notes they are slanderers of Pope and praisers of men in authority. They have already been introduced as such in the fourteenth chapter of *Peri Bathous,*[41] and what is emphasized in the poem and its notes is their creation of lies, of false and fantastic realities extending from birthday odes to John Rich's harlequinades.

The "Testimonies of Authours" is an even more remarkable addition. The pedantic scholar Martinus Scriblerus lists and quotes, one after another, all the attacks on and defenses of his author, Pope, arguing that the former are by those who do not know him and the latter by those who do. Implicitly Pope's response is being explained in terms of the lies, slanders, and fabrications, as well as truths and flatteries, which have been uttered about him.

But *The Dunciad* at the same time establishes the true fame of the Dennises and Theobalds, and the "Letter to the Publisher" explains the necessity for a dunce, even in the obscurity of poverty, to be "call'd by his right name," Theobald or Cibber and not Homer or Virgil.

The agon between Pope and the false fame of dullness is carried over to the page itself, for Scriblerus is promulgating the opposite procedure from Pope's own metamorphosis of duncery into poetry. He is writing the truth, in fact, is a partisan of Pope because Pope happens to be his author; and yet his "truth" is embedded in Theobaldian pedantry. The text itself is the poet's activity focused on the dunces; the frame structure, whose subject is the poet, is in the hands of a pedantic dunce. The agon (which is not, of course, really an agon but a purposeful juxtaposition to Pope's advantage) is carried out visually as well as verbally on every page, where the poetic text is beautiful, clear, balanced, well leaded, in large type, while at the bottom of the page, like a kind of sediment, are Scriblerus's notes, busily explaining why these people are here and who they are, in cramped, double-columned, dense, grayish pedantry. The poet's metamorphosis of dullness into beautiful verse at the top of the page is parallel to the reclaiming of the verse for dullness by the commentator at the bottom of the page.

The fourth book of 1742, and the final 1743 *Dunciad* in four books, complete the large enveloping action.[42] In the three-book version, Settle, now a spirit in the lower world, prophesies the fulfillment of Dulness's empire to the contemporary poetaster Theobald in Pope's ultimate version of the Pollio vision. But in the 1743 *New Dunciad* the poet himself, as if continuing from the conclusion of the two dialogues of the *Epilogue to the Satires,* opens the fourth book with his personal plea to Chaos, the only remaining muse, to suspend a moment her sway, and, lifting Settle's words from the end of Book 3, ends with his own experience of the darkening world (and without the mitigating ambiguity of the ivory gate through which Settle's vision passes).

Thomas Gray's *The Bard* (1757) ends with the last surviving Welsh bard declaiming from a mountaintop a prophetic curse on the monarch Edward III, who has killed all of the other bards—a curse that projects the War of the Roses; after which he leaps into the chasm beneath, sounding the cry at the end of *The Dunciad* when Chaos "lets the curtain fall; / And Universal darkness buries All":

> "Be thine despair and sceptered care;
> "To triumph, and to die, are mine."

He spoke, and headlong from the mountain's height
Deep in the roaring tide he plunged to endless night.

The distinction is maintained in this way between the man, the mortal poet, and the immortal poem (or prophecy). We read that the man is obliterated but he survives as a true prophecy, as a projection, and not in the present.

The gist of Pope's ending was that the world—George II and Cibber—have won but that the poet's defeat is also a triumph in so far as his verses will survive. In Gray's poem this satiric apotheosis becomes the tomb sentiment that the monument celebrates the dead but victorious; only the order is reversed, no longer "to die and to triumph" but to triumph and then to die. The movement toward self-destruction and death, from a satiric toward a memorial structure, is accompanied by the change (again like Pope's) of the poet's theme from human nature to art, or more specifically to the writing of poetry.

At the end of *The Bard* the poet utters his curse to the king and leaps into the abyss. Strangely anticipating these lines, *The Progress of Poesy* (1754) ended with the present and contemporary poet said to be "Beneath the Good how far—but far above the Great." And he reappears later in the story of Baldur's death at the end of *The Descent of Odin* (1768) when

> substantial Night
> Has reassumed her ancient right;
> Till wrapped in flames, in ruin hurled,
> Sinks the fabric of the world.

Gray's elegies on the Bard, the Poet, and Baldur (also, I suspect, reflected ironically, self-deprecatingly, in the plunge of his favorite cat) are the mourning and funereal version of the satiric projection of Pope's *Dunciad* and Swift's *Verses*.

ASIDE from the embarrassment of the Homer–Shakespeare scandals what was there in *The Dunciad* that required explanation? When we compare Pope and Curll, both metaphorically "Renew'd by ordure's sympathetic force" (2.103), we must conclude, to judge by Curll's case, that *this* maggoty corpse no longer regenerates. It can only be metamorphosed in the Ovidian way. And, as we have seen, this involves first killing and then reconstituting the stigmatic material, trying in the process to alter its essence for the better, specifically into an instrument of art. The poet finds himself in the role of the satyr who makes the ostensibly unprovoked attack, observes the metamorphosis by the muse, and then adapts the results to the larger ends of poetry.

Pope states this violence in the conventional terms of punitive satire. The vocabulary of the prefatory "Advertisement" and "Letter to the Publisher" is of "crime," "correction," "punishment," "infliction" of pain, and "destruction."[43] The case made in "The Hero of the Poem" is more specific:

> Having then so publickly declared himself *incorrigible*, he is become *dead in law* (I mean the *law Epopoeian*), and descendeth to the Poet as his property: who may take him, and deal with him, as if he had been dead as long as an old Egyptian hero; that is to say, *embowel* and *embalm him for posterity*.   [p. 265]

By the law of the epic (and punningly of Pope), the satirist thus kills the dunces in order to immortalize them in art. This violence is one more phenomenon that has to be explained and calls for the framing documents.

Death is the unspoken subject of *The Dunciad*. Virgil's fourth *Georgic* was unblinkingly about death. The double consequence of the Fall was labor and death. The first offered an opportunity as well as a curse; the second was unequivocal loss, and can only be dealt with by compensation or displacement. Death was also at the center of Pope's Ovidian fiction of the poet, in which the same art that produces the everlasting artifact also kills the living nature for which the artifact substitutes. Alongside the symbolic putting to death and embalming of the dunces there is the obsessive subject of the death of the poet himself and the survival—or afterlife—of his text.

The text is always presented as the monument—sometimes literally a tomb—for the transient half-life of dunces. As in the poems on Eloisa, the Unfortunate Lady, and Cleopatra, the fear of Time, sweeping away the poet as well as the world around him, is contradicted by the confidence that the poem itself, which is being read, will survive. The triumph of Vice at the end of the *Epilogue to the Satires* 1 is followed by the final couplet:

> Yet may this Verse (if such a Verse remain)
> Show there was one who held it [Vice] in disdain.

And the fourth book of *The Dunciad* ends with a victory of Chaos which nevertheless is inscribed in couplets that Pope clearly hopes will remain a bulwark against Chaos and Time.

If physical death—or (in duncical terms) obscurity—is frightening, the fragile immortality of the poet within his poem is even more so. One almost suspects that by giving the dunces and their works a strange afterlife Pope is continuing to reassure *himself* beyond the central conviction of his own poem's immortality.

In summary, Pope takes what are clearly unaesthetic materials—by which we mean not only nonliterary materials but perversions of conventional (i.e., classical) aesthetic objects, in effect gothicized versions, and materials that fall outside the range of the classical norms, including personal stigmas. He treats them by ridiculing and satirizing them, but also by regarding them as georgic compost or Ovidian raw material. The result is still dubious enough, however, to require the most elaborate explanation, framing, and surrounding. These three stages add up to a process moving away from morality in the direction of aestheticization and autobiography.

The strongest claim for Pope the Ovidian poet arises here. Pope's claim to be empirical and georgic must be put up against the question of whether his emphasis falls less on renewal than on memory, and less on memory than on its active, optative form, metamorphosis. The latter, a mode of power, raises the poet from farmer-gardener to demiurge.

By turning the apocalyptic vision from Settle's words into the words of the poet, by introducing poet-centered epigraphs, climaxing in the 1743 epigraph in which he is only a severed (iconoclasted?) head being devoured by the "yawning" jaws of the dunces, Pope also connects himself with the lost age of Charles I and its sad sequel in the rule of the Saints. This figure is summed up in the Miltonic Bard of *Paradise Lost*. Book 4 recalls the great invocations to Books 3 and 7 (light-blindness and Milton isolated among the Belials of Restoration London). *The Dunciad* originates with Milton's image of chaos, "a universal hubbub wild / Of stunning sounds and voices all confused," a place where we find "Rumor . . . and Chance, / And Tumult and Confusion all embroiled, / And Discord with a thousand various mouths" (2.951–52, 965–67). But it is in fact "Hell" that "at last / Yawning receiv'd them [the fallen angels] whole, and on them clos'd" (6.871–75). Adding somnolence to the sense of "yawn," Pope has the world encompassed by regressive sleep, the diabolic aspect of chaos, and conflates the earliest time, before creation, with the final end of all things.

The parallel with *Paradise Lost* makes it appear that the dunces carry out the same parodic action as Milton's Satan, a pseudo-Aeneas trying to transfer his empire from the ruins of Troy to Italy. And Pope's use of the bard reminds us that if the ostensible hero of Milton's epic is the Son who volunteers to redeem fallen man, his human analogue is the Bard who is carrying out his own equivalent of the Son's redemption on language and history in his epic. Pope places himself—by the intervention of all the frame texts, but as well by the closing of his epic with the fourth book—in the same role.

Literature that draws upon, builds upon literature, was of course part of the classical modus operandi, but Pope projects a literature that is also *about* literature—or, alternatively, in the case of the dunces, about *non*-literature. One way was to make the poet's past, his precursor or the coming to terms with his precursor(s), his subject— either in the Augustan sense of using and imitating past models or in the post-Augustan sense (inaugurated, I believe, by Pope) of writing about that past, making poetry out of the problem of dealing with that past, or out of the act of writing itself (whether or not to write, what to write), developed by Pope in his last Horatian imitations. That seems to be the choice; augmented in Pope's own case—exemplified in the end of his *Dunciad*—by the choice between writing (like Orpheus) and (like St. Cecilia) not writing at all.

Like Cervantes' *Don Quixote* (and the various imitations of it, in particular Swift's *Tale of a Tub*), however, *The Dunciad* forces us to distinguish between literature that takes as its subject "literature" (canonical literature) and that which takes "sub- or non-literature," that is, the writing of "hacks." Pope's subject, from the 1720s onward, is larger than that—it is fame, reputation, praise-blame, satire, and poetry itself—but it also includes the nonliterary in a meaningful, if negative, way.

What follows from *The Dunciad* are the assumptions that an epic like *Paradise Lost,* and so the greatest "literature," can no longer be written—at least in part because of the Walpoles, Cibbers, and George IIs, the contemporary politicians, poets, and monarchs. And so the poet absorbs and makes them—and their nonliterary writings—his subject; or more particularly, the myths and lies they weave around the poet himself.

Of course this is, in Bakhtin's terms, a reflection of the "new" genre, the novel (which "novelizes" other genres in its wake).[44] But I

use Pope to suggest a larger phenomenon in England which subsumes, as in a way it partly prepares for, the narratives of Fielding
and Richardson, as also of Hogarth. In these (rather than Bakhtin's)
terms we can see Fielding benefiting from the Popean utilization of
high literature and nonliterature and related forms of the low and
unacceptable. His rehearsal plays, which followed directly on *The
Dunciad Variorum*, picked up and materialized Pope's implied allegory
and constructed a dramatic scene that Pope himself then returned to
in his *New Dunciad*. Fielding carried this scene into *Jonathan Wild* and
Joseph Andrews (1742–43) in the actual utilization of low materials
within a controlling structure of art and order. He even writes about
his hero Tom Jones as a sturdier, healthier Pope surrounded by lies
and rumors, but by analogy also about the novel *Tom Jones* he is writing (and about his own rakish life as well).

THE POPEAN OTHER

The enveloping fiction of provocation and response informs many of
the satires that intervene between the 1729 and 1743 *Dunciad*s. The
"advertisement" to the *Epistle to Dr. Arbuthnot* (1734/5) explains that
Pope had written some observations on the times in a poem but "had
no thoughts of publishing it," until he was attacked "in a very extraordinary manner"—"not only my Writings (of which, being publick, the Publick is judge) but my Person, Morals, and Family"—by
Lady Mary and Lord Hervey. Within the poem itself it is the slanders
("lies") of Sporus (Hervey) which elicit the climactic utterance of the
satire.

But a new Horatian figure, the adversarius, begins to emerge. As
he needs an anti-Pope gesture before he can respond, Pope also
needs the indifference of those who would let vice alone or come to
terms with it before he can give vent to the indignation that adequately captures the false world. Faced with vice itself he can often
remain silent. In fact, he never shows himself simply responding to
vice—though in conversation with a "friend" he recalls doing so. It is
only when a Sporus slanders with his lies, or when a "friend" urges
moderation, silence, or flattery of the evil—thus showing the consequences of accepting vice—that he must speak out.

In the Horatian imitations the provocation of the slanderer is
moved into the background and its place of prominence taken by
the flatterer. The first imitation, of Horace's *Satire* II.i (1732), is

presented once again as a response, in this case to the attacks on his *Epistle to Burlington* of the year before. But having been grossly maligned because of imagined satire (supposedly aimed at the Duke of Chandos), the poet is now being advised by his friend Fortescue ("F." = either Friend or Fortescue), a lawyer, against writing anything else that smacks of satire; write praise instead, he is told. This advice allows Pope incidentally to summon up grotesque images of Hanoverian eulogy. But the caution urged by Fortescue has the larger effect of drawing him further out, until the warning for his personal safety—"Alas, young man, your days can ne'er be long, / In flower of age you perish for a song!"—prods Pope into the powerful climactic declaration, beginning "What? armed for Virtue when I point the pen, / Brand the bold front of shameless guilty men . . .," for which in effect the poem was written.[45]

William Fortescue is symptomatic of the "friend" who now begins to appear in Pope's satires because he was a friend of Walpole as well as of Pope. In the late 1720s he had exerted efforts to keep the two men on polite terms and was in fact, to use Mack's words, "his own and Walpole's long-time intermediary—who would speak with the grave accents of Horace's Trebatius but at the same time with the arguments of the government gazetteers."[46] Dr. Arbuthnot is a more normative "friend" than Fortescue, closer in function to Clarissa in *The Rape of the Lock,* but he advances the pattern established with Fortescue by advising Pope to avoid naming or using living examples and warning him of the personal dangers involved in writing satire. But Pope must name. He is condemned, in this instance like Midas's wife, to act naturally: "Who can't be silent, and who will not lie."

In the *Epilogue to the Satires* the "friend" comes close to being the subject. In all these climactic satires evil emerges as the state of mind of acceptance, the unwillingness to question the idol or the idolatry: the peaceful prosperity of Walpole's long reign, where money and prosperity are sufficient, and art and literature are either forgotten or turned to praise of the regime. This is the same bland acceptance of a new ruler and universal sleep and darkness at the end of *The Dunciad,* together with the same lone cry of the poet who sees the truth.

The effect in the *Epilogue* involves the interaction of P., F., *and* Walpolian vice. The end toward which each dialogue moves is the grand outburst Pope utters, but the subject is this interaction, with the crucial voice now that of the "friend." The voice of commonsense and reason has become utterly despicable, the voice of prudence, of shiftiness, of those who join the forces of evil without admitting it, in short, the Other. He is asking for a quiet, peaceful world of flatterers in which satirists do not cause trouble or threaten the status quo by attacking men in place: wait until they are out. The figure of Vice is defined in terms of her acceptance or rejection by others—by the great, by the "friends," by "Fame," or by Pope. For Vice is dangerous only if "Greatness own her," and she is defined only in terms of the great, their flatterers, and the nonsatirists whose acceptance is a necessary condition of her being. Pope represents (and, judging by the last lines of the first dialogue, he is nearly alone) another world of truth, passion, and satire.

He is ironically accepting the role urged upon him by the "friend" when, in Dialogue 1, he describes a world in which satire has a bad name, flattery a good, and the low is taken to be the high, vice to be virtue, and to rise is to fall and vice versa. Here is the pseudo-Pollio at its most powerful, with the removal of distinctions and oppositions, mountains sinking and valleys rising, lambs and lions lying down together. At the end of the first dialogue Pope abandons the ironic impersonation, and in the second dialogue resumes his role of true poet, intensifying the distinctions and making oppositions clear, establishing high as high and low as low, and good *versus* evil. Turning to the whole system of fabrications that is the court, he says:

> The Muse's wing shall brush you all away:
> All his Grace preaches, all his Lordship sings,
> All that makes Saints of Queens, and Gods of Kings,
> All, all but Truth, drops dead-born from the Press,
> Like the last Gazette, or the last Address.   [ll. 223–27]

Though an adversarius appears physically in a few of the Horatian satires, such a figure is present explicitly or implicitly in almost every one of Pope's imitations. Even where there is no overt intermediary to elicit his response, Pope suggests the same effect by printing the lines of "delicate" Horace he is imitating on the other side of the page—materializing them over there as a stimulus to a stronger moral vein as well as a source of historic and literary authority. Where Horace's text still applies, we find opposite a literal translation. Where it does not apply, Pope forces the reader to compare his own modernized line.[47] Where in *Satire* II.i Pope speaks out for himself—utters his "mighty rage"—there is simply blank space on the opposite page where Horace's text is printed.

In the opening of Dialogue 1 of the *Epilogue to the Satires*, with its subtitle "A Dialogue Something like Horace," the "friend" begins by accusing Pope of having stolen all his good lines from Horace, but he himself (as Pope points out in a footnote) is the one who steals the only two lines from Horace in the poem: *he* is the Horatian, advocating a Horatian prudence to Pope in the next verse paragraph:

> But *Horace,* Sir, was delicate, was nice;
> *Bubo* observes, he lash'd no sort of *Vice;*
> *Horace* would say . . . [etc.]

It is, of course, also a comment on Pope's satiric object to write a Horatian satire that turns out Juvenalian (or Persian). To evoke the Horatian mask and then prove too large for it, too Juvenalian, is one way of producing passionate response as well as of characterizing the intermediary who provokes it.

The Other who appears in Pope's satires is always external and concrete.[48] The "dialogue" between poet and Other cannot be confused with a Socratic dialogue which involves a certain equality of speech, with the ironist asking questions of his opponent that eventually elicit a response expressing the ironist's own view. Pope's procedure is almost the reverse of Socratic; the opponent elicits the response from the poet himself. The form is far less dialogue than a speech of his own, and the adversarius's function is to provoke the poet, by his words or his mere presence, to the intensity of response which raises the poem above mere exposition. The method is, in fact, parallel to that of Pope's Pollio-visions. The values of the adversarius (whether foe or friend) are questioned and shown to break down under their own load of internal contradictions. But the process is one of creation as well as destruction, and the poet's act of response includes an act of redefinition, which takes the form of a remetamorphosis of folly into truth and poetry.

The adversarius ultimately tends to become conflated with the "You" of the addresses to Cobham, Bathurst, and Bolingbroke. These patrons descend in one sense from the unattainable "You" of the "Summer" pastoral, but in another they are separated off (as Bathurst is from the Man of Ross = Pope) into an Other. Even Milton serves this purpose: Pope needs *Paradise Lost*, now an unattainable ideal and/or a museum piece, in order to write his contemporary version, *The Dunciad.* The relationship between Pope and either his "friends," his Bolingbrokes and Burlingtons, or his poetic models is not a matter of analogy approaching unity; resemblance is less important than the relationship of stimulus and response. The Other is rather something that is already understood or apprehensible, something that is already *there,* by which something new, less readily apprehensible, can be posited which supersedes or corrects the other.

There is always an Other in Pope's world whether he be Homer, Virgil, or Horace; but (even in his translations) this is always a slightly, or markedly, different presence—a too-heroic world or perhaps a too modestly satiric one, but always one that by its difference defines, prompts, and justifies his own in both its similarities and divergences. Take the letters he planted on Curll to make him bring out his piratical edition, the sine qua non for the "correct" edition Pope then published. The latter could only come into existence once a false simulacrum was in existence, as the true image of a weeping Cleopatra could only follow a correction of Augustus's statue of her. One other example among many is *The Key to the Lock* (1715), a work that, while not at all changing the true meaning of *The Rape of the Lock,* produced a counter or additional satiric meaning about contemporary politics, while at the same time satirizing the sort of pedantry or converting imagination (i.e., the attacks on the *Rape*) which could find such preposterously inflated meanings in an innocent poem. The *Key* is only meaningful in relation to the *Rape,* and yet it is a totally independent work because now the stimulus it presupposes is *"The Rape of the Lock"*—in quotation marks, reconceived. In the same way, at each stage of *The Dunciad*'s development something is taken as the real, and this provokes, causes, defines, brings about something else—a sequel, a correction, an explanation—which exists only in relation to it, but once in existence—published and read— becomes a thing itself in terms of which something else is then elicited and defined. The immediate stimulus for *The Dunciad* is presumably Dryden's *Mac Flecknoe,* not because it is a literary source but because Pope corrects and completes it. Every poem exists as a response to another poem in one way or another—whether it is by a friend (Homer, Horace, or Virgil) or by an enemy (Dennis, Hervey, or Theobald). Every poem uses in the georgic sense, or metamorphoses in the Ovidian sense, the matter of these other poems.

It is as if Pope has at every stage to prove his own position to himself by provoking it from something extant, as if without the actual presence of another person or object the sense of his own identity lacks firmness. This is related to the neoclassical stance of seeing reality as a relationship to something already understood, something ontologically and epistemologically secure, however unsatisfactory in itself. The Augustan mode of poetry involves a drawing out or discovery of meaning in an existent rather than the creation of a new object or identity. Pope's identity, and that of his poetry, is seen only as an inference from real, known figures or poems—alike and different in various degrees—or as an extension or realization of them.

Beginning with the paradigm of the *Messiah,* Pope's particular strategy is to take something known and metamorphose or restore it, draw out the true but hitherto unrecognized meaning. Following from the lesson of *The Temple of Fame,* he puts his own Horatian verses on the page opposite Horace's to show that he is again consulting the Genius of the Place, continuing the Horatian entelechy into the 1730s, and establishing for his time the true fame of the Horatian text. He builds on, or brings out the potentialities *as he sees them,* thus producing not exactly a translation or a poem by Pope but rather (if we refer to the Other as X) an X prime or $X + P$ or $X - P$; but never merely P. Paraphrased, these symbols become the Homer of the eighteenth century; or Horace rendered appropriate for the Age of Walpole; or Bolingbroke (in *An Essay on Man*) but less "great" as well as less fallen, less in need of consolation; or Bathurst but a Christ figure, or the Man of Ross but a poet. His own poems may be understood in the same way: once written, *The Dunciad* is regarded as an object that must itself be properly given an "honest fame."

But even this explanation does not cover the friction we feel between Pope and the Other that always reduces it ultimately to an opponent. He has *exceeded* both Virgilian and Horatian models (both of them patronized by the Emperor Augustus), and in a characteristic mock epitaph, to one who was *not* to be buried in Westminster Abbey (as he knew he would not, being a Roman Catholic), he writes:

> Heroes, and Kings! your distance keep:
> In peace let one poor Poete sleep,
> Who never flatter'd Folks like you:
> Let Horace blush, and Virgil too.[49]

In most cases, at least as we approach the satiric end of his poetic spectrum, the Popean meaning is not so much a drawing out of the other's capabilities as a reaction against the Other. It takes a Horatian stance at least partly wrong (or outdated), or a *Dunciad* attacked and misunderstood, to produce Pope's own work, as it takes a property split down the middle by a highway to produce Pope's grotto with its particular symbolic perspective on his peaceful garden on one side and the busy Thames traffic moving toward London on the other. Or perhaps, within the context of iconoclastic discourse, we should conclude that his own inbred Catholic "idolatry" was displaced onto the classical texts, but this was qualified by such factors as his sense of the orthodoxy of iconoclasm, his own quite unclassical body, and (to judge by *The Dunciad*) his deep-seated gothic predilections. As his treatment of Horace shows, the classical text allowed him to keep the idol but distance and correct it.

Chapter 3

The Aesthetics of Revolution/Restoration: Byron and Wordsworth

THE BODY POLITIC OF LORDS ROCHESTER AND BYRON

If names are significant in a book about change, whether revolutionary or counterrevolutionary, the names of Pope and Byron create a frame consisting of one poet whose surname designates the supreme pontiff of Roman Catholicism (and whose enemies never let him forget this), and whose Christian name, attached to the monosyllable, grandiloquently makes the connection with Alexander the Great, and shortened (as Pope shortened it to a signature) to A. Pope, allows for a hostile reference to imitation and plagiarism ("A.P−e"). The other is a poet whose name is always written to indicate his rank: never anything but *Lord* Byron, with also the romance sound of *Byron* and the memory of the many generations that bore the title (strictly, the less euphonious *Baron Byron*).

Pope and Byron hang together for other reasons, however: Byron devoted much energy, especially in the years when he was writing *Don Juan*, to defending Pope—not only against the anti-Popean poets of the Lake District but against the Wartons and Bowleses, against anyone who regarded him as less than one of the handful of great English poets. Byron saw his own poetry as a continuation of Pope's ethical poetry—the poetry of "truth." Although his actual poetic practice may owe as much to the poetry of Swift, he did not think so himself: and I believe partly because he saw his poetry as a poetry of art and civilization—the poetry of a lord—rather than the consciously slumming, iconoclastic poetry of the Dean of St. Patrick's. On the other hand, the lordly stance allows Byron to reach as low or as high as he wishes, recognizing the shared values of aristocrat and plebeian against the money-oriented merchants in the middle.

From one point of view—most vigorously argued by Malcolm Kelsall in *Byron's Politics*—Byron appears to be a largely passive figure enmeshed in the political discourses of his time.[1] These included, first, the Whig discourse (or the old discourse of civic humanism) in which the aristocrat was still trying to mediate between monarch and people in a time of revolution, when he could not identify with Mirabeau and Lafayette—the aristocrats who started the Revolution as an attempt to correct the imbalance of power between monarch and nobles—certainly not with Robespierre and Marat, who took the Revolution away from the aristocrats. Even Napoleon was no longer viable once he crowned himself emperor and set out to create a pseudonobility of his family and marshals. In other words, Byron, at the time he writes the final cantos of *Childe Harold* and conceives *Don Juan,* is living in an England—in fact has fled it—in which a mad king has been replaced by a foolish regent. In both England and his place of exile, Italy, counterrevolution is in control and the potential revolution, such it is, centers not in a reforming Whig lord but in the mob. In England the Peterloo marchers, from Byron's point of view, are no better than Wat Tyler's mob, and in Italy the carbonari are disorganized and unreliable.

Don Juan is therefore a story of a young Byronic aristocrat who is cut off from his homeland and a society in which he supposedly has a place (though events in Canto 1 suggest that he doesn't fit in there either) and is forced to function in the space between absolute despots and disorderly crowds. In the terms of this study this is the space between idols and iconoclasts, and it has become a largely passive space: in the company of despots he becomes a minion (a concubine's lover, or a queen's), and from the Wat Tylers he can only protect himself (as with the highwayman who attempts to rob him on Shooter's Hill) by blowing their brains out.

Juan's automatic reaction to the highwayman relates to another part of the aristocratic discourse, that of honor and dueling, which Byron falls back upon in emergencies—particularly when he finds himself in the Popean situation of having his honor impugned. As

Pope first administered an emetic to Edmund Curll and then wrote up the episode, so Byron responds first with a challenge to a duel (forgetting all the *Spectator*'s talk of antidueling) and second with the words of a satire. The difference lies in the fact that Pope materialized a satiric metaphor, Byron gestured an aristocratic code.

The central aspect of the aristocratic discourse on which Byron draws is the discourse of body. His inscription of his honor on the bodies of malefactors is based on the topos of the king's two bodies, politic and private; it existed for Byron, as it did for John Wilmot, earl of Rochester, primarily in terms of a parallelism and rivalry between monarch and noble, which had been materialized in the earliest phase of the French Revolution and survived into the nineteenth century in the relationship Byron never lets us forget between the old mad King George III and the young vigorous Lord Byron.

The English poetic tradition inherited by Pope was one that had lost its natural center in the monarch. Pope's major poems, it could be argued, are representations of the cultural and moral vacuum created by the Hanoverian monarchy. Gone was the monarch as the mystical body that both governed and healed, and his replacement was the false idol of a prime minister, Walpole, whose power lay with the progressive money interests. All that the poet like Pope could turn to was Walpole's opponents, the responsible landed aristocrats and, at a somewhat lower social level (but acceptable in the company of the responsible lord), the poet himself.

But to understand the tradition Pope was reconstructing we must look back to the poetry of the reigns of James I and Charles I. There is a sense in which poetry, and especially drama, in a court-centered culture is *about* the monarch. Dominated and determined by his particular body and its functions, both public and private, the theater makes him its protagonist. This became demonstrably clear during the great outburst of literary activity in the Elizabethan, Jacobean, and Caroline periods: most obviously in court masques, of course, but reflected in various ways in poetry and even in popular theater.

Emphasizing the absolute dichotomy of "private/public" for the king, Christopher Goodman, the Puritan apologist, wrote long before the Civil War that if rulers failed in their duty they would "be accounted no more for kings or lawful magistrates, but as private men: and to be examined, accused, condemned and punished by the law of God."[2] With the trial and condemnation of Charles I this doctrine became real: he was judged not by his own but by a different law, and for this to happen, he had to become a private citizen, just as the private men who judged him became public.

After the Restoration the situation was therefore more strained—by memories of a king's body desecrated, by the embarrassing presence of the new king and his court, and by the replacement of the private court masques with nothing but public theater. The latter, though some of the time dominated by court tastes, and occasionally written for the court, was essentially a public theater that was carried to the court for royal performances. The figure of the monarch continued to dominate the drama, at least into the 1670s, but it now took bizarre forms.

Dryden wrote his early heroic dramas about such monarchs as Charles II with brothers resembling the duke of York; the plays reflected anxieties of the succession and the brothers' shifty religious allegiances. In *The Indian Queen* (1665) Dryden, in collaboration with Sir Robert Howard, created a hero who starts out rash and self-centered, learns virtue from his rival-friend Acacis and his beloved Orazia, and grows from individualism to social responsibility. His story echoes Charles II's: a youth spent in harsh and insecure exile, ending in restoration to his rightful throne. At the center of the play is the theme of usurpation and restoration spanning two generations, and this is a world in which rebellion and civil war are always just around the corner.

The Conquest of Granada (1670), following close on the heels of the Earl of Clarendon's fall, was dedicated to the king's brother the Duke of York, prefaced with a discussion of the mixed hero that focuses on the real virtues of York and introduces as its fictive protagonist Almanzor, a hero whose womanizing would at least have permitted some spectators to associate him with York—or, for that matter, with his brother the king. In the second place, the kingdom of Granada is governed by a weak king, Boabdelin, who has allowed factions to divide his country—factions roughly recalling the court and country parties and their equivalent religious sects—and cannot control them. Worse, Boabdelin has a brother, Abdalla, and the succession is a crucial issue in the disastrous civil warfare that ensues.[3]

There is also a foreign threat in the army of Ferdinand and Isabella: the relationship between a small kingdom and its larger predatory neighbor, of course recalling England and France, momentarily draws together the opposing factions. But due to the irreparable divisions of factions and of command, Granada falls, serving as an admonition to the audience about the political future of England. The central paradigm, however, is the three figures of the king, his brother, and the heroic stranger, a *true* king, who saves the country—though sullying his reputation by changing sides and giving way to lustful behavior. I do not think that the political allegory, certainly a characteristic of most writing of whatever sort at this time, is as important as the dominant figure of the monarch and his brother. This is still a drama, court oriented, which reflects its monarch as the most important fact of imaginative life. He is the figure, as we have noticed, who fills the empty space left by the holy figures in the iconoclasted idols.

Dryden, of course, had many excuses if confronted with objectionable parallels: none of the parallels were exact and the allegory was never consistent. Almanzor and the York-figure Abdalla are given the sexual promiscuity, not the Charles-figure Boabdelin. At worst, Dryden would have admitted that Boabdelin and Abdalla were *bad* versions of the English brothers, and Almanzor an idealized version of the Duke of York; Ferdinand and Isabella are an idealized version of the brothers, and so on. Abdalla's lust, for example, can be contrasted with Ferdinand's respect for heroic love, Boabdelin's impracticality with Ferdinand's practicality. He would have admitted, however, that the issues raised by the plays were central to problems of English government in 1670.

The Rehearsal, a comic version of *The Conquest of Granada,* produced a year later by the Duke of Buckingham and collaborators who opposed the York faction and therefore Dryden, parodied the allegory. Here again there are two brothers, a kingdom usurped by their gentleman usher and physician (senile figures, recalling the "old boys," Clarendon and Arlington, whose service went back to before the Civil War), and the same themes of usurpation and restoration. The allegory is more precise now, and Dryden himself, as author, appears in the role of the play's author Bayes, who, while alluding to his poet laureateship, also catches his political analogue Henry Bennet, Earl of Arlington, the principal secretary of state for foreign affairs and Buckingham's rival in the Cabal.

Buckingham's parody also draws our attention to the conflict between the gentleman professional and the lordly amateur. The "court wit" was everywhere in evidence in the Restoration court, touting the notion that the nobler the birth the better the poem. Buckingham and Rochester happened to be brilliant writers, Rochester a figure as important in his way as Dryden. The motivation for their attacks on

Dryden was partly because all three of them *were* talented. But the bitterness was probably political (as James Winn shows[4]); Buckingham and Rochester were strongly anti-Yorkist and Whig in their bias, and for them Dryden seemed a time-serving parvenu. Moreover, Dryden left himself open to their most barbed attacks by imitating precisely the kind of lordly behavior which was beyond his means and temperament. This behavior extended from (as they pointed out) his feeble attempts in company—and in some of his plays—to be aristocratic-witty ("To frisk his frolick fancy, he'd cry, 'C—t,'" Rochester wrote) to his taking a young actress for his mistress (as they all did, up to the king himself). Finally, in the words of an ironically titled pamphlet, *The Friendly Vindication of Mr. Dryden,* "Mr. *Dryden* writ as well as any man that could write no better." Dryden was not a hit-or-miss careless wit, who was burnt out young, as were Buckingham and Rochester, but top scholar at Westminster School, honor student at Oxford, winner of all the prizes, and poet laureate (in that sense in the succession of the conscientious dullards Davenant, Shadwell, Nahum Tate, Eusden, and Cibber—and, for Byron, Southey).

It was into this class division that Pope sought in one way to insert himself (nonlaureate) and Swift (not-bishop) in another. Rochester, feeling no such insecurity, occupying a space very near the monarch himself (as virtually an adoptive son), could speak frankly about a body dedicated to high living. Thus the centrality of the king's body— by which I mean its reflection in the heroes of epic and tragedy— figured also its synecdoche, in this case Charles II's sexual organ, the center of fertility/sterility in England, the creator of bastards scattered broadside but of no legitimate heir at a time when the next in line was an avowed Roman Catholic. His sexual organ was celebrated in Rochester's notorious "Lampoon" as his scepter—and as the invisible center of energy in the mock-heroes of Wycherley's *Country Wife,* Etherege's *Man of Mode,* as well as Rochester's *Ramble in St. James's Park* and *The Imperfect Enjoyment.*[5]

But the figures (in Etherege's *Man of Mode* and Wycherley's *Country Wife*) of Dorimant and Horner, in one sense reflections of the merry monarch, more precisely represented the aristocratic alternative to the monarch who satirizes, places, and replaces him: sometimes with active potency, sometimes as a satiric perspective, and sometimes as a sad mirror image of his "expense of spirit in a waste of shame." Rochester maintained the parallel between his own sexuality and the monarch's, while privileging his own freedom as against

Charles II's mechanical and self-consuming lust. But he also, as he grew older, used his own poxes and physical debility to reflect the decline of the body politic in the greater world.

For if there is the king's public-private body, there is, in the case of a lord who is also a satirist, Rochester's own public and private body. In words spoken to Gilbert Burnet during their conversion dialogues (on Rochester's deathbed) it is not difficult to detect the satirist's defense that it may take an evil man to detect evil in others, but only out of a desire to revenge his honor:

> A man could not write with life, unless he were heated by Revenge; for to make a *Satyre* without Resentments, upon the cold Notions of *Phylosophy*, was as if a man would in cold blood, cut men's throats who had never offended him.[6]

"Heated by Revenge" are Rochester's operative words. But there is another interesting remark, dropped to Mr. Giffard, his tutor:

> My Ld. had a natural Distemper upon him which was extraordinary, . . . which was that sometimes he could not have a stool for 3 Weeks or a Month together. Which distemper his Lordship told him [Giffard] was a very great occasion of that warmth and heat he always expressed, his Brain being heated by the Fumes and Humours that ascended and evacuated themselves that way.[7]

One recalls the conventionality of the metaphor of evacuation as it extends from medical treatises to Burton's *Anatomy of Melancholy*, Swift's *Tale of a Tub*, and even Fielding's *Tom Jones*.[8] But it is not always centered in the physical body of the poet; it does not always so permeate the poet's writings as in the case of Rochester. Impersonating the Earl of Mulgrave he writes to Dryden (O.B., "Old Bays") that "Perhaps ill verses ought to be confined / In mere good breeding, like unsavory wind," and concludes:

> What though the excrement of my dull brain
> Runs in a costive and insipid strain,
> Whilst your rich head eases itself of wit:
> Must none but civit cats have leave to shit?

And this is very close to the sense of his own argument (in the persona of Horace) with Dryden in *An Allusion to Horace*, where, for example, in the lines, "Yet having this allowed, the heavy mass / That stuffs up his loose volumes must not pass. . . . ," he is criticizing

Dryden's "looseness" against the norm of his own costiveness, as Horace did with his precursor Lucilius.

The "warmth and heat he always expressed," however, refers to both sexual and literary activity, linking the two, emphasizing the naturalness of both but also the particular situation of a body for whom catharsis (of either sort) has a special meaning.

Horace says he writes satires to ward off insomnia ("verum nequeo dormire") and Pope responds to a fool or a knave as "Bulls aim their horns, and Asses lift their heels." But Rochester tells us he "never rhymed but for [his] Pintle's sake." Unlike Pope, who was "dipp'd in ink" as his baptism into literature, Rochester says he "dip[s his] pen in flowers" (semen or menstrual discharge).[9] The symptoms he describes are, needless to say, those of melancholy, for which the natural outlet is ordinarily sexual fulfillment. But the ethos he describes—the discourse he invokes—is one of a royal body that historically centers on sexual (and their obverse, excremental) concerns.

It is a revealing fact that the best of the anticourt satirists were also, like Rochester, "court wits" who, though having gone over to the Opposition, shared Charles's libertine skepticism, had helped to give his court the bad name at which they now leveled their satires, and could speak as insiders who had seen the sordid reality. The closeness of the opposition satirists to the subject—almost a filial closeness, anticipating the time when the opposition would be centered around the monarch's eldest son—gave a peculiar poignance to the body imagery employed.

Obscenity, though at the center of Rochester's best poems (satiric or amatory), almost never appears alone; it is the private half of a basic analogy between public and private life. Sexuality offered the most impressive symbol available for the private world. Kingship is the subject of the *Scepter Lampoon:* Louis XIV's kind of kingship is compared with Charles's, the one a game of war, the other a game of love, and the conclusion is, "All monarchs I hate, from the thrones they sit on, / From the hector of France to the culluy of Britain." They share a common lack of serious purpose, abdication of the duties of kingship, and a frenzied, compulsive, and altogether pointless activity.

The analogy between war and lust remains implicit, but our attention is focused in the larger part of the poem on Charles and the second half of the comparison, which becomes an equation of his scepter with his sexual organ (and, by implication, Louis's scepter with his sword). Since the king *is* in an important sense the state, public and private life are one, and the king's body is the body politic; and so quite appropriately for Charles, "His scepter and his prick are of a length." The vehicle of the metaphor—as befits an effective lampoon—is taken from the material of the tenor or subject: Louis did wage pointless wars and Charles did have numerous whores. The metaphor is based on a physical resemblance and on a causality between private and public actions. The whore "may sway the one who plays with th' other," and, in effect, Charles's lust determines his policy; conversely, his policy is characterized by the changeableness of his passion. And so when Rochester says that Charles's lust is now so jaded that Nell Gwynn can barely arouse it to action, he is saying the same for Charles's rule of the country.

Rochester begins the *Scepter Lampoon* with a contrast of war and lust, which could appear to be public as opposed to private activities (war is traditionally a public duty of kings).[10] By equating them he not only exposes the frantic meaninglessness of Charles's lust (this is the part that adheres to Charles from the "war" half of the equation), but also reduces the idea of war to a level with whoring. The official view was that war was public and whoring private, that a king's public acts were separate from his private. Charles is supposed to have replied to Rochester's lines "He never said a foolish thing, / Nor ever did a wise one" that *he* was responsible for his words, his ministers for his actions. Rochester demonstrates that they are a unity.

Rochester's poetry projects a world in which the two areas of experience, public and (illustrated by sexuality) private, are for all practical purposes one. In *Timon* a bore's attempt to lure a gentleman to his dinner party is compared to a whore's soliciting; the meat and carrots served are arses and dildoes; the lady's question to Huff ("if love's flame he never felt") is answered, "Do you think I'm gelt?"; the diners lapse into heroic verses about war from plays, which lead into talk about actual war (Huff and Dingboy at dinner are the equivalent of kings and generals and admirals conducting the war), and a squabble among the diners ends with a "peace" treaty. The correspondence appears in the most incidental imagery. In *The Imperfect Enjoyment* the speaker's sexual organ would "invade, / Woman or Boy";[11] it "Breaks ev'ry stew, does each small whore invade." In all of these "whore" is associated with a perversion of natural feeling which reflects on a similar perversion in the great world of politics and statesmanship. So too the social world of wit and poetry: in *Satyr against Reason and Mankind* the distrust of wits is like that accorded whores by the clients who fear the consequences of their pleasure; and in *Artemesia to Chloe* "Whore is scarce a more reproachful name / Than poetess."

The distinction between nature and its perversion points to the meaning of Rochester's sexual metaphor. In the example of Charles and Louis the terms are freedom (nature) and license (perversion). Charles's behavior is to the ideal (or in his terms, the romantic illusion) of kingship as uncontrolled lust is to love.

In *The Imperfect Enjoyment* the poet, who has equated his monarch's sexual organ and scepter, addresses his own organ in order to curse its impotence—but with a distinction:

> When vice, disease, and scandal lead the way,
> With what officious haste dost thou obey!
> Like a rude, roaring hector in the streets
> Who scuffles, cuffs, and justles all he meets,
> But if his King or country claim his aid,
> The rakehell villain shrinks and hides his head.

The activity of the "roaring hector" is exactly that of the debauching soldiers in *The Disabled Debauchee;* and any old whore *versus* the woman he loves is the private part of a comparison with king or country, street fights, and civil chaos. But the poem is not about whores and street fights but the untrustworthy organ, which can succeed with whores but not with the poet's true love (and, by the terms of the comparison, cannot serve his king and country as it ought).

When he talks about what may have been a personal problem of impotence, he is of course talking about a much larger issue, which he can feel so strongly because of the analogy to his own plight. The king's body (body politic) is manifest in the microcosm of the body-Rochester. This king represented to Rochester and his countrymen a particular situation of a monarch who is able to father innumerable bastards on mistresses or whores but cannot father one legitimate son and heir to the throne;[12] thus leaving the country open to the central crisis of his reign, a crisis of succession. Thus by the late 1670s politics was dominated by the Exclusion Act and threats of rebellion, with the apprehension of rule by either a bastard or a Roman Catholic. *The Imperfect Enjoyment* is based on a contrast between the gentlemanly sexual prowess that satisfies all women of the lower orders but fails to function with the one loved (socially equal) woman.

The Imperfect Enjoyment is an adaptation of Ovid's *Amores* 3.7, which celebrates the impossibility of controlling the flesh. But though it recalls the speaker's past successes with other women, it makes no distinction between them and the present one; this one is a whore, and so presumably were all the others. In Rochester's poem the whores are contrasted with the true love in whose arms he now lies, as lust with romantic love. In effect, Rochester says that not only do we have no control over our bodies, but they can satisfy only the pattern of lust, not the patternless complexity of love. This is an extreme statement, which even Swift does not approach, of a Strephon who has no need to get into Chloe's dressing room; under the most felicitous circumstances he could not bridge the gap between ideal and real—"soe great a disproportion" is there, as Rochester wrote his wife, "'twixt our desires and what is ordained to content them." [13]

Something is to be said about the relationship between the impotence (sexual and moral) celebrated in Rochester's poems and the profligacy or license of the mistress who is merely (in the words of the *Ramble in St. James's Park*) a "passive pot to spend in" or "The joy at least of a whole Nation" ("On her no Showers unwelcome fall, / Her willing womb retains 'em all"). The receptivity of the woman is matched by the "looseness" of Rochester with any passing whore, of other "lovers" such as Charles II, and, to extend the metaphor, of such writers as Dryden (in the *Allusion to Horace*). For impotence/constipation is a general malady of Rochester/Charles, who in important matters say wisely but act foolishly, while in casual encounters with the world are guilty of mere "looseness." The custom of respect or "love" is the trap in which such as Rochester and the king, and many of his subjects, find themselves when confronted by "king" or "loved one" or any hallowed ideal. The organ will not respond. But the only alternative to the costive, in love or art or politics, is the loose.

Impotence—or rather feigned impotence used to secure the pleasure of other men's wives but masking an inability to love—is the subject of Wycherley's *Country Wife* (1675). For Horner's pose of sexual impotence (like Rochester's poetic one) is a symbol of his real moral impotence, and with him the moral (and social and political) impotence of English court society. The sense in which Horner is really impotent is like that in which Jonson's Volpone was really (morally) the sick man he pretended to be. In 1675–76 Rochester's career comes to a climax, or a watershed: his greatest poems are written around this time and he begins seriously to extend the writing of his poetry into the living of his life, looking toward his conversion and death. It is also the time when the two great comedies of the Restoration, *The Country Wife* and *The Man of Mode*, are first performed, reflecting Rochester/Charles II both mimetically and metaphorically. We know from contemporary evidence that Rochester was seen as the model for Dorimant,[14] but Horner is equally Rochester, because Wycherley makes him a symbol in precisely the way that Rochester was making himself one. The most immediate analogue recalling Rochester's *Disabled Debauchee* is Harcourt's remark that Horner, like "an old married general, when unfit for action, is fittest for counsel" (3.2). Horner is a symbol that combines the repletion or retention with the covert release by both sexual and satiric catharsis that we have seen in Rochester's satire. The pose of impotence is a device for exposing the lust of the hypocritical women and the complaisance of their husbands, an outlet equally for his sexual and for his satiric satisfaction. The satire depends on the private-public analogy of Horner and the world, as of sex and china, which is painted, decorated, and collected to conceal its earthy origins and its humble function of satisfying hunger.

What these comedies demonstrate, however, is that the central position of the monarch is being taken over by the poet himself. I think it is significant that, though neither Horner nor Dorimant is more than "Mr.," the model for the figure is a lord, and one closely associated with the monarch. Horner is both monarch and lord, but the figurative impotence, the ability to couple with his subjects' wives and daughters but not with his legal or loving spouse, and the witty nonchalance of the saying as opposed to the cruelty of the doing, were primarily references to the idea of the merry monarch. Indeed, as Rochester must have realized, his own self-image is only a reflection of that monarch—or a reaction to it, an antiself in some ways but in more ways a mirror image.

"Kings and Princes," Rochester wrote to Henry Savile, "are only as Incomprehensible as what they *pretend* to represent; but apparently as Frail as Those they Govern." [15] It is certainly noticeable that Rochester attacks in others (in particular Charles) what he comes around to attacking in himself. The protagonist of *A Ramble in St. James's Park* and *The Imperfect Enjoyment* could have been either Rochester or Charles II: as the kind of projection of omnipotence in Bajazet (of the *Very Heroical Epistle in Answer to Ephelia*) could have been of the illusory power and real impotence of either. Their mutual impotence and inability to relate public and private life become the insight that one must be satisfied with whores and linkboys; Rochester turns this knowledge into a private version of the body politic metaphor, an image of the whole world's decline that looks forward to Swift's use of his own body in his Irish poems. Rochester must have seen himself as a representative man (certainly so by 1676, when Dorimant appeared), fully as representative as the king. And it is at this point that he begins to project his alternative selves—versions of damnation, pride, and conversion. When he inquires of the postboy the way to hell, he is told: "The readiest way, my Lord, 's by Rochester." That is, by way of the city of Rochester, toward the sea and France, but also by *playing* the Earl of Rochester, or by his example, or by being himself.

Rochester's masquerade as Alexander Bendo is reminiscent of Horner, who derives in more ways than one from Volpone, another actor whose repertory included the role of mountebank as a self-disguise to expose politicians and clergymen and other more respectable mountebanks. In Rochester's (Bendo's) words, "the Politician is, & must be a Mountebank in State Affairs, and the Mountebank no doubt . . . is an errant Politician in Physick."[16] Bendo begins by distinguishing true physician and quack but then blurs them into one, together with politicians and clergymen. Rochester's impersonations transform the private man momentarily into the public; they extend from mountebank and city merchant to naval hero, peer sitting in the House of Lords, rake "some years always drunk, and . . . ever doing some mischief,"[17] coward refusing to duel with Mulgrave, and atheist turned convert.[18] Etherege and Wycherley recorded some aspects of the impersonation, as later Gilbert Burnet and Robert Parsons recorded the drama of conversion and a "good death," mixing life and art in a way that is central to Rochester. But the great dissimulator, as Rochester was aware, whose secret treaties with Louis XIV were the subject of intense and prolonged speculation, was of course once again the monarch himself.

Rochester's two earliest surviving poems, of 1660, associate him and Charles II as son and father. He was born into a relationship with the great world of the court, and specifically with Charles II: his father, Lord Wilmot, had saved Charles at Worcester. In that scene Wilmot was to Charles as father to son, and Rochester becomes, in his own terms at least, both son and brother (or alter ego) to Charles. Whether Rochester wrote these verses of 1660 (he would have been only thirteen), or whether they were revised or even dictated by his mentor Robert Whitehall, nonetheless the two poems express the essential relationship that emerged. The king took over the dead father's role, supervised Rochester's education at Oxford, his grand tour, his life at court thereafter (navy and pension), and chose a wife for him. But this father/brother was also a slave to his lusts, and his energies were scattered when they should have been focused on his duty, queen, kingdom, "son," and subjects—and so it is no surprise that Rochester wrote attacks on the king which could have been di-

rected at himself and eventually, in his last years, went over to the
Opposition—which was, of course, centered on the crisis of the Suc-
cession, the replacement of the brother York with the bastard son
Monmouth.

The poems show Charles II, the father surrogate, transformed
from a threatening figure to the other side of the poet, the harmless,
impotent, castrated, uxorious man—the costive man of wise words
and bungled deeds, safer in the country but always yearning for the
city. We do know that Rochester's mother's ancestral sympathies were
Puritan, while his father (whom he can have met no more than once,
when he was eight) was the staunchest of cavaliers, who served
Charles until his death, separated from his wife and son. Perhaps the
father, in that one return, seemed a threat to the son's own monopoly
of his mother, or a threat to his own identity. (When he returned that
once he was traveling in disguise on a secret mission directing Royalist conspiracies to undermine the Puritan Commonwealth.) Presumably something of Rochester's association with his father and his
father's glamor persisted in the life at court in London and at sea, but
Rochester always followed it with a return to the country to be near
his mother, to meditate and write (although keeping Woodstock at
hand in which to live like a cavalier).

BYRON's self-portrait is in more than one respect based on Pope's
rather than Rochester's. Pope's self-portrait was based on Milton's,
the figure of the poet as set off from other men, a responsive and not
a representative figure. Milton's blindness (as well as, we might add,
his Puritan self-righteousness) isolated him but also gave him an insight denied to others; Pope's Roman Catholicism and his sickly, deformed body did the same. But for Rochester (as to some extent for
Swift) the poet's body was paradigmatically related to his world—to
the Body Politic, to the monarch, and therefore to all the citizens who
make up the Body Politic. The illness of his body private does not set
him off from society but is an indication of the decrepitude or decline
or impotence of the Body Politic. In the poetry of Rochester the poet
figure implicates himself because he remains an aspect of the monarch. The idea of the poet (or the nobleman) as corrective to the
monarch is confused in Rochester's political poetry with the idea of
the poet/lord as representative—as hopelessly tainted by analogical
association with Charles II as his monarch/father/nation.

The discrepancy between monarch and nation, or nobleman or
poet, became, as I have said, emphatic in the 1720s. And the royal

line of Dunce the First followed by Dunce the Second culminated in the old mad dying George III and the scapegrace Prince Regent (seemingly a reincarnation of Charles II, a "restoration" of Charles I/ George III). The line of the poet Pope, who had left no heirs, was resumed by the young vigorous *Lord* Byron, who happened to be both aristocrat *and* poet. And the opposition of old mad king and young handsome lord was as symbolic as could be imagined. Byron had caught the English (and European) imagination as the Byronic poet-adventurer-lord. Once in exile—in Italy, as Swift had been in Ireland or Napoleon on St. Helena—Byron fictionalized the greater bodily agon in the poems, plays, journals, and letters of his last decade.

The aristocratic discourse of making, informed by talk of swimming, gambling, orating, and acting, is explicit in Byron's letters and journals, implicit in *Don Juan*.[19] The emphasis is on the spontaneous, the physical, and chance. In "Detached Thought" No. 33 on gambling Byron states his preference for dice:

> I was very fond of it when young—that is to say of "Hazard" for I hate all *Card* Games even Faro. . . . For I loved and missed the *rattle* and *dash* of the box & dice—and the glorious uncertainty not only of good luck, or bad luck—but of *any luck at all*—as one had sometimes to throw *often* to decide at all.[20]

Something of the same reliance on chance can be found in his account of acting and oratory, which focuses lovingly on his friend of the previous generation, Richard Brinsley Sheridan. Sheridan never initiated but always reacted, his every word a rejoinder to whatever position the last speaker took: "his former compliment had been drawn out by some preceding one—just as it's reverse was by my hinting that it was unmerited."[21]

But while the pose is aristocratic, the gravitational pull is literary. Whereas symbolically, and by lip service, the universe of Byron's time remained regio-centric, in fact the number of orbits or worlds of symbolic value—as of power, aspiration, and influence—had increased. Literature offered an independent and competing universe to which the crown itself could be seen as circling in orbit. Replacing the monarchical model, as Byron himself demonstrated, was the literary one, especially when supported by the lordly.

The chief discourse for Byron, however, remained that of the body, equally a sign of his political conservatism and his literary heritage. He compared wit to soda water, but the reference also shows how closely he connected his wit to his stomach and indigestion (the dozens of bottles of soda water he calculates he drank during a night following dissipation). Wit is closely allied to effervescence but also to change in the primary sense of physical decline—of the body's deterioration with age.

In this sense, as with Rochester, there was a tendency to mirror as well as polarize the monarch. The poet's stigma replaced, indeed took on an almost Christological sense of redemption, the monarch's. By the time *Don Juan* came to be written Byron felt (or self-dramatized) himself to be aging, world-weary, and mortal, looking back equally on his own and on the French Revolutionary past—as George III, if he still had his wits, might have looked back on his reign—and seeing both with a mixed sense of outrage and mourning. But it may also be that the malaise of aging (of being past thirty) which hangs over *Don Juan* is another displacement for the larger issue of the poet's own stigma: the "madness" Lady Byron had supposed, or the "badness" she had concluded, or the mysterious guilt Byron had been writing about in one form or another since the oriental tales of around 1815.

Byron's stigma derived not from royal madness but from Miltonic blindness, which had covered (or atoned) for Milton's more heinous stigma of being a regicide. Like Milton, Byron conflates the roles of God (or monarch) and Satan. The continuum—the public equivalent of his Miltonic blindness—was his situation of being defeated, outcast, and excoriated, the consequence of his bold patriotism. Pope, like Milton, passed himself off as the insider who had become, alone in his integrity, an outsider. But there had also been Pope's hump and his Roman Catholicism—as later, though fictionalized, there had been the by now thoroughly humanized stigmata of Tristram Shandy and Laurence Sterne. Each had its sexual dimension, at least as remarked by Byron, who even liked to recall Milton's trouble with his wives (Dedication to *Don Juan*, stanza 10). In each case it is the bodily disability that causes the writer to write. He would have remembered the story of Rochester's going a month without a bowel movement and then evacuating both physical and poetic matter simultaneously. But closer to Byron is the Shandyan writer/protagonist who suffers a bodily disability, which he attributes to the outside world (of self-contained parents, incompetent men-midwives, careless maid servants) and must explain, clarify, and somehow control by writing about it: as he writes of his uncle Toby's parallel situation, "The history of a soldier's wound beguiles the pain of it."

Although he invokes the iconoclastic Milton as the great precursor (especially when attacking the idolators Southey and Wordsworth) and models his plot on Sterne's, Byron acknowledges Pope as his master. Pope himself, as a no longer esteemed poet in the sentimental age of the Lake Poets, prompts vigorous defenses that link his poetry with Byron's. The "Dunciads" of both Byron and Pope show monarchs complemented by duncical poet laureates, Cibber and Southey. But when Byron goes to Pope's defense he always takes off from remarks about Pope's deformity and sexuality—innuendos linking Pope and Martha Blount or Lady Mary Wortley Montagu, questions of sexuality which derive from his deformity.[22] Byron's real interest in Pope—though ostensibly located in the "ethical poet," the poet of truth rather than Wordsworthian intoxication—is always triggered by the ambiguity of Pope's deformity (and presumably his bad personal reputation: spider or wasp, parallel in its way to Byron's).

Pope, he notes, was "at least aware of his deformity, as indeed deformed persons have in general sufficient wit to be." And again: "It is also another unhappy dispensation of Nature that deformed persons, and more particularly those of Pope's peculiar conformation, are born with very strong passions."[23] When Byron wonders about the sexual attractiveness and potency traditionally associated with dwarfs, hunchbacks, and other deformed people such as Pope (he cites the amorous advantages of deformity in the Marechal Luxembourg and John Wilkes), he is most probably thinking of his own limp.

The sexual stigma he acknowledges is love (for which read sex) outside marriage, carried as far as the taboo of incest, which may also cover for homosexuality.[24] But sexual truancy is probably for Byron the more acceptable stigma, the one over which he has control, concealing the physical one over which he has no control, for which he is not personally responsible. In his personal writings he can talk about his lameness in terms of another's (the young Henry Fox):

> But there is this difference, that *he* appears a halting angel, who has tripped against a star; whilst I am *Le Diable Boiteux,*—a soubriquet, which I marvel that, amongst their various *nominis umbrae,* the orthodox have not hit upon. [*Letters and Journals,* 10.136]

Lameness cannot appear alone; it is accompanied by angel or devil, by some moral or—implicit also in the reference to Lesage—satiric dimension. In his poems this duality is simplified to a private sexual transgression, which is then publicly and politically charged with the French Revolutionary mixture of heroism/guilt and virtue/crime.

He consciously draws on James Mackintosh's *Vindiciae Gallicae* (1791), which had used these terms to defend the "excesses" of the

French Revolution against Burke's *Reflections.* Mackintosh had asked the rhetorical question whether "our sentiments, raised by such events so much above their ordinary level, become the source of guilt and heroism unknown before—of sublime virtues and splendid crimes?"[25] In Byron's case the symbolic stigma—the transgression—has both public and private functions: the *Lara* fiction of the guilty secret, finalized in Manfred's incestuous sin and Cain's curse, draws upon the Gothic convention of secret and festering sin, the actual personal secret of homosexuality and incest, and, primarily in *Don Juan,* the public virtue/guilt of "revolution."

IN the *Epistle to Augustus* Pope set up Swift, the poet, Dean, and Drapier, as a royal substitute in Ireland for the lamentable George II in London. Pope and Swift simply show the falling away, the appalling discrepancy, and the necessity of turning to a completely different center of authority. As Swift himself tells us when he renders himself as low and decrepit as possible, in order to replace the dead idol of kingship it may be necessary to turn plebeian and descend far below kings *or* prime ministers. *Lord* Byron, however, believes that the king must be replaced, as historically he was in England, whenever he does not live up to his duties vis-à-vis his nobles: whether he is an Edward II, a Richard II, a Charles I, or a James II, seen from the point of view of the nobles, kingship is replaced by lordship. Thus Byron substitutes himself, a "true" (one of his favorite Popean words) for a false idol, a living for a dead one. But historically this iconoclasm had to fit itself into a pragmatic series of substitutions that included Robespierre and Napoleon: thus Napoleon is replaced by *Lord* Byron, and—if this were not enough—the author of *Childe Harold* by the author of *Don Juan.*

In Canto 11 of *Don Juan* Byron explains that, though he did not seek "of foolscap subjects to be king,— / Was reckoned, a considerable time, / The grand Napoleon of the realm of rhyme" (55). He then jokingly qualifies this by placing Sir Walter Scott before him and Moore and Campbell before and after him; by calling *Don Juan* his Moscow and *Marino Faliero* his Leipzig. But the points he is making are serious: he equates himself with the macrocosm of politics (sometimes specifically with Napoleon) and he is extremely interested in the metaphor of poetry as power.[26] It is the latter that leads him into speculation on—pleased amazement at—the notion that Keats could have been "killed off by one critique" or "snuffed out by an article" (11.60; also in the letters). But the work that will free him from the Napoleon–Childe Harold impasse is the low and disreputable *Don Juan*.

The passage in Canto 11 is followed in stanzas 74–75 by the "life of a young noble," who in the House of Lords mediates "Between the Tyrant's and the Tribune's crew," or the forces of the monarch and the mob. The discourse of lordship (with its mutuality of public and private lives) takes the form of seeing oneself as mediator between monarch and people, tyrant and mob, master and chattel (or property). But the fiction this mediation takes for Byron is amorous.

There are long passages in the letters and journals in which Byron melds his concerns with the revolutionary movement and his on-going love affair. Waiting for some word of the commencement of revolution in January 1821, he intermingles at every stage the possible revolution in Italy, his love affair with Teresa Guiccioli, and his need to escape boredom (8.14–19). His discourse partakes, as with Rochester, of the old Petrarchan metaphor, "but then he was in love—and that is a martial passion" ("Thought" No. 36; 9.26), but its frame is always political, and it takes on the specific fiction of a romantic triangle.

He projects the triangle of Castlereagh, Thomas Paine, and Byron, followed by Count Guiccioli, Teresa, and Byron: one is public and political, the other private and amorous. The first involves reaction and radicalism (or revolution), the tyrant and the mob, mediated by a lord; the second, the Italian situation (as he tells us frequently in the letters) of the *cavaliere servente*, involves the convention of the aging husband, his young wife, and her young lover—in this case actually living on the upper floor of the Guiccioli palazzo in Ravenna. The elements are age, tyranny, possession (property owner); youth, rebellion, femininity (the property); and the interloping young yet aging Lord Byron.

The parallels are by no means exact, but they keep running through Byron's mind in the journals and the letters of 1819–20 and reappear in *Don Juan*. He is writing Cantos 3 and 4 at this time, the story of Haidée, of sorrow at their separation: Canto 3 is about the intrusion of Lambro, the father, and the expulsion of Juan, the death of Haidée, and the subsequent withering of the Paradise they have lost. This is the canto where the attack on Wellington was first to have appeared; it still retains the attack on Wellington's laureates and surrogates, the poets Southey and Wordsworth. Canto 4 then describes the slavery into which Lambro has sold Juan—leading into a new conformation, another version of the Lambro–Haidée–Juan triangle in the harem situation of the sultan, Gulbeyaz, and Juan. All of these, of course, refer back to the first and paradigmatic romantic triangle in *Don Juan*, in Canto 1, with Don Alfonso, Donna Julia, and Juan. But in that case there were also Don Alfonso, his earlier (and perhaps continuing) lover Donna Inez, and Juan: Donna Inez and Donna Julia, Juan's mother and lover (Alfonso's lover and wife) overlap, in a sense substituting for each other. Don Juan's actual father, being dead and out of the story, is replaced in both triangles by Don Alfonso, who collapses the roles of father and husband.

The first, surprising case of iconoclasm in *Don Juan* is literally Juan's father, Don Jose: "unluckily, Don Jose died." Like a jar (characterized by "frailties"), his marriage destroyed, he is depicted in a scene of iconoclasm:

> Standing alone beside his desolate hearth
>   where all his household gods lay shivered round him:
> No choice was left his feelings or his pride,
> Save Death or Doctors' Common—so he died.   [1.36]

The act of killing him—the poet's act—is noteworthy because Jose is one aspect of Byron himself. He is married to Donna Inez, the equivalent of Lady Byron; regarded by her as mad, then as bad, and disowned; and, at the point where Juan's allegorical referent Byron himself left England for Italy, Jose simply dies. (The close friendship between him and the narrator is remarked: "That I must say, who knew him well.") But the destruction, which is in some obvious sense a self-destruction, is attributed to his contemporaries and in particular his wife.

Thereafter Juan is shown living in an iconoclasted world: his father is broken and his education is one of censorship and bowdlerization of literary texts. The "filthy loves of gods and goddesses" are avoided and the editions of classics are "expurgated by learned men":

> but, fearful to deface
> Too much their modest bard by this omission,
>   And pitying sore his mutilated case,
> They only add them in an appendix,
> Which saves, in fact, the trouble of an index.   [1.44]

They stand "staring" there "Like garden gods [i.e. Priapus]—and not so decent either" (45); the object being "to destroy / His [Juan's] natural spirit" (50). This then is the form iconoclasm takes now: break but save, file away, and store the offending part; restore it (in the manner of *Dunciad* 4) as part of a pedantic scholarly structure.

Byron's cuckolding and killing of the figure who at this point corresponds to himself is curious, as is the placing of both functions, of husband and father, in the cuckolder of Jose, Don Alfonso. Later, in the Haidée episode, Lambro also serves (or takes upon himself) both functions. Thereafter, however, while a young girl remains part of the grouping (including, later, of Leila with Catherine the Great), the older woman, first functioning in Donna Julia, becomes a *much* older woman, Queen Catherine (fiftyish like Don Alfonso), and Juan himself becomes the younger party, the literal possession, who has to find ways to break away—in this case spatially, by traveling to England.

Byron, in his thirties, remains the mediator. For what has happened is that Byron himself, meditating on age and death, has closed the gap between the young lover and the old party. Typically he writes to Kinnaird (18 January 1823): ". . . on the very verge of thirty five.—I always looked to about thirty as the barrier of any real or fierce delight in the passions—" (10.87–88). His self-epitaph is of his thirty-third birthday.

The political allegory, we see, takes the form of a lover between old husband and young wife—in life (embodied in Byron's letters and journals) and in *Don Juan*. In the journal he was keeping in the early months of 1821 the two roles alternate (sometimes line by line): one moment he is a supporter of the carbonari and the next Teresa's lover. In *Don Juan*, however, this dichotomy emphasizes the difference between Byron and his protagonist. It is Juan who mediates between a husband and a wife, while Byron, the jaded past-thirty narrator, mediates (in both age and function) between Juan and the husband. Both characters originate in Dryden's heroic plays by way of Rochester's satiric poems, in the great lover, invented to complement the figure of the merry monarch (and his amorous brother-heir), of the aristocrat who serves as mediator, champion, successful warrior, always between the monarch and his unruly people. Juan, in short, prefigures the movement in the poetry of *Don Juan*—thematic and actual—from iconoclasm to memorialization or the constructing of an epitaph for a tomb.

THE AESTHETICS OF GLEANING IN *DON JUAN*

>   and I would say "fie on 't,"
> If I had not perceived that Revolution
> Alone can save the earth from Hell's pollution.   [*Don Juan*, 8.51]

> There was a modern Goth, I mean a Gothic
>   Bricklayer of Babel, called an architect, . . .
>   . . . [who] produced a plan whereby to erect
> New Buildings of correctest conformation,
> And throw down old—which he called *restoration.*   [16.68]

Byron's discourse of poetry making, in so far as it partakes of iconoclasm and georgic renewal, draws upon the determining subtext of the French phenomenon that renamed them revolution and restoration. By 1818 when Byron began to write *Don Juan,* the French Revolution meant its whole plot, beginning, middle, and end. On the face of it, he did not appear at a time when he could write as a revolutionary iconoclast. It was the early euphoric stage of revolution that saw the replacement of the old with the new calendar, of cathedrals with temples of reason. For Byron the poet of *Don Juan* iconoclasm was a historical process he could only look back on and analyze.

From his historical vantage—post-Thermidore, post-Brumaire, post-Waterloo—political iconoclasm had only replaced the idol with a contemporary leader (living, secular, successful). Louis XVI had been iconoclasted by the French Revolution, only to be replaced by Robespierre and Robespierre by Napoleon; and the idol (Emperor) Napoleon was iconoclasted by the Duke of Wellington only to be replaced by Louis XVIII. Renaming was only an exchange of names: not merely an exchange of church and state, of cathedral and temple, but of king, first consul, emperor, and now king again, and duke. Wellington is a central presence in *Don Juan* (first introduced following the description of the carnage of Ismail) because he is an iconoclast, restorer of icons, and himself an icon. Thus he shares with Byron, though as false to true, the double roles of icon and iconoclast (of both monarch substitute and monarch breaker), and embodies the iconoclastic process that Byron represents in *Don Juan.*

The memory of iconoclasm in England lay, so far as Byron is concerned in *Don Juan,* in the Henrician replacement of pope by king, and the concrete memory of this replacement was the abbey turned into a country house. The center of Canto 13, the center of Juan's adventures in England, describes the iconoclasted abbey that became (has now been for generations) the country house of the Amundevilles: Norman Abbey. It carries an additional charge for Byron because he has based it on his own ancestral estate, Newstead Abbey— about which he had written a poem in his youth, when he left it to make the Grand Tour (*On Leaving Newstead Abbey,* 1806), and which in 1818 he was forced to sell in order to make ends meet. This act of dispossession took place while he was writing the earlier cantos of *Don Juan*. Representing Newstead Abbey in Canto 13 (written in 1823) therefore registers a continuing iconoclasm, but an iconoclasm (like that in France) carried out by forces and by parties other than the poet.

Byron chooses to represent Norman/Newstead as the sort of great country house that had symbolized Whig politics since the days of Walpole. Kelsall sees the assumptions very much the same in Byron's day, and therefore concludes that Byron is still writing as essentially an anti-Walpole Whig.[27] Following upon the positive description of Parliament in Canto 12 (at least as of 1789), the country house appears to be an equally positive symbol. And yet, seen against the tradition of country-house poems (Jonson's *To Penshurst*, Carew's *To Saxham* and *To My Friend G.N. from Wrest*, and Marvell's *Upon Appleton House*), Norman Abbey sounds, as an ongoing social phenomenon, closer to the Tory heaven of *The Vision of Judgment*. While the Amundevilles' hospitality is emphasized, we notice that it does not extend beyond the house guests to the country folk; and that these house guests—designated merely Lords A, B, and C (contrasted in the same stanza with the soldiers killed defending their country)—make Norman Abbey sound more like Squire Allworthy's Paradise Hall, which housed Thwackum and Square and the Blifils, than Penshurst or Saxham. Even the emphasis on the Norman genealogy suspiciously recalls the bastardy that Thomas Paine noted was at the origin of so-called legitimate succession in England. In short, the Amundevilles are presented as Norman Abbey's present, appropriating, restoring "possessors," and Byron associates himself with the pre-Reformation dispossessed owners.

Norman Abbey is also the place where expectations call for yet another romantic triangle to materialize. The descriptions of Lord Henry Amundeville and his wife Adeline, in particular the details that suggest autobiographical reference, prepare us for Juan's new affair. But it does not materialize, and when Byron breaks off the narrative he is describing a romance between Juan and the Duchess of Fitz-Fulke. Nevertheless everything in the narrative of *Don Juan* up to this point leads one to expect—and Byron's journals and letters support the expectation—another older man, cold, distant, and correct, with a *cavaliere servente* relationship between Juan and Adeline. The abbey, in this sense, carries along with associations of the past, associations of marital property.

The significant detail offered in the first panoramic view of the country house concerns its setting: "it lies, perhaps, a little low, / Because the monks preferred a hill behind, / To shelter their devotion from the wind" (13.55). This is a sly comment on the parallel between the subservient monks and the trimmers who acquired and have held onto the property in the intervening centuries sheltered from "the wind" of changeable monarchs. The low-lying position of the monastery-mansion is set off in the next stanza by the "high woodlands" (i.e. the "hill behind"), "where the Druid oak / Stood like Caractacus," the ancient king of the Britons who held out for nine years against the Romans before being carried off a prisoner to Rome.[28] In this way the hills, the woodlands, and the ancient British hero emerge somewhat larger and more impressive than the briefly mentioned mansion that is an iconoclasted monastery: the one implies a struggle for freedom, the other Henry VIII's appropriation of church property and his parceling of it out among his henchmen.

The architectural element that draws the poet's attention is the "grand arch, which once screened many an aisle," a "glorious remnant," the one *un*-remade element of the iconoclasted ecclesiastical structure. The destruction of the aisles was, we are told, "a loss to Art," but the surviving arch compensates: alone, it "yet frowned superbly o'er the soil, / And kindled feelings in the roughest heart . . ."—rhyming "art" with "heart" (59). This remaining fragment resembles and recalls the Druid oak: iconoclasm and time have withdrawn it from the world of art (to the world of heart), rendering it virtually a part of nature.

The next element to be described is the empty niche (60) which once contained the figures of twelve saints: "fallen, not when the friars fell, / But in the war which struck Charles from his throne." The poet has moved from the Druid oak to Caractacus to the "glorious remnant" of the "grand Arch" and finally to the "gallant Cavaliers, who [like Caractacus] fought in vain"—those members of Byron's own family, who fought for the royalist cause, Charles I and his court "who knew not to resign or reign."

Two sets of iconoclasts now emerge: the generation of Henry VIII and his mercenary crew who transformed holy sites into property, monasteries into mansions, and then the roundheads who seized and defaced Norman Abbey in the Civil War. The defenders of the twelve saints were therefore Byron's ancestors, the cavaliers who "fought in vain" and for a cause that betrayed them by its own folly (a monarch "who knew not to resign or reign"). The twelve saints "fallen" at the hands of the roundheads are, of course, parallel to Charles I "struck . . . from his throne," as Caractacus and the cavaliers, the defenders of ancestral lands, are parallel to Byron.

But there is one niche, "a higher niche, alone," once again a lone survivor like the Druid oak and the arch, which was beyond the reach of the roundhead iconoclasts, where a Virgin and Christ Child remain intact:

> Spared by some chance when all beside was spoil'd;
> She made the earth below seem holy ground.
>   This may be superstition, weak or wild;
> But even the faintest relics of a shrine
> Of any worship, wake some thoughts divine.   [61]

These "thoughts divine" are hardly the sentiments of an iconoclast. And yet they have been associated with the most iconoclasted, the least restored parts of the monastery. In stanza 62 Byron describes the broken window:

> Shorn of its glass of thousand colourings,
> Through which the deepen'd glories once could enter,
> Streaming from off the Sun like seraph's wings,
> Now yawns all desolate. . . .

The window has not, in the iconoclastic manner, been replaced by transparent glass but has been left empty—and so while there is no obstruction to vision, it is not a view but a sound that Byron notes: no visual image but a sound like that produced by a natural amplifier, a sort of gigantic aeolian harp. A sound was also the central sensory perception in *On Leaving Newstead Abbey:* "Thro' thy battlements, Newstead, the hollow winds whistle." There too the sound suggested a medium more expressive than words—or than finished architecture—equivalent to its source in the broken opening, unobscured by glass whether stained or clear. Like the iconoclast, Byron constantly reduces spirit to matter (in its most common form, fiction to "truth") and this takes the form of progressively replacing image with word, word with voice and gesture, seeking a presence which compensates for the absence of the visual image or word on the page: "When, ere the ink be dry, the sound grows cold" (51).

We should note that the words "gone to decay" were applied in *On Leaving Newstead Abbey* not just to any ruin but to "the hall of my fathers." The words "hollow winds whistle" did not carry a positive sense there as they do in *Don Juan;* they were used nostalgically to recall the "once smiling garden" in which the rose had been "choak'd" by the hemlock and thistle. Inside, the escutcheons and shields of the Byron barons are "the only sad vestiges now that remain" (the word "sad" echoes in the opening stanzas of Canto 13). "No more" are the words, carrying the now familiar *sic transit gloria mundi* theme, evoking loyalty to the king, the battle of Marston Moor, and the purpose of the ancestors ("The fame of his fathers he ne'er can forget") which are supposed to give courage to the present Lord Byron, their heir, when he is abroad.

> That fame, and that memory, still will he cherish,
>   He vows, that he ne'er will disgrace your renown;
> Like you will he live, or like you will perish;
>   When decay'd, may he mingle his dust with your own.

The ancestors survive for him in their iconic funerary monuments—in the human, patrician effigies that were spared the iconoclastic fervor. Worship of idols had become worship of Whiggish self and family and, as we have seen, memory of the affiliation of the ancient (or not so ancient) British ruling class with classical Rome. In this regard it is revealing that Byron (whose evocations of Horace also depend on the mediation of his English precursor Pope, and often with Pope's words) makes his family connection not with the Romans but with their unsuccessful British opponent Caractacus.

But the sequence of human breakage and natural decay is what interests Byron. A polity or an abbey is broken, the parts are patched into a domestic dwelling, and the ruins are transformed by corrosive force of time into objects of spiritual and aesthetic pleasure. This transformation based on the forced collaboration of man and nature is then remade, first by the Amundevilles. Before the partying begins Byron describes Norman Abbey as a "mix" of past and present; the monastery that has been made over into a mansion is a "mixed Gothic" admired by "artists." Finally, all of the above is remade an object of meditation on the immense spectrum of change that is *Don Juan*.

If the passage in Canto 13 describes, as I think it does, a process of poetic making as well as (in excess of) a model Whig country house in the post-Waterloo era, then the emphasis is not on the transformation of sacred into secular, or the naturalizing of the sacred, but on its survival: on the transformation of the ecclesiastical ruin, by iconoclastic hands but also by time and weather, which produces something more as well as less beautiful than the original building, in particular beautiful sounds that are perceived and remade into a specifically aural art by the poet.

Although the conclusion is aural, oral, the sound of a voice (an aristocratic voice), nevertheless the metaphor Byron pursues is visual.[29] His description of the ruined arch takes us back to the first stanza of the canto, in which the poet's subject is said to "soar high and solemn, / As an old temple dwindled to a column." This is the first suggestion of how art accommodates iconoclasm: here the temple is reduced ("dwindled") to a single remaining column, but this ruin also permits the temple now, in its single column, to "soar high and solemn." Sixty-seven stanzas later Byron addresses himself to the effect of the "Gothic Babel" monastery-mansion: halls, chambers, galleries "joined / By no quite lawful marriage of the arts," but

> when combined,
> Formed a whole which, irregular in parts,
> Yet left a grand impression on the mind,
> At least of those whose eyes are in their hearts.   [67]

There is also a gothic fountain on which the composite faces of monsters and saints may be confused, which has become (was not in Gothic times) an emblem of "man's vain glory, and his vainer troubles":

> The spring gushed through grim mouths of granite made,
>   And sparkled into basins, where it spent
> Its little torrent in a thousand bubbles,
> Like man's vain glory, and his vainer troubles.   [65]

The gothic fountain recalls the one purely natural element in the landscape (back in stanzas 57–58), the lake and stream. The wanderings of the stream leading into the pellucid lake adumbrate, among other things, the meandering of Byron's form, which also relates to the rambling ad hoc structure of the abbey.

With its combinations of monster and saint, of architecture and nature, the fountain leads into the description of the mansion itself in the following stanzas: This is the remade part, "reformed, replaced, or sunk, / And [which] spoke more of the baron than the monk" (67). The "cloisters still were stable," we are told, "The cells, too, and Refectory," with "stable" meaning both still standing in place *and* transformed into a stable, monks replaced by horses. This is the first iconoclastic metamorphosis that is remarked, but it is followed by parallel ones within the mansion's picture gallery: from "Steel Barons, molten the next generation / To silken rows of gay and gartered Earls," and thence to ermine-clad judges, and finally allegorized in the paintings of martyrs, landscapes, and genre scenes, all transformations of life into art.

In his essay of about the same time attacking William Lisle Bowles (and defending Pope), Byron explains why the towers of Westminster Abbey are aesthetically preferable to a shot tower. Though he claims that it is only a matter of the shot tower's "architecture" being "inferior" to that of the great abbey, what interests him emerges in the next sentence:

> Turn Westminster Abbey or Saint Paul's into a powder magazine, their poetry, as objects, remain the same; the Parthenon was actually converted into one by the Turks, during Morosini's Venetian siege, and part of it destroyed in consequence. Cromwell's dragoons stabled their steeds in Worcester cathedral; was it less poetical as an object than before?

He may or may not mean *while* the horses were stabled there, but the picture he gives us is of a cathedral-stable, that is, of a cathedral iconoclasted into a stable. As in Wright of Derby's *Blacksmith's Forge* (fig. 21) it is in fact the juxtaposition of cathedral and stable which interests in the picturesque result of iconoclastic remaking—in Bentley's illustration of Gray's churchyard (fig. 1), the parish church set into the old iconoclasted abbey. Byron puts iconoclasm in its political dimension—property stolen, ruined, made picturesque, a "mix"—but also in its aesthetic dimension.

The ruined but unrestored arch (or the temple dwindled to a column) is one form taken by Byron's iconoclasm, and the monastery-turned-into-mansion the other. The poem *Don Juan* is characterized by fragmentation and mixed-patching; there is figuratively a "killing" and restoring of life to the "dead"; there are discontinuities. But, as in the case of the Virgin and Christ Child, Byron shows a nostalgia for wholeness, for the time before the iconoclasm. And the extraordinary violence, the sheer breakage in which Swift seemed to take pleasure, is foreign to Byron the heir and late owner of Newstead Abbey. Thomas Paine's image in *Common Sense* of George III's statue being ground up into dust and reconstituted as ammunition is very different from Byron's representation of George III in *The Vision of Judgment:* though dead (as well as blind and imbecile) George nevertheless ends singing psalms in a British heaven controlled by

Tory angels. Byron's is a vision not of grinding-to-dust but of the wholeness recalled by the remaining ruinous part—a vestige that has escaped Duncical triumph and restoration. *The Vision of Judgment,* the allegorical equivalent of *Don Juan,* recreates the fourth book of Pope's *Dunciad,* and like Pope, Byron the poet survives only because he embeds the duncical vision in the amber of his poetry. *Don Juan* is not a Swift poem about the inefficacy of writing. It is, like Pope's *Dunciad,* about successful remaking, in poetry if not in politics, but out of poor, second-class, long-since iconoclasted materials, and by a method largely dependent on an understanding of the relation of chance to change (as in the cast of dice).

Idolatry then—or pragmatic iconoclasm which ends in another idolatry—is the folly permitted by Napoleon, reestablished by Wellington, and celebrated by the turncoat poets Southey and Wordsworth. In the passage on Wellington that opens Canto 9 (and originally opened Canto 3) Byron sets up the Wellington figure as an antipoetic maker who props up the old regime; Wellington is the great restorer:

> You have repaired Legitimacy's crutch,—
>   A prop not quite so certain as before: . . .
> And Waterloo has made the world your debtor—
> (I wish your bards would sing it rather better.)   [9.3]

What Wellington *might* have done (or Napoleon before him) would have brought him proper "fame" (that Popean term once again): "You might have freed fall'n Europe from the Unity / Of Tyrants, and been blest from shore to shore" (9).

Parallel with the general/politician Wellington is the poet Southey, the laureate who celebrates this counterrevolution. Both are like a cobbler or tinker, "botching, patching," "cobbling at manacles for all mankind" (Dedication, 14), who is finally realized in the architect of Norman Abbey who

> produced a plan whereby to erect
> New buildings of correctest conformation,
> And throw down old—which he called *restoration.*   [16.68]

What the Revolution calls for at this stage is an act of sublimation, displacement, repetition, relocation, or some other way of coming to terms with its losses and disillusionments. This stage of the process, though in a sense it reminds us of the naming substitutions carried out by the iconoclast, is very different in one important particular. In iconoclasm the antiartist is the active agent, breaking and remaking. Byron is the intransitive patient mourning a breakage and a loss that have been carried out by others (by the state, by God, by Wellington and the Southeys and Wordsworths).

From Byron's point of view, what begins (or was formerly) a process of breaking and remaking becomes an act of mourning for, seeking a memory of, the breakage or loss—as well as, in some ultimate aristocratic nostalgia, the wholeness before the breakage and loss. *Don Juan* stands for, as it represents, a later stage of revolutionary process involving not just loss of any kind or loss for loss's sake but loss of the ideal, or hope, and of youth (and with it of love): in short, embodying disillusionment with that time when it was very joy to be alive, for which Wordsworth also tries to compensate in the immensity of *The Prelude*.

THE account of Norman Abbey is placed in the context of change. The changing seasons and the end of the Parliamentary term signal the time to visit the Abbey (42 ff.), which then is described in terms of Henrician iconoclasm and temporal transformation. The subject that connects politics and poetry is change: on the level of consciousness, the artist's manipulation of his materials, and on the natural level mere flux; at one extreme political revolution, with its devastation, but remaining as a constant referent in the poem (as in the age), and at the other the patching and propping restoration by Wellington and Southey. Change is the motion of the turncoat, turning over his creed; whereas the stabilizing intent of poetry (or virtue) is "To keep *one* creed," "a task grown quite Herculean" (Dedication, 17). The still point of the moving circle, therefore, is something like the Virgin-Child who has survived iconoclastic revolution, and personally the enduring memory which survives (as genealogy as well as poetry does) the divestments of property and of government. In poetry it is the immortal line, in both the sense of the poetic line and of the poetic genealogy of Milton, Pope, and Byron.

The French Revolution implies the extremity of violent change described by Mackintosh in *Vindiciae Gallicae*. Mackintosh was careful to attribute revolutionary change not to an individual plotter (as the counterrevolutionary writers claimed) but to "general causes influencing the whole body of the people" (p. 31), nor to the unruly Parisian mob so much as to the whole body politic, the whole of nature shifting its ground. One aspect of change educed by Mackintosh was its extreme rapidity, so quick that "Doctrines were universally received in May which in January would have been deemed treasonable, and which in March were derided as the vision of a few deluded fanatics" (p. 20). A second was its violence. But Mackintosh argued against Burke's appalled reaction to the notion of attempting "to establish order from principles of confusion, or, with the materials and instruments of rebellion, to build up a solid and stable government"—that is, Burke's belief that "beauty is achieved through orderly means only." On the contrary, Mackintosh asserts (in a Romantic melodramatization of Hogarth's aesthetic of modernity), beauty can be achieved *only* through excess and misery—and he insists, further, on the mixed or alloyed nature of the result in which the good is mingled with the bad, the wonderful legislative acts with the "excesses and miseries at which humanity revolts."[30]

While by Byron's time it was impossible for him to accept these formulations as any longer applicable to the French Revolution, they could still appear relevant to the writing of postrevolutionary poetry and not unrelated to Pope's formulation about making a beauty from a blunder.

The second aspect of change is personal, physical, and psychological. For if *Don Juan* is a *Dunciad* in its use of iconoclasted materials, it is also, most centrally, a Popean apologia for the poet. But the apologia takes the form of obsessive talk about death, aging (middle age), and memory. The great *ubi sunt* passages (the anaphoras, "where is . . ." and "I have seen . . ."), which began in Canto 11, always relate the public and the private, the decline of England and Byron's own decline now that he is past thirty. A change in love ("Juan mused on mutability, / Or on his Mistress—terms synonymous," 16.20), for example, connects the love of a private citizen Juan with the nonpassion of the public "eunuch" Castlereagh.

Change in this sense means youth becoming middle age; the deaths of friends, the evocation of the contemporary deaths of Keats and Shelley, of Byron's own past-thirty years. The middle-aged Catherine the Great of Canto 10 pursues the young Juan, in the same way that the first-person speaker seeks a relationship with his allegorical protagonist. On the other side are displayed the fiftyish Wordsworth and Laureate Southey, and the old king. "Carotid-cutting Castlereagh" as well as the king die and their deaths are celebrated in the course of *Don Juan*'s composition. Though he was anything but moribund, Wellington's fame is embodied in his projected "tomb in Westminster's Old Abbey" (9.2). Death and mourning complete every metamorphosis Byron foresees in *Don Juan*.

Byron anchors his theme in the obvious association of revolution and death. The French Revolution had fostered this association, first in the killing of its own, one faction after another, in a seemingly suicidal process, but then also in the wars that followed by a sort of inevitability from revolution. The theme was summed up in the Rowlandson drawing of Napoleon and Death sitting looking at each other over a corpse-strewn battlefield—and in the whole immense *Dance of Death* Rowlandson published in 1814 and 1815 just before Byron left England. The account of Wellington at the opening of Canto 9 leads into a Dance of Death.

The third aspect of change resides in the poetic transformation brought about by wit. Quick, glancing, bubbling (soda water or uncorked champagne), it extends for Byron from the ottava rima stanza into epistolary correspondence, a mode parallel to *Don Juan* except for the lack of rhyme. This liveliness is polarized with Wordsworth's slow gradualism, his leach gatherers and little girls who seem to be turning to stone or disappearing into nature—as also with Keats's "mental masturbation" and Southey's vulgarizing Cibberian flattery.

But the opposition also includes Byron's own pre–*Don Juan* poetry, to which he often refers—the *Childe Harold* and *Corsair* mode that made him famous. The Horatian/comic/Italian/Popean mode of *Don Juan* has to resist the change—the restoration—to the *Childe Harold* mode urged by his publisher John Murray and such close personal friends as John Cam Hobhouse, even by his mistress Teresa Guiciolli who persuaded him to stop writing *Don Juan,* and exemplified in the poetry of his own contemporary works *Manfred* and *Cain, Marino Faliero* and *The Two Foscari*, which express the same anxieties as *Don Juan* in another, higher, more conventional, or less (in that sense) iconoclastic genre.

The literary model for the joining of autobiography, death, and other forms of change, with writing that seeks the immediacy of gesture was the other presiding literary figure (with Pope) in *Don Juan*. I mean Laurence Sterne, whose prose style is the best precursor of Byron's prose and to some extent his terza rima style; whose subject was the way to deal with change (which for him meant death); and whose novel was a huge work of mourning for that imminent death. One recalls the old dying Tristram, the author—a reflection of the aging, ailing Sterne—who writes about the young innocent Tristram. One recalls the threat of women in the innocent Shandy homosocial household—Mrs. Shandy, Tristram's Jenny, and, above all, the Widow Wadman—and the emphasis on the father-mother figures, the aging family, and its (literally) crushing effect on young Tristram. Indeed,

Byron's idea of ending Juan's life on the guillotine recalls the more innocent accident of the sash window on young Tristram's sexual organ. But above all, one recalls the whole problem of writing—linking death and, holding it off, Tristram–Sterne's writing, related also (in Book 7) to escaping from England and traveling on the continent.

At the center of *Tristram Shandy* was Sterne's equation of innocence with impotence, and therefore the impossibility—if not undesirability—of sexual love: its relation to the Fall, innocence, and Time-Death. Like *Don Juan* it could be argued that *Tristram Shandy*, far from being iconoclastic, represented the anxious attempt to hold off change—change in the form of aging, impotence, and death. Sterne's enumeration of the deaths of Bobby, LeFever, Toby, Trim, and Walter recalls the obsessive listing of deaths in Byron's poem (and in his journals and letters).

But at the same time it is impossible to overlook the addition to old Sterne and old Byron of the young Tristram, Byron, Juan, and so on (including the young Napoleon): those who do bring on change or carry it out. Thus the central question of *Don Juan* at least is whether the poet/hero uses the forms, myths, fictions, "truths," to stave off the reality of death, or whether they use him, constantly containing his "liberty" as the revolution has proved to be contained by the counter-revolution. After all, both Sterne and Byron make quite explicit the connection between themselves and, ultimately, Don Quixote (as does also, of course, Wordsworth in Book 5 of *The Prelude*). Don Quixote is the hero—the old hero—whose story opens Canto 13, which is called the "saddest" of tales:

> Because it makes us smile: his hero's right,
> And still pursues the right;—to curb the bad
> His only object, and 'gainst odds to fight
> His guerdon: 't is his virtue makes him mad!
> But his adventures form a sorry sight . . .   [9]

If there is a process at work in nature—in the world described by Byron—it is one that moves back and forth from order to disorder, with its fulcrum a transgression and fall. Canto 10 opens with the linkage of Sir Isaac Newton, the poet, and the common factor of discovery; the connector is the ambiguous and paradoxical apple, the cause of both our fall and (with Newton's discovery) our rise again. And so by implication, Byron's discovery too involves apples, fall, rise, transgression, and discovery of a new world. Revolution itself is the model with its fall from innocence and the inevitable return of the father (whether Donna Julia's husband or Haidée's father). And the drama we witness is of Byron looking back on the French Revolution—on his own youthful "revolution," on Juan's youth—and obsessively memorializing: thus producing memory (unabused) images, while at the same time attacking, iconoclasting (we might say) the cant of idolatry (Napoleon, Wellington) and the idolators (Southey, Wordsworth) of the abused images.

THE consequence of breakage and change at the hands of others is (perhaps naturally for a reader of Pope) a metaphor of georgic renewal, in particular an alternative to political restoration. It begins with the assumption of a few surviving shards like the broken arch. The sorting out of the guests at Norman Abbey, that "heterogeneous mass" (as he calls it), into "a specimen of every class" leads into the striking metaphors of stanzas 95–97: the poet in this situation of classification has "to cull"—but "there is *nought* to cull / Of Folly's fruit; for though your fools abound, / They're barren, and not worth the pains to pull." He is referring to such barren names as the Duke of Dash and the Countess of Blank (Adeline, we recall, lives in Blank Square). But the metaphor becomes explicitly georgic in the next stanza (96):

> But from being farmers, we turn gleaners, gleaning
>   The scanty but right-well threshed ears of Truth;
> And, gentle reader, when you gather meaning,
>   You may be Boaz, and I—modest Ruth.

And concludes at the beginning of stanza 97: "But what we can we glean in this vile age / Of chaff, although our gleanings be not grist." He has gone from the georgic farmer[31] to—all that's feasible in "this vile age"—the gleaner, one who follows in the wake of the harvester, picking up whatever he can, whatever is left (even when the "gleanings" are not "grist" for a poetic mill).

We already saw, in the description of Norman Abbey, iconoclasm from the point of view of the cavaliers, in short the iconoclasted Roman Catholics and royalist lords. It is possible that in Byron we see another version of Pope's dialectic of iconoclasm and georgic regeneration, where the latter term (what was in fact the Popean solution) has now bifurcated into (1) the restoration work of the politician patching and repairing the old discredited regime and (2) the work of the poet, which is only gleaning—Ruth following Boaz, as Byron follows Wellington and Southey.

The gleaner is a new poetic figure. Perhaps in Popean terms the gleaner is the poet who tries to make a beauty from a blunder, but in Byron's Popean terms, he is the person who gathers the "truth"—that is, what is left in the wake of the (Napoleonic, then Wellingtonian) harvester. There is an analogy between what the gleaner gleans and the ruined abbey arch, but the harvester is better known as (Byron's repeated term) the mower, the Grim Reaper Death. (Byron even refers once to the "Grim Reader.") The poet is literally writing of and out of what remains, the "truth" of "fact," or what remains in the wake of the Revolutionary scenario from 1789 through 1815. This is the grim reaper who follows upon the description of Wellington in Canto 9 (which follows upon the massacre of Ismail), who appears opposite Napoleon in Rowlandson's print and opposite a long series of social types in his *Dance of Death*.[32]

A knot of references and half-formed metaphors in Canto 9 has already connected georgic and iconoclasm, reducing georgic to something close to gleaning. Here the process is projected beyond the breaking to the later unearthing, an unearthing somewhere between the farmer's unearthing of old swords in the first *Georgic* and an anthropological dig. The passage begins in stanza 24 with a statement of the poet's "plain, sworn, downright detestation / Of every despotism in every nation" (the reference is to Catherine the Great), and then goes on in the next stanza to make the distinction made repeatedly in the letters between Byron himself and the plebeian demagogues who control the mob. What they do is

> to pull down every steeple,
> And set up in their stead some proper stuff.
> Whether they may sow scepticism to reap Hell,
> As is the Christian dogma rather rough,
> I do not know.

The practical iconoclastic process of pulling down and setting up instead is followed by the sowing and reaping we associate with georgic, but presented not in its Virgilian but its Christian form, "As ye sow, so shall ye reap," which brings in the context of the Fall—and foreshadows the stanzas in Canto 13 about "gleaning."

Then, in stanza 31, Juan turns his attention to his "little charge" Leila, whom he saved from the carnage of Ismail. Byron compares her future (and Juan's) to the road along which they are bumping in a carriage: it is beautiful because left to "lovely Nature's skill," but since Nature's "no paviour," it consists of rocky ruts. Continuing the metaphor, God is the freeholder of this beautiful but intractable land, a "Gentleman farmer" among renters who can no longer afford to pay rent in the wake of the war. The confusing pronoun "he" in stanza 32 can apply to either God or Juan as (once again) Adam, "the first of what we used to call / 'Gentlemen farmers.'" The application, whoever the referent, is to the making of passable highways and canals, and thence back to sowing and reaping and to the inappropriateness of the term in the aftermath of the Napoleonic (or Catherine) wars and the counterrevolution. The "gentleman farmer" is

> a race worn out quite,
> Since lately there have been no rents at all,
> And "gentlemen" are in a piteous plight,
> And "farmers" can't raise Ceres from her fall.
> She fell with Buonaparte:—What strange thoughts
> Arise, when we see Emperors fall with oats!   [9.32]

The emphasis on "Fall" is unmistakable, a connection with all of the earlier allusions to the Fall (going back to Juan and Julia and Haidée). Farmers lose their crops with the "fall" of emperors and stock prices—and these are the result of wars as frivolous as the one Catherine the Great has just concluded at Ismail.

In this context, the war is the old pregeorgic war, and the only thing "gleaned" or salvaged from the destruction of Ismail is Leila,

> the sweet child
> Whom he [Juan] had saved from slaughter—what a Trophy!
> O! ye who build up monuments, defiled
> With gore . . .

She, like the Christ Child of 13.61, was also "Spared by some chance when all beside was spoiled." But the startling added word "trophy" precipitates the passage on "monuments" and the following stanzas in which the georgic farmer gleans a few pretty girls (as earlier on the seashore, "some pretty shell," 18): "one life saved, especially if young / Or pretty" (34) is preferable to "the present laurels" or "Fame" of the poet.

With "build up" still hanging on from the earlier georgic discourse, Byron projects a "trophy" or "monument" that is "built up" out of defilement, in the manner of the fourth *Georgic*. The referent is Leila but also the road and canal of stanza 31 and the "fallen" farmer of 32, and thus becomes "relic" when the poet loses the train of his thought in 36 and says the lost thought

> will one day be found
> With other relics of "a former World,"
> When this World shall be *former,* underground,
>   Thrown topsy-turvy, twisted, crisped, and curled,
>   Baked, fried, or burnt, turned inside-out, or drowned,
>   Like all the worlds before, which have been hurled
> First out of and then back again to Chaos . . .   [37]

that is, all of the deluges and wraths of God which are reaped by humankind following their sowing (cf. 25). The monument/trophy/relic will be found in the same way (mixing classical and anthropological examples) titans, giants, and mammoths will be unearthed—and these "fellows of about / Some hundred feet in height, not to say miles" (39) suggest the portly George IV, whose unearthing will make "the new worldlings" "wonder where such animals could sup!" These "great relics" of buried monarchs are essentially broken idols, with further metaphors activated by "dug up" and "burial." The titans of the Golden Age have been "pulled down" (25) and in the Iron Age that has followed, Juan and Haidée before, Juan and Leila now, those like Byron who have survived the French Revolution, are the

>   young people, just thrust out
> From some fresh Paradise, and set to plough,
> And dig, and sweat, and turn themselves about,
>   And plant, and reap, and spin, and grind, and sow,
>   Till all the arts at length are brought about,
>   Especially of War and taxing. . .   [40]

(Following the passage on gleaning in canto 13, we read in 14.78: "Adam exchanged his Paradise for ploughing, / Eve made up millinary with fig leaves. . .") Ploughing and digging (the sweat of the fallen, georgic world) have led to the arts, but they have also led to war and taxation once again—and back, with stanza 42, to the court of Catherine the Great, Juan's latest keeper, and the "reaper" of the bloody massacre of Ismail.

All of this takes place in a pair of contexts, the first of the Christian Fall and the second, in stanza 49, of the politician Castlereagh, from whose public utterances sense must be "gleaned": "that odd string of words"

> Which none divine, and every one obeys,
> Perhaps you may pick out some queer *no* meaning,—
> Of that weak wordy harvest the sole gleaning.

Between the two passages Byron discusses (41 ff.) his own aleatory poetic method, based on the assumption that "I never know the word which will come next."

In Canto 12 the handler of gold has also replaced the georgic farmer: the bankers and usurers, the survivors of change and revolution, "the true Lords of Europe" (6), as opposed to the old nobility, which includes the poets (cf. 11.55 ff., 13.100), or even the monarchs whom the bankers, not the nobility, now control. (In 11.75 they were shown to control the "young noble" too by his purse strings.) The georgic metaphor is introduced in the discussion of gold (40), where Byron notes how public opinion (the work of publishers and blue-stockings) believes it is "immoral" to "show things really as they are, / Not as they ought to be." It is therefore the "virtuous plough" of Southey–Wordsworth

> Which skims the surface, leaving scarce a scar
> Upon the black loam long manured by Vice,
> Only to keep its corn at the old price.

This "vile age" is not a time for sowing seeds. But it has proved to be a great time for mowing, and so the poet's function—in an icono-clastic age—has become that of a gleaner.

"Truth," in the formulation Byron repeats most often, is a georgic function, part of its ethos of use, acceptance, revitalization, on the basis of "truth" as opposed to invention. Fiction and imagination (associated with drunkenness, with the Lake Poets) must be replaced by "truth" (associated with Pope, the ethical poet). The removal of imagination/inebriation, like the removal of the stained glass from the church window, reveals "truth"—by which Byron means both facts not fiction and the workings of humans in ethical situations. Within Norman Abbey is the Gothic pile. Or the cathedral or palladian palace is turned into a common stable.

Connecting the truth-fiction opposition with the georgic assumptions, he writes (15.88–89):

> Apologue, Fable, Poesy, and Parable,
> Are false, but may be rendered also true,
> By those who sow them in a land that's arable.

Here he comes close to saying, as Defoe did in his defense of *Robinson Crusoe* as history, that his story is true because it is an allegory, that is, made of his own life. The georgic metaphor then continues that it is therefore "wonderful what Fable [i.e., when so planted, in truth] will not do!" Then: "'T'is said it makes Reality more bearable: / But what's Reality?" But he means here not that fable makes reality more bearable but that truth and reality are different things.

In *Don Juan* "truth" is summed up by the story of the Russian officer whose heel is seized and held by the teeth of a dying Moslem (8.86):

> 't is the part
> Of a true poet to escape from fiction
> Whene'er he can; for there is little art
> In leaving verse more free from the restriction
> Of Truth than prose, unless to suit the mart
> For what is sometimes called poetic diction,
> And that outrageous appetite for lies
> Which Satan angles with for souls, like flies.

The point is that poetry needs "the restriction / Of Truth" to curb its penchant for satisfying "that outrageous appetite for lies." (Implicit, of course, is the recognition that one form of lies, Satan's falsehoods, has been about Byron—and is one reason that he, like Pope, writes.[33])

In 14.13 he affirms that his muse "by no means deals in fiction: / She gathers a repertory of facts," but he adds: "Of course with some reserve and slight restriction, / But mostly sings of human things and acts—." He rhymes "facts" and "acts"—indeed, "fiction" and "restriction" (cf. 8.86). This is his basic definition of truth, as of Pope's ethic poetry. He adds two Popean asides: that "too much truth, at first sight, ne'er attracts," suggesting that some fiction is needed; and that if his poetry's subject were "only what's called Glory," he'd then write a more fictive poetry.

The subject of truth is brought up one final time at the beginning of Canto 16 with the subject of the Norman Abbey ghost. The monastery-mansion passage is completed in Cantos 15 and 16 with the ghost story. And at the same time the subject of truth, fact, fiction, and belief (in the impossible) is summed up: Byron says, first, that his work is the "most sincere that ever dealt in fiction" (2); second, that his muse "treats all things, and ne'er retreats / From anything" (3); and third, that (in 4) "of all truths which she has told, the most / True is that which she is about to tell"—that is, about a ghost. And the reason, of course, is that the ghost turns out to be only the amorous Duchess of Fitz-Fulke.

The scene takes place in the hall of ancestral portraits, the gothic ornament that "remained," "all / That Time has left our fathers of their Hall" (16). What is actually "left" turns out to be the ghost of a monk himself—a ghost only, which proves to be in fact the Duchess of Fitz-Fulke dressed as a monk in order to seduce Juan. The sequence recapitulates the whole erotic course of iconoclasm/fetishism from Swift's rotting Celia to Hogarth's Venuses and Apollos in *The Analysis of Beauty:* the monk is revealed to be (or is demystified into) the amorous woman; the deceived, terrified spectator of the ghost is the object of her love and seduction. The iconoclasm is carried out by her, not by Juan, except in so far as his probing touch reveals its "truth." Juan, as he approaches the ghost/Fitz-Fulke, is "eager now the truth to pierce"—in the sense of getting at the facts—but in the next stanza, the words "Juan put forth one arm—" echo the ending of Sterne's *Sentimental Journey* and prepare us for the kind of penetration that is going to take place when he gets under the robe.

Adeline Amundeville's song about the Black Friar, delivered the morning after Juan's first encounter, has to do with the appropriation of the monastery:

> When the Lord of the Hill, Amundeville,
>   Made Norman Church his prey,
> And expelled the friars, one friar still
>   Would not be driven away.
>   2
> Though he came in his might, with King Henry's right,
>   To turn church lands to lay,
> With sword in hand, and torch to light
>   Their walls, if they said nay;
> A monk remained, unchased, unchained,
>   And he did not seem formed of clay.

The monk unites marriage and death beds, returning to curse the Amundeville heirs: "When an heir is born, he's heard to mourn" (interesting that this is sung by Adeline); "For he is yet the Church's heir, / Whoever may be the lay. / Amundeville is Lord by day, / But the monk is Lord by night" (4–5).

This is a reversal of the well-known story in *The Monk* (by Byron's friend M. G. Lewis) of the Bleeding Nun, when the waiting lover turns out to be a ghost. The question that remains is: was the first appearance in the hall a real ghost and the second, entering Juan's bedroom, Fitz-Fulke (who has had the idea planted in her head by the talk at breakfast) or was she the first as well, and on the second night got up the courage to enter his room? Byron wants to have it both ways, with the inclusion of ghosts in a "true" world. He introduces the Columbus-discovery metaphor once again, relating the subject of spirits to "the limits of the coast" of the world explored by Columbus (16.4; cf. 14.101). His subsequent talk about "credo quia impossibile" and "believe" suggests an opening up or extension of the sense of "truth," but of course only later, in a Radcliffian ambiguity, to reconfirm mundane Popean truth. And, to judge by the story of the "ghost," truth is simply the revelation of love under a monk's cowl, seduction under ghostly terror; and this amounts to yet another form of change.

These associations of mutability bring *Don Juan* back, at its moment of breaking off, to revolution. In his "Thoughts" Byron connects his aging and physical decline with the weakness of his memory and its distortion of "truth" by imagination; but he makes two significant exceptions: "—I except indeed—our recollections of Womankind—there is no forgetting *them*—(and be d—d to them). Any more than any other remarkable Era—such as 'the revolution'"—to which he adds, as if to qualify the original conjunction of love and revolution, "or 'the plague'—or 'the invasion' or 'the Comet'—or 'the War' of such—and Such an Epoch."[34] But clearly the first two are the important ones, love and revolution, those private and public paradigms of change.

WORDSWORTHIAN RESTORATION

> These beauteous forms,
> Through a long absence . . .
> . . . [have passed] even into my purer mind,
> With tranquil restoration . . .   [*Lines* on Tintern Abbey, ll. 22–23, 29–30]

> I would give,
> While yet we may, as far as words can give,
> Substance and life to what I feel, enshrining,
> Such is my hope, the spirit of the Past
> For future restoration.   [*The Prelude* (1850) 12.282–86][35]

The Byronic enemy was Southey, the author of the revolutionary play *Wat Tyler* who became poet laureate. Because of Southey's change of political sympathies, Byron associates him with both the Peterloo mob, Marat, Robespierre, and Company, and the opposite counterrevolutionary forces of reaction, seeing him as the literary propper-up of tyrants, the Cibberian laureate, and the hireling praiser of kings. Wordsworth follows as a trailer, because it could be argued that by accepting an official employment he was also, on a smaller scale, another Southey; because he had not hidden his disillusionment with the Revolution after initial enthusiasm; because in *The Excursion* of 1814—the work to which Byron refers in *Don Juan*—this former revolutionary sympathizer apparently praised religion and order; and because it could be argued that the Idiot Boy, Goody Blake, Simon Lee, and the other vagrants of *Lyrical Ballads* were the sort who made up the revolutionary mob led by Marat and Robespierre.

In Popean terms, the basic disagreement between Byron and Wordsworth is between truth, proper fame, and the ethical poet on the one side and lies, romance, fantasy, and inebriation on the other. Byron extends the argument to the artifact versus the natural scene:

> Art is *not* inferior to nature for poetical purposes. What makes a regiment of soldiers a more noble object of view than the same mass or mob? Their arms, their dresses, their banners, and the *art* and artificial symmetry of their position and movements.[36]

By extension, the regiment of soldiers is also more poetic than a savage "described by William Wordsworth himself like the 'idiot in his glory.'" This statement, which appears in Byron's attack on Bowles, represents the antiiconoclastic, the Popean position. Byron further argues that canals, ships, and buildings are more poetic than oceans and mountains, that it is the ships that make the ocean poetic or sublime. And if art is superior to nature as ships and buildings are to oceans and mountains (of the sort described by the Lake Poets), then discussing ethics is superior to walking around the lakes. It is worth noting that Byron's examples—army and navy—retain a political dimension in an argument that might have sought neutrality.

Byron writes of the silliness of *Peter Bell* and his "little boat" (3.98), but the charge that matters is in stanza 100, where he asserts: Wordsworth writes of "'Pedlars,' and 'boats,' and 'waggons!'" that have replaced the ethical and political subjects "Of Pope and Dryden." Wordsworth's poetry, he says, echoing *The Dunciad*, is "trash of such sort [that it] not alone evades / Contempt, but from the bathos' vast abyss / Floats scumlike uppermost" (3.100). The Lake Poets are "Jack Cades / Of sense and song" in relation to the establishment poets Pope and Dryden—and Byron. They are subversive, indeed revolutionary in that they "hiss" above the graves of Pope and Dryden and "sneer at" them, while counterrevolutionary in that they do so in the name of George III, Wellington, Restoration, and the status quo in European politics.

Byron was right that Wordsworth was for "restoration"; right also that his wagoners and vagrants were related to the sansculottes. What Wordsworth referred to (looking back from 1815) as "breaking the bonds of custom," and what Hazlitt referred to as Wordsworth's "levelling" of his characters, can be regarded as a specific reference to the "liberty, equality, and fraternity" of the French Revolution which subsumes the English tradition of iconoclasm in poetry. But what he does not notice is that the Wordsworth of *The Excursion* was already writing about "restoration" in the first edition of *Lyrical Ballads* in 1798.

Lines written a few miles above Tintern Abbey, like the first book of *The Prelude,* tells the story of Wordsworth's abandoning his idle wandering among vagrants for the writing of poetry—first of lyrical ballads embodying the vagrant experience and then of poems concerned with the problem of writing or not writing about vagrants. It is an early example of the obsessive rewriting of his own story in the 1790s which includes, as well as *The Prelude* as a whole, the stories of the Wanderer, Solitary, and various others in *The Excursion.* Basically this is the story of his personal and public experience in the early 1790s and of his recovery from them.

The *Lines* serve as a tailpiece and commentary on the sansculotte ballads of *Lyrical Ballads.* Placed at the end the poem speaks for Wordsworth himself, not for the impersonator or slumming wanderer of the ballads. The full title *Lines written a few miles above Tintern Abbey / On revisiting the Banks of the Wye during a Tour, July 13, 1798* has been taken to reveal within the poem proper the absence of vagrants, poor farmers, and polluted water.[37] But, while the poem is about absence, it is rather the absence that Wordsworth now feels and is trying to "restore" of those "wild," "ecstatic" days—perhaps that time when he *felt* the need of doing something about the poor vagrants, but also when he was young, "revolutionary," and in love. (The most repeated word in the *Lines,* besides "wild," "again," and the like, is "love.")

I agree with recent critics that the public scene is implied in the private experience. There is no way of getting around the significant date of 13 July 1798, the day before Bastille Day; the "revisiting" of the spot on the anniversary of this occasion; and the repetition of "five years," which puts the date of the earlier experience in the pivotal year of 1793 when Wordsworth's hopes in the Revolution were finally dashed by the Terror, followed by the fall of Robespierre and the rise of Napoleon. I have no doubt that the "wreathes of smoke," the "silence," and the "uncertain notice" of "vagrant dwellers in the houseless woods" are his own *mea culpa* for what he did not do, or for what remained to be done, just as the "hermit's cave" (hermits and philosophical types have *chosen* their place) may recall the literary alternative, what he *has* done, which is to withdraw in order to write the poems of this volume. He offers not a repression but a conscious glimpse—like the "wretches hang that jurymen may dine" of *The Rape of the Lock*—of political and social reality, as much a part of what he has to deal with in his "restoration" as his former youth and passion.

In the same way, the "summers" followed by "long winters" of the opening lines suggest that in the last five years the bad times have overbalanced the good, wars and disillusionment have followed the initial joy of 1789. Therefore he now has to find the "blessed mood, / In which the heavy burden of the mystery, / In which the heavy and the weary weight / Of all this unintelligible world / Is lighten'd."

The two landscapes, then and now, present and remembered, are precisely the same. In "the mighty world / Of eye and ear, both what they half-create, / And what perceive," the difference is only in himself. His words associate past, love (and dread), wildness ("aching joys" and "dizzy raptures," "ecstasy"), and hope (implicitly the Revolution). He accomplishes his recompense-restoration by distancing that time as one of "unripe fruits," "the hour / Of thoughtless youth," and by offering compensation: "other gifts / Have followed, for such loss, I would believe, / Abundant recompence."

His sister Dorothy, associated with the "wild eyes" and "wild ecstasies" (with Jesus the Good Shepherd, "For thou art with me"), was also there five years ago. She seems to serve as a substitute, her experience for his own: her "wild ecstasies shall be matured / Into a sober pleasure," as his love has been turned into a "holier love" or "deeper zeal." It would seem that Dorothy stands for all that is not said in the poem about Annette Vallon, her and Wordsworth's child, and the desire to wander from home.

That he now writes "a few miles above Tintern Abbey" was a conscious choice, and not, I suspect, because he wanted to get a few miles above the polluted part of the Wye but because he wanted to cite yet distance himself from the iconoclasted ruins of Tintern Abbey. The poem is about—the same subject as *The Prelude*—the move from

iconoclasm to "nature" as "restoration," "recompense," and "matured . . . sober pleasure." If the writing of the poem is situated a few
miles above/beyond the iconoclasted ruins of the abbey, in the layout
of the book it is situated beyond the "ballads" and their "levelled"
characters.

The absent ruins of Tintern Abbey anticipate Wordsworth's account of St. Mary's Abbey in *The Prelude*, Book 2, as this asks to be
compared with Byron's account of the ruined Norman Abbey in
Canto 13 of *Don Juan*. (There can, of course, have been no cross-
pollination between *Don Juan* and *The Prelude*, but the parallels are
instructive of differences.) Wordsworth brings in the ruined abbey as
part of a sequence of recollections from his youth: first, a "rude
mass / Of native rock" has been removed by modern developers, "and
in its place / A smart Assembly-room usurped the ground / That had
been ours" (ll. 33–40). Then, moving back to a time not long after
the original rock, the boys encounter "some famed temple where of
yore / The Druids worshipped," and, finally,

> the antique walls
> Of that large abbey, where within the Vale
> Of Nightshade, to St. Mary's honour built,
> Stands yet a mouldering pile with fractured arch,
> Belfry, and images, and living trees;
> A holy scene!   [ll. 102–07]

Wordsworth regards the ruin, as Byron does, as "A holy scene"—and
in fact it is a "fractured arch" that he singles out to stand for the
whole ruin:

> the cross-legged knight,
> And the stone-abbot, and that single wren
> Which one day sang so sweetly in the nave
> Of the old church, that—though from recent showers
> The earth was comfortless, and, touched by faint
> Internal breezes, sobbings of the place
> And respirations, from the roofless walls
> The shuddering ivy dripped large drops—yet still
> So sweetly 'mid the gloom the invisible bird
> Sang to herself, that there I could have made
> My dwelling-place, and lived for ever there
> To hear such music.   [ll. 117–28]

What he remembers is the sound; in this case the "faint / Internal
breezes, sobbings of the place / And respirations" of Byron's ruin are

augmented by the sound of a bird's song. The sequence, which began with a rock turned into a modern assembly room, ends with the description (as if iconoclasted from the abbey) of a tavern, "a splendid place" with a "bright fire." The other facts stressed are that the tavern's name on its signboard has "dislodged / The old Lion and *usurped* his Place"—a case of image being replaced by words. It is a place of "refreshment," where what they eat is emphasized. Yet, like the original preiconoclasm abbey, it is a place of "foolish pomp."

Each of the brief episodes that open Book 2 of *The Prelude* follows the sequence of the *Lines* on Tintern Abbey. Each begins with the boys' "tumult," "games," "revelry," and "uproar," accompanied by such adjectives as "feverish." The first culminates in a passage beginning, "Ah! is there one who ever has been young," which anticipates the more famous passage in Book 11 celebrating the French Revolution: "Bliss was it in that dawn to be alive, / But to be young was very Heaven!" (ll. 108–09). This evocation of joy and "wantonness," however, is followed by the "tranquilizing spirit" that succeeds youth, the "vacancy between me and those days."

Childhood, associated in the later books with revolutionary youth, takes the twin forms of "infantine desire" (or love) and "conquest," and other verbs such as "usurp" denoting politics; and this riotous youth is transformed into the "some other Being" that the poet has now become. Descriptions of "boisterous" "giddy motion" are succeeded by the lines: "the time approached / That brought with it a regular desire / For calmer pleasures" (ll. 48–50).

If we look more closely at what is involved in the "giddy motion," we see that these sports center on the "rude mass / Of native rock" now transformed into a "smart Assembly-room" that has "usurped" the rock's place, replaced that revelry with a different, more civilized kind of revelry (sedate dancing, but—suggesting the tension that remains in the mature poet—to the "scream" of the fiddle). The rock—it is mentioned at the end of the passage, but then picked up again forty lines later—was named for the old "Dame" who sold the boys sweets there. The Dame introduces the theme of eating, which becomes insistent in the following passages. So to love and conquest Wordsworth adds physical hunger, finally satisfied in the tavern's "refreshment," which is accompanied by the boys' play and "bursts of glee" (l. 164, a Wordsworthian version of the inebriation associated by hardier souls with the Revolution).

Before the boys visit the abbey they row a boat on Lake Windermere and visit an island with "the ruins of a shrine / Once to Our Lady dedicate, and served / Daily with chaunted rites" (ll. 62–65): in the shade of which they rest, "all pleased alike, / Conquered and conqueror." These words precede the realization that resting in these ruins the giddy, boisterous motions are "tempered" and changed to a "quiet independence of the heart."

The notion of the iconoclasted ruin as refuge, literally as a home, a place to return to and live in, connects the shrine and the abbey. The passage (ll. 78ff.) opens with the question of money and school routine, frugal meals and "vigorous hunger," preceding, intensifying by contrast, the holiday. The money thus saved is spent during the holiday, the subject of these passages, on food (bought from the Dame) and on renting horses: an interesting conjunction of appetite and Gilpinesque movement, now joined with the old woman and the ruined church. It is the horse rental, the riding off on horses, which takes the boys to the "distant" "adventure" (l. 100) of the Druid temple and then, in much greater detail, St. Mary's Abbey.

The ruined abbey, like the island shrine, serves Wordsworth as "safeguard for repose and quietness" (l. 114), a strange echo of Reformation iconoclasm. This abbey, in the Vale of Nightshade, was left in ruins, not domesticated like Norman Abbey. But now it serves that purpose for the boys: for a moment they pause there, their horses graze on "the smooth green turf," and "that sequested valley" becomes for them a "safeguard for repose and quietness." The ruins themselves become (or are interpreted by Wordsworth as) a place where the poet "could have made [his] dwelling-place, and lived for ever there." Instead, however, the boys remount their horses and ride through the ruins. "In wantonness of heart," they "left" all that "repose and quietness" that could have been a "dwelling-place." There is a sense of desecration in the words: "through the chauntry [we] flew / In uncouth race, and left the cross-legged knight, / And the stone-abbot"—*and* the singing wren: this is an iconoclastic replacement, as in the letters that replace the icon on the tavern signboard, but it sacrifices the living bird and its song as well as the dead images. And the sequence ends inside the tavern, that "splendid place" which is also, however, associated with "foolish pomp" of a sort that remains also in the towering ruins of the abbey.

Youth *and* revolution are on the poet's mind. The scene is recalled much later in Book 10, at the point where Wordsworth recounts how he learned of the fall of Robespierre. First he describes the ruined Romish chapel, then the "variegated crowd" on the beach, and the cry "Robespierre is dead!" The last is followed by the explicit memory of the occasion described in Book 2 when he visited the Vale of Nightshade and "St. Mary's mouldering fane," of "the stone-abbot," and of the "joyous band of schoolboys" (ll. 596–603). The scene is the same, but now there is no memory of the singing bird. Instead the poet goes straight to the boys riding across the sand to the sounds of hoofbeats: the line is word for word the same: "We beat with thundering hoofs the level sand." I take this to mean that the peaceful sound of singing in the ruin has been replaced—as it was then replaced—by the sounds, not just of the boys racing "in wantonness of heart," but now, in the context of the 1790s, of an army rushing into battle. The conjunction of youthful "joy," ecclesiastical ruins, failed revolution, and warring armies is the fulfilment of the earlier passage: youthful exuberance then, revolutionary war now.

The Prelude, beginning as it does with the Miltonic "The earth is all before me" (1.14), sums up much of what we have said about the artist laboring in a postlapsarian world. When the poet contemplates the labor of "reading or thinking" he summons up the familiar trope:

> either to lay up
> New stores, or rescue from decay the old
> By timely interference;   [1.115–18]

and he tells us that his recovery of the past will be difficult because there is

> No little band of yet remembered names
> Whom I, in perfect confidence, might hope
> To summon back from lonesome banishment.   [1.161–63]

He is seeking an act of restoration, the form taken by reconstruction after a time of revolution.

In Book 1 the act of walking as merely following the road ahead—the metaphor of wandering that Byron found offensive—is tested against the alternatives of labor and reconstruction associated with the farmer. But enclosing both alternatives is the primary *felix culpa* task/freedom of choice itself, which becomes the subject of *The Prelude*. And, joining the Miltonic with the classical Choice of Hercules, as David Simpson has shown, Wordsworth is torn between industry and idleness.[38]

The childhood story of the woodcocks and boat stealing are introduced as analogues to the poet's adult frittering away of his time instead of writing his epic. The dilemma is set in motion by the pivotal lines echoing the parable of the Talents:

> Unprofitably travelling toward the grave,
> Like a false steward who hath much received
> And renders nothing back.   [1.267–69]

The following passages are prefigurations of this false stewardship linked to the fault of wandering, idleness, and forms of thievery. But they are not all bad, for memory has been set going:

> though mean
> Our object and inglorious, yet the end
> Was not ignoble.   [1.328–30]

And what is "not ignoble" is the experience—in fact the memory—of hanging "suspended by the blast that blew amain," of "hanging alone," on a "perilous ridge," listening to the "strange utterance" of the wind (ll. 485–91). But part of that memory is the guilt, which is another aspect of the general sense of guilt that permeates Book 1, extending from childhood thefts to young adult idleness, holding back (as yet) the public equivalent in the young man's excursion into revolutionary politics and adult sexuality.

Wordsworth is worrying in Book 1 about his "gift" of poetry, and so his "service" or labor, which is based on the postlapsarian "liberty" of deciding whether to wander or to work—or combine them in the shape of encounters with wanderers—; whether to be a "home-bound labourer," bound to his "hermitage," or to follow a "pleasant loitering journey." And if the former, then the choice becomes also one of the proper subject: not myth, history, or romance, those Byronic subjects, but reconstruction. In short, his subject will be the reconstitution of those "wanderers of the earth" like himself and the "vagrants" he meets (finally arrived at in 13.155ff.). But this is the act we have described running from Milton, Defoe, and Pope to Byron himself; and it is possible to argue that in the public, allegorical poems, *The Excursion* and *Don Juan*, the real subject is reconstruction of the poet's childhood and young adulthood, his *earlier* self critiqued by a later. Wordsworth's discovery of "wanderers" applies to himself in *The Prelude* but also to himself and the "vagrants" he meets in *Lyrical Ballads* in one sense and in *The Excursion* in another.

Thus the *Prelude* of 1805 and 1850 is a heroic attempt to restore those memories designated "spots of time," first put down in the 1799 draft, and subsequently related to history, the French Revolution, and other partially suppressed memories and facts, suffused with the feeling of guilt, displaced onto various other objects, but perhaps best summed up as compensation for loss through laboring to reconstruct. Thus from the most distant past there are the "spots of time"; then the mountain-climbing, sight-seeing episodes from the Cambridge years; the French Revolution; and finally the subsequent years of recovery, which lead up to the writing of Book 1. These were the years of walking, meeting vagrants, writing about the encounters, writing *this* poem ("Six years have I . . ."). And the form taken in Wordsworth's case—not all that different from Pope's in his *Dunciad* and Horatian imitations—is that of the bare memories *plus* their gloss, explanation, and secondary revisions, that is, their recuperation (in the sense of the bird's eggs and the boat).

I shall take the most famous of Wordsworthian cruces in *The Prelude*, the episodes of the Simplon Pass, Gravedona, and Mount Snowdon, and from them work back to the simple, marginal, elemental, and "iconoclasted" scenes from which they derived. In the passage describing the way he ascended the Alps at the Simplon Pass Wordsworth could easily have evoked a wonderful sight, followed by the disappointment of the conclusion when he is told, "we had crossed the Alps," and then opened up into the glorious memory he had retained. But he chooses rather to describe the hope and expectation as he and his companions climb. "For still we had hopes that pointed to the clouds" are words that, in the context of Book 6, his visit to France, the celebration of the French Revolution, and the disillusioning passage describing its effects on the Grande Chartreuse, apply as well to the Revolution as to the ascent of the Alps. The latter can be said to allegorize the former: one is private, the other public in the basic mode laid out in the 1805 *Prelude*.

Thus imagination, not memory, is evoked because there was nothing at all there to remember—only expectation (hope, desire) followed by disappointment. The passage is about the discrepancy between the experience and the reconstruction of it, based on the frustration of hope and expectation rather than on what was actually seen. From Wordsworth's own perspective it is a story of compensation—not displacement but simple compensation. It illustrates how there was, mixed with the "soft luxuries" of the dreaming and gathering flowers as they walk, "something of stern mood, an underthirst / Of vigor" from which, in the Simplon experience, "how different a sadness / Would issue." The message is that "hope" is not tied down to brute experience. One can see the failure of the French Revolution, as of the expectation of a view from the top of a mountain, but: "With hope it is, hope that can never die . . . something evermore about to be." This is, as the passage admits, pure "imagination." In the terms of the note to *The Thorn*, it is "the faculty which produces Impressive effects out of simple elements," which is there called a component of "superstition." In *Prelude* 6 it ends in the bizarre simile that carries the poet off in imagination to Egypt and Abyssinia.

Abyssinia reappears in the next scene of discrepancy, the night at Gravedona on Lake Como. The poet remembers Como as "a treasure" kept in "Abyssinian privacy," which suggests that both references include the Happy Valley of Johnson's *Rasselas* (to which Johnson attached the usual allusions to Adam's departure from Paradise) and that the question Wordsworth is asking throughout these books of *The Prelude* is how to be happy once out of the Happy Valley and in the fallen world.

In the Gravedona episode the church bells signal the expectation "that day was nigh" and that, following a path along the lake, Wordsworth and his companion "should behold the scene, / Hushed in profound repose" of a sunrise. Instead it proves to be the middle of the night (they misinterpreted the bells), they get lost, and when at last they try to sleep they are kept awake by the stings of insects. This experience is one of confusion, uncertainty, annoyance, and strange shapes and noises that cannot be interpreted in the darkness. It is less a disappointment of expectations than a thrust into a strange and unaccountable experience. The imagination has much material to work on, but a description of the experience itself suffices—"such a summer's night" is all Wordsworth can say of it, and then: "But here I must break off . . ." He is now back again in the world of *Lyrical Ballads*, which strips away, breaks, and removes the ornament (poetic diction), returning to the bare, the common object.

In the poem *Nutting* (pub. 1800) the boy's excess violence, so often commented on by critics, is no more than the way the act of nutting seems in the boy's imagination (or rather the man's as he looks back and writes) when he has come to the grove with the intention of gathering nuts and found it a silent untouched paradise. Within that context, his simple act of nutting seems to him sacrilege; his imagination expands the act to the status of a rape. Unlike the episode in the Simplon Pass, the event of nutting and its surrounding did exist. Memory has been augmented by imagination, but both the quiet grove and the apparently rapacious nutting were *there*. In the Simplon Pass passage Wordsworth describes a discrepancy, which points to an absence: there was, where he expected something, *nothing*, and imagination later—he stresses the fact, much later—seemed to compensate as imagination would also reviewing the similarly disappointing story of the Revolution. The result is a powerful pathos, especially in so far as we feel ourselves still outside the poet, something of a Byron witnessing an act of fetishization. Repeatedly we see Wordsworth making a stock or stone substitute for a spiritual entity—quite the contrary of the iconoclasm of *Lyrical Ballads*.

The Simplon Pass and Mount Snowdon passages are connected by, among other things, the repetition of the word (encountered earlier in the context of the ecclesiastical ruins of Book 2) "usurped." In the Snowdon passage it is part of an elaborately developed metaphor of rule ("majesty," "sovereign") in which the apparent ocean ("a silent sea of hoary mist") has "usurped" the actual Atlantic, "that appeared / To dwindle, and give up his majesty." Whereas the sky, on the other hand, suffered no "encroachment," and, within a true hierarchy, the "full-orbed Moon" in "her sovereign elevation" (versus "the inferior stars") looked down on the ocean, "all meek and silent." For the usurpation is of course carried out by the light of the moon, which has transformed the mist into an illusion of an ocean. But the actual usurpation has only been displaced onto the effect of moonlight from the poet's compensating imagination. Only a rift in the mist reveals the true ocean in the "roar of waters" far below (and far distant).

In the interpretive passage that follows, the scene is described, echoing the Simplon passage, as a "type": before "types and symbols of eternity," now "the type of a majestic intellect" and "the emblem of a mind / That feeds upon infinity" (6.639, 14.66–71); but the mind is again envisaged as "one continuous stream" (like the "waters, torrents, streams" of the earlier passage). The metaphor of domination which connects Simplon and Snowdon tells us again that the (poet's) mind "loves / To exert upon the face of outward Things" its "supremacy" and "power"; it affirms the prevailing discourse of power, usurpation, revolution, and restoration.

These passages on the poet's own power then are the other end of the general human imagination, "that glorious faculty / That higher minds bear with them as their own," which produces revolutions in both politics and poetry. To say that "they build up greatest things / From least suggestions" is to relate the phenomenon to *The Thorn*'s doctrine of "the imagination" as "the faculty, which produces impressive effects out of simple elements." The difference is that in one case the poetic effect is in the making itself; in the other it is in the glossing and interpreting. In this sense, the iconoclast poet of *Lyrical Ballads* is lost in Wordsworth's vision of human imagination in *The*

Prelude. Nevertheless, the iconoclastic French Revolution remains even here in the background, informing and, in itself, explaining the need for the imagination: "For this alone ["this freedom"] is genuine Liberty." The imagination remains, at least in origins, in the service of the experience of the French Revolution (public)—and of Annette Vallon and her child (private, equivalent to, type of, the public experience). The imagination retains its sense in the prefaces to *Lyrical Ballads* of the ability to metamorphose simple minimalist objects, whether political or personal.[39]

In French Revolutionary practice then Wordsworth sets out to break, destroy, and replace. First, he finds an equivalent to the experience of the Revolution in his affair with Annette, in his ratio of experience through time to memory and imagination; second, he writes in the "revolutionary" mode, as in *Lyrical Ballads,* where he "revolutionizes" subject matter, turning it on its head, rejecting aristocratic, ruling-class, dominant-culture materials in favor of poor subculture subjects. But then, in the light of the first, his revolutionary experience, he must, as a maker, either fetishize the bare object or gloss it, comprehend it or justify or compensate for it (or its loss through time and memory), with "imagination."

This is the way Wordsworth restores the sense of loss in the French Revolution and in his French love affair, by recovering the experience through expansion and vision in his poetry; as in ideology, in both poetry (on the level of plot) and public life, he supports the restoration of the *ancien régime.* So the basic model gives us the elemental experience (Revolution, Vallon), to which are added time, memory, and imagination, which "restore" the experience by assimilating it to a time before the "revolution" (the child's spots of time).

The juxtaposition in *Lyrical Ballads* of the ballads and the elevated *Lines* on Tintern Abbey draws attention to the structure we have been describing: the imitation of simplicity in the ballads in addition to the process of restoration that takes place in the interpretation of them. And so in *The Prelude* "the coarser pleasure of my boyish days" in the spots of time as in the affair of France/Annette is followed by the way the experience is seen through the calm, compensatory imagination. In other words, the spots of time, the coarse pleasure, the childishness, and iconoclasm, metamorphosed by imagination in *Lyrical Ballads,* are retained in *The Prelude* but turned into a justification no longer for the spot of time (or experience reduced to a spot of time) but for a theory of imagination. This I take to be the process of Wordsworthian restoration.

Part II

Chapter 4

The Aesthetics of Modernity: Hogarth

THE SLEEPING CONGREGATION

The practical effects of English iconoclasm by the 1730s are both "illustrated" and embodied in Hogarth's engraving, *The Sleeping Congregation* (1736, fig. 2). We see an Anglican church with no graven images. Roman Catholic idolatry has been expunged. The stained glass of the windows has been replaced with clear glass. In the one remaining piece of stained glass, however, the cross has been replaced by the royal cross of St. George. The only trace of art is the disjointed angel who now serves as a supporter of the royal arms.[1]

Hogarth shows that worship has only been displaced from images of God to the monarch—from the *Dieu* of the royal motto, now lost behind a pillar, to the *et mon droit* which is all that remains, along with the lion-supporter of the royal arms: as much later, in *Gin Lane* (1751), he represents the steeple of St. George's Bloomsbury, which in fact carried not a cross but a statue of George I (and by a bit of false perspective, he replaces the cross *and* royal icon with the simulated—secularized—cross of a pawnbroker's sign).

At a more popular level, the displacement is from devotion to the image of the Virgin or any other icon to the sleeping young woman (with an exposed bosom) who, dozing with her prayer book open to the service of Matrimony, has displaced her own worship to thoughts of a husband. From the clergyman's point of view, *she* is the idol. But

2. William Hogarth, The Sleeping Congregation *(1736), engraving.*

for the majority of the congregation spirituality has been replaced by—or returned to—sleep. As if the image itself of somnolence were insufficient, Hogarth adds the word—the word of God according to Matthew 2.28: "Come unto me all ye who labour and are heavy laden & I will give you Rest."

Hogarth dramatizes a series of displacements, showing them to be as idolatrous as the images that were stripped from the church, and he does so by means of a representation that is itself an iconoclasm. His satiric message is that not only art but all trace of religious feeling has disappeared from the church. The cracks in the wall are indicative of the general decrepitude of the ecclesiastical structure.

There are two points to which I want to draw attention. Like Swift, Hogarth identified idol with the metaphor of "Harlot" associated in the language of the Bible with idolatry: harlots are those who forsake the true God and follow idols and false gods (Isa. 1.21). In Hogarth's engravings the themes of imitation and fashion are modern equivalents of, in religious terms, idolatry. Worship of the woman by herself and by the men of her society as a "Harlot"—and the "idols" of society by the woman—is the subject of his first and paradigmatic series of engravings; and in this respect he is building upon Swift's progresses of a harlot in *The Progress of Beauty* and *A Beautiful Young Nymph Going to Bed*. The woman, herself an idol to the men (in Plate 2 she is compared to the Ark of the Covenant), idolizes everything from her own mirror to the paintings and prints on the walls of the various quarters in which she lives. And like an idol, she becomes increasingly inanimate, losing life and individual identity, until she is only a vague shape in a sweating blanket and then in a coffin dead and transformed, by a final irony, into a parody of a Eucharistic table surrounded by her twelve mourners.

Idolatry is quite literally the theme of his satires: either the idolatry of any object that is denied its physical reality or the idol as a godless, that is, a lifeless statue. Therefore the somnolent figure of the pretty young woman in *The Sleeping Congregation* is being worshiped by the clergyman whose eyes should be on the Word of God before him. We shall pursue the central figure of the woman: for Swift an idol to be broken, for Hogarth an idol to be broken and remade, as she progresses from the Harlot to Shakespeare's Miranda, the Poet's wife, and the milkmaid outside the Musician's window.

There is a second aspect of iconoclasm in Hogarth's practice which deserves comment. Whenever he represents (in one of his interiors) an old master painting of a religious subject, either he chooses one in which the deity does not appear or he excises the deity. In *A Harlot's Progress* 2, in the painting of Uzzah being struck down by an angry Jehovah, he replaces Jehovah with a human priest who stabs Uzzah in the back; in the first plate of *Marriage A-la-mode* he copies Domenichino's *Martyrdom of St. Agnes* closely except for the singular omission of God in the upper quarter of the canvas. The elimination of Domenichino's God presumably reflects the patron who chose (probably commissioned) the copy of the original which hangs on his wall: he thus sees *himself* as replacing the deity in the painting—and/or as not envisaging a heavenly reward following martyrdom (in this case of his son and daughter-in-law). But with hardly an exception God or any form of divine providence is totally excluded from Hogarth's contemporary scenes.

The substitution in *Harlot* 2 of a human priest for the deity raises the question: who is obliterating the deity, the denizens of contemporary London society or the iconoclast Hogarth? If the former, the strategy is part of Hogarth's satire on the time-serving clergymen which extends from the corrupt priests of *South Sea Scheme* and *A Harlot's Progress* 1 and 6 to the remote church steeple of *Gin Lane* capped by the statue of the monarch and the alternative Methodist church of *Credulity, Superstition, and Fanaticism* in which somnolence has been replaced by fanaticism.

But in *The Sleeping Congregation* the name of God, apparently excised in favor of the king's, is in fact only concealed by a trick of Hogarth's composition: the *Dieu* may still exist if we could see through the church pillar that blocks it out. The satirist is pointing out something about this church, but it is *his* point—his comment on the clergy and not manifested by an act of replacement by the clergy themselves. The iconoclasm is his; the idolatry theirs. He is making a picture that is itself an act of iconoclasm, first in the sense that it directs its own destructive energy at the royal motto and the subservient, lax, and lecherous clergy; and second in the sense that it does itself, by an act of aesthetic framing, physically conceal the name of God.[2]

Hogarth, in short, would seem to accept here and elsewhere in his work the article of Anglican orthodoxy, expressed in 1559 by Matthew Parker but reiterated in Hogarth's time by the Bishop of London, Edmund Gibson. In Parker's words:

> Last of all, as I do utterly disallow the extolling of images, relics and feigned miracles, and also all kind of expressing God invisible in the form of an old man, or the Holy Ghost in the form of a dove, and all other vain worshipping of God, devised by men's fantasies . . .[3]

We know Hogarth's disdain for painters of angel heads levitated by wings and old bearded men designated as God.[4]

Iconoclast is not an inappropriate term to apply to Hogarth, a descendant of Scottish Presbyterians who was born into a dissenter community of London. Though a maker of images, his primary theme in his art is the falsity of images—yet at the same time his theme is also the inevitability and power of the proper, "unabused" images. Hogarth is the important figure in the tradition of English iconoclasm because he was the graphic artist who lived its experience or aesthetic. His work, more than anyone else's in the century, embodied the great advantage of images over writing: that they can stir deep and subtle feeling in readers at all levels of sophistication, whereas words quickly lose a large part of their audience when the text rises above or drops below a certain level of elegance and complexity. Thus the power of Hogarth's visual images in the period was recognized by politicians as well as writers; indeed they served as one model for the forms of prose fiction in the decades that followed. But they also dramatize the iconoclast's fear/attraction to graphic images, and in a number of ways problematize, and so in one way aestheticize, the process or act of iconoclasm itself.

In a sense, Hogarth's *Sleeping Congregation* is replacing the canonical religious painting that has been iconoclasted from the walls of the church with a representation of its absence and the substitution of a contemporary, commonplace, living image (at the same time substantiated by words). For some results of the tradition of iconoclasm, evident to anyone walking through a gallery of British art, are the physical destruction of medieval painting and sculpture, the virtual nonexistence of subject painting by English artists, and quite possibly the abrogation of an English tradition of graphic art. The heritage of English iconoclasm was a frame of mind suspicious of all the visual arts, and more particularly of the tradition of continental popish art, as leading to worship of the Whore of Rome. This frame of mind contributed to the Puritan dissolution of Charles I's great art collection and explains the mere trickle of commissions of religious paintings in the eighteenth century, including the irony that Hogarth must represent the bare church and its disinterested congregation rather than the religious scenes painted by his continental precursors.

Calvin's words were taken seriously in England:

If it be unlawful to make any corporeal representation of God, still more unlawful must it be to worship such a representation instead of God, or to worship God in it. The only things, therefore, which ought to be painted or sculptured, are things which can be presented to the eye. . . . Visible representations are of two classes—viz. historical, which give a representation of events, and pictorial, which merely exhibit bodily shapes and figures. The former are of some use for instruction or admonition. The latter, so far as I can see, are only fitted for amusement.[5]

The result of this "sacramental realism" for an artist in seventeenth- and eighteenth-century England was to paint as compensation mere (from the point of view of continental theory) portraits, landscapes, still lifes, and local or contemporary history. These were the sacramental-realist versions of the idolatrous paintings of Counter-reformation artists, and the English artist found his spokesman in Hogarth, who represented "things which can be presented to the eye," commonplace objects and events, including *The Sleeping Congregation,* which served a useful, that is, a moral purpose.

One source for *The Sleeping Congregation* may have been the universal sleep that concluded the third book of Pope's *Dunciad Variorum* (1729). Such sleep is the final reduction of meaning, religious and aesthetic, in the contemporary world. (And Hogarth's print formed part of a sequence that included *The Distrest Poet,* with its allusions to *The Dunciad,* and *The Enraged Musician.*) But the primary inspiration, I suspect, was Swift's poem *Baucis and Philemon* (1708), where the humble, material, utilitarian, commonplace, and lived-in objects are shown to be the point of origin for idolatry. The "miracle" performed by the visiting saints turns the dining table into an altar, and thereafter the kitchen into a church, Baucis's cooking pot into the church's bell and Philemon's bed into the church's pews and his easy chair into the pulpit. Swift replaces Ovid's Olympian gods by saints— retaining both popish associations and memories of the local "saints" who had governed England during the Puritan Commonwealth. These "saints" proceed to transform the humble cottage upward into a (perhaps THE) Church, but with every item obviously translatable back into its plebeian source:

> The groaning chair began to crawl
> Like an huge snail along the wall;
> There stuck aloft, in public view,
> And with small change a pulpit grew.
>
> . . . .
>
>   A bedstead of the antique mode,
> Compact of timber many a load,
> Such as our ancestors did use,

Was metamorphosed into pews;
Which still their ancient nature keep,
By lodging folks disposed to sleep.   [ll. 85–88, 101–06]

A pew is reduced to a bed, an altar to a table; or a bed is raised to a pew. Both pew and bed are for sleeping, as both altar and table are for eating and drinking, and an easy chair, like a pulpit, is for palavering. The effect, the base trope, is the reduction of something with a (supposedly) spiritual significance to its physical and material reality.

In the same way John Gay, and later Henry Fielding, reduce prime ministers and other "great men" to thieves and great ladies to whores in another, gentler version of the Calvinist emphasis on the significance and exemplary nature of physical and visible phenomena—which replace, and are obviously more interesting than, the abstraction. The literary progenitor of these works was French, Paul Scarron's *Virgile travesti* of 1648, which should be compared with its English equivalents, Charles Cotton's *Scarronides*, a more radically reductive work, and Samuel Butler's *Hudibras*. Significantly, Cotton's and Butler's long, diffuse, and dilated poems are not merely a series of frissons (as when Dido is reduced to a fishwife) but rather homely retellings for the popular or for the sophisticated-popular audience in the manner exemplified on one level by *Robinson Crusoe* and on another by *Gulliver's Travels*. The practitioners of the travesty mode share with Calvinist iconoclasts, as well as with the scientists of the Royal Society (Robert Boyle and others), a delight in the ordinary and local, whether it is the scum on a bucket of water or the behavior of cowherds or London pickpockets or merchants. Calvin's "sacramental realism" is, after all, merely invoking the function of Christ's parables, which also used the material world to set forth and represent higher truth. He is doing no more than returning us from images of spirit to the common parabolic matter that represents it— which cannot possibly be turned into an idol.

We can now ask how the iconoclastic process as the transformation downward to something common and useful relates to the other model, the removal of a barrier. We have noticed the tendency, following the destruction, not to replace: to take out the opaque stained glass and leave the window transparent; for Hogarth (in *Boys Peeping at Nature* of 1731, fig. 14) to remove the veil covering Nature's lower parts; or for Capability Brown to take the gods out of the landscape garden and leave it bare. This procedure is, however, essentially no different from reducing a spiritual entity to a commonplace equivalent; the disguise has only been removed and the "Body of Christ" revealed to be a piece of bread. Both involve the removal of an intermediary. To replace it with a low, common, subculture equivalent is only another way of talking about the removal of the stained glass that conceals the real landscape—or the real loaf of bread or dining room or bedroom.

REMAKING THE CLASSICAL CANON

At the same time that Bentley was executing his illustration for Gray's *Elegy* (fig. 1), Hogarth was writing and illustrating his aesthetic treatise *The Analysis of Beauty* (pub. 1753). In the first of the two illustrative plates (fig. 3) he represents a sculpture yard, containing (from left to right) the Farnese Hercules, the Antinous, the Venus de Medici, and the Apollo Belvedere, and in the background the Laocoon and in the foreground the Vatican Torso. These sculptures were the great works of the classical canon of taste around which the artist's imagination had circled from the Renaissance onward—which he copied in his academies, arranged into his own compositions, and from which he drew his standards, ideas, expressions, iconography, and forms. These sculptures were collected, copied, and revered for their ancient historical associations and—above all—for their ideal beauty. The authority of these sculptures was still in the 1750s nearly absolute.

English country gentlemen arranged copies of these sculptures in their houses and gardens, not just to signify their "taste" (the taste of a connoisseur) but their continuity with the ideals of ancient Rome. What we can only call the ruling class found social and political support in Rome, as the poets, from Dryden and Pope to Samuel Johnson, found moral and literary support—which in turn was adopted by their "betters" in the roles of patron, politician, and gentleman of the "Roman Stamp."[6]

There was Thomas Coke, who built a house, Holkham, with a temple shape, Roman down to the bricks, which were specially baked in the Roman shape and color. The entrance was a gigantic hall shaped as a Roman basilica, its colonnade of African marbles recalling the Temple of Fortuna Virilis in Rome, and its entablature from the portico of the Temple of Antoninus and Faustina. The message was that Coke had inherited Roman ideals, had devoted himself to public virtues, and had collected the symbols and memories of past

3. Hogarth, The Analysis of Beauty, *Plate 1 (1753), engraving.*

authority. And so the entrance hall was lined with statues, and the original plan was to have placed the colossal Jupiter, the prize of his collection, on a pedestal in the middle of the stairway. A sculpture gallery was given prominence in the floorplan of the house, and the rooms in general were designed to show off antique sculptures.

Down the road from Holkham was Houghton, the country house of Sir Robert Walpole himself. Equally Roman in style—that is, Vitruvian by way of Palladian—this was the grandiloquent pile that has been identified by some scholars as the Timon's Villa of Pope's *Epistle to Burlington.* Walpole offers a more political example than Coke. First, there was the portrait of the Great Man by the contemporary sculptor Michael Rysbrack, looking like a Roman bust—it is hard to say whether of the Republic or the Empire, whether a Cato or one of the decadent emperors, a Nero or Vitellius, but clearly Roman, in a toga—a toga inscribed with the Order of the Garter.

A more subtle and interesting case was the memorial sculpture Sir Robert's son Horace commissioned after the death of his mother,

Lady Walpole, in 1738 (the same year as the bust of Sir Robert). At his instruction, the Roman Filippo della Valle represented Lady Walpole as the well-known Roman sculpture usually called *Livia, Wife of Augustus,* but also known as *Pudicity.*[7] Walpole may have seen the sculpture in Rome in the Villa Mattei, but prints of it labeled *Pudicity* had been published from 1704 onward. It was usually identified with both names, *Livia* and *Pudicity:* the reason for the association was probably the modest veil worn by Livia on the reverse of Roman coins. But it was also sometimes identified as Sabina and both Faustinas. The point was the same, that she was the consort of a great Roman statesman—Augustus then, Sir Robert Walpole now; Livia then, Lady Walpole now. On a somewhat more personal level, however, Horace Walpole must have focused his attention on the reference to Modesty, which for him would have separated Lady Walpole from her husband, his mother from his father, emphasizing her virtue in a marital relationship in which Sir Robert consorted with his mistress, Maria Skerrit, until, with Lady Walpole's death, he promptly married her: as Pope commented in his first *Epilogue to the Satires,* now Vice had been owned and could ride in a Roman triumph, with Virtue, where Vice ought to be, dragged behind her chariot. Horace Walpole was evoking with this sculpture both an empress and a chaste matron—the one perhaps to honor his father, the other to satisfy his own deep feelings for his betrayed mother.

These exemplars of beauty were, in short, a powerful mode of self-validation based on Roman-Imperial values: control and power, public service and sovereignty, the embodiment of a ruling-class ethos. Though hardly new with the eighteenth-century English, they carried an especially defensive, and therefore powerful, charge in the age of the early Hanoverians. One peculiarly transitional feature was the totally contradictory uses to which the Roman artifacts and imitations were put, depending on party and circumstance, whether the associations were meant to be republican or imperial. Sir Robert sought republican associations with the bust of himself by Rysbrack, while his opponents in the *Craftsman* saw imperial pretensions. In the same way, he would have read the monument to Lady Walpole in one way (wife of a great Roman), the friends of his son Horace in another (poor Lady Walpole!), and Pope and *his* friends in yet another (which included both of these readings plus some sense of the gossip about the free amorous life Lady Walpole herself enjoyed while "suffering" under her husband's infidelity).

In the second plate of *A Rake's Progress* (fig. 15), Hogarth shows the Rake in a brothel: he has broken the mirror that contains his own self-image and cut out the faces of the Roman emperors that decorate the walls, saving only the image of Nero, with whom he thus associates himself. Whether or not Hogarth intends an allusion to Walpole himself, he refers to the folly of the Englishman who associates himself, for better and worse, with the ancient Romans.[8]

The canonical images Hogarth represents in his Sculpture Yard meant authority, in all its senses, from the associations of Rome-Italy (the authority of the connoisseur, of the art treatises, of so-called taste) to Roman Catholic to Stuart-absolutism. By 1753 when *The Analysis of Beauty* appeared, the Pretender was living in Rome under papal protection, and his brother was a cardinal. Virtually all of these canonical sculptures in their originals (the exception being the Venus de Medici) were part of the papal collection in the Vatican. The one nonclassical work is a tomb sculpture of a magistrate with a full-bottomed wig and heavy robes. There were no such monuments in Westminster Abbey in the 1750s—though the monument eerily anticipates the monument to Lord Mansfield erected in the 1780s. But there *was* a place where such monuments did abound, and that was St. Peter's in Rome.[9] Hogarth's magistrate is given a papal monument to suggest the "infallibility" falsely associated with magistrates and, by extension, "judges" of art—as well as a climax to the Roman sequence from Republic to Empire to "Holy" Roman Empire.

The indigenous English tradition of art Hogarth had founded in the 1730s asserted a much greater interest in national, local, and particular English representations and themes than those of foreign, remote, Roman Catholic Italy. Time had brought into question the use of these sacred casts in the academy, where students were forced to master their every curve before being allowed to draw from life. Scholarship was beginning to draw attention to these canonical sculptures being in fact copies, composites, sometimes even forgeries. The Venus de Medici, for example, was the most copied of all the canonical sculptures, and (aside from questions of its own authenticity) it was known that the plaster casts were generally taken from aftercasts rather than the original in the Uffizi.

Of the art academies with which Hogarth was associated, first as student and then as master, extending from Vanderbank's to Thornhill's to Hogarth's own St. Martin's Lane Academy, we know two facts: that he insisted on drawing from the life—including shorthand notations of unposed figures observed on the streets of London—and that at the same time he carefully salvaged and transmitted the collection of casts, which would have included all of the canonical sculptures shown in the *Analysis,* Plate 1—a set of casts that eventually served the new Royal Academy after Hogarth's death.

Like the Rake in the brothel, the owners of the canonical sculptures could arrange them in their gardens into symbolic patterns to celebrate public, or more usually private, matters. At Stowe, for example, sculpture was arranged to satirize the Walpole ministry. Hogarth's setting, however, is not a country-house garden. It is Henry Cheere's statuary yard at Hyde Park Corner, one of a chain of such yards that ran from Park Lane to Half Moon Street, each producing objects of lead and stone, mostly for English gardens: ornamental vases and dolphin fountains, statues of shepherds and shepherdesses, marble funerary monuments, and above all copies of classical sculptures. While giving his friend Cheere a free advertisement, Hogarth also uses Cheere's business as a type of the commercialization of foreign art works which dominated English culture and the fate of these canonical sculptures. Here they are lead castings stored awaiting sale and delivery, *prior to* their disposition in gardens and country houses.

For next to—juxtaposed with—these canonical sculptures Hogarth has two human figures. One holds a book of anatomies reduced to geometric diagrams while gazing at the Venus de Medici, a figure of beauty in which (as the text informs us) art and nature join; the other is a posturing dancing master correcting the stance of the Antinous, an example of nature rendered artificial and art that is natural. This foppish figure was a recognizable portrait of John Essex, a well-known dancing master (author of books on deportment analogous to the anatomy book that is being contrasted with the Venus de Medici).

Within his text Hogarth uses Antinous to illustrate the "utmost beauty of proportion"; this statue "is allowed to be the most perfect . . . of any of the antique statues" (pp. 81–83). It was reproduced in the art treatises of writers from Bellori to Audran in measured illustrations of the proportions of the ideal human body, and Hogarth uses it, quoting du Fresnoy's words ("a fine figure and its parts ought always to have a serpentlike and flaming form," p. 6), to illustrate the serpentine Line of Beauty, the basic principle of his aesthetics.

But the juxtaposition with the contemporary dancing master raises more particular questions of the Antinous than the aestheticians, connoisseurs, and collectors were accustomed to ask. If we identify

John Essex the dancing master, we also acknowledge (something not mentioned in the art treatises but evident in the history books) that Antinous was the minion of the Emperor Hadrian, deified and celebrated throughout the ancient world in versions of this statue erected by the emperor in memory of his drowned lover. The Christian Fathers were outraged by the emperor's making a god of this boy who seemed to them no more than a male whore. In the context of Hogarth's composition in 1750s London then, he is being approached—perhaps indecently propositioned—by the effeminate dancing master.[10]

In much the same way, the Venus, representing Beauty but also withholdingness (she is a "Venus Pudica," a Modest Venus, trying to conceal her private parts from view), is here exchanging amorous looks with the Apollo Belvedere, while Hercules's back is turned in both his partial and full-length forms.[11] What is revealed beneath the canonical assumptions of these sculptures is a romantic triangle and an undercurrent of human desire. Even Hercules's "labors" (both sculptures were said to show him resting after his "labors") in Hogarth's new context become sexual labors—and so Venus, insatiable, no longer fitting the descriptions of this "Venus Pudica," of (in Joseph Spence's words) "decent Bashfulness . . . spotless Modesty and Chastity . . . Sweetness, Beauty and Delicacy and Air of Youth," is the Venus who betrays Vulcan with Mars. Spence had noted of her, "if she is not really modest, she at least counterfeits modesty extremely well."[12]

The Apollo Belvedere had already been used in little scenarios of this sort. The statue was thought to have accompanied the Diana the Huntress as part of a group depicting the story of Niobe's Children, and in gardens he was placed with statues of Ceres or Flora so as to augment female with male beauty or Fruitfulness with Wisdom. In Hogarth's statuary yard he is placed in a double gestalt, one involving him romantically with Venus, and the other placing him politically. He seemingly knocks on the head an eighteenth-century statue of a stage Brutus who is (again seemingly for it is only a rolled speech he holds) stabbing in the back Julius Caesar, who appears to fall forward because a rope is hoisting his statue for crating—or onto a gallows.

If we extend this political parallel, we see that Hogarth has placed a Roman emperor's pathic on the left and in the middle the assassination of Julius Caesar, with the avenging of his murder by the Apollo Belvedere, whose pose also recalls the most famous antique statue of the Emperor Augustus.[13] It is worth noting that the Apollo Belvedere had already been used in England as an aristocratic portrait model: in 1748 Allan Ramsay painted his *Chief of McCloud* in the Apollo pose, and as Hogarth was writing *The Analysis of Beauty*, Joshua Reynolds was painting his *Commodore Keppel* as another, more stately Apollo Belvedere.

In all of this play Hogarth is presenting the statues' unofficial, private, off-duty selves. A crucial concept of *The Analysis of Beauty*, *play* was the antithesis of the civic humanist authority, duty, and responsibility to which lip service was paid by both ministerial and opposition politicians. This authority was based on wealth and property, which included most notably (and symbolically) these sculptures. Thus these sculptures, which had formerly had abstract allegorical significance projected onto them, now have projected onto them the repressed human desires of their purchasers/owners. Hogarth's Sculpture Yard is only a realization of the sculptures' *real* meaning—or formation— in the gardens where they are now being placed: not as virtues and heroic figures, as *figurae* in any Platonic sense, nor as decorative accompaniments or learned allusions, but as personal meaning—or, more generally, as erotic *mis*readings. Hogarth is asserting that the canonical sculptures were now in the 1750s essentially empty signs waiting to be filled by the experiential interpretations of the first passerby because their conventional code (aesthetic and iconographic) had no counterpart in the objective world.[14]

Hogarth reads the sculptures—or rather forces us to read them— as an unfolding sequence: first, in the conventional code of the connoisseur, as ideal beauty and political authority; second, as an arbitrary iconography in which one statue, one human being, is called Venus, another Apollo, another Hercules. Then he empties them of their iconographic as well as their aesthetic significance by placing them as lead copies in a sculpture yard, thus turning them into *vanitas* symbols, memories of a lost time—and so into commercial objects waiting to be sold and crated and delivered, and therefore subjected to yet another context. Finally, he places them as if in an existential situation, with a human who is both bystander and actor, so as to force us to read them within the unequivocally empirical sensory data of everyday London in the eighteenth century, which fills the now empty signs—or, more specifically, aesthetic forms—with a particularly "modern" meaning: a meaning, however, which does not entirely replace those others but ironically augments them.[15]

The deadness of the old code is emphasized as the eye moves from the Venus and Apollo, the Brutus and Caesar rightward to the climactic object: a tomb sculpture of the sort found in Westminster Abbey. This is a magistrate with a full-bottomed wig and heavy robes (which in the *Analysis* text designate dignity, artificial and often unearned) with a pentecostal flame atop his head and at his feet a mourning putto holding a square signifying justice. However, in the existential context of the scene the square recalls a gallows (like the one Caesar is being hoisted upon), and the putto's tears are for the wretches he has hanged rather than for the deceased judge, whose judgments evidently produced only the ruins depicted around the base of his tomb—ruins equally consequential in the causal sequence that runs from Venus to Brutus to Caesar. This sequence, framed by memorials to Antinous and to the dead magistrate, imposes a sense of the memorial and dead which equally applies to the Venus, Brutus, and Caesar.

On the other hand, at the far left of the sequence the live John Essex, dancing master, imbues them with the fitful half-life of contemporary London. If the natural form of the Antinous shows up the fashionable pose of the dancing master, himself the author of manuals formulating body movements into dance and deportment, the natural (contemporary) costume, gesture, and expression of John Essex enlivens (or forces) the statues into particular human relationships. The general range of the examples in the *Analysis* and around the illustrations emphasizes the commonplace, which runs on a spectrum from smokejacks, candlesticks, table and chair legs—to corsets and ladies' legs—to the curves of the concupiscent female body in action, a Venus or (in Plate 2, fig. 4) a Woman of Samaria or an adulterous wife.

There is no question that *The Analysis of Beauty* plate expresses Hogarth's idea of how to revitalize English art by infusing new, contemporary life into old forms, old myths, old iconography, and old canons. The illustration expresses a doctrine Hogarth does not stipulate in his text: the Venus and the Apollo are, seen in one way, paradigms (or more specifically memories—memorials) of beauty. But seen in another way they are infused with human feelings, desires, and deceptions (to use Spence's word, "counterfeits"). Something that appears to be an art object is naturalized or popularized; something seen as a public political act (bashing the murderer of a dictator) is implied to be a private act of passion. What is revealed as the living reality of the aesthetic object is not precisely moral wrong but human desire.[16]

Characteristically, however, Hogarth builds his demystification

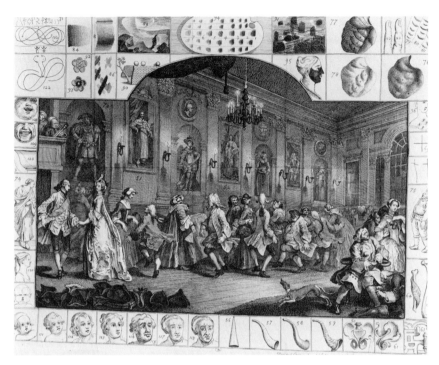

4. Hogarth, The Analysis of Beauty, *Plate 2 (1753), engraving.*

upon ancient authority (as he claimed in his subscription ticket for *A Harlot's Progress* to be only following Aeneas/Virgil in seeking out his "ancient Mother," fig. 14). Not only do the figures of Venus and Apollo remain, still an integral as well as vestigial part of the meaning, but the existential dimension of the human gestures is supported by emblems drawn from the old iconography: the love of Venus and Apollo is indicated in one way by the pair of doves mating at Venus's feet and in another by the predicament of Laocoon entangled with both the serpentine coils of passion and the serpentine lines in which Hogarth found beauty.

In a more general sense also Hogarth draws for support upon the doctrines of the antiquaries who commented on the canonical sculptures. The Abbé Raguenet, in his *Monumens de Rome* (1700), described the classical sculptures as depicting "states which are neither Life, nor Death, nor Agony, such as the Niobe who is neither alive nor dead nor dying but turned to stone." [17] The Dying Gladiator represents "the very moment from Life to Death, the instant of the last breath." Raguenet suggested that the power of the great canonical sculptures lies in their showing better than any others the transitional states of expression, gesture, and being. This was a view still shared by Hogarth, as earlier by Watteau, whose garden sculptures are often indistinguishably stone or flesh. (In this sense, the Statuary Yard is simply a parody of Watteau's gardens and their sculptures in his *fêtes galantes;* as *Marriage A-la-mode* 1 with its paintings is a parody of the interior in *L'enseigne de Gersaint.*) The moment of transition is the moment shown in Hogarth's examples: Apollo turning or reaching out, Venus caught unawares and modestly covering herself, and Laocoon and his sons being crushed to death by the serpent. If we compare the Apollo Belvedere as he appears, for example, in the plate of Spence's *Polymetis*, with Hogarth's, seen from the same direction but reversed, we will notice that Hogarth has turned his head to profile. This gives a sense (to anyone knowing the plaster casts, or Spence's volume) of inclining as if by magnetic attraction toward Venus and also of being in movement from one position to another and in transition from one state of being to another.

Also interesting, first, is that Hogarth, as usual, does not bother to reverse as he engraves, and so the sculptures appear turned about, in a sense estranged; and second, that he shows the sculptures from views and angles that suggest that he copied them not from the engravings (which do not show these views in most cases) but from the casts in the academy, where he could walk around and observe from every angle. His purpose seems to be partly to show them in unaccustomed views—or, more to the point, at the moment of turning from one to another, in transition.

These transitions fit into the spectrum of shapes, aspects, and attitudes of the human body which is the chief point of Hogarth's illustrative plate as it serves his text: from the candlesticks, corsets, and table legs to caricatures, anatomical diagrams, statues, and a tomb effigy, from a human overdressed dancing master to the man in the foreground looking at Dürer's rules for drawing the human figure. Hogarth evokes the graded series in the physiognomic treatises which illustrated the progressive degrees of the passions as they change from the tranquil to the vehement.

In Hogarth's painted and engraved work leading up to the *Analysis* these classical sculptures fit into a larger context, of Old Master paintings that depicted Old Testament cruelty and New Testament martyrs. Hogarth turned to the canonical sculptures of the sort he would deal with in the *Analysis* plate in *Strolling Actresses Dressing in a*

5. *Hogarth,* Strolling Actresses Dressing in a Barn *(1738), engraving.*

Barn (1738, fig. 5): the central young woman is playing the role of Diana. We know this not only because of her headdress but because of her pose as the famous Diana the Huntress (another of the canonical sculptures). This woman is frozen in the pose, her right arm reaching back to take an arrow, her left holding a bow, but the gesture is meaningless because both quiver and bow are missing (as from a broken statue), and the iconographical signs are inappropriate to this buxom, attractive young woman with her skirts down around her ankles. The woman is quite unsuited to the role of the virgin huntress, the goddess of chastity. She could serve as a point of origin for one of the best-known sentences, and in many ways the epitome, of *The Analysis of Beauty:* "Who but a bigot, even to the antiques, will say that he has not seen faces and necks, hands and arms in living women, that even the Grecian Venus doth but coarsely imitate?" (p. 83).

In Hogarth's own terms, the revelation is the living, breathing, sensuous reality that is beneath—and preferable to—even the greatest but dead art object. The living actress can transcend the role that has been imposed on her by the manager of her troupe because she retains her own slovenly, concupiscent nature, at least until she goes back on stage.

The more usual situation, however, which Hogarth explores in his print series, concerns the collector who redefines him or herself by the choice of the objects collected. In the second plate of the *Rake's Progress* (fig. 15), the Rake is shown standing beneath an old master painting he has collected, which shows the Judgment of Paris: Paris choosing among the goddesses Minerva, Juno, and Venus; or Wisdom, Power, and Beauty. Beneath this picture he has bought, the Rake lives out its plot, trying to choose among all the allures of upper-class London life. And like Paris (we see in the next plate) he chooses Venus. As Paris's choice of Venus led to the rape of Helen and the Trojan War, the Rake's own leads to the financial, moral, and physical ruin of himself and others. Again, the young countess in *Marriage A-la-mode* collects paintings of sexual indulgence in classical myth and in Old Testament story. In the fourth scene she has just purchased a sculpture of Actaeon, who symbolizes in this context her treatment of both of her men: Actaeon's antlers refer to her husband whom she is cuckolding, and his death prefigures the deaths of both husband and lover.

As I have said above, idolatry is quite literally the theme of Hogarth's satires: either the idolatry of any object that is denied its physical reality or the idol as a godless, that is, a lifeless statue. Pagan images of Diana or Venus, though of less a concern to the Puritans than images of deity, did have in common with the "idol" their deadness and pastness or remoteness from nature and experience. And it was for this reason that Hogarth fastened on them: indeed, in his time, as so many of his engravings show, the idol that could not be found on the walls of a church tended to be found in the country houses of rich collectors, connoisseurs, and self-seeking politicians.

Hogarth associates "idol" with old, dead art, with copies and forgeries, as well as with contemporary fashion, as opposed to a figure of voice, sight, and breath, who is the living and breathing woman he tells us in *The Analysis of Beauty* is more beautiful than the most perfect antique Venus. Thus the culmination of the idea of dead matter out of which is fashioned a false deity appears in the lead statues Hogarth shows being sold in the statuary yard at Hyde Park Corner. That these are dead statues is emphasized by the framing of the series with Hadrian's memorial to the dead Antinous at one end and by the Westminster Abbey tomb at the other: death, emptiness, and all the qualities associated with the idol in Psalm 115 are here. Then, having established their deadness, Hogarth reanimates them in much the same way that Calvin insisted the actual miraculous presence of Christ's body and blood, both the notion and the image, the wafer and the Mass, must be replaced with the common bread people ate in their daily lives.

Hogarth's aim in his *Analysis of Beauty* was to extend the aesthetic (1) from ancient Greek sculpture to modern London women (from gods and goddesses to contemporary humans), (2) from nature to such commonplace man-made objects as the candlesticks and corsets he showed on the borders of his *Analysis* plates, and so (3) in a more general sense from Idea to labor and making. These objects were made for general consumption, commonplaces of any Londoner's experience, exactly repeatable and intended for "mass" distribution—like his own mass-produced engravings.

The *Analysis* plates themselves were presented as mere illustrations of the text—that is, of those more elevated words, ideas, aesthetic concepts. Yet Hogarth's effort, by putting his richest intellectual content into these graphic images, is to designate this reading structure, this combination of forms for the eye and for the mind, to follow as aesthetic.

FEMINIZING THE HERO

The most general sense of antiheroism (which I have connected with Hogarth's emphasis on play in the *Analysis*) was summed up at mid-century in David Hume's preference for the useful and agreeable over the heroic or "enthusiast" gesture. An example in his *History of England* (1754) was his criticism of the Earl of Strafford for preferring the significant moment of self-martyrdom to a continuing life of useful effort—and so sacrificing not only his own life but probably his monarch's as well. On the other side, in the theater (and acting manuals), as well as in the aesthetics of Shaftesbury's *Judgment of Hercules,* and in the aristocratic civic humanism he preached, there was the continuing preference for the "pregnant moment," or "the exceptional moment in a person's life as decisive," as opposed to the everyday experience, the life lived outside official or heroic offices. In acting as in painting, this moment implied the "artificially elevated style" as opposed to "the natural style [that] will reject theatrical gesture because [the poet] does not want to estrange man from his everyday existence."[18] The latter was of course itself a *style* of acting, but it was also part of the belief (shared by George Lillo and Fielding) that even a crime must be judged as part of the person's whole life, and not as a momentary aberration or a single poorly performed role.[19] Hogarth's "comic history paintings" still (in both theatrical and aesthetic terms) represent the significant moment, the decisive action. Moral choice at a given moment remains for Hogarth the center of human experience. But that moment, as a heroic action, is being seriously questioned: it is, among other things, being transformed from public to private, from political to sexual desire, and from male to female.

The "hero" in this period is reconstructed by breaking the image of the classical, mythological, historical, Old Testament hero and replacing him with an antihero, or a hero manqué, a denial of the possibility of old-fashioned military heroism in this time (beginning with Milton's Satan, Butler's Hudibras, Pope's Belinda) or a Horatian rather than a Homeric or Virgilian figure, advocating an ideal of retirement rather than epic energy. The hero of satire simply recedes as the fools and knaves fill the foreground, pushing him out of the way, destroying him, or rendering him obsolete. But there is a sense in which the georgic also renders the hero obsolete, by replacing him with a farmer who, unconcerned with heroic highs and lows, knows the way to deal with life on a day-to-day, season-by-season basis. The farmer, however, does not exist except as a replacement for the hero.

As we saw in Pope's Horatian imitations, a better answer was a *New* Testament figure, Christ or, more usually, St. Paul (as in Steele's *Christian Hero* or, in painting, in the Raphael Cartoons of the Lives of Sts. Peter and Paul), and/or a passive victim, the oppressed of either satiric or sentimental fiction, who is often a woman—sometimes a saint, often a Magdalen figure (Calista, Jane Shore, Eloisa, and Hogarth's Harlot)—a woman who loses her virtue and suffers for it. The two sides of this last figure eventuate in the 1740s in Richardson's Pamela, who saves her virtue and benefits, and Clarissa, who loses hers and dies but benefits in the afterlife and the memories of survivors; and in Fielding's burlesque heroes, running from Tom Thumb to Shamela to Joseph Andrews, all of whom (as Jill Campbell has shown) are in striking ways feminized.[20]

All of these figures retain memories of (are in fact defined iconoclastically in terms of) the original "heroic" image, whether Achilles or Aeneas or Louis XIV or the Duke of Marlborough, which remains either as a contrast or an upward aspiration. Our subject is England in the years of Walpole's power, when he was being unsuccessfully attacked by a concerted machine of Opposition propaganda, represented as the *Prime* Minister, the "Great Man," in other words as a brazen modern version of a hero—vulgarized, degraded, but with the power and the will, with (as Pope would say) the ear of the monarch that raised a mere liar into a dangerous Satanic force. Walpole was the Great Man who in fact, as Pope and then Fielding show, is only a Jonathan Wild who escapes hanging, serving a monarch who himself is presented as something less than a heroic figure, uncouth, foreign, uncharismatic (no longer speaking English or touching for the King's Evil). And yet this Walpole figure is so firmly entrenched in contemporary ideology that his Greatness is the unthinking model for any young man or woman who embarks on life in London.

As we recall, drama and poetry of the seventeenth century were imaginatively conditioned by, and centered on, the monarch. The poet's concerns derived from the character or myth of the particular monarch. But after the death of Queen Anne the king was no longer accessible or viable as a plot center. The magic had gone out of the icon, itself originated as a substitute for the religious icon of Christ. The Jacobite king was a rebel inside England, and the Hanoverian was a remote, German-speaking prince who preferred living in Hanover. As an apparent figurehead, his role was taken over by his "steward" or "prime minister," Walpole.

In the 1720s–1740s Walpole assumes (usurps, in the *Craftsman* idiom) the place of the monarch in the literary imagination. Walpole is in fact where the poet or painter goes for his protagonist and plot (for the career of his "hero"). Implicit is the shift from one sort of protagonist to another: from a ruler who is a synecdoche for the state, symbolically its Body Politic, to a peripheral figure, a low, iconoclasted, parodic version of a king. He is also, it needs hardly be added, more appropriate as a subject for writers of prose fiction and painters of "modern moral subjects" than for the practitioners of high art. Fielding, in such plays as *Tom Thumb,* used Walpole and the Walpolean career as an imaginative center. If, as has been suggested, Walpole is the model for Hogarth's Tom Rakewell (in *A Rake's Progress* 1-4), then it is as if Walpole's is the *typical* life or career of the time and so must inform any "progress" that is supposed to be typical.

By 1726 the satiric image of the Great Man was being attacked by the *Craftsman* and Bolingbroke's pamphleteers, as well as by such artists as Swift and Pope. Hogarth entered the fray in that year, just as

6. *Hogarth,* The Great Seal of England *(1728), engraving on silver.*

the *Craftsman* was founded, but by 1728 he seems to have been quieted, momentarily at least, by the commission—presumably from Walpole himself, or with his approval—to engrave the plate known as the Walpole Salver, made from the Great Seal of England melted down at the death of George I (fig. 6). The seal would have represented for a supporter of the Opposition both the delicious moment when Walpole was finally dismissed from his offices by the new monarch and the disappointment that followed when he was reinstated. The design shows Hercules balancing two worlds, two circles (in fact two sides of a coin, but represented as two globes), containing the two sides of the Great Seal. Hogarth may have intended some comment by turning around the figure of Justice to face away from the king. But the main point is that he shows Hercules—in effect Walpole, the subject of the Salver—in an Atlas pose holding up both the monarch and the Great Seal. Envy and Calumny are chained at his feet (perhaps also in the secondary satiric sense of censored). The image is positive, indeed flattering: Walpole must have been delighted to see himself celebrated as Hercules, Heroic Virtue, and would not have objected to the trope suggesting that he holds up the monarchy—as in some ways he did. This was the reality Walpole made clear to George II on his accession, which caused his (at the time reluctant) reappointment as chancellor of the exchequer.

I describe this minor design in such detail because it precedes by only a year Hogarth's commencement of work on *A Harlot's Progress*. The *Harlot* was Hogarth's first great popular triumph, which established his reputation and set the course for his subsequent career. It also embodied one of the central mythic images of eighteenth-century England: the loss of female innocence, a sexual fall, precipitate decline, punishment, and death. What I want to notice is Hogarth's manipulation of the paradigm of Hercules as Heroic Virtue, the figure in traditional history painting who was used to elevate Alexander the Great or Louis XIV or William III or the Duke of Marlborough. This paradigm hovers over the first scene of the *Harlot's Progress*, where the Harlot, the clergyman, and the bawd are parodies respectively of Hercules, Virtue, and Vice, based on the graphic tradition of Hercules's Choice, in particular the image Shaftesbury prefixed to his influential essay *A Notion of the Historical Draught or Tablature of the Judgment of Hercules* (1713, fig. 7), which sought to improve the art of history painting. It advocated choice, and in particular Hercules's, as the subject of contemporary history painting.[21]

I apologize for once again recalling the Choice of Hercules and the *Harlot*, but I seem to return to the subject in every book I write. The question of what Hogarth is doing with the classical and Christian allusions in the *Harlot*, in particular the reduction of the stories to a popular retelling, appears with each reading in a different light. This time I want to examine the process as a form taken by Hogarth's Protestant-English iconoclasm, which destroys the Hercules, the Virgin Mary, and religious myths of heroic kings and virgin queens, replacing them with the literary story of a Polly Peachum and the true factually based story of a contemporary woman, Ann Bond.[22]

Hogarth has subverted the heroic paradigm by transforming Hercules into a passive young woman from the country (fig. 8); and by making Shaftesbury's rational, argumentative, winning Virtue into a clergyman who has turned his back on the young woman in order to read the address of the bishop of London, Walpole's chief adviser on ecclesiastical preferment. Pleasure, who is supposed to be languid like the clergyman, is in fact vigorously and successfully persuading the young woman to follow her own depraved way of life. But the important thing to notice is that Hercules has been replaced by this young woman (the familiar story of the girl from the country, specifi-

TREATISE VII.

VIZ.

A NOTION of the *Hiſtorical Draught* or *Tablature*

OF THE

Judgment of *Hercules,*

According to PRODICUS, *Lib.* II. *Xen. de Mem. Soc.*

―――――――――――――――Potiores
HERCULIS ærumnas credat, ſævoſque Labores,
Et Venere, & cœnis, & plumâ SARDANAPALI.
Juv. Sat. 10.

Paulo de Mattheis Pinx.   *Sim. Gribelin ſculps.*

Printed firſt in the Year M.DCC.XIII.

7. *Paulo de Mattheis,* The Judgment of Hercules, *title page of Shaftesbury's* Notion of the . . . Judgment of Hercules *(London, 1713).*

8. Hogarth, A Harlot's Progress *(1732), Plate 1, engraving.*

cally, in the scandalous story of 1730, Ann Bond, hired at an inn yard
by a bawd disguised as a gentlewoman, and turned over to the rake
Francis Charteris): Hercules is reduced to helpless femininity, as opposed to active male power and strength.[23] She is a travesty, but also a
softened, sentimentalized (precisely in the sense of feminized) version of Hercules.

Equally important, Hogarth has displaced the active Herculean
(and he means specifically, in the 1730s, the Great Man attributes) to
the supporting characters, the men who destroy the young woman.
The woman, stigmatized by her *un*respectable profession, is destroyed by their male respectability as clergymen, magistrates, prison
warders, and physicians. Even the rake Colonel Charteris is "respectable" (referred to in the newspapers and pamphlets as another Great
Man) because he was a known friend of Walpole's whom the prime
minister had just contrived to reprieve from his capital conviction for
the rape of Ann Bond.[24]

How Hogarth characterizes this deheroicized figure is of interest. Politically Hercules was associated in France with Henry IV and in England—in paintings by, among other artists, Hogarth's father-in-law Sir James Thornhill—with William III. When Shaftesbury selected the Choice of Hercules as the central fiction of history painting, the highest genre available to a painter, he was also—undoubtedly, given his own politics—using both the notion of choice and the figure of Hercules for their Whiggish associations. Hercules's choice between Virtue and Pleasure was familiar to English schoolboys from their earliest classics texts. Hercules was a central ideal of the discourse of civic humanism to which Shaftesbury laid claim for English politics as well as art. Indeed, the civic humanist focused on Hercules-of-the-Choice when the surviving classical sculpture was the Hercules at rest after his labors. In one of the temples at Stourhead, for example, Henry Hoare placed the latter Hercules in a choice situation by posing him between sculptures of Ceres and Flora, equivalents of Virtue and Pleasure.

Hogarth had picked up the Hercules-in-modern-dress, specifically theatrical dress, from the third act of Gay's *Beggar's Opera* (1728), where Captain Macheath pivots between his two "wives," Polly and Lucy, singing, "Which way shall I turn me," in a dramatic parody of Hercules's hesitation between his two women. Hogarth illustrates the scene in his series of *Beggar's Opera* paintings executed between 1728 and 1730 (figs. 9, 10). He shows Walker the actor who played Macheath at the moment when Macheath has assumed the pose of Hercules choosing, but the particular overbearing pose Walker-Macheath adopts, legs spread and arms folded on his chest—quite unlike the Hercules Shaftesbury had Paulo de Mattheis paint for his frontispiece—resembles the Walpole of satiric prints, and indeed portraits, of the time. Walpole, like Macheath, had two "wives" and was, as we have noted, at the last moment, "reprieved" by George II and retained as his first minister; this was just a few months before *The Beggar's Opera* was produced.[25]

So the transformation that takes place in the first plate of *A Harlot's Progress* carries with it memories of Walpole-Macheath, but displaced in this first scene from the Harlot to versions of Walpole, the bishop of London—Edmund Gibson, Walpole's man—and Francis Charteris, another Walpole man—a procedure that continues through the remainder of the plates, as one Walpole man after another appears in person or by allusion as an exploiter or threat vis-à-vis the Harlot.

As to the *non*-Hercules, the softened and feminized hero, the

9. Hogarth, The Beggar's Opera *(1728), painting.*

Harlot: If she derives by iconoclastic travesty from Hercules/Macheath, she descends in a direct visual line from Polly Peachum, the pretty but easily deluded girl who fell for Hercules/Macheath—and, played by Lavinia Fenton, won the hearts of the first-night audience with her singing of "Oh Ponder Well," offering the pathos and prettiness that played such a large part in the impact of Hogarth's visual image of the Harlot. Hogarth apparently started with a painting of the third scene (fig. 11)—and I have no doubt that what excited the response that encouraged him (as George Vertue tells us[26]) to fill in the rest of the story was the piquant juxtaposition of a pretty young rosy-cheeked Polly Peachum in these sordid surroundings (already the medicine bottles on the window sill imply that she is diseased within, however lovely on the outside).

In Hogarth's graphic work we notice that he consistently emphasizes and shows sympathy for the subculture marginality of dogs, children, blacks, apprentices, whores, and criminals but keeps them marginal; with a single exception, and that is the plebeian young woman. Indeed, the most important process in *A Harlot's Progress* is the feminizing of the heroic male—and the moving of heroism out from this central female figure into the villainy of the males surrounding and preying on her.

Now in his first thought for *A Harlot's Progress* he has centralized Polly and displaced Macheath into the over-zealous harlot hunter, the Walpole-supporter Sir John Gonson. For this scenario Hogarth turns to the place where Polly *is* made central, Gay's sequel to *The Beggar's Opera*, the ill-fated *Polly*, suppressed by Walpole before its first rehearsal in December 1728 but published in April 1729. This play follows Polly as she pursues her wayward husband Macheath to the West Indies, where he has been transported, has escaped, become a pirate, and is living with his new wife, Jenny Diver. Here Hogarth found the situation that bridged the fictions of *The Beggar's Opera* and *A Harlot's Progress*. At the beginning of Act I we are

10. Hogarth, The Beggar's Opera *(1729), painting.*

11. Hogarth, A Harlot's Progress *(1732), Plate 3, engraving.*

introduced to the bawd Trapes talking with a rich old man Dukat about how she lures young women who have just arrived off the boat from England into service, where they are seduced or raped by such as old Dukat. She has just procured Polly in this way for Dukat, and a scene follows in which he tries to seduce and then rape her.

This is, of course, the trio we encounter in Plate 1 of the *Harlot's Progress* (fig. 8) in Moll Hackabout, the bawd Mother Needham, and her employer Charteris (who, by the time Hogarth was conceiving the *Harlot,* had been tried for the offense of Mr. Dukat, condemned to death, and reprieved with the aid of his friend Walpole). So I would add the play *Polly* to the newspaper accounts of Colonel Charteris, memories of Steele's account of the young woman being approached by a procuress in the *Spectator* (1710), and various other sources: including, I suspect, the parallel story of Lavinia Fenton (the actress who played Polly) who was seduced and lured from the stage into keeping by the Duke of Bolton—a relationship that Hogarth emphasized in his final version of the *Beggar's Opera* painting (fig.

10). This is perhaps the most important because the Harlot can only be understood as a strange amalgam of Hercules-Macheath and Polly-Lavinia.

But Hogarth invokes another paradigm—not a classical, heroic one, now carrying a negative charge, but a Christian one, based on the *New* Testament Protestant art that was more acceptable to the English. In relation to the figures of the bawd and Charteris standing in the doorway, the young woman from the country in Figure 8 recalls the composition of the Virgin Mary with St. Elizabeth in a *Visitation* (fig. 12; I illustrate with a Dürer engraving, but there are many similar compositions of this trio). And she reminds us of an *Annunciation* (fig. 13, which also appears in Plate 3 of *A Harlot's Progress*, fig. 11). This allusion does a number of things, but for our present purposes it complements the classically heroic Hercules with the New Testament story (as it does the *Old* Testament stories in the pictures that hang on the walls of the rooms). It may historicize or naturalize

12. Albrecht Dürer, The Visitation, *woodcut from the* Life of the Virgin *(1511).*

13. Dürer, The
Annunciation, *woodcut
from the* Life of the
Virgin *(1511).*

the Biblical story, but it also serves to soften and feminize the heroic
ideal that was expected in history painting of the sort that Hogarth
was trying to remake for a modern English audience. (He made his
program explicit in *Boys Peeping at Nature,* fig. 14, his subscription
ticket for the series, with a central female figure of Nature-Diana of
Ephesus.)

In particular I see behind Hogarth's image Milton's primary un-
dermining of the classical Choice of Hercules (indeed, the whole
idea of classical heroism) with a woman and a rationally arguing and
winning Vice (like the bawd, successfully seducing). The hero who,
in a positive sense, underlies the Harlot—and presumably Pope's
Belinda and later Richardson's Clarissa—is Milton's Eve.[27]

The two facts to be stressed are, first, the need for the vestigial, by
which Hogarth means the negative heroic paradigm, the classical
Hercules *as well as* the contemporary woman, in the definition of the
protagonist—and, second, the middle term that connects the two elements. This middle term (going back to the dichotomy of Lavinia
Fenton–Polly Peachum) is acting or role playing, which served for

the early eighteenth century as a trope for the coercive force of manners, fashion, or social forms. The Harlot herself is an "actress" in the sense that she is a country girl who replaces her true, natural identity with the false, assumed role of a "lady"—as, for example, she appears beating hemp in Bridewell in the dress of a lady, as earlier she attempted to maintain a ladylike identity by keeping history paintings and portraits (in engraved copies) on her walls and having tea served by a decrepit servant. Acting serves as the middle term between the heroic and the real for Hogarth, as also for Fielding, not only in his farces and ballad operas (derived equally from Gay, Pope, and Hogarth) but in his novels, and for the Richardson of *Clarissa* as well (in both Lovelace's and Clarissa's letters and the theatrical poses they transmit).[28]

Unlike the Harlot, the strolling actress Diana (of 1738, fig. 5) is not choosing, does not fall, and is not a Hercules manqué. She is a natural woman bursting through the role of Diana, the everyday erupting in the pregnant moment of the drama. To see the way in which this figure came about, we have to notice again that in his painting of *The Beggar's Opera* Hogarth combined two scenes of Act III, Macheath as Hercules choosing between his two "wives" *and* the two wives, Polly

14. Hogarth, Boys Peeping at Nature *(1731), engraving.*

and Lucy, pleading with their respective fathers to free Macheath: so to a male gestalt of choice he added a second gestalt, of feminine mediation.

The Harlot then shows the male action of choice imposed (as an inappropriate role) on a young woman in 1730s London. It is the Harlot's tragedy that she gets her roles confused and behaves as if she were a Hercules instead of a Polly, choosing rather than mediating. But it is a comment on society that she is forced into such a role in the first place—both in the travesty sense that the men can no longer play anything but villains and in the aesthetic sense that she *is* a woman. This makes her a harlot and then, when she exerts her freedom of choice again in her keeper's house and takes a younger lover, she is cast out, and her descent thereafter is as short and certain as Eve's.

In Hogarth's second series of prints, *A Rake's Progress* (1735), the protagonist is likened (fig. 15) to Paris making his disastrous choice

15. Hogarth, A Rake's Progress *(1735), Plate 2, engraving.*

16. Hogarth, A Rake's Progress *(1735), Plate 4, engraving.*

of Venus over Wisdom and Power (Paris appears significantly in an old master painting Rakewell has collected, which hangs prescriptively above him on the wall). But Rakewell has none of the vulnerabilities of the Harlot except for being in a mild way, like her, an outsider (he is an outsider merely in the sense that his father was a rich merchant while he wants to be a rich gentleman). The Rake can himself be Hercules/Macheath, abandoning his Polly (his Harlot) in the first scene. The Polly part is now played by a separate character, very like the Polly who pursued the faithless Macheath all the way to the West Indies. She is Sarah Young, who, deserted and marginalized in Plate 1, mediates between the Rake and his creditors in Plate 4, ministering to him up to the bitter end (fig. 16).

The male, the Herculean, the negative aspect of the Harlot therefore goes off into the Rake, the male Squanderfields of *Marriage A-la-mode,* and the Tom Idles and Tom Neros of Hogarth's popular prints of the late 1740s. In the late 1730s, however, immediately following the *Rake's Progress,* Hogarth painted a series of New Testament history paintings, a corrective to those Old Testament scenes his characters like to collect—and a sublime equivalent of his modern histories. He followed these with a series of satires concerning the artist, which led in turn into the aesthetic theory of *The Analysis of Beauty.*

In the New Testament histories the protagonist has become quite literally Steele's Christian Hero, Christ himself in *The Pool of Bethesda* (in St. Bartholomew's Hospital). But this male figure follows iconographically, visually, and thematically from the female figure of Sarah Young (and so Polly Peachum)—who, by this time, was also appearing in smaller history paintings as Shakespeare's Miranda vis-à-vis Prospero and Ferdinand (i.e., Ferdinand is Macheath and Prospero is Mr. Peachum). She stands, like the strolling actress, in the center of the picture, and the man, the poet or musician, is on the periphery behaving in the manner of the Harlot or Rake.

With *Scene from 'The Tempest'* (fig. 17), however, the polarity has changed: Ferdinand *and* Prospero are on one side of Miranda and on the other is the ugly, grotesque, plebeian Caliban, Prospero's *slave* (versus the genteel Ferdinand whom he tests with errands). In short, Hogarth is sketching out the opposition he explores in later works— in *The Enraged Musician* but also in *Industry and Idleness*—between bourgeois order, patriarchal and coercive, and plebeian energy and disorder.

But before turning to the aesthetic meaning of this woman, I must mention the personal dimension. We notice that a number of Hogarth's compositions involve a courtship, with a lover who is a parvenu outsider, a father who is a ruler or a nobleman, and a daughter who is in love with the youth. In *Industry and Idleness* the industrious apprentice effortlessly courts and wins both daughter and father-master (possibly not in that order). But in the earlier works there is always trouble: Ferdinand is at first repudiated by Prospero; Death is in contest with Satan for Sin and vice versa; and, at the end of his career, Sigismunda (in his painting of Boccaccio's heroine) defies her father to take the lower-class Guiscardo, all, in this case, embodied in the tragic figure of the woman.

It is necessary to recall Hogarth's elopement with Sir James Thornhill's daughter Jane early in 1729 and the stories of a prolonged estrangement before a reconciliation (they date the reconciliation as late as 1731 or 1732, but I take their emphasis to be on the importance of the estrangement to Hogarth, who *talked* about it). The relationship between Hogarth, a sort of apprentice, and the great Thornhill (who also thought of himself as great), with the coura-

17. Hogarth, Scene from Shakespeare's 'The Tempest' *(c. 1736), painting.*

geous act we must attribute to Jane: all this serves as a kind of subtext for these works.

We must therefore ask: Did Hogarth, at the same time that he followed the political analogy of Walpole–Hercules–Macheath, associate himself (as Boswell did) with Captain Macheath in relation to Polly and Mr. Peachum, that is, in relation to his wife Jane and his father-in-law Sir James Thornhill? If so, this would explain why he later uses this configuration to illustrate scenes that are closer to his own situation (in *Scene from 'The Tempest,'* for example, and, most strikingly, in *Industry and Idleness*) and why he is so intrigued by the Polly figure. First he treats her realistically or demythologizes her (in *A Harlot's Progress*) into the Polly of the sequel who *doesn't* escape the clutches of Trapes and Dukat, and then developing the love-idealistic-faithful aspect of her in Sarah Young—with implicitly in the background an *un*faithful Macheath. (There are of course obvious parallels between the stories of *Polly* and Shakespeare's *Tempest,* which may also have led Hogarth to his *Tempest* painting.)

All we can say is that this was a scenario that interested Hogarth, or he would not have painted it so often. It does not, however, appear in his progresses or overtly comic-history works; rather he explores this stigmatic subject in his more sober historical paintings, especially those based on literary texts. Only in *Industry and Idleness* does it appear among the comic series, and here the happy story of Goodchild is fatally compromised by the parallel story of Idle, the one with Hogarth's own puggish face, and by the ironies in Goodchild's success story. It is possible, of course, that Hogarth is most interested in the rebellious woman—the Harlot who rebels against father, family, and Church—summed up at the end in the single figure of Sigismunda.[29]

In *The Distrest Poet* (fig. 18) the beautiful wife is the mediator who tries to deal with the outside world of torn trousers, unpaid milkmaids, unfed babies, and hungry dogs, in order to serve her deluded husband, lost in the role of "poet" and a poem *On Riches*. As in *Strolling*

18. Hogarth, The Distrest Poet *(1736), engraving.*

THE ENRAGED MUSICIAN.

19. *Hogarth,* The Enraged Musician *(1741), engraving.*

Actresses, where Hogarth returns to his original subject of actresses and juxtaposes the real people with their roles, the beautiful young woman bridges the worlds of reality and role playing. She appeared earlier in the drummer at the center of *Southwark Fair* who infuses the sweaty reality around her with the dreams of the signboards and costumed actors above as well as the natural hills of the countryside beyond.

Finally, in *The Enraged Musician* (fig. 19) she is the beautiful milk-maid with a bucket on her head, bridging the orderly "artistic" world of the Musician, with his notes on staves based on harmonic laws, and the discordant cacaphonous world of the lower orders (including a poster for the perennial plebeian songs of *The Beggar's Opera*). She delicately lifts her skirt to avoid the boy's urine stream. Her mouth is open, uttering sounds that we presume are natural but not gross like those of her companions. Her beauty and grace are surely intended to suggest that her voice, which among the sounds of nature is art, is more beautiful than the Musician's violin because less constricted by the conventions imposed by treatises and connoisseurs. The polarities are not just art and nature, the overordered structures of the poet or musician and the chaotic disorder of bill collectors and street noises, but British high culture and the subculture types of the London streets.

The extreme statement that explains the other, milder versions is Hogarth's painting *Satan, Sin, and Death* (fig. 20), in which the wife or milkmaid is Sin, the mother/daughter, as she tries to relate Satan, the rebel/father/lover, to that unknowable shapeless chaos called Death, who is both son and lover as well as a father in his own right.

Satan, Sin, and Death is best understood by recalling Hogarth's interpreter of *Paradise Lost,* Jonathan Richardson, a friend and member of the Slaughter's Coffee House group, who read parts of his *Explanatory Notes . . . on Milton's 'Paradise Lost'* to the assemblage in 1734 and, as I have argued elsewhere, probably planted in Hogarth's mind the idea of painting the Satan, Sin, and Death scene.[30] But Richardson's primary contribution to the interpretation of *Paradise Lost* was the introduction of the term "Mediator" for the Son and mediation for the central metaphor of the poem. The result was an original analysis of Milton's theology, but more significantly for our purposes, a fiction of the Son mediating between the Father and his creation.

To see the significance of this interpretation for Hogarth, we need to recall Addison's formulation of an aesthetics of the beautiful, sublime, and novel in his "Pleasures of the Imagination." In *Spectator* No. 417 (28 June 1712) he had attempted to apply these categories to *Paradise Lost:* the great (or sublime), he decided, was embodied in the War in Heaven, the majesty of the Messiah, and Satan and his fallen angels; the beautiful in Pandemonium, Paradise, Heaven, the angels, and Adam and Eve; and the novel or strange in the creation of the world, the metamorphoses of the fallen angels, and the "surprising Adventures" of Satan as he searches for Paradise. Now in these terms, Richardson's interpretation serves as a solution to the vexed question of whether *Paradise Lost* centered on the beautiful or on the sublime. As Leslie Moore has shown, in Richardson's interpretation the Son mediated "a new aesthetic between sublimity and beauty in *Paradise Lost*"—that is, between (in Addison's terms) the greatness of the Father (and, in a different way, of Satan) and the beauty of Adam and Eve and Paradise.[31]

20. *Hogarth,* Satan, Sin, and Death *(c. 1736), painting.*

In his description of the "Invocation" to Book 3, in order to define his visual sense of this Mediator, Richardson uses the words "a *Shape Divine, Presence Divine,* a *Bright Vision,*" and describes the "Picture" that Milton draws of him: "Milton has Suppos'd Him Visible, though not as Cloath'd with Flesh (So he appear'd not in Heaven till after the Ascension) but as Mediator" (p. 100). The primary characteristic of the Mediator kept in view by Richardson (himself a painter) is this visual quality. Glossing "Blaz'd forth unclouded Deity" (10.65), he writes: "That Glory which in the Father was Invisible, is in the Son Express and Manifest. This is his Mediation" (p. 443).

The underlying fact is that Richardson the painter concludes with the wish that "*Rafaelle* had Attempted This and had Succeeded in it as when he painted Christ a Child" (p. 100). This was precisely the sort of challenge that Hogarth insisted on accepting. And what he has done is to adopt the metaphor of mediation. It was, we have seen, a subject implicit in the *Beggar's Opera* painting which served as the basis for his *Satan, Sin, and Death,* as it did for his *Scene from 'The*

Tempest'. But in 1734, when Richardson's *Explanatory Notes* were published, Hogarth had access to authoritative concepts that he could develop in the paintings that followed.

Of the various implications I want to note first that in the demonology of the Opposition satirists there were bad male mediators: the estate stewards, including Walpole himself mediating between monarch and people (as an estate steward did between landlord and tenant, cheating both), and in the *Beggar's Opera* painting Polly's father, Peachum the fence.[32] The connoisseur-critic was another bad mediator, between art and nature, spectator and artist, consumer and producer. Mediation of a negative sort, the mediation of the bawd dressed as a gentlewoman (representing the notion of "lady" or, with the Rake, "gentleman"), was the subject of the *Harlot's Progress,* as it was of the *Rake's*. The female then, as in the case of Polly or later Sarah Young, was available to serve as the corrective, a privileged, a good version of mediation.

Second, in this painting Hogarth has applied mediation parodically to (what Richardson had called) the "Allegory which contains the Main of the Poem," Satan, Sin, and Death. For Sin mediating between Satan and Death parodies Richardson's idea of the Son mediating between Father and creation.[33] The gesture of reconciliation has hardened into one of separating vicious opponents, and the woman is now unambiguously the central figure. The context makes it clear that the father and lover/son are fighting for her. They are not only held apart by her but are contending for her favors.[34] *Satan, Sin, and Death* is the painting in which Hogarth exposes the deepest level of conflict in his *Beggar's Opera* and *Tempest* paintings.

But this is not to exhaust Richardson's metaphor of mediation. His words describing the Son as expressing a "Mediatorial Sweetness and Sublimity" (p. 101) must have stuck in Hogarth's mind. In aesthetic terms, this means a figure that Hogarth can call Beauty mediating between the sublime and the novel or strange. This female figure finds her ultimate resting place, now in both word and image, in the Venus of the Statuary Yard of *The Analysis of Beauty* who comes alive again in the usual Hogarthian triangle of husband-father and lover.

Finally, I want to note the religious aura. Hogarth could have heard Richardson's text read in time to have painted the mediation of Sarah between the Rake and his creditors in the fourth scene of *A Rake's Progress*. The oil that overflows the lamplighter's tin, apparently annointing the Rake's head, serves as a metaphorical gloss on Sarah's "angelic" intercession, which provides him the opportunity to repent, and recalls the "old man's" words to Doctor Faustus: "I see an angel hover o'er thy head, / And with a vial full of precious grace, / Offer to pour the same into thy soul, / Then call for mercy, and avoid despair" (13.74–77).

The female figure blurs the line between Polly, Mary, Miranda, and the Poet's wife: the last two are both painted in blue, the Virgin's color, and placed in compositions reminiscent of a Nativity and/or Adoration of the Magi.[35] Richardson makes his position clear: he has replaced the Marian intercessor with Christ the Son. But what is Hogarth's position?

For Pope the classical as well as the biblical worlds lived in a positive way in each canonical sculpture. He read these typologically in relation to the New Testament, as the Fathers read Ovid or Virgil. But the classical world was more specifically the renewal of classical Rome in Renaissance (Counterreformation) Rome, where it meant imperialism, continental ideals of art, and a form of Christianity which has been degraded by English Protestant iconoclasm. What Pope means by Rome is classical Rome but in some idolatrous sense Catholic Rome as well. For example, his grotto invoked Numa's visits with the *genius loci,* but also Christ's sepulchre. He had a stone representing the five wounds of Christ over the garden entrance, and over the river entrance a stone crown of thorns: both, it was believed, were taken from dismantled chapels. Grottos, moreover, remained within the tradition of early Christian (and recusant) refuges from oppression.[36]

Pope puts into his poetry a good deal of God, Christ, Mary, and the saints, which both Swift and Hogarth—and of course Addison and Steele—take pains to leave out or change into contemporary equivalents. For Pope the cross around Belinda's neck is reduced to a piece of jewelry and her neck is the object of "adoration" (as it is in Hogarth's *Sleeping Congregation*), representing a sad reduction of the cross and the Marian breast by English Protestants.

The Popean parody of a Pietà in *Dunciad* 3 is *not* a scene that alludes to *Paradise Lost*. To Pope it would have signified continental religious art, probably Roman Catholicism itself, carrying a positive charge; to Hogarth, for example in *Rake* 8 where he invokes the same image, employing Sarah Young as Mary and Tom Rakewell as Christ, it is a parodic reference to Counterreformation baroque art, its mysteries and mystique, its iconography, and its mythologizing, into which the Rake has sentimentally absorbed himself, as he did earlier into the classical image of Paris choosing between Venus and Minerva (Plate 2, fig. 15).

Returning to Hogarth's Mary-figures, we may wish to conclude that in England at this time it doesn't matter; Mary is not a matter of much importance theologically. Or perhaps Pope and Hogarth are both trying to retain some vestige of the old icon, Mary and Christ, in an iconoclasted society. These figures stand for what has been lost. Closer to the truth, Pope retains the Christ-Mary relationship in *Dunciad* 4 as an ideal, now lost in Dulness and Cibber, whereas Hogarth regards (as Addison and Steele would have) the image itself as Roman Catholic, continental, and idolatrous—as, we see, he may also have regarded the "Mary" of his *Harlot's Progress*.

THE "LOVE OF PURSUIT"

Hogarth wrote his *Analysis of Beauty* within two contexts: the first was one of aesthetic theories. In his "Pleasures of the Imagination" essays Addison laid down the basic terms of beautiful, great, and uncommon or novel (which would be called picturesque by Gilpin, Uvedale Price, Payne Knight, and others): these were the affective categories within which Hogarth constructed his theory of "beauty." There was also the aesthetic theory of Shaftesbury and Francis Hutcheson. Hutcheson's *Inquiry concerning Beauty, Order, Harmony, and Design*, the first part of *An Inquiry into the Original of Our Ideas of Beauty and Virtue* (1725), followed Shaftesbury in arguing for the equation of beauty and virtue. But Hutcheson developed his own argument that we "discover" beauty in an object when it presents "a compound ratio of uniformity and variety," that is, variety *in* uniformity, with the emphasis on uniformity.[37]

The second context in which Hogarth wrote his *Analysis of Beauty* was his own practice—his "comic history paintings" (as Fielding called them) or "modern moral subjects" (his own words) of the 1730s and 1740s. This double context led him to bifurcate his argument, discussing principles of what he called beauty in his text and illustrating—in precisely the manner of his "modern moral subjects"—these principles in the accompanying plates. But "illustrate" falls short of the actual effect, which is of complicating, questioning, problematizing aesthetic principles. There are, for example, places in his text where Hogarth is at pains to delimit the "precise Line of Beauty," ruling out all others; whereas in Plate 1 (fig. 3) the dozens of chair legs or stays, each with a slightly different curve—which in the text must be reduced to the "one"—imply instead the copious variety within uniformity.

Hogarth's "beauty" applies to two overlapping areas: one is the aesthetic experience of a spectator, an epistemological beauty, a way of knowing, and the other is the beauty inherent in an object.

The aesthetic experience of beauty starts for Hogarth not in Addison's beautiful, the response a spectator has to soft hilly serpentine landscapes but in Hutcheson's definition of it as the spectator's pleasure of discovery—of discovering or recognizing uniformity in variety (e.g., as one's eye moves from a triangle up to a square, hexagon, octagon, and duodecagon). Hogarth greatly increases Hutcheson's emphasis on discovery—that is, on process as part of the aesthetic experience—and reverses Hutcheson's order of priority: it is the pleasure of discovering not uniformity but variety.

Hogarth calls his beauty "a composed variety," but adds that the more variety the more beauty (pp. 35, 57). In a typical Hogarth composition (like the second *Analysis* plate, fig. 4) one's first impression is of the framing verticals and horizontals, the diagonals, of a closed perspective box; then of the chaotic crowd of dancers moving within its bounds. The architectural closure only regulates but does not subordinate the serpentine and irregular lines and shapes that lead the eye here and there, from object to object, never quite allowing it to rest. For Hogarth it is a principle of the most basic sort that geometrical structures should not finally regulate the vital Lines of Beauty of life.

As a larger application, recall the twelve plates of *Industry and Idleness* (1747) with their simple contrast of two apprentices, one named Goodchild and the other Idle. In one of the rejected passages in the *Analysis* manuscript Hogarth argues that "Fitness excites a pleasure equal or similar to that of truth and justice[; and] uniformity and regularity, are pleasures of contentment," in other words the sort of balanced, clear-cut morality of *Industry and Idleness*. "Variety," on the other hand, "excites the lively feeling of wantonness and play," and "Intricacy" excites "the joy of pursuit." These qualities Hogarth opposes to "Simplicity and distinctness," which are "like the pleasure of easy attainment" (pp. 170–71). Thus, as defined by a single plate, *The March to Finchley*, and by the series *Industry and Idleness*, Hogarth's method is essentially the exciting *discovery* of variety in apparent uniformity by means of a "lively feeling of wantonness and play" of the mind.

Among other things, Hogarth is invoking Locke's dismissal of innate apriori ideas by the experience of sensation, the Lockean "understanding" whose "searches after truth are a sort of hawking and hunting, wherein the very pursuit makes a great part of the plea-sure."[38] The terms "pleasure," "delight," and "satisfaction" are linked to "pursuit," with the metaphor of "the hunter's satisfaction" "to find and follow truth." And Locke's authority was particularly apposite for Hogarth because of his equation of the understanding and "the eye." In the same way, Locke's words about the mind's "power to re-peat, compare, and unite [simple ideas], even to an almost infinite variety" point to Hogarth's emphasis on variety over uniformity. Ex-perience is said by Locke to be "painted" by fancy on the "white paper" of the mind—"painted on it with an almost endless variety."[39]

The basic terms Hogarth applies to this epistemological beauty be-gin with curiosity, surprise, incongruity ("contrast"), and pursuit. His chapter "Of Intricacy" is about the "reader" of the work of art. "Pur-suing is the business of our lives," he writes:

> This love of pursuit, merely as pursuit, is implanted in our natures, and design'd, no doubt, for necessary, and useful purposes. . . . It is a pleas-ing labour of the mind to solve the most difficult problems; allegories and riddles, trifling as they are, afford the mind amusement.[40]

Intricacy, linked with the ancient topos of life as a hunt, "leads the eye a wanton kind of chase" and produces, in the context of "fitness" and the whole composition, beauty. His terminology based on "the love of the chase" surely draws upon Locke's view that "the very pur-suit makes a great part of the pleasure." Perhaps recalling *Tom Jones*, Fielding's verson of pursuit, in which the reader is continually invited to search out motive and causality, Hogarth adds: "and with what de-light does it follow the well-connected thread of a play, or novel, which ever increases as the plot thickens, and ends most pleas'd, when that is most distinctly unravell'd?"[41]

In the first plate of the *Analysis* the principle of intricacy is specifi-cally connected by Hogarth with an attack on secondhand forms and experience: the canonical sculptures, represented by lead copies in a merchant's storage lot, are returned to life. From this case we may formulate the subject of the "comic history painting": "the surprising alterations objects seemingly undergo through the prepossessions and prejudices contracted by the mind.—Fallacies and prejudices strongly to be guarded against by such as would learn to see objects truly!" (p. 25). This is one of the pleasures intricacy produces: the ability "to see objects truly." In the works leading up to 1753 the question of the viewer's choice, which grew ever more complicated and ever more Hogarth's own, in fact became the question of seeing objects truly. Thus in *Marriage A-la-mode,* and perhaps in the popular prints that followed, it may be accurate to say that moral instruction is subordinated to the importance of interpretation.

But the "intricacy in form" in beauty, we read, "leads the eye a *wanton* kind of chace." So to problem solving and pursuit (or the metaphor of the chase) Hogarth adds the particular kind of pleasure or play designated as wantonness. The viewer's searching and pursuing mind is excited or inspired by the undulating shape of the figure, just as the viewer's feeling of sublimity might be elicited by the great object, a mountain or ocean. But the example Hogarth gives us, over and over in one form or another in the *Analysis* as well as in his graphic works, is not the mountain or stream but the attractive woman in a situation of courtship or dalliance: "the many waving and contrasted turns of naturally intermingling locks" (also "wanton ringlets"), he writes, "ravish the eye with the pleasure of the pursuit" (p. 45). Here the epistemological aspect of beauty joins the definition of the beautiful object, typically the woman, and more particularly the amorous woman. I quote one summary passage (adding emphasis):

> A lock of hair falling thus across the temples, and by that means *breaking* the *regularity of the oval,* has an effect *too alluring* to be *strictly decent,* as is very well known to the *loose and lowest class of women . . .* [p. 52]

We can see all of these elements, in different degrees of tension, beginning in the subscription ticket for *A Harlot's Progress, Boys Peeping at Nature,* where Beauty is telescoped with Nature, Truth, and the earthy and sexual (fig. 14). There Venus was not a sculpture of a Venus Pudica but a fertility idol, the many-breasted Diana of the Ephesians. By the time of the *Analysis* Hogarth makes Beauty the "variety" of the undulating serpentine line; nevertheless in the design on the title page he emphasizes serpentine by showing the line standing upright with a small serpent's head, and directly above it the book's epigraph is taken from *Paradise Lost:*

> So vary'd he, and of his tortuous train
> Curl'd many a wanton wreath, in sight of Eve,
> To lure her eye.   [9.516–18]

This conjunction of Eve, Satan, and the Fall (extended in the text to another amorous temptress, Cleopatra) is the clearest acknowledgment Hogarth makes that his aesthetic, centering on woman and the serpent (who, we recall, at first walked upright) as graceful forms, must focus morally on the scene of man's temptation and fall from another kind of "grace": a *moral* as well as aesthetic grace is at stake. The original power and vision of beauty are inseparable from the original sin: as, for example, in his earlier painting of Milton's snaky sorceress Sin, and later, in his last engraving, *Tailpiece, or The Bathos* (1764, fig. 24, below). Here he attempts to connect the Line of Beauty with the ancient worship of Venus, represented (as he shows) by some of her votaries as simply a serpentine line coiled around a cone.

But also involved is the process of reading, summed up in Milton's warning in *Paradise Lost* against the shortest way (which I think Hogarth was invoking when he said "simplicity and distinctness" are "like the pleasure of easy attainment"). Sin and Death may build a "broad and beat'n way" from earth, but this smooth and easy path, Milton reminds us, leads directly to hell. So also in Book 9, Satan promises Eve speed: "If thou accept / My conduct, I can bring thee thither soon," and when Eve is won over, he makes "intricate seem straight" and guides her "swiftly" to the forbidden tree. At the center of the aesthetic experience for Hogarth is the matter of Miltonic choice, where, as in *Paradise Lost,* the audience must, like Eve and Adam, pause between conflicting interpretations and choose. But the form this takes is that a confident presentation of a doctrine is suddenly compromised by a troubling simile or off-center trope, calling it into question.[42]

Within his text Hogarth recalls how he introduced the subject of the serpentine line in conversation as a bait to trap stupid artists and ignorant connoisseurs. And, as I have suggested, he connects this more encompassing sense of beauty with the lady's lock of hair which entangles men in the same way that Hogarth's text entangles the reader (drawing upon memories of Belinda's locks, whose "labyrinths," "slender chains," and "hairy sprindges" trap men).

Accordingly in the first illustrative plate (fig. 3) Venus appears square in the center of the foldout, and she is turning to catch the Apollo Belvedere's eye while the Farnese Hercules's back is turned, creating a romantic triangle. Some kind of love-play as well as an example of pure form is also implicit in the relationship between the effeminate dancing master and the statue of Antinous. And in the second plate (fig. 4), in a situation exactly parallel to that of the Venus–Apollo–Vulcan, the young bride is receiving a love note from a young man behind the back of her aging husband: a scene that invokes the amazement of Sancho Panza, a marginal figure outside the scene, intermediate between the romantic triangle and the spectator. In both cases the female figure formally represents beauty, and the discordant immorality is revealed less as an ironic contrast or admission that beauty and morality may not (as in the simple Shaftesburyian equation) always go together, than to suggest that beauty requires both of these elements: a play of beauty with, against, and around morality.

To return to my quotation, the "regularity of the oval" of the female face is needed, but also the "breaking" of the oval with the lock of hair, and this is because the effect is "too alluring to be strictly decent"—a phrase that leads Hogarth naturally to introduce the "loose and lowest class of women" such as the Harlot, and that sense of the fallen associated with Daughters of Eve and the lifting of Nature's shift in *Boys Peeping*.

Hogarth's "beauty" is very different from Addison's, and Burke's a few years after Hogarth's treatise, which associate its soft curves with the mother's breast and an experience of a quiet, passive, and regressive childhood experience. Hogarth consistently emphasizes the connotations of disobedience, rebellion, and entanglement in beauty—and, at the same time, a function of mediation between a stereotype of "beauty" and disorder (or "sublime"). In *Tailpiece, or The Bathos* (fig. 24) the sublime (Burke's sublime) is represented as the breaking of serpentine continuities, replacing sensuous and intellectual connections by negation, exhaustion, and stasis.

Hogarth's "beauty" was in fact an attempt to find a middle way between the static order of Shaftesbury and Francis Hutcheson and the stark uncontrollable chaos of the sublime (which Burke's interpretation later confirmed for him). While he calls his solution beauty, it remains closer to Addison's attempt (in *Spectator* No. 412) at a middle term, "whatever is *new* or *uncommon*," which

> fills the Soul with an agreeable Surprise, gratifies its Curiosity, and gives it an Idea of which it was not before possest. [Its virtue is] to vary Human Life. . . . It is this that recommends Variety, where the Mind is every Instant called off to something new, and the Attention not suffered to dwell too long, and waste it self on any particular object.

The "final cause" of the novel or uncommon is the pleasure "in the Pursuit after Knowledge," the need "to search into the wonders of [God's] Creation."[43]

Both Addison and Burke agreed that the sublime refers one for-

ward to ultimates, to a confrontation with an exercise of power, while
the beautiful refers one nowhere beyond the self and repose. Hogarth
took the active aggressiveness of the sublime and combined it with
the undulating form of the beautiful and called it beauty. He parallels the undulating shape of the figure with the viewer's searching
and pursuing mind—just as the great object is paralleled by (or elicits) the viewer's feeling of his inability to encompass sublimity. We can
see here the same claims he made for his modern history, that intermediate genre which privileged nature over art and advocated an
active search for fundamentals. We can also see how emblematic are
his images of the pretty young woman between the aristocratic (or
pseudoaristocratic) artist and the plebeian chaotic crowd.

The main difference between the novel or uncommon, which
Hogarth called beautiful, and the "picturesque" of Gilpin, Price,
Payne Knight, and the others, is that Hogarth's focuses on the human
body and human artifacts, while their focus is on nature.[44] Contingency is the disruptive principle of both, but in the picturesque it is
subsumed under merely temporal change: leave a landscape alone
and it will grow into picturesque shapes.

It is significant that Gotthold Ephraim Lessing in *Laocoon,* his great
treatise on the differences between graphic and verbal art, quotes a
passage from the *Analysis* which sums up Hogarth's aesthetics of the
modern. This is the passage in which Hogarth explains that the Apollo
Belvedere "calls forth surprise" in the beholder because "upon examination its disproportion is evident even to an untrained eye": its
feet and thighs are "too long and wide for the upper parts." It is, of
course, first necessary that there be that element of "surprise," but
then it follows, "if we examine the beauties of this figure thoroughly,
we may reasonably conclude, that what has been hitherto thought so
unaccountably *excellent* in its general appearance, hath been owing to
what hath seem'd a *blemish* in a part of it."[45]

Thus the woman at the center of *Strolling Actresses* (fig. 5) plays
Diana or Chastity in the play, but she also smokes a pipe, drinks ale,
lets her neckline plunge, and drops her petticoats around her ankles
to reveal enough thigh to endanger any Actaeon in the vicinity. She
is, in short, an attractive young woman (who *attracts* a Peeping Tom),
but a disreputable Diana. The figure simulates sculpture—the young
woman is in the pose of Diana the Huntress; and with both sculpture
and woman come the ideas of an interjected contingency—the woman
as Diana, as a piece of sculpture suddenly enlivened, of Diana with
her petticoats about her ankles.[46] With the Venus of *The Analysis of*

Beauty the middle term of acting becomes, by way of expansion, the term "art," in the sense of copy, forgery, and "fake." The Harlot and Rake were bad actors, and these objects are as inauthentic as were those human beings. But the heroic norm—along with the aesthetic and authentic—is once again transformed into a contemporary and particular and very human gesture, based on sexual desire.

Both of these elements, of the particular and the general, are necessary for Hogarth's idea of beauty (i.e., variety in apparent uniformity), which is summed up in the sentence in the *Analysis* which prefers the "faces and necks, hands and arms in living women" to those of the "most perfect antique Grecian Venus." In short, both the uniformity of the Grecian Venus and the unenclosable variety of the living woman are required for beauty. This general assumption appears throughout the *Analysis*. At the very outset, for example, Hogarth writes that beauty is a "subject generally thought to be a matter of too high and too delicate a nature" for discussion. Why artists have achieved beauty despite the lack of writing on the subject has been, first, by "the mere dint of imitating with great exactness the beauties of nature" and, second, by "often copying and retaining strong ideas of graceful antique statues" (pp. 3–5). The point is clarified by the words of Abraham Cowley, in the Preface to his first two Pindarics: "I have seen originals both in painting and poesie, much more *beautiful* than their natural objects; but I never saw a *copy* better than the *original*, which indeed cannot be otherwise." As this suggests, it is not so much a question of beauty and nonbeauty as of original and copy, with the original always superior. But both the original and the copy, the natural object and the ideal artifact, are necessary.

For Hogarth, beauty requires the accidental or contingent detail as well as the immutable principle, the exception as well as the rule— what Charles Baudelaire would refer to as the contingency of modernity.[47] For Hogarth accident meant various human and "modern" or contemporary particularities including (as his allusions to *Paradise Lost*, Eve, and Cleopatra suggest) sin: which clearly distinguishes his aesthetic—and its modernity—from the reactionary aesthetic of Shaftesbury, Richardson, and Reynolds.

This aesthetic also included, with sin, the voyeurism we have noted in the presence of the peeping putti, Actaeons, and clergymen. In *Strolling Actresses* at least, where the spectators to the print are admitted backstage, the Actaeon serves as a surrogate for the inquiring, playful, pursuing eyes of the rest of us. So to the elements of the ideal, canonical sculpture and the human woman, we must add the peeping spectator's "pursuit."

By "modern" Pope began by meaning the denial of the hegemony of the Ancients. Those qualities, life, and artifacts characterized by their contemporaneity which are not sanctioned by the term "ancient" first fell under the scrutiny of the satirists but then more sympathetically of other writers. In this sense Pope's *Dunciad* was the first "modernist" poem, but Hogarth's prints went on to explore modernity, and his *Analysis* was the first attempt to define an aesthetics based on Pope's sense of the modern. It is, of course, anti-Popean. Hogarth recognized the potential for liberation in new forms of mechanical representation, in the infinitely repeatable engraving, and accordingly in the happenings in the streets of London which are newsworthy in the sense of both immediate and mechanically reproducible. This is quite different from the fastidious distaste Pope demonstrates for these phenomena—represented for him by the dunces, seen against the nostalgic memory images of Aeneas and Turnus, Sarpedon and Glaucos—which become for Hogarth the unassimilable shocks of contemporary urban life.

For modernity then morality and beauty are quite separate; and indeeed *praxis* is an essential element—the proper moral action implicit in the rhetorical intention of the artist and in the practical response of the spectator. This *praxis* Hogarth means to be antithetical to the disinterestedness, the detachment, required by the aesthetic of Shaftesbury and Hutcheson and, a few years later, of Burke. But *praxis* here refers to the act of being drawn by the Line of Beauty from one revelation to another, as the "veil of Truth" is withdrawn to reveal what had before been concealed by custom, society, and ideology. *Praxis* has more to do with interpretation and visual pleasure than with social or moral action. It depends on the element of play, for the aesthetics of modernity involves, as the replacement for morality (which has been first separated from beauty), something like mental play with the dichotomies of—for example—morality and beauty, form and content, appearance and reality. This thematizing and problematizing, replacing clear-cut right-wrong alternatives, I would argue, serves the function of disinterestedness in a process of aestheticization of materials that are not usually thought of as aesthetic objects.

HOGARTH's initial notion was that civic humanism, with its image of a male aristocratic hero, seems to call for an antidote in the form of a feminized plebeian society, a bourgeois society. But then, in the 1740s, he goes deeper and seeks an antidote to the bourgeois society itself in apprentices and genuine subculture energy—the energy of the Enraged Musician's noise makers *without* mediation.[48] What we notice is that in the popular prints of 1747–51 the young woman disappears in a simple contrast of order and disorder or good and bad, Goodchild and Idle, without any middle term, or the good boy and Tom Nero of the *Stages of Cruelty*. The industrious apprentice has *married* the master's daughter now; she appears only with Goodchild, never appearing with either the father/master or the other apprentice; and in the *Stages of Cruelty* she is simply murdered by her lover Nero.[49] Following from *Marriage A-la-mode* in 1745, the opposing terms have become essentially parent against child, without any room for a pretty mediator.

She has been taken out and transported into Hogarth's aesthetic theorizing, to figure more ambiguously in the pretty-but-immoral women of the two plates of *The Analysis of Beauty*. It may have been around this time that Hogarth painted the single head and shoulders of *The Shrimp Girl* (London, National Gallery); he was also painting bright, rosy-cheeked faces in portraits, but when the pretty young woman appears again in a subject painting she is either the sexually threatened woman of *The Lady's Last Stake* or the suicidal Sigismunda.

The reading structure changes accordingly. As the center of the composition is emptied of the pretty young woman or replaced by a simple unmediated contrast between opposites, the spectator's role naturally increases in importance (moving toward the emphasis on spectator cooperation in the *Analysis*). From the first the "reader" was crucial, divided into common reader and "reader of greater penetration,"[50] but by the 1740s, with *Industry and Idleness* and the popular prints and *Paul before Felix* among the paintings, the audience divides into one consisting of patron, master, and father, capable of reading at the simple moral right-wrong, crime-punishment level of meaning; another consisting of the servant-subculture-apprentice audience, which sees straight to the subversive antimaster message. (The "reader of greater penetration" by this time may have the privilege of seeing or encompassing both these points of view within a larger overview.) This strategy functions as another part of the general tendency to break down unities, not to seek them, and to fragment audiences outside, as the figures within the picture are fragmented.

Hogarth's turning his attention to aesthetics from the late 1730s into the 1750s would at first seem a turning away from the problems of the real world, and especially odd in the same years he was making his most subversive socio-political prints. But what he came out with in *The Analysis of Beauty* was a claim for beauty precisely *in* the common, the everyday, the fallen, corrupt, and subculture world—of screwjacks and unfaithful wives—seen related to the ideal antique Venus or the "Perfect Line of Beauty." It is an aesthetics not of nature but of man-made forms of utility, recalling the iconoclasm of *Analysis*, Plate 1, which extends from the canonical sculptures to the common utensils, the corsets and candlesticks of the marginal diagrams. What at first looks like a process of abstraction turns out to be a search that reveals beauty in the Harlot and poor London milkmaids.

The political message of *The Analysis of Beauty* is the elevating of this world of variety, liberty, and subculture above the old doctrines based on unity and order: Shaftesbury's nature as order, harmony, and proportion; Hutcheson's uniformity and regularity; Palladian orders in architecture; and "whatever is is right" in politics. We have to notice the synonymy of what we might call the increasing radicalism of the popular prints—the increased play within apparent systems of order, the breakdown of large overarching narratives with small independent and unpredictable ones—in both politics and in aesthetic doctrine. And so that Hogarth was writing the *Analysis* at the same time he was producing the "popular" prints is not surprising.

Chapter 5

The Aesthetics of Mourning: Wright and Roubiliac

THE EMPTY TOMB

I once was a member of a group of historians who met annually to discuss the historian's use of visual objects. At one memorable meeting we examined a painting by Joseph Wright of Derby, *The Blacksmith's Forge* (1771, fig. 21). Looking at this painting a facetious historian suggested that the boy leaning toward us in the foreground was trying to light a cigarette. There was much concern about the time of day portrayed. When did a blacksmith shop close? Is it winter or summer? If, as the moon might suggest, it is after hours, is an emergency therefore implied? If the emergency is a broken horse-shoe, as the pictorial evidence seems to indicate, why is one being forged when a supply of ready-made horseshoes is visible on the wall at the rear? Is not the ingot on the blacksmith's anvil too large for a horseshoe?

What fascinated me, however (aside from the picture's prompting questions of this sort), was the one feature that all the historians were bothered by and kept returning to: the intensity of the light was far in excess of the apparent source, the ingot. One historian said there had to be a furnace or some other source of light out of our range of sight in order to explain the brightness.

I appreciated this puzzlement because these historians, though

21. Joseph Wright of Derby, The Blacksmith's Forge *(1771), painting.*

they had not read my essay on Wright of Derby, confirmed my thesis in the best possible way: that the light generated by the ingot is a modern equivalent of the supernatural, a substitute or displacement for a Nativity or some other transcendent event.[1]

Most art historians still prefer to see Wright as his modern cataloguer Benedict Nicolson did, as a "Painter of Light" whose paintings never leave the spectator "in any doubt as to what is meant."[2] The light for Nicolson designates a naive realism, a faith in empiricism and the technology of both industry and art: "To maintain that Wright transported his forges into imaginary settings," Nicolson writes, "is to misunderstand his whole approach to industry, which was a reverent acceptance of things as they were."[3]

Frederick Cummings provides a second example of a faith in what I shall call for lack of a better term Wright's ontological security. Unlike Nicolson, Cummings recognizes that "it is unlikely that any forge he visited would have been housed in a crumbling basilica reminiscent of Botticelli's shelter for the kneeling Virgin and Child in a Medicean 'Adoration of the Magi,'" but such differences only reveal the similar ontological concerns of the two scholars. The Nativity or Adoration architecture is secularized according to Cummings, who views it as creating "a setting of Roman grandeur for . . . modern steel-forgers," a subject outside the range of official art in the 1770s.[4] Blacksmiths, of course, were not laborers but traditional English craftsmen. One of the striking facts about Wright of Derby, whose reputation has him celebrating the Industrial Revolution, is that he habitually represents not modern technology but ancient crafts; not modern scientific experiments but ones that are "unscientific," remote, popular, and odd (involving alchemists, orreries, and air pumps). If the Industrial Revolution is in any sense alluded to in *The Blacksmith's Forge*, it is through a foreshadowing of industrialization by a memory of the ancient craft of the blacksmith.

All of these scholars, intent on seeing Wright as either "scientific" or proto-Marxist, overlook the excessive intensity of the light source or regard it merely as a bourgeois way of elevating unaristocratic subject matter. (The other aspect, the darkness surrounding the source of light, I shall take up later.) Behind them is Wright himself, the primary empiricist, who left a written program for his painting:

Two men forming a bar of iron into a horseshoe, from whence the light must proceed. An idle fellow may stand by the anvil in a time-killing posture, his hands in his bosom or yawning with his hands stretched upwards, & a little twisting of his body. Horse shoes hanging up ye walls, and other necessary things faintly seen, being remote from the light. Out of this room shall be seen another, in such a farrier may be shoeing a horse by the light of a candle. The horse must be saddled, and a traveller standing by. The servant may appear with his horse in hand, on such may be a portmanteau. This will be an indication of an accident having happened, and show some reason for shoeing the horse by candlelight. The moon may appear, and illumine some part of the horses, if necessary.[5]

"It is gratifying to know that we see in the pictures what he saw," says Nicolson. The passage reveals Wright to be an artist in the candlelight tradition of Gerrit van Honthorst and Georges de La Tour, and it shows that at some point he wanted to tell a story—or felt he should tell a story—in his painting. But the revealing phrase is "if necessary": "The moon may appear, and illumine some parts of the horses, if necessary." Among the numerous discrepancies between Wright's stated program and his finished painting, the horse is not illuminated by a moon but rather by a guttering candle, whose precarious flickering is pointed to by one of the figures. Wright does not verbalize the topos of the Ages of Man he adopts in the final composition, nor the structure, out of the art manuals, of the spectrum of *l'expression des passions*. But most interesting, he does not mention that the blacksmith has set up his forge in an ancient iconoclasted church. If the blacksmith's craft projects us forward into the Industrial Revolution, it is also projected, by the structure in which he is lodged, back to the Age of Faith—or Superstition, depending on the point of view. The ingot partakes of all three dimensions.

The most remarkable thing about Wright's words is their almost total irrelevance to the picture he painted. It is as if, still stuck in the iconoclastic tradition (which he is in fact tacitly illustrating), he is afraid of putting into words what in fact goes into the image. The words are for the public; they hold at a distance the terrifying (to him perhaps, or to his patron) image that emerges on the canvas.

The double aim then is to paint the local and to paint in the great tradition of continental (Roman Catholic) history. So Wright paints a blacksmith's shop but in the setting of a ruined, towering ecclesiastical structure; he arranges the figures in groups suggesting the Ages of Man and intensifies the light coming from the ingot beyond the possible in order to suggest the sense of a Nativity with shepherds and wise men. By contrasting his man-made source of light with the natural light of the moon, he qualifies the "supernatural" sense of the former, in effect bringing it down to the "miracle" of manpower.

The presence in Wright's work of traditional structures such as the Ages of Man has been demonstrated by Cummings in another painting, the portrait of Brooke Boothby (1780–81, fig. 22). In this case an appreciation of naturalistic detail and high finish does not satisfy Cummings, who observes the disquieting effect of the work and then traces its source. Boothby's dark dress is elegant, but also incongruous in this wooded scene—as is his reclining on the ground. He lies meditating in this quiet glade, his back turned upon the distant sunlit

22. *Wright,* Brooke Boothby *(1780–81), painting.*

meadow, the destination of the spectators' eyes. These are details that Cummings has identified in the iconographical tradition of melancholy. Recalling Elizabethan miniatures, Burton's *Anatomy of Melancholy,* and poetry of the mid-eighteenth century, Cummings identifies Boothby as a melancholic.[6]

There is more to the portrait, however, than the melancholy pose. Boothby also holds a volume titled *Rousseau,* which has been identified as the manuscript of the first dialogue of *Rousseau, Juge de Jean-Jacques,* entrusted to Boothby by Rousseau himself for publication in England. In the context of the Rousseauian doctrine of the superiority of nature over society, Boothby is posed as Rousseau's hero St. Preux, solitary in the forest near Lake Geneva, in the most popular of all his works, *La nouvelle Héloïse.*

But he has closed his Rousseau with a negligent fold, and he lies so near the picture plane that he has in effect blocked out, or turned his back on, nature itself (except for a few flowers). Even stranger, although there is a stream between the Boothby and the spectator, Boothby is seemingly pressed against the picture plane; the leaves around him—even the tree trunks at some distance from the picture plane—are scumbled so as to seem close to the spectator's eyes: which I would sum up as the artist's attempt to suggest the simultaneous immediacy and withdrawal of Boothby.

To a contemporary Englishman (and undoubtedly to Boothby himself, an enthusiast of the subject), the figure would have suggested a reclining figure on a funerary monument. As Cummings has recognized, melancholy and tomb sculpture coincide in this pose: reclining thus, "his right arm supporting his head, [was] the traditional motif of melancholy reflection especially as found in tomb portraits from Sansovino's Cardinal Sforza (Rome, s. Maria del Popolo) to Thomas Carter's Chaloner Chute of 1775."[7]

There is, of course, a question of priority: which came first, the topos of melancholy which is used on funerary monuments or the tomb pose of the deceased which is appropriate to the topos of melancholy? In the 1780s it seems likely that the image of the reclining figure on a tomb was the more common experience. But a conflation of the two was available in Gray's *Elegy Written in a Country Churchyard,* where the "hoary-headed swain" recalls the poet in the pose of both the melancholic in a forest glade and the reclining figure on a tomb sculpture inside the country church:

> "There at the foot of yonder nodding beech
> "That wreathes its old fantastic roots so high,
> "His listless length at noontide would he stretch,
> "And pore upon the brook that babbles by . . .   [ll. 101–04]

These lines could serve as Wright's motto. Gray's poem is about the relationship between the monument outside and the ashes—of the great or the lowly—inside. And ultimately he uses the epitaph as a synecdoche for the monument, the words covering an unknowable absence by implying an unearthly imminence.

Though the portrait of Brooke Boothby, with every feature delineated in precise clear-focused detail, is so different from the Blacksmith's glowing ingot, in fact Boothby is a figure of equal ambiguity. The man Boothby in all his particularity is qualified by the poses of the melancholic solitary, of Rousseau's romantic St. Preux, and above all of the dead-yet-alive figure on a tomb.

Before asking what it may mean to portray Boothby in this way, let me turn to a literal representation of a tomb, one of Wright's more schematic paintings, *Miravan Opening the Tomb of His Ancestors* (1771, fig. 23). Miravan, according to the story, read the inscription on his ancestors' tomb, "a greater treasure than Croesus ever preserved," to

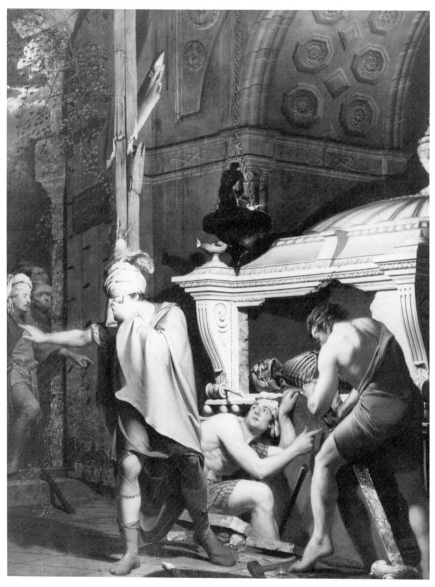

23. *Wright,* Miravan Opening the Tomb of His Ancestors (1771),
painting.

mean that the inside was filled with gold. He broke open the tomb but found instead of wealth only his ancestors' bones—which, however, conveyed to him the wisdom that the "treasure" referred to in the inscription was "eternal repose."[8] But what *is* the wisdom he learns? It is not merely that the greatest treasure is "eternal repose"; it is also that to achieve this wisdom is precisely to violate the "repose" of his ancestors who inscribed the wisdom. Such ambiguity lurks in the literally hollow, empty tomb, at the center of the scene.

The moral is being revealed to Miravan— and Miravan *and* the moral to the spectator, including the observer who, having helped him break open the tomb, points out the skeleton to Miravan, who averts his eyes. Miravan's gesture of covering his eyes suggests, among other things, a progression from the outward form of the tomb to the interiorization of its significance in the spectator's mind. He is like the spectators we saw within and without *The Blacksmith's Forge* responding in various conflicting ways to the glowing ingot on the blacksmith's forge. Thus the tomb is both hollow receptacle of bones and dust and—something in excess of that—not merely moral wisdom but what we have referred to as problematization. In this case we can be more precise by seeing that term within an enactment of iconoclasm, the idol broken in order to reveal the truth, either in its shards or empty transcendence.

In this painting two concerns characteristic of Wright's art are added to that juxtaposition of the scrupulous detail of presentation and the questionableness of a central object. First, the extension of the architectural form of the sarcophagus to the mausoleum in which it is housed, and, by implication to any human dwelling, implies the instability of all human structures, or at least of the relationship between inside and outside. A complex linking of observers to a central object, which is not what it first seems, induces a recognition of the questionable state of their responses as well. Miravan may be the positivist historian, as the slick surface and sharp detail were intended for his eye before he broke open the tomb. Now that it is broken Miravan and the other spectators beyond him respond to the full suggestiveness of that tomb. What separates this painting from the others is that Wright portrays the moment in which its emptiness-yet-fullness is established, recognized, and internalized by the spectator.

The dissolution of an immediately perceived solidity, both of objects and persons defined in their relation to objects, is a recurrent feature in the experience of Wright's scenes. Miravan's tomb is a useful point of departure because the tomb in western tradition is a place of transition, where a dead body is placed—a *transi* as the French called it, held by embalming pathetically and temporarily against decomposition but of course decomposing inside the tomb while another aspect of it survives in stone on the outside and a third is assumed to be ascending to heaven. The common French tomb structure of the fourteenth to seventeenth centuries was two-layered, on the top an idealized figure of the man as he was in heaven (i.e., remembered, idealized), and below the *transi* in process of decomposition as he was in fact underneath the slab. The English tomb was a simpler structure, relating only outside to inside, and summed up in the injunction, common in funeral sermons, to look inside the beautiful tomb of the rich in order to see the sordid reality: in Ben Jonson's Cavendish epitaph, the "polish'd stones" of the monument "only hide" the "flesh, and bones [which] will turne to dust."[9] Miravan's discovery is therefore only literarily—in terms of the story Wright quoted in his notebook entry on the painting—about the absent treasure, present bones, and edifying moral concerning "eternal repose"; more deeply it reveals the hope that something else will be found there, in the manner of the opening of Christ's tomb, not the bones and dust that we know, especially in the scientific age of Wright, to be there.

In the second place, that oil lamp, whose feeble light illuminates the scene, is itself an inversion of the dominant architectural form of the sarcophagus and mausoleum, and its limited light implies a comparison with the greater scene opening out from the shattered architecture. Miravan's arm, instinctively thrust away from the enclosing tomb, leads out of such fabricated, lamplit interiors to a vague but extensive natural landscape illuminated by the natural light of a full moon.

Usually included in Wright's subject pictures is a contrast between the human and the natural, the man-made and the unchanging, as in the ingot, the lamp, the illuminated air pump and the real sun or moon—or Brooke Boothby's elaborate pose and the natural world on which he (with his various artificial poses) has turned his back.[10] Above all, there is the painting of Arkwright's factory at night (private collection): the factory small, deep within a natural setting, with the moon off to the side, but with the exact repetition of innumerable lighted windows. The effect, often sinister, is to further put in question the authenticity of the central object (ingot, lamp, factory); but its ontological status is always set off against the spectrum of subjective responses in the spectators to the scene. In fact, Wright's concern for the subjectivity of perception, his recognition of the inadequacy of reason to define experience, is frequently as observable as his intense interest in clarity of expression, in the technique of craft, and in the application of reason to the representation of nature. In Wright, as in many eighteenth-century English writers and artists, these two concerns are equally compelling.

WRIGHT's paintings pose for us an aesthetic experience from the second half of the century. Let us recall what we said in the last chapter about Hogarth's aesthetics. In his *Analysis of Beauty* plates he makes a series of assertions that contradict the aesthetic principles laid down by Shaftesbury, Hutcheson, and Jonathan Richardson, in particular the equation of aesthetic and moral qualities in the work of art: (1) that the image of beauty, in the canonical figures of Venus, Apollo, and others, does not correspond to virtue but to passion and adultery; (2) that these canonical sculptures of western art are now in 1753 essentially empty signs waiting to be filled by the existential interpretation of the first passerby on Hyde Park Corner. His intention is to infuse new, contemporary life into old moribund forms in order to revitalize English art; and this involves (3) the association of these sculptures with funerary effigies. He thus imposes a sense of the memorial on these sculptures at the same time that he enlivens them with associations of desire and passionate behavior in contemporary London. (4) These are in every sense transitional figures, moving in contrary gestalts between the alive and dead, between aesthetic and moral categories.

(5) As he ridiculed the static equation of formal and moral beauty, he also rejected the disinterestedness Shaftesbury attributed to the "moral sense" (in *Moralists* 3) that takes pleasure in both aesthetic and ethical harmony. This detachment within the aesthetic experience, which is distinct from either the moral or the purely existential experience, has become central in the doctrine of Edmund Burke. In his *Philosophical Enquiry into the Origin of Our Ideas of the Sublime and Beautiful* (1757), where he defines beauty as "love" without desire, and sublimity as "terror" without danger, the Burkean spectator has to be aesthetically, by which he means physically, distanced from frightening objects or phenomena, which "are simply painful when their causes immediately affect us." They are better held at one or two removes—by a safe platform over an abyss or by the perspective that allows us to see over the shoulders of participants. Such objects, he says, "are delightful when we have an idea of pain and danger, without being actually in such circumstances ourselves."[11]

24. Hogarth, Tailpiece, or The Bathos *(1764), engraving.*

If Hogarth is one stage of aesthetic theory, Burke is a second, as can be seen by comparing Burke's description of the sublime with Hogarth's interpretation of it in his *Tailpiece, or The Bathos* (1764, fig. 24). The form again is that of a funerary monument in Westminster Abbey, perhaps a cross between Louis-François Roubiliac's Hargrave Monument, with images of Death and Time and tottering masonry (fig. 33), and Rysbrack's reclining Sir Isaac Newton. Hogarth's reclining Time is surrounded by emblems of mortality and Burkean sublimity—broken, burning, discontinuous, and decaying objects, including shattered Lines of Beauty. Hogarth could be specifically illustrating Burke's image of sublimity "in images of a tower, an archangel, the sun rising through mists, or in an eclipse, the ruin of monarchs, and the revolutions of kingdoms." The spectator's mind is, as Burke says, "hurried out of itself, by a crowd of great and confused images" (p. 62). But what Burke regards as sublimity Hogarth clearly designates chaos, or (as he put it in the *Analysis*) "variety uncomposed, and without design, [which] is confusion and deformity."[12] Hogarth's application of "Bathos" to Burke's "Hupsous" is a return to the aesthetic assumptions of *The Dunciad.*

But the difference we cannot avoid noticing between the image of the *Analysis of Beauty* plates and the *Tailpiece* is that one is still comic, the other is memorial, even funerary: Hogarth knows he is at the end of his life and is making a tailpiece for the folio of his engraved works, his earthly memorial, one that recalls Pope's farewell at the end of *Dunciad* 4 (as later Gray's in *The Bard*). Those broken objects, and that image of Father Time breathing his last surrounded by decay, are Hogarth's program for his own funerary monument. But if Roubiliac shows the Resurrection in the Hargrave Monument, Hogarth stops short with the stage of breakage, the End of All Things. Indeed, further associating himself with the farewells of Pope, Swift, and Gray, he had preceded his drawing of the *Tailpiece* by wiping out his official self-portrait in the frontispiece to his folios, *Gulielmus Hogarth,* and replacing it with the face of a bear (his brutish attacker, Charles Churchill).[13]

What Hogarth depicts as the end of all coherent values Burke sees (at the moment at least—perhaps less so later when the French Revolution emerged to test his theory) as, with proper distancing, the highest sort of aesthetic object. For Burke, the affect alone testifies to the power of the object; and this is a natural rather than artifactual object. Autonomous, it is essentially without agency or authorship. This sort of aesthetic object comes as a striking correction to Hogarth's manufactured objects such as smoke jacks and corsets, let alone the elaborate "machines" of his own paintings and engravings. Indeed, it is important to emphasize that Burke is answering Hogarth. A post-Hogarth Burke may seem strange for readers of Weiskel, Hertz, and Ferguson, but in fact it is as truthful to see Burke from the direction of his precursor Hogarth as to look back on him from the retrospect of Kant.

Burke's beautiful, like Hogarth's, is embodied in the woman and is also connected with domestic, bourgeois objects and values, with making and with utility. The features of this beautiful are labor and repetition (literally embodied in the repetition of Hogarth's engraving process), custom and society. This sense of society as the beautiful is of course Hogarth's world, which is being broken apart by the power of mere affect in the *Tailpiece:* that is, by the sublime, embodied in the male who exerts power and represents an aristocratic, warlike ethos. The affect of the sublime experience is submission to someone more powerful than you; and so Burke presents us, in his paradigm of terror, with the spectator (or Burke) confronting and confronted by Milton's Death; then a page later by Milton's Satan.

Burke presents these confrontations sequentially as examples of comparative power. He consciously chooses the confrontation of Satan and Death in Book 2 of *Paradise Lost* but then avoids the oedipal situation, the Satan-Sin-Death relationship, by breaking it into two separate segments—by holding them somewhat apart—of spectator-Death (from Book 2) and spectator-Satan (from Book 1), and by eliding—suppressing altogether—the middle term, Sin the female domestic (mother, daughter) mediator who is the center of Hogarth's aesthetic structure.[14]

In short, we can say that Burke does pick up Hogarth's sense of the beautiful, embodied in the mediating woman we have traced in an earlier chapter, and augments it with the sublime, which is privileged against it as male subordinates female. Thereafter, in his *Tailpiece, or The Bathos,* Hogarth gives back his own version of Burke's sublime as antagonist to the beautiful (in another version of *The Battle of the Pictures,* where *his* modern history paintings had been battered by old masters). The opposition is derived from his own playing off of the feminine beautiful against the largely male crowd, disorder, subculture images and noises in *The Enraged Musician* and the other artist-satires of the 1730s and 1740s; but now, partly with the advent of Burke's *Philosophical Enquiry* and partly with the new political dimension of Hogarth's *Election* and *Times,* Plate 1, this playing off has taken on a threatening aspect. Burke's sublime is destroying Hogarth's beautiful as the Pittites and Wilkites are destroying England.[15]

There is another significant point of contact between Hogarth's and Burke's aesthetics. Burke tells us that people are rendered dull by their "constant use" of the codified stimuli of their environment, and that the effect of this "constant use is to make all things of whatever kind entirely unaffecting . . . our natural and common state is one of absolute indifference" (pp. 103–04). Burke draws two conclusions from this assumption: one, that when these "constant" stimuli are removed—are no longer present—they *do* become, by their very absence, affecting; and two, that therefore absence and its alternative (or concomitant) "novelty," or "noticeability" in an object, are the factors that stimulate to an aesthetic response.[16] In other words, Hogarth's construal of "beauty" as the novel and surprising may serve as a bridge for Burke into his more demarcated aesthetic experiences of the beautiful and the sublime. For Burke there is beyond, or complementing, Hogarth's modernist aesthetic of immediate contemporary presence one that posits absence as its chief affective characteristic.

In short, Burke theorizes what we have called an aesthetics of mourning, though he does not call it that. His "obscurity," the necessary ingredient of the terrible, is darkness, night, "popular tales" of goblins and other unvisualizable creatures, in short, a deprivation or absence: the *un*known rather than the known—what he calls "our ignorance of things" (p. 61).

WILLIAM Collins also built his major poems around the figure of the mediating muse. Emerging in the last years of Pope's life, Collins writes almost entirely on the subject of how and whether to write a poem—of what subject matter (including some of those recommended by Philips and Tickell) and the way to get started. And with him emerge the dark poets who write about themselves and why they cannot write; with their obscurity formulated in the 1750s by Burke's aesthetic of obscurity/sublimity.

So Collins writes poetry about the problem of writing. Pope had picked up the subject from his second career model, Horace, but by way of *The Dunciad* made it his own. In the same way, Collins made Pope *his* career model, beginning with pastoral (the *Persian Eclogues* of 1742) and shaping them like Pope's to end with decline into the fallen, georgic world.[17] As one might expect, however, the decline is closer to *Dunciad* 3 than to the "Winter" pastoral: the Turks (like the Goths) are overrunning the pastoral realm in a kind of political imperialism that returns in the great *Odes* (pub. 1747). But like Pope, Collins's "literature" is again both literary and nonliterary writings.

Collins's *Odes* develop in their own way two Popean fictions.[18] One is of a "Progress of Poetry" that is a westering, in effect a progressive colonization by the Goths that now precludes the possibility of any longer writing poetry,[19] and the other, for our purposes the more significant, is of a fruitless, impotent relationship between the poet and a goddess-muse.[20]

Collins's distinctive version of *The Dunciad* has the goddess-muse flee, her place usurped by Dulness or the literalization of Dulness in optical obscurity. The function of Collins the poet is to try to fill this empty space—first of course scooping it out to make it empty—with a nonpoem that is about not writing a poem. Like the other artists we have been dealing with he creates a space that is both abandoned and in some sense transcendent. He suffers belatedness in the sense that he has come *after* the goddess-muse has fled. But the fiction is also anti-Popean in the sense that it tries to build on the very obscurity that, with the goddess's departure, has overcome clarity and reason, masking or designating the empty space left by the Astrea figure.

Following from this, not an anxiety of influence but the sort of suicidal absence-making we have examined in the poetry of Swift and Gray is the subject of Collins's odes—not conflict but the sense of absence following conflict, or the question of what the poet can do after the goddess-muse has fled, the veil has been replaced, and war and chaos have returned to England. For another significant fact about the odes is that they are about poetry *and* political subjects. They are odes to peace, mercy, and liberty—primarily referring to the War of the Austrian Succession and, within England, the Rebellion of '45 and its bloody aftermath: as if these were now in some sense historical correlatives to the final images of *The Dunciad*.

In the final manuscript *Ode on the Popular Superstitions of the Highlands of Scotland* (written 1749–50) the word *colonize* refers specifically to Scotland in the devastating wake of the '45. The "progress" in the sense of progressive politics is that of imperialism or colonization: and so Scotland is the prime example of the "solution." Scotland is an empty, proverbially barren and inhospitable land, now literally decimated, which serves as one of Collins's "fancy lands" whose emptiness is filled with folklore and superstition, a contemporary substitute for the lost Golden Age: both emptiness *and* fullness, since the Bard never left that remote wilderness. Thus for Collins the problem was the way to reconcile Greek, Christian, Renaissance, European, and Roman Catholic with national, local, patriotism, Shakespeare, Otway, and others. The solution was always in favor of the local: how to write poetry in England in the 1740s—as Hogarth's question was how to paint in England in the 1730s–1740s. A solution, for Collins, was to replace the muse with an elf or a goblin—those "tales of Goblins and Fairies" recommended by Tickell—thereby spiritualizing the landscape, making it a tomblike container. The subject itself was embodied in an unfinished, fragmentary poem: Throughout, Collins also reflects a fear of art—of completion, probably of "labor" in the sense that we have employed the word, but including the efficacy of words themselves. Broken form reflects the subject of the odes.

One way of dealing with the emptiness left by iconoclastic breakage was a picturesque patchwork of the old and new, of the sort we saw in Richard Bentley's illustration for Gray's *Elegy* and in Wright's joining of iconoclasted abbey with contemporary blacksmith shop. Another, illustrated by Gray's poem itself and by the odes of Collins, was to worry about the iconoclasted emptiness: a response summed up by a poem of Thomas Warton the Elder, *Verses on Henry the Eighth's Seizing the Abbey-Lands, and on Queen Anne's Augmentation of the Livings* (in *Poems*, 1748). Charissa, the spirit of England (or religion in England), flees when Henry VIII despoils the church lands:

> She view'd, she mourn'd, she fled her rifled Isle,
> While ravenous *Henry* gave a Loose to Spoil.

Warton ostensibly writes of spoliation—appropriation of property— rather than iconoclasm, and finds the issue resolved when Queen Anne "rais'd the drooping Priesthood from the Ground" by granting the First Fruits. But the central part of the poem is about the problem of writing poetry, that is, about the empty, deserted, stripped holy buildings and lands, now only occupied by ghosts, and the preserve of poets. In the holy ground "where Saints and Martyrs lay interr'd," for example,

> Here in still Deep of Night are Peasants fear'd,
> When the tall Ghosts stalk slow with Steps unheard,
> When moaning Cries the lonesome Ruins fill,
> So pitiful they howl! and shriek so hollow shrill!

The passage goes on and on (ll. 102 ff.), describing an emptiness created by iconoclasm, which is now being filled by superstition, ghosts, a *genius loci*, and even picturesque creatures ("Now browzing Goats, and lowing Oxen stray, / O'er mould'ring Pillars creep the blushing Vine," and so on). Warton's projection becomes a clear alternative to the iconoclastic barrenness in Collins's *Ode on the Popular Superstitions of the Highlands*.

AT the center of Burke's discussion is a painter-poet contrast that privileges the poet: the painter makes things too risibly clear, too visible, too *present;* whereas (and this was, of course, Collins's insight) the poet's words *create* an absence or ignorance, whose very power lies in their inability to specify what is there or is not there. This ignorance, unspecified and confused by words that do not correspond to things, Burke calls the sublime. If, as I suspect, Hogarth's *Satan, Sin, and Death* (fig. 20) was the occasion for Burke's invidious comparison of the painter's and poet's account of Death (and by implication Satan and Sin), the response of the *Tailpiece* is the more explicable. By the 1760s and 1770s painters (as well as the poets Collins and Gray), and especially such painters as Wright of Derby, were attempting to achieve Burke's sublime "obscurity" by painterly means.

Burke's assumption that there is nothing sublime in nature but only in our apprehension of it (of a "scene" or "landscape" our apprehension frames out of it) postulates a uniformity of response and a continuum of the object and the responding subject.[21] But, as Hogarth's response to the "sublime" object in the *Tailpiece* suggests, one comes away from Burke's *Philosophical Enquiry* suspicious that there is only a conventional object and a conditioned subject ("the greater attention and habit," the more cultivated the taste, Burke argues, "the more uniform the response to the sublime object" [p. 22]). Even in Shaftesbury's phrase "Harmony perceived as beauty" we recognize "perceived" as the operative word, for with all his platonic optimism Shaftesbury was still thinking within the English empiricist tradition. And this relationship between subject and object is not very different from the one supposed by David Hume:

> Euclid has fully explained all the qualities of the circle; but has not in any proposition said a word of its beauty. The reason is evident. The beauty is not a quality of the circle. . . . It is only the effect which that figure produces upon the mind. . . . In vain would you look for it in the circle, or seek it, either by your senses or by mathematical reasonings, in all the properties of that figure. . . . Till such a spectator appear, there is nothing but a figure of such particular dimensions and proportions: from his sentiments alone arise its elegance and beauty.[22]

The essays in Hume's *Essays, Moral and Political* (1742) are set out perspectively, each with a different voice: he tells us in the "Advertisement" that "a certain Character is personated," of an epicurean, a stoic, a platonist, and a skeptic. In practice, however, these are arranged to make a single argument.

For the literary tradition we need go no further back than Sterne's *Tristram Shandy* (1759 ff.), which Wright was reflecting in his subject paintings of the 1760s before he made literal illustrations for *A Sentimental Journey* in his *Captive* and *Maria* paintings (1770s). But in both novels Wright found a structure in which an object, or some misunderstood word, is responded to in comically different ways (with different understandings of it) by different people: the problem being the same one Burke dwelt upon (and Locke introduced), the intractability of words. The fact of brother Bobby's death, like so many other things in *Tristram Shandy*, has no independent existence of its own. Book 5 begins with an account of the word "whiskers" which has no stable meaning and so eventually gravitates to the sexual sense—which is also "death," making way for Bobby's—and Book 5 ends with the well-known employment by Walter Shandy of auxilliary verbs to establish the reality of a white bear nobody has ever seen. The dead and never-glimpsed Bobby is nowhere to be found in the funeral oration of his father, Walter Shandy. He is finally evoked—or rather not he but his death—not by words but only by Corporal Trim's dropping of his heavy dark, claylike, tomblike hat—a hat which later, unsurprisingly in the world of this novel, is turned into another sexual symbol. As in Hogarth's *Analysis of Beauty,* Sterne finds under every aesthetic or monumental structure a trace of human desire— in this book that, we should also recall, is one enormous funerary memorial erected by Tristram to himself and his father, mother, uncle, and friend Yorick. Yorick's death was marked by a black page and the epitaph "Alas Poor Yorick," a symbol of both fullness and emptiness which is hard to match in the monuments of Roubiliac and Wilton. *Tristram Shandy* is simply the most complex, ambiguous, and profound example—because, I suspect, it is written in the greater tradition of English literature—of the sort of structure I have been analyzing in English painting.

Sterne owed a great deal to Hogarth, not least his emphasis on the visual and sensible scene, his insistence on a spatial and associative reading structure. But the Hogarthian scene of response (derived from the art historical formula of *l'expression des passions*) was centrifugal, the only common element being self-interest. The biblical model was the parable of the Good Samaritan, with Levites and Pharisees recoiling out of self-interest, but with a single Good Samaritan to minister to the wounded man. In the same way, the Harlot's sickly bunter and the Rake's Sarah Young introduce the possibility of a sentimental attachment in an unfeeling society, which heralded the sort of scene that Sterne and Henry McKenzie made famous in their novels.

Sterne's scene usually involves a victim—Tristram, Yorick, Toby, or Bobby—but the occasion is always something empty or absent: dead Bobby or empty words or Tristram himself, but if an absence also in some sense one transfigured by the spectator's sympathy. The novel Sterne wrote is quintessentially a sketch of a few lines which the reader's fancy is asked to fill in, as he fills in the blank page with the Widow Wadman's features, or in *A Sentimental Journey* Yorick fills in the lady's face which he cannot see in front of the remise in Calais. The novel is all suggestion, asking for an active participation of the reader which stands in striking contrast to the failures of communication within the novel, among its characters.

Wright's paintings should be situated between the somewhat different modes of *Tristram Shandy* and *A Sentimental Journey.* The former is about *un*relatedness and demonstrates the unrelatedness of society by focusing on the most apparently related of all groups, the family, in the most restricted of places, Shandy Hall and the bowling green ("a world in a small circle . . . of four *English* miles diameter"). The comic effect of this incongruity would have been lost, and less would have been demonstrated, had Sterne shown unrelatedness in a picaresque narrative. The reader is drawn into *Tristram Shandy* to be confused and to personally experience the unrelatedness Sterne is also proving on the level of his characters and their milieu. The emphasis throughout is on the conventions of society and the way they prevent communication by choking the natural, primitive, intuitive, and sympathetic impulses, which appear only as isolated, exceptional moments such as Trim's dropping of his hat or the brief sympathies that pass between Walter and Toby: As the result of a misunderstanding, Toby blows smoke in Walter's face, Walter starts to cough uncontrollably, Toby leaps up to help his brother, thus causing excruciating pain to his wounded groin, and both brothers suddenly join in a moment of sympathetic understanding.

A Sentimental Journey, on the other hand, is about just those isolated moments of relatedness. But now they are the subject and are presented in a picaresque narrative where one would least expect to find relatedness, and Yorick is among not his family and friends but strangers and foreigners, and in time of war between his country and theirs. In *Tristram Shandy,* even Volume 7, in which Tristram's journey anticipates Yorick's, the emphasis was still on the constricting forms of travel books and topographical studies which get between the traveler and his experience (again with a few exceptions such as the dance with the nut-brown maid). In *A Sentimental Journey,* this aspect is represented by the unsociable travelers Smelfungus and Mundungus, and they are peripheral, mostly offstage texts (like Tobias Smollett's very different *Travels through France and Italy*) which set off the real subject. The reader here is intended to join in the sympathetic evocations of Yorick, re-creating them as his or her own:

an experience quite different from the harried, delayed, and waylaid frustration of the earlier novel.

In Wright's scenes the air pumps and orreries were merely excuses for a social gathering. The responses of the spectators assembled are centrifugal in that (unlike say the responders to Jean-Baptiste Greuze's paralytic) each is carried off into his or her own thoughts, according to age, type, and proclivity. But Wright shows, by way of the empty/ transcendent object, *both* the divergences of response and (yet) the common bond of sympathy. However wildly eccentric the reading of the object, it does draw the different people together, making of them one subject.

Ten years before *Tristram Shandy* appeared, its tragic counterpart, Richardson's *Clarissa,* was published. Here the unfeeling self-absorption of each member of the family served to destroy poor Clarissa, as on a somewhat lower level Tristram suffers the destruction of his homunculus, his name, his nose, and his sexual organ (implicitly, in the near future his life). Only the body of the dead Clarissa draws together the fractious members of the Harlowe family. She and her coffin become another of those baffling central objects. Pure sensibility in a Clarissa (or a Tristram or McKenzie's Harley) is virtually impossible within the fiction of an unfeeling world of competing interests and prejudices. But it is hopefully projected, by both Richardson and Sterne in their different modes, out onto the spectator, who has a role of peculiar importance in relation to both novel and picture.

WRIGHT's paintings are about and embody the relation between a stimulus and a response, but the question is whether the thing at the center is only empty, a vanitas emblem or the result of a Humean skeptical-empirical reduction, science purged of its mystery and returned to a conventional status; or whether it is an ambiguous object embodying both nothingness and transcendence or in some sense even transubstantiation; or whether, instead, it is the quintessential act of iconoclasm, reducing what was once transubstantiation to common experience—the Christ Child to a blacksmith's ingot in the 1770s.

What the object-spectator relation confirms is that once Humean skepticism has cleared away the pretensions of reason, it seeks a positive area of agreement in belief based on the relative strength of feelings operating within a range of subjectivity narrowed by the categories of custom; and this is what Wright visually represents. Wright's *Experiment with an Air Pump* (1767–68, fig. 25) shows a glass

25. *Wright,* An Experiment with an Air Pump *(1767–68), painting.*

sphere enclosing a bird on the edge of extinction, attempting to pro-
long its life—and a spectrum of sometimes anxious, sometimes apparently unconcerned responses by the spectators to the experiment:
all however, whether child, lover, or old man, are held together by
the phenomenon of the bird.

The proof of the vacuum will be the asphyxiation of the bird in the
airless glass sphere. The spread-winged bird, lit so dramatically and
centrally, has to be in some sense a replacement for the Paraclete of a
prescientific tradition. It may be the ultimate answer to the iconoclastic churchmen's attack on "the Holy Ghost in the form of a dove,
and all the vain worshipping of God, devised by men's fantasies."[23]
And it is remythologized in the same way that Hogarth revived classical statues by placing them in contemporary situations in his *Analysis
of Beauty* plate. But the bird's exact function and status remain more
doubtful than those of Hogarth's statues.

The emphasis in Wright's painting seems not so much on transfor-
mational iconography as on another sort of mutation, from the surface of the glass sphere to the vacuum within, from a living bird to

inanimate matter, that is, primarily from beauty to death (as from passive bird to active male scientist). As if illustrating the moment the Abbé Raguenet referred to in classical sculpture, "the very moment from Life to Death, the instant of the last breath," Wright's point is the ephemerality of the bird but more precisely its hovering on the margin of life and death, in the control of the scientist. The boy is shown lowering a birdcage to receive it after the experiment: the bird *will* survive. But the bird, like the old man, like the young couple's love, and even like the children, embodies a moment of transition between states of being like that of the Dying Gladiator or Niobe. As well, of course, it embodies a transition between bird and some kind of an eighteenth-century Paraclete.

Wright's fascination with transmutations appears as an almost compulsive feature of his work. His iron forges and smithies, for example, show none of that detail of metal-working machinery, of stock forms, shapes, and products so carefully chronicled in the plates of Diderot's *Encyclopédie*. We perceive, in contrast to Diderot's documentation, an appearance that undoes our conceptual expectations, replacing our faith in the solidity of objects with an experience of transmutation. In his late series of burning cottages and Vesuvian eruptions, which demonstrate his mastery of light, Wright makes use of this mastery to undermine our faith in a stable ontological center in our relationship to apparently unchanging objects.

The validation of the both-and quality of the object-in-transition is in the expressions of the spectators. Candlelight, as artificial light, plays traditionally on spiritual contexts for illumination; the object illuminated, in *vanitas* scenes, reveals, ironically, the transience of beauty and pleasure. Take the case of the early paintings that show a girl reading a letter by candlelight: it is the letter that is transfigured by the light, and its reflection in the girl's face indicates the power not of that phenomenologically trivial object but of her reading of it. Something is in the letter (we presume only "sweet nothings") which in fact expresses desire but is reflected as love on her transfigured face and anger on a second lover's as he discovers in her heart desire for another man.

Wright may be thought to have reduced Hogarth's statuary yard to a single art object and changed the predominantly moral-aesthetic contrast in Hogarth (and in another follower, Johann Zoffany) to a more elemental contrast of man-made and natural objects. In his *Academy by Lamplight* (1768–69, fig. 26) he takes as a model Hogarth's satiric subscription ticket, *Boys Peeping at Nature* (1731, fig. 14). The

26. Wright, An Academy by Lamplight *(1768–69), painting.*

idol being covered, unveiled, in both senses of veil (conceal, protect the senses), and responded to worshipfully or in other ways is a model for the situation of Wright's *Academy by Lamplight.* All of the virtue or vice, the beauty or ugliness or sublimity, indeed the reality or art of the object itself, is in the perception of the living viewers within and without the painting (at least one of whom has fallen in love with the statue). One of the points of the parallel position in the series of paintings of the orrery and the sculpture of the Gladiator with the views of Vesuvius erupting is that a similar range of response is elicited by a mechanism or a work of art as by a natural object.

We might also explain Wright's paintings as a conscious reaction to the Reynolds figure of the 1750s and 1760s who poses and dresses and in some Reynoldsian sense *is* a god, goddess, or hero. Reynolds is consciously elevating these figures as a painter in the tradition and style of his canonical models Michelangelo, Raphael, and Titian. The ontological security of even a portrait like Reynolds's *Mrs. Siddons as the Tragic Muse* (1784, Huntington), an actress in a role, is stunning compared with the insecurity of *Brooke Boothby*. Reynolds's figures and their poses, costumes, and settings are unified by the clear synonymy of forms and brushwork; while Wright's every detail emphasizes contingency and difference. Although this can simply be called realist painting or portraiture, I think we have seen enough of Wright's subject paintings to know that his subject is an ontological uneasiness, whether in the direction of transcendence, negation, or only difference.

In order to connect Wright's fables with larger issues of the time, however, I am going to argue for another explanation: that he finds his deeper reverberation of transcendence by building on a branch of the portrait tradition for which *Brooke Boothby* can stand as an example. I am not suggesting that all of Wright's many portraits function in this way, but only that *Brooke Boothby* overlaps with his history paintings in a way that allows us to ask whether Wright paints from different assumptions than those enunciated by Reynolds. While Reynolds ostensibly paints the living image, Wright finds a model in the tradition of funerary sculpture.

Both are attempts to use the artist's image in order to hold something that is passing or will be lost through aging or death, to maintain its presence while acknowledging its absence. But the funerary sculpture is more immediately an image that tries to recover something that is irrecoverable. An image can outlast what it represents—it has a survival power denied to humans, though it is trivial set against the objects and forces of nature.

In portrait painting the perceiver—the patron, the subject, or, even later the survivors—can take pleasure in the imitation and in the beauty of the image. Funerary sculpture builds into its image, if in no other way than through the presence of the sarcophagus and inscription, the stronger aesthetic pleasure of catharsis resulting from the ambiguous jointure of beauty and death, or the memory of a loved one and death, or fullness and absence. It may be that such artists as Wright (following Burke) realized that it is possible to elicit the feeling of beauty or sublimity in the spectator *because* of the loss or absence objectified in the empty object—and internalized by the mourner.

Angelica Kauffmann's *Cleopatra Decorating the Tomb of Mark Antony* (fig. 27) is a literal transference of the funerary convention into paint, of which the primary source was Poussin's *Et in Arcadia Ego*.[24] But Wright again shows us the implications of the structure: one form is the widow kneeling by the body of her dead husband within a tomblike tent (1789, Yale Center for British Art) and another is the young woman in the fable of the origin of painting who traces the profile of her sleeping lover on the wall just before his departure for the wars (Washington, National Gallery). The woman mourning her dead husband is the conventional funerary symbol, whereas the woman outlining the profile of her sleeping but present lover is mourning in a more special sense: she is herself creating his monument. If the other paintings are fables of the function of the art object in relation to the response of spectators, this one is a fable of the artist himself. There are no spectators; there is not yet an absence, though the preparation for mourning, for filling the absence, is at hand.

We might call this the fable of portrait painting. It can be done by a careful copying that recovers and preserves something experienced, loved, and lost (or feared to be passing). In these terms we can see Wright's *Blacksmith's Forge* not as Cummings's elevating of "modern steel-forgers" but rather as a preservation of the lost blacksmith—as within the scene the ingot is a preservation of an even more remote loss—mediated by the "survivors" gathered around. Again, we might see Reynolds as the Englishman who tries to use the classical canon not (in Hogarth's or Wright's way) by abstracting principles of form but by treating the sculptures and paintings as though they were themselves the departing lover and copying out their forms as tried and true sepulchres in which to inter the living figures of friends and patrons.

Reynolds's portraits rather than Wright's painting of the widow and the dead soldier lead to the related phenomenon of all those paintings of deathbed scenes so popular from Gavin Hamilton's *Death of Hector*, based on Poussin's *Death of Germanicus*, to West's *Death*

27. *Angelica Kauffmann*, Cleopatra Decorating the Tomb of Mark
    Antony *(R.A. 1770), painting.*

of General Wolfe and John Singleton Copley's *Death of Lord Chatham* or
Death of Major Pierson. In West's painting the mourners are all in harmony with one another, sharing a common grief, which (sharing
Burke's assumptions) is objectified in Wolfe's body. But the center of
the composition is also—as has often been noted—based on a Pietà,

and so there is a sense of joy in the observers and transcendence in the dead body. Wolfe dies at the moment of the British victory of Quebec and the rise of the British Empire. (The painting was made ten years after Wolfe's death when all the political consequences were clear.) West is doing something quite different from Wright—celebrating rather than analyzing—and yet the very composition of the Pietà, the very grief of the mourners, now express an alienation from the man Wolfe who is no longer that but something like a funerary monument in relation to the bones within and the mourners without.

Being deprived by death or disaster is part of the experience of these paintings. In all of them the object is of an ambiguous status; and the emphasis is on the responses of the periphery, which has lost touch with its object of desire, and yet has internalized a closer, transcendent contact, which is the tenor of the aesthetic experience.

Gavin Hamilton found in Homer and Poussin a vehicle for his contemporaries' concern with transcendent subjects (the death of a hero at the moment of victory, or at the moment of defeat given a spiritual victory) in an immanent world, imperialist England in the 1760s. No major English art followed that particular line of development, but the potentiality was there all the same. In France Jacques-Louis David learned from the precedent, and a great tradition of painting followed, centered on the morally and spiritually ambiguous act of revolution against constituted authority, in a Brutus, a Horatius, a Socrates, and eventually a Marat.

I am suggesting that the form adopted and explored for beauty in the 1760s and 1770s was the pathetic response (among other responses) to a center of emptiness and/or transcendence, or the one becoming the other, and that a model—or at least an analogue—was tomb sculpture, which was per se a filling of absence, a surrounding of emptiness, a representation of transition. The aesthetic is now attached to, or in congruence with, the pathetic, and by means of the epitaphic inscription on the tomb, with the moral. Wright's paintings are merely a more sophisticated, self-aware version of these monuments. They are about the aesthetic experience as developed by Shaftesbury and Hutcheson and remorselessly analysed by Hume. The reactions projected by the apothegm "Beauty is in the eye of the beholder," materialized, look something like a Wright subject painting—and in turn reflect upon the straightforward, unself-conscious demonstration of the tomb sculpture.

In the mid-eighteenth century the tendency I detect—to engage in the modes of making, breaking, and remaking (and the aesthetic

experience that follows)—is followed by a reaction that finds pleasure in monuments—in precisely the "unabused images" the Calvinists had spared—and in memory. This was the other side of iconoclasm:
if one aspect was to destroy the idols, the other was to preserve memory; to enjoy an aesthetics based on memory, compensation for loss,
focused most intensely on the dead, but allowing the dead to stand
for all that is absent or lost.

THE WOMAN ON THE TOMBSTONE

> Of all thy blameless Life the sole Return
> My Verse, and Queensb'ry weeping o'er thy Urn.
> [Pope, *Epistle to Arbuthnot*, ll. 259–60]

The great majority of sculptures in England were funerary monuments. After the Reformation and the powerful tradition of iconoclasm that followed, there were no religious icons, relatively few
statues of kings and heroes and little or no opportunity for self-
expression in sculpture. As portraiture offered English painters the
greatest opportunities, so funerary monuments offered English sculp-
tors the freest play, but also the limiting assumptions, with which to
develop their aesthetic powers. A history of these monuments would
yield the same aesthetic principles I have outlined above in painting.

Sculpture itself, as opposed to painting, was a mode—Roman in authority—for stabilizing, eternalizing, as well as politicizing, fame. The
idea of sculpture, as transmitted by the Renaissance, was summed up
in the words monumentality, elevation (literally a figure raised on
a high pedestal), fixedness, permanence, and the embodiment of
power. As Byron said, speaking of his own bust by Thorwaldsen, "A
picture is a different matter . . .—but a bust looks like putting up pretensions to permanency—and smacks something of a hankering for
public fame rather than private remembrance."[25] Whereas painting
(as in the portraits of, for example, Titian or Rubens) attempted to
approximate these qualities but always contradicted the apparent
permanence of sculpture and so the power it tried to embody, with
the shimmering and shifting patterns of color and chiaroscuro—as
did poetry to an even greater degree with the slipperiness of its words.

The two traditions of English sculpture in the first half of the century corresponded, as David Bindman (following Edgar Wind) has

shown, to two opposing camps of politics and aesthetics: one, whose exemplar was the Rysbrack who sculpted Walpole, can be associated with Shaftesbury, classical Rome, civic humanism, and the taste of the connoisseur. The other camp, whose sculptural exemplar was Louis-François Roubiliac, associated itself with the various terms I have grouped around Swift, Hogarth, and Fielding.[26]

An obvious way to put in question the civic humanist statue is to emphasize the funerary nature of sculpture; indeed to sculpt the dead on tombs rather than the great living "heroes" in public squares; further, to reduce their figures on the tombs to the periphery or to a pendant profile on a medallion, centralizing a mourning woman or an allegory of Time, Death, and the mourner. Or if one must make living portraits, the sculptor may show them not as heroic public men but in their private, out of office, relaxed, unbuttoned aspect.

The two kinds of subject for which Roubiliac was renowned were intimate, casual portraits and emotionally charged funerary allegories (the great examples of which still dominate Westminster Abbey). Both avoid, except in an allegorical mode, the single significant moment whether of action or death, moving the attention to the extended passivity of mourning.

The portraits include his supreme achievement, the many portrait busts, noted for the intensity of their likeness and aliveness, but also, moving toward the funerary monuments, the full-length statues of the living *and* the dead—George Frideric Handel, Sir Isaac Newton, and William Shakespeare. In these the liveliness of the living (as well as the unofficial) is recovered in death; the portrait precedes or transcends death. Roubiliac's trademark is the dangling foot, the half-off slipper, the bulging-open coat, unbuttoned, revelatory, opening before us in the belly of the Great Man. If his living Handel in Vauxhall lets his coat hang open and his slipper dangle, the dead Handel in Westminster Abbey slouches over the edge of his monument; the moment of transition between composer and private citizen has become the transgressed edge of life and death.

The relaxed living figure of the dead was not invented by Roubiliac. It was introduced to England by Guelfi's cross-legged James Craggs in Westminster Abbey (1727), but was best known in Scheemakers's Shakespeare (1740, fig. 28), also in the Abbey. As Nicholas Penny says, " a concern to portray the deceased in a pious or devotional posture is not particularly conspicuous in grand monuments erected in England during the first two-thirds of the eighteenth century."[27] But

The Cloud-cupt Tonire
The Gorgeous Polaces
The Solemn Temples,
The Great Globe itself.
Yea all which it Inherit.
Shall Dissolve;
And like the begideps fabrick of a Uifion
Leeaue not a wreck behind.

28. *Peter Scheemakers, Monument to Shakespeare (1740), sculpture.*

the source of this pose is what I want to indicate: the antique *Pothos* or "longing" statue (attributed to Scopas) which was thought to be a funerary monument, perhaps because longing was an appropriate funerary sentiment.[28] It presumably represented the yearning or desire of the mourner, but in England this was translated into an image of the dead as caught in a moment of casual indifference—a private, personal matter that in some sense stimulates the *Pothos* in the mourner who remembers this aspect of the deceased. It is, I presume, a confusion of the figure who longs (mourns) for the deceased and the figure of the mourned, longed-for deceased. On the other hand, there were cross-legged statues illustrated in Bernard de Montfaucon's *Antiquités*, the Medici Mercury, for example, and the informality may have been intended as primarily a memory of the deceased when alive.[29]

That something of the ambiguity of this figure on a funerary monument was recognized is evident if we recall first Hogarth's Antinous, the model for an ancient monument to a lost beloved, and second Gainsborough's tongue-in-cheek portrait of David Garrick in the cross-legged pose of Scheemakers's Shakespeare but with his arm proprietarily around the frozen bust of Shakespeare against which he leans. Gainsborough's conflation of poses and images implies that Garrick regards himself as both "longing" for the lost Shakespeare and longed-for by his own spectators, as both proprietor of Shakespeare and (though still living) a monument in his own right.[30]

The ambiguity (of life-death, celebration, commemoration, and nature-art) which is apparent in the simple standing figure is allegorized in the grandest monuments in Westminster Abbey. If Roubiliac's first way of dealing with the hero was to represent him in undress, the other was to render the deadness or pastness of heroism in allegory. John Wesley placed his sculpture accurately when he wrote that his Hargrave and Nightingale monuments are the only truly Christian ones in Westminster Abbey. What he meant was that they are not in the classical idiom of Rysbrack's monuments to Newton and Stanhope, which memorialize a hero, but deal with the ordinary Christian life, the situation of death, and the response to loss in a local way. These monuments were, appropriately, accused by Shaftesbury, Jonathan Richardson, and Reynolds of being in (gothic) bad taste, tainted by Roman Catholicism.[31]

What Roubiliac was making in the 1750s was the sculptural equivalent of Hogarth's enterprise in the 1730s and 1740s. These relate to Hogarth's history paintings as the cross-legged standing figure does

29. *Louis-François Roubiliac, Monument to Lady Elizabeth Nightingale (1761), sculpture.*

to Augustan portraiture. (Hogarth learned himself, in the portrait way, from Roubiliac's full-length lounging sculpture of Handel.) Roubiliac was a close friend (his bust of Hogarth convinces that *this* was how Hogarth looked) and represents the same assumptions about art. Roubiliac's Nightingale monument of 1761 (fig. 29) sums up the Hogarth tradition in the idiom of the monument. It is constructed of three figures like those in Hogarth's painting *Satan, Sin, and Death* (fig. 20), itself a genteel echo of the conversation-picture situation of lover, daughter, and father in the *Beggar's Opera* paintings. Roubiliac's version has Mr. Nightingale pathetically trying to intervene between his wife and Death brandishing a deadly dart. But seen from the far left, the wife is between the two; once again the woman seems to be mediating between her husband and Death. The spectator to this confrontation with death as an example of terror and obscurity is the individual passerby in the aisle of Westminster Abbey. There is no pedestal, and so we are on the same level as Death emerging from a metal door that seems to open directly out of the wall. This is the same gate Death fought over with Satan, but in the aisle of the Abbey it appears to be an extension of the sarcophagus above, and we are primarily aware of the empty darkness beyond the door which indicates the whole edifice as one great hollow shell.[32]

THE reclining figure on the sarcophagus, most impressively present in the Rysbrack–Kent memorial to Newton and the Roubiliac memorial to the Duke of Argyle (Westminster Abbey, fig. 30), was a replacement of the old recumbent figure, and in a way a more dignified version of the seemingly alive figure who stands upright cross-legged. The reclining figure is alone, retrospective, and (if you will) melancholy, but above all *transitional* between the states of life and death, and observed by one or more spectators (in the manner of Wright's tomblike compositions).

In Chester Cathedral there is an inscription to John Vernon, dated 1797 (aged 72) which problematizes in this way the relationship of the deceased and the erector of the monument:

> Polite, learned, ingeniously upright,
>   To the best of Husbands
>   ANN, his afflicted Relict,
>   Erected this,
>   She departed this Life March 22nd 1812
>   Aged 88.

30. Roubiliac, Monument to John, Duke of Argyl (1745—49), sculpture.

We are reminded that the tombstone of the husband, inscribed by a grieving widow, is in time going to be—as she and we know—her own as well.

There is a bed tomb in Worcester Cathedral (by Epaphanius Evesham) which shows the widow reclining, her surviving husband resting on his elbow watching her. Two of their children, one on each side, are included. This is the tomb of Anne, wife of Sir William Waller. Sir William erected the tomb for her, but when he himself died he ended up, as it happened, not with her but in the Tothill St. Chapel in Westminster. The irony underlines the fragility of the survivor's role: he/she is certainly sooner or later going to join the deceased, but at the moment, on the bed tomb, he/she is both alive and dead. Alive at this moment, when the mate has died, but dead soon, perhaps before the monument is completed; certainly without disturbing the sculptural relationship that will remain between the two, the deceased and the survivor.

The monument in Worcester Cathedral (by John Bacon) for Richard Solly (d. 1803, aged 33) shows his mourning widow and three children bending over the sarcophagus, on the side of which we read: "Absent from the Body / But / Present with the Lord." It is this drama of absence/presence that these monuments try to embody: we see the surviving family represented, and we see the sarcophagus which represents—literally contains—the deceased and yet (as the inscription tells us) is at the same time empty and, transcendently, filled.

These are, of course, the echoes we catch in Wright's *Brooke Boothby* (fig. 22; he was himself an active planner of funerary monuments for others[33]) and in Wright's other paintings of objects that are in a state of transition. In Wright's own time the popular funerary monument showed *Pothos* as a kneeling figure, praying or mourning the deceased, often mourning over an urn. This is most often a woman, an idealized widow or allegorical figure. Joseph Wilton's monument to Lady Anne Dawson (1769–74) shows the urn with her husband and son approaching to be met by an angel assuring them by its gesture that the soul of the deceased has risen to heaven. The urn, like Christ's sepulcher, is empty because of the implied transfiguration, but (as in the tomb of Miravan's ancestors) the fullness is imparted to the mourners.[34]

The mausoleum represented in *Miravan* was by this time a common burial place in England. Hawksmoor's at Castle Howard, completed in 1742, was the first in Western Europe since antiquity, and another of his Roman allusions. Several followed in the 1750s and

1760s, and dozens in the 1770s and 1780s;[35] so that Wright's representation draws on the added importance given by the mausoleum to the family tomb. By enclosing tombs within a similarly tomblike structure, dimly lit, often from an opening in the ceiling, the architect—and so Wright the painter—extended the ambiguity of life-death to the inclusion of a tomb/house which was architecturally a small version of the great country house in which the family lived (in some cases indistinguishable from a casino or small temple in the park).[36]

WE have looked at the Venus in Hogarth's Sculpture Yard, noticed her centrality—or rather the centralizing of a marginal figure—and her associations with on the one hand idolatry and on the other a funerary or memorial mood. Primarily, however, we saw the hero feminized. This mediator reappears on tombstones in the inscriptions and in the sculptures of the more ambitious monuments. These, the surviving and most legible stones, are inside churches, on tablets affixed to the walls accompanied by modest—sometimes not so modest—bas-reliefs and sculptures. Here is an example—much abbreviated—of a long and complex saga from one wall of Bath Abbey: Edward Temple, d. 1787, is initially identified as a commissioner of H. M. Navy, and the remainder of the inscription reads:

> He married Ann Sophia, Daughter of Sir William Temple Baronet of Kempsey in the County of Worcester: by whom he left no surviving Issue. As the last token of Conjugal affection and regard She hath caused this marble to be erected March 20th 1787.

The widow's inscription, in which the father-in-law's name figures as prominently as the deceased's, may even imply (at least to readers of eighteenth-century novels) that Temple married above himself and died a failure to perpetuate his wife's distinguished line. In any case, it was the woman who erected the monument to her husband's memory, who emerges as the living protagonist of the inscription.

There are many tombstones that are more about family genealogy than about the deceased husband: "By the Death of this Gentleman an ancient and respectable Family in Ireland became extinct," we read on the tomb of Lt. Col. Robert Walsh Esq., d. 1788. But more interesting is rather the presence (in the inscription) of the "inconsolable widow" grieving over the loss of Robert Walsh and/or of an heir.

The very long inscription to the memory of Herman Katencamp in Bath Abbey sums up such inscriptions, and I shall quote it entire:

Sacred to the Memory of Herman Katencamp Esquire. / Many Years His *Majesty's Consul General* for the Protection of Trade / in the two Sicilies and in *Spain*. / He assisted & maintained with Dignity, Firmness, and incorruptible Integrity / the Liberty and Privileges of the British Flag. / Many brave Seamen, / who, but for his Energy and Perseverance in the Performance of his Duty, / would have perished in a Foreign Land, / are now living to serve their Country & bless the Memory of their beneficent Protector. / His Charity was unbounded: / Friendless Strangers of whatever Nation never left his Door without Relief, / and were frequently heard to exclaim, / "This Man is indeed Representative of his Country." / His Manners were amiable: His Disposition warm sincere candid and affectionate. / He never injured or offended any Man: and never witheld, even for a moment, / his Pity and Forgiveness from those who offended him. / His Mind, strong clear and comprehensive, was cultivated by a liberal Education. / His Faults were but as transient Shades on his many and brilliant Virtues, / which rendered their Possessor an Honor to Human Nature. / His Widow, the Partner of his Bosom for thirty-four Years, / knows what she has here written to be a true, though faint, Portrait of the excellent Man / to whose memory she consecrates this poor token of Gratitude and love.

The monument (dated 1808), by the sculptor John Bacon, shows a woman grieving over an urn, decking it with flowers; her mourning robe reaches from her head to cover the urn. The earlier part of the inscription reads like a paraphrase of Fielding's description of Squire Allworthy early on in *Tom Jones*. But these words about Herman Katencamp are attributed not to a normative author, an omniscient narrator, but to an interested female party, who identifies herself near the end, perhaps sounding the way Pamela's epitaph for Mr. B. might have sounded.

The elements of these typical late eighteenth-century monuments are: the deceased, the sculpture, the inscription, and the relict who erected the monument and dictated the inscription, whose name and role are admitted only at the end, in a sort of revelation, creating a perspective on what has gone before. The inscription consists of her words; the monument is therefore about her grief *and* about her husband's virtues and his parting, death, and absence. She is erector of the monument (and, we might say, "carrier of the flame"), but also survivor and mediator between the dead and the living.

A more familiar type of epitaph had the dead speaking to the living. Philippe Ariès, in his history of the customs of dying, identifies this basic form as early as the twelfth century: "What we were, you are. What we are, you will become."[37] One of the most beautiful examples in English is Ben Jonson's *Charles Cavendish to His Posteritie* (cited above). There are dozens of variants still legible on New England headstones from the end of the eighteenth century:

> Death is a debt to Nature due,
> As I have paid it, so must you.   (1795)
>
> As you pass by and cast an eye,
> As you are now so once was I.   (1799)[38]

This message is addressed to a stranger, not a friend of the deceased, who is asked to pause as he/she walks through the graveyard and to "better understand, by means of this visible example, the great Pauline lesson of death. This is a very ancient tradition of the *contemptus mundi* and the *memento mori*."[39]

I have found none of these on surviving English tombstones of the period. But the form I have identified is equally ancient. In the Grosvenor Museum in Chester one finds a surviving stela from Roman England which reads: "To the spirits of the departed, Curatia Dionysia. She lived 40 years. Her heir had this made." Then came the Christian tradition of the admonitory epitaph, and in the sixteenth and seventeenth centuries the individual begins to be subordinated to his family. The voice, inscription, or personality of the testator now becomes that of his family. In the first place, as Ariès says, the "affection of the family—conjugal, parental, or filial love—was beginning to replace the noble official merits [of the individual] in the changed world of epitaph writers" (p. 230). In the second place, the epitaph began to be divided into two distinct parts: no longer the message to the living and prayer for the dead, but the "first . . . devoted to the eulogy, the biographical notice of the deceased, the second to the survivor who commissioned the epitaph and laid the monument. For example, the long accounts of [one such hero and his family] are followed by this signature: 'His father ordered this marble, which will provide for posterity an eternal monument to the virtue of so worthy a son and the grief *of so worthy a father*'" (pp. 230–31). In the third place, the rise of the "affective family," held together by affection rather than patriarchal authority, began to place more emphasis on loss—on lost children, for example—and on love. The emphasis shifted to "the regret of the survivors, especially of the family," and (particularly noticeable in England after reading Ariès's predominantly French epitaphs) from military heroism to love and its public aspect charity.

31. Roubiliac, Monument to George Lynn (1758), sculpture.

32. Roubiliac, Monument to Richard Boyle, Viscount Shannon (after 1755), sculpture.

33. Roubiliac, Hargrave Monument (1757), sculpture.

The feature that stands out in the mid- and late-eighteenth century in England is a feature not remarked by Ariès: the emphasis on the widow, who in most case survives her husband, a woman who mourns over the dead. Her centrality to the fact of death and mourning, though strongly implied in the epitaphs, is manifest in the sculpture that accompanies the more opulent monuments.

The prominence of the female figure has many sources. Simply on the strength of actuarial tables, the mourning figure is most often female. Another source is, of course, the suppressed Roman Catholic figure of Mary the Mother, the very prototype of maternal mourning and intercession who should have been long iconoclasted but in this form returns (as she did in Hogarth's paintings and prints). We can find analogues on the one hand in the antiheroism of the She-Tragedies of the 1700s which replaced a king with a domestic heroine and on the other (as we saw in Chapter 4) in Hogarth's engraved "modern moral subjects" of the 1730s.

But the woman on the tomb is decidedly not dead, not a Jane Shore or Calista but Hogarth's (and Burke's) beautiful, domestic, social woman—mediating between life and death. Though we know she will die, she continues to live in the context of her tomb function. She weeps for the dead, but she is no Antigone figure, who entombs herself; she remains with us, a part of the world, as we would expect her to given the Hogarthian (and indeed Burkean) aesthetic of the beautiful. There is accordingly—as even the example of Roubiliac shows—not a "sublime" tomb sculpture; rather even the grandest tombs of the 1750s and 1760s are "beautiful" and "modern." By the heroic imperial age of the 1770s and 1780s the huge monuments to Fox, Pitt, Nelson, and Wellington are adumbrated in such tombs as the one to Lord Mansfield in Westminster Abbey, which seems a strange materialization of the papal tomb of a magistrate in Hogarth's *Analysis*, Plate 1.

The two most prominent figures of the sculptural tradition of funerary monuments had been the recumbent figure, the deceased, and the figure kneeling in prayer—who was sometimes an intercessor, more often an image of the deceased him/herself. The wife appears, when she appears, recumbent beside her husband (or kneeling next to him praying). At the end of the seventeenth century, one of the recumbent figures begins to rise on an elbow and regard the other—thus indicating who is the survivor, the erector of the monument, and the mourner. Among the small number of opulent monuments in English churches, this mode became fairly common in the eighteenth century, but the more "popular" or modest form taken by monuments showed (in order of increasing complexity) an urn, a draped urn, and an urn mourned over by a woman. She may be identified as the widow or she may be only an allegorical figure, but she fills, in the little drama of family and gender, the role of a wife. There is a monument in Bath Abbey to the memory of Sir Richard Hussey Bickerton, Bt., d. 1832, erected (the inscription explains) by his widow. The sculpture (by Sir Francis Chantrey) shows a woman grieving against a plinth on which sits a draped urn bearing his name; on the plinth his profile is represented parallel to hers.

In the great monuments executed in England in the 1750s and 1760s by Roubiliac the woman—sometimes wife, more often allegorical figure—comes to serve as an intercessor, mourning his passing and clinging to the symbolic urn (figs. 31, 32). But she also serves upon occasion as part of a particularized romantic triangle, suggesting, even when not representing, husband, wife, and (the third figure) Time-Death, that Other who threatens the security of the domestic pair (fig. 29).

Indeed Time threatens the stone itself in which the group is represented: for the message of the artist who sculpted this elaborate group has now been added to the epitaphic structure. The drama is now one of permanence and transience in the particular terms of art and nature: the struggle of the figures in the sculpture with the forces of change and dissolution is augmented by the struggle of the sculptor (whose name also appears on the monument), working in lasting stone that is placed in a public area where future generations can be counted on to see it, with the same forces of dissolution. So there are the deceased, the surviving widow, and the sculptor/artist— all named and placed in an agon with Time and Death.

About the same time, Hogarth was representing Father Time as the true iconoclast. In *Time Smoking a Picture* (1761) Time is gnawing at the Torso Belvedere, surrounded by broken statues and mutilated paintings. From Hogarth's point of view, Time is two things: the connoisseur's accomplice, lopping off arms and heads of antique sculptures with his scythe, darkening paintings with the smoke of his pipe (a Dutch emblem of transience), and connecting the two by running his scythe into the canvas to make a great tear; in effect he makes art by destroying it. But Time also figures Hogarth the iconoclast of antique art, who in the Sculpture Yard enlivens dead art and replaces the idolized with the new, local, commonplace, and useful.

Chapter 6

The Aesthetics of Possession: Reynolds, Stubbs, Constable, and Others

LABOR AESTHETICIZED—PAINTING POSSESSED

Sir William Blackstone wrote in his *Commentaries* (1766) on the "Rights of Things":

> There is nothing which so generally strikes the imagination, and engages the affections of mankind, as the right of property . . . that sole and despotic dominion which one man claims and exercises over the external things of the world, in total exclusion of the rights of any other individual in the universe.[1]

Not that property-possession is itself a new subject for scholars of art. It has been extensively utilized by John Berger, Raymond Williams, John Barrell, and others.[2] Beginning with Berger, however, the center of interest has been the property owner—the patron who commissioned the portrait of *his* Last Duchess, *a* nude, or his (or someone else's) landscape, thus taking possession of it. If, as in the case of Barrell, some attention is paid to the artist who executed the representation, it is largely focused on the spoken or unspoken instructions of the patron-owner, whether this is a person or a hegemony. Barrell deals with the artist only in so far as he is trapped in a determinist net of ideology.

My concern is with the artist himself and his strategies, successful or not, as an active party to the contest for possession of the representation. I use "possession" as my term rather than property because it extends beyond the legal ownership implied by "property." As Blackstone wrote: "The right of possession (though it carries with it a strong presumption) is not always conclusive evidence of the right of property, which may still subsist in another man"[3]—that other man being possibly the artist, as opposed to either the person who commissioned the picture, the owner who is its subject, or yet an Other who acquires it and uses it in some personal way.

"Possession" then means "control or occupancy of property without regard to ownership": my emphasis is on "occupancy," the ancient definition of property, which is sometimes an issue in contention between the artist and his patron. But I also prefer the word "possession" because of its secondary meaning of "a domination by something (as an evil spirit, a passion, or an idea)," or "a psychological state in which an individual's normal person is replaced by another." I am thinking of the portraits and history paintings, "old master" paintings and sculptures, represented by Hogarth as possessions that also possess the collector.

We are all aware of the notorious laws in eighteenth-century England which made theft a capital offense (murder a lesser one). This property consciousness supported the tendency to define oneself in terms of one's property—and to intimate the paradox that one *is*, or at least is dominated by, "possessed by" one's property.

What allows us to focus on the artist as possessor—indeed what allows us to employ a discourse of property in eighteenth-century England—is the authority of John Locke. Of primary importance is the way Locke accounted for the way man came by, or acquired a right to, his property. His *Second Treatise on Government* (pub. 1704)[4] was written in reaction to Robert Filmer's argument in *Patriarcha* (1680) that property right derives from Adam's original inheritance from God, that is, from the "supposition, that God gave the World to *Adam,* and his heirs in Succession, exclusive of all the rest of his Posterity."[5] By contrast, Locke places man's right to property in his labor.

Property, as defined in Chapter 5 of the *Second Treatise,* begins with the premise that "*labour* put a distinction between" the land a man "encloses" and the "common" or "waste" land: "*As much Land* as a Man Tills, Plants, Improves, Cultivates, and can use the Product of, so much is his *Property.* He by his Labour does, as it were, inclose it from the Common" (32, p. 332). This amounts to a service tenure, and one that, to begin with, embodies the georgic assumption of labor n a postlapsarian world based on "tilling," "planting," "improving," and "cultivating." Georgic principles also govern—or correspond to—Locke's picture of the mind in the *Essay concerning Human Understanding* itself (1690), that blank sheet or empty room on which simple ideas are projected.[6] Art is therefore discovery and utilization, not creation. Man's "power,"

> however managed by art and skill, reaches no farther than to compound and divide the materials that are made to his hand; but can do nothing toward the making the least particle of new matter, or destroying one atom of what is already in being.

This passage leads both to the conclusion that man for all his pride is only "a worm shut up in a cabinet," which underlies Swift's satiric imagery, and to the georgic assumptions of Pope's poetry.

In Locke's terms, we are all the workmanship of God, and the distinction he makes is between creating (and so absolutely owning) something and, what all men can do, "working" it in the manner of the georgic farmer. Men are God's "Property, whose Workmanship they are, made to last during his, not one another's Pleasure." And so the metaphor of God-the-Maker introduces at the highest analogical level the idea of the proprietary authority of workmanship (as opposed to mere occupancy). The metaphor of God and Man as master and servant, on the other hand, continues to imply a relationship like that in the Parable of the Talents ("Servants of one Sovereign Master, sent into the World by his order," and so on), which can taper off into the relationship of patron and dependent.[7] Making, property, and dependence are inextricably linked in Locke's model. Thus if *labor* is one term that describes ownership for Locke, *stewardship* is another: "we are *pro tem* custodians and managers of God's property—we have, if you like, leasehold interests for life, or, better, we are put in as managers."[8]

Locke's evaluation of work is antithetical to Shaftesbury's remarks about mechanical labor. As Alan Ryan has pointed out, when Locke uses Aristotle "it is with none of Aristotle's emphasis on the way trade and every day work disqualify a man from politics,"[9] that is, making, or mechanic labor, is not a disabler for Locke as it was for Shaftesbury and his tradition.

On the other hand, although Locke certainly implies that "property detached from a concern for its proper use" (that is, merely collected) is excessive, his insistence that rights are based on property could also be taken to imply the advantage of accumulating property. And this accumulation, of course—of house, estate, and collections, all expressing conspicuous consumption—is what comes to define the Whig magnate. Both the artist-maker and the purchaser-collector coexist uneasily in Locke's system.

For Locke's vocabulary also emphasizes the "otherness" of the common land and the aggression that is implicit in the act of cultivating, working, and enclosing—in short appropriating. As one classical scholar has said, in the *Georgics* "man's violent imposition upon the natural world deserves as much stress as his cooperation with it." [10] The key terms Locke uses in his *Second Treatise* besides "labor" and "improvement" are "inclosure," "subdue," and "appropriate." [11] And they are only intensified when he produces the example of the deer that is the property of the Indian "who hath killed it" (and of the fish that is the property of the fisherman who "catches" it). "Before the Appropriation of Land, he who gathered as much of the wild Fruit," says Locke, "*killed, caught,* or *tamed,* as many of the Beasts as he could" (37, p. 336, my emphasis).

Locke permits us to look at eighteenth-century English art through a discourse of property in which the users are pitted against the makers: the spectators, connoisseurs, and critics, as well as the owner, patron, and connoisseur, with their belief in the primacy of idea, *disegno,* and intellectual distance vs. the painter or poet and the primacy of the labor or touch of his hand and the *self*-possession of the art object.

Speaking of the poet or painter, rather than "possess" we might say "reclaim" or even "redeem," depending on which discourse we think most appropriate. But in the historical context of a credit economy, possession refers first to property and the landowner; second, it refers to labor and the laborer who makes a product that is therefore *his* property. The situation is complicated, however, by the presence of two other figures: the merchant or middleman who buys and sells the product and the stockjobber, who has no concrete product at all but only manipulates someone else's product—and not as an object but only as marks on paper. The last two figures (who become the protagonists of Adam Smith's economics) fulfill the villainous role of bad steward or mediator we discussed in Chapter 2. It was very much a part of Pope's strategy to link the You or Friend (the lawyer Fortescue), who tries to bring him and Walpole together, with the stockjobber who mediates between the mode of production and the investors and speculators.

Writing and paper center on two loci in Pope's poetry. *The Dunciad* celebrates the results of the printing-publishing boom, as the *Epistle to Bathurst* celebrates the results of the advent of paper money and paper credit, the founding of the Bank of England, the South Sea Company, and the innumerable stock companies that followed: "blest paper credit" is the socio-political, the criminal version of the bad birthday odes that flatter and the scurrilous lies that malign Pope. The ideal becomes that lost time when Cato would have had to carry his bribe in the form of a huge bag of gold or an unwieldy herd of cattle. And those solid material objects remain in the account of the ideal, the Man of Ross, who moves landscapes, erects churches, feeds the poor, and heals the sick, as well as specifically driving out money changers.

The passages in Pope's poetry concerning forged checks and other documents, paper money, stocks, and bonds are centered in the *Epistle to Bathurst* but scattered throughout the Horatian satires and epistles. Japhet's forged will is the refrain of *Bathurst,* and the lines "Let *Budgel* charge low *Grubstreet* on his quill, / And write what e'er he pleas'd, except his *Will*" (ll. 378–79) connect with the bad plays and poems in the *Epistle to Dr. Arbuthnot* which shade off into "Fib, or Sophistry" (l. 91), as satire becomes lampoon and fiction becomes the "Lye" (l. 302). In other words, "a Lye in Verse or Prose [is] the same" (l. 339), and forged wills are the same as Sporus's lies.

Whereas Pope himself, the writer of poetry, "stoop'd to Truth, and moraliz'd his song." Truth is the opposite of lie, but truth is also something more than the "paper credit" of Pope's poetry. In the crucial passage near the end of the *Epilogue to the Satires,* Dialogue 2, truth is the muse (by implication the poet's "Sacred Weapon") who "shall brush . . . away" the fabrications, flatteries, and lies, leaving only truth (ll. 220–27). Truth is the fame that the poet, if he handles his words and sheets of paper properly, reveals, just as Sporus uses his "paper credit" to hide it. It has a reality independent of Pope's poetry; and at the end of his career Pope is asking himself whether, for the sake of his own salvation, to devote himself to poetry or truth, writing or living:

> Heav'ns! was I born for nothing but to write?
> Has Life no Joys for me? or (to be grave)
> Have I no Friend to serve, no Soul to save?   [ll. 271–74]

As these lines in the *Epistle to Dr. Arbuthnot* suggest, Pope is *not* the Man of Ross. His poetry, however devoted to revealing fame or truth, is still part of the mediating printed paper world of *The Dun-ciad* and *Bathurst* as opposed to the life of nature and deeds of the Man of Ross or St. Cecilia (see above, p. 75).

As Pope realized, there is a dangerously close analogy between the stockjobber and the poet himself. He defines himself as a good me-diator—between nature and art, Horace and his own text, and so on. But while that is an easy enough position to maintain (one Pope con-stantly restates), he retains the stigma of the manipulator of paper as opposed to real objects.

WE shall pursue the example of the poet Pope (and then, for con-trast, the painter Hogarth). Pope—a Roman Catholic, dispossessed of property, and without wife or heir—extolls the alternative to pos-session as self-possession. But by doing so (in his imitation of Hor-ace's *Satire* II.ii and *Epistle* II.ii) he keeps within the discourse of property, retaining the memory of Virgilian-Horatian dispossession. He drags in his friend Swift and has him say: "I wish to God this house had been your own," attributing to Swift an admonition about Pope's alienation of property rights. Swift's blunt assertion provokes Pope to the final realization ("What's Property, dear Swift?") that for him the choice between active life in sophisticated London society and rural retirement, contemplation, and simplicity is resolved by his necessarily fragile hold on property.

Here Pope has forced even his friend Swift into the role of Other, of materialist adversary, by putting thing-property words into his mouth, while implying that for himself "property" is something in-ternal, to be "cultivated" and "improved" spiritually rather than in the land. In both the satire and the epistle, however, while Pope *says* that dispossession of things is corrected by a spiritual self-possession, he *shows* that the self-possession rests upon the possession of his Ho-mer copyright and of the Homeric text—and later the Horatian—which he has made his own, Popean text (as self-possession also rests on the possession of a friend like Swift). In a reversal of iconoclastic practice, he attempts to turn the material copyright or the Homeric profits into spirit. Swift himself in his writings, and even Pope's "Swift," uses "property" only in order to break out of the discourse of property altogether, saying in effect, "Poor Pope, employ another form of discourse more appropriate to such as you and I."

The theme, which permeates Pope's later work, is expressed in terms of textual possession, whether by copyright or literary appro-priation. *Satire* II.ii (1734), for example, is specifically designated not an imitation but a "paraphrase," first because, whereas Horace describes Offelus, his ideal of the propertyless man, Pope sets off Bethel (his Offelus) by putting his words in quotation marks—thus further setting off Horace, whose text is printed on the opposite page. Second, whereas Horace spends the last part of the satire explaining Offelus's abstinence by virtue of the political appropriation of his property, Pope at that point switches from quotation to his own voice, therefore to his personal dispossession by the lack of heirs, impending death, and implicitly the dispossession of a Roman Catholic (made explicit in the imitation of *Epistle* II.ii which followed), and so his own Popean alternative of self-possession. And in this alternative he has carefully set himself off from (some distance above) Offelus, while at the same time appropriating Offelus's Roman context of civil war, political dispossession, and personal isolation.

In Pope's imitation of Horace's *Epistle* II.ii (1737) the basic Popean terms *use, property, mind,* and *imitation* share the Lockean vocabulary of mind and property: each makes the "common" land into property by *use*—by cultivating, working, and enclosing it. The Lockean vocabulary of aggressive appropriation dominates this imitation.

One of the accusations that dogged Pope following the *Odyssey* scandal was that he plagiarized, and the accusation was only intensified when he turned to "imitating" Horace. The *Verses Address'd to the Imitator of Horace* (1733) by Lord Hervey and Lady Mary Wortley Montagu asserted that the imitations were failures of both creativity and the dubious art of copying:

> Who can believe, who view the bad and good,
> That the dull Copi'st better understood
> That *Spirit,* he pretends to imitate,
> Than heretofore that *Greek* he did translate?
>   Thine is just such an Image of his *Pen,*
> As thou thy self art of the Sons of Men . . .[12]

These *Verses* served to prompt, in Pope's usual action-response pattern, the *Epistle to Arbuthnot* and the opening of the *Epilogue to the Satires* 1, where the adversarius accuses P. of theft from Horace ("don't I see you steal?"), when in fact the only two lines in the poem that *are* by Horace are those of the adversarius. But the accusations of thievery, declining powers ("Decay of Parts, alas!"), and incompetence (Horace "was delicate, was nice") dealt with in the *Epilogue* become the manifest subject of the imitation of *Epistle* II.ii.

Here Pope starts from the Hervey-Lady Mary contrast of his poetry, a distorted "Image of . . . [Horace's] *Pen*," and his body ("thy self"), a distorted image of "the sons of Men," which he materializes by printing his imitation opposite the Horatian original on facing pages of his text. The first version of the image-copy relationship is the story of a father and his erring son ("My only Son") who was once "caught . . . in a Lye" and has been known "to steal."[13] The son himself is property—in Pope metaphorically and in Horace literally a slave; and whereas Horace's boy (not a son) is a runaway, Pope makes his a thief, like the poet who "steals" from his father Horace. But the verbs connected with the patron, the Colonel to whom the poem is addressed, also refer to his "taking" Pope's poems when they are not forthcoming, as the patron in the story "took the graceless lad" despite the warnings, yet is now complaining of his theft.

The theft-property theme becomes more emphatic as Pope moves through the story of the thief acquitted by Sir Godfrey Kneller and the parallel stories of the poor old soldier whose property is stolen, Achilles whose slave-lover Chriseis is stolen by Agamemnon, and Pope's own father whose estate is confiscated (in a literalizing of the political dispossession of the latter part of *Satire* II.ii) by the Protestant William III. The old soldier reacts to the theft of his money with the familiar Popean action-response pattern:

> This put the Man in such a desp'rate Mind,
> Between Revenge, and Grief, and Hunger join'd,
> Against the Foe, himself, and all Mankind,
> He leapt the Trenches, scal'd a castle-Wall,
> Tore down a Standard, took the Fort and all. [ll. 37–41]

Pope's father, who taught *his* only son to distinguish right from wrong, and whose example in the face of poverty provided a more valuable patrimony than the "Right Hereditary" (l. 64) of land cut off by England's laws, corrects while paralleling the mercenary Frenchman who sold *his* son. By identifying Achilles as "Peleus' Son," Pope compares his own situation and that of Homer's hero, whose wrath was aroused by Agamemnon's tyrannical seizure of his rightful share of the spoils of battle (which happened to be a woman). And King William is an implacable taker in the further sense that he interrupted both the private and the public line of property, the proper hereditary descent of Pope's inheritance as well as of the English throne. At the same time Pope's transformation of the story serves as the contrasting case of his own privileged utilization of the property available to him, the Horatian text.

But the greatest thief of all, transcending the personal and political realms, and leading into the meditation on self-possession in the remainder of the poem, is Time: against whom Pope's poetry emerges as that property beyond the reach of either monarch or Death. As the family metaphor is meant to imply, the Popean text has been inherited by lineal descent, not stolen, from Horace. Implicitly the misshapen text Lady Mary and Hervey satirized as copy and as bastard is reconstituted in *Epistle* II.ii as the actual words of Horace (the father) and Pope's (the son's) utilization of them. Both the Horatian and Popean texts, the word and the spirit of Horace, have demonstrably survived the ravages of Time on the facing pages.

The basis of property—whether Horace's, Pope's father's, or Pope's own—is in labor. Thus Pope contrasts William III's real theft with the use of the land by his father—and so, in the following passage, of Homer's text by Pope the translator—"But (thanks to *Homer*) since I live and thrive, / Indebted to no Prince or Peer alive," ll. 68–69— and so of Horace's text by Pope the imitator. The legal and financial dimension of the copyright is followed once again by the juxtaposition on the page of Horace's text and Pope's use of it, which establishes his right to the property. As Locke tells us, what is at stake with any "common" is "some nobler use, than its bare Preservation" (p. 311), and the Popean utilization of the Horatian "common" includes correction and supplementation. Following Locke, Pope is setting up against "Originality," invention, or creation (processes left to God) a concept of property based on "use". And in the process he is turning the mistaken notion of his own theft into (as he so often does) personal loss, theft, and confiscation at the hands of the Other.

But what in reality does "property" (as in "What's Property, dear Swift?") mean in these satires? It is difficult not to acknowledge that Pope proposes self-possession by in effect possessing—appropriating—his friend Swift (who did not appreciate the borrowing), as he has also, we have seen, appropriated Horace, Horace's Offelus, and indeed Bethel under cover of a metaphor of familial inheritance.

WE began by looking back at Pope for whom property meant, on the one hand, his possession of his own works as source of profit and as establisher of his identity, and on the other, within the context of those works, his possession of Horace and Virgil. In the case of Hogarth, "property" meant the right of the artist to his painted or engraved work. Specifically this meant the artist and engraver, as opposed to the dealer. But the extension was easily made to the original work of art, whose ownership (to follow Locke) derives from the artist's labor, as opposed to the antique sculptures and old master paintings and copies gathered (sold, bought) by the collector or dealer. The latter were mere property, unrelated to a living transaction between painter-medium and a patron or purchaser *from* him— rather, objects that had been removed from the context of their making to the collector's gallery by way of the dealer's (or before that the copyist's) shop.

First, Hogarth's "work" embodied the Lockean valuation of labor as self-expression. The objects he makes are, in short, *self*-expressive, virtually an extension of the self. But at the same time these works are *per se* salable, transferable within a market society. They are an extension of the artist's self but also an alienable version of that self. And so with the sense of ownership comes an accompanying anxiety—and, in Hogarth's case, a need for extra assertion.

The symbolic act of Hogarth's professional career was the Engraver's Act (known as Hogarth's Act), which guaranteed to him the possession of his own engraved works, as opposed to their possession by a patron or printseller; instead they could be distributed to a wide audience, while at the same time remaining his own both in the sense that he derived profit from his own labor and in the sense that he could establish his own context for his works, and therefore their proper meaning.

For Hogarth then property means legal ownership and financial profit, but also, and more important, the determination of its meaning. The latter he sought to accomplish by creating his own context for his product. This context he created by engraving his paintings, selling the engravings himself, providing explanations, and arranging them according to his own plan in folio collections (to be continued after his death through the copperplates he bequeathed to his widow); and with the paintings themselves by establishing their setting vis-à-vis a public audience, not a private collector.[14]

This external establishment of meaning would count for nothing, however, without the internal. *Within* the works he starts with the classical canon; as in the *Analysis*, Plate 1 (or, for that matter, *A Harlot's Progress*), he recontextualizes the canon, making it his own by reanimating it as one of his "modern moral subjects." But he goes further and thematizes the situation itself of property owning, making a satire on the collectors and purchasers. He draws upon the civic humanist notion of luxury as the source of corruption, while at the same time subverting it: *luxuria* in his scenes becomes the civic-humanist collecting of ancient art as objects of *virtu*.

As we have seen, in the Statuary Yard he first invokes the whole area of possessions, pointing to the transformation of art into merchandise—the result of an organized art market, which includes copyists, art-fakers, and connoisseurs devoted to false attributions. The art is transformed by being removed from its original setting and by obliterating history in the sense of both function and context—by replacing its history with canonical and aesthetic formulae. An altarpiece is iconoclasted, not into a pig trough or a doll's cradle, but into a decorative trophy, an item in a collector's gallery, an investment or self-glorification, or merely interior decoration. Thus, with the development of collections and the development of public exhibition space (influentially accomplished by Hogarth himself), what emerges is the ambiguity of the work of art as to its ownership and its meaning. As Hogarth shows, the canonical works can be placed in a garden, gallery, or church, or represented in an engraved copy, or *within* an engraved copy of a gallery or garden, in Hogarth's engraved copy of copies of copies.

Having invoked the area of possessions, Hogarth then shows that only he, the artist, can establish the context of the canonical sculptures—the Venus de Medici, Apollo Belvedere, and so on—and therefore their meaning. Granted, a purchaser of these sculptures can in a private sense establish a context by placing them thus and so in his landscape garden. But Hogarth can do so publicly: and in this sense he has taken possession of the canonical sculptures by changing, "modernizing," their meanings, and making them a part of his aesthetic of the modern.

In Hogarth's terms this is to say that the deepest meanings of the work of art lie beyond the private delectation of the aesthete or the privileged possession of the collector. They are accessible rather to a public—those people who can see the painting exhibited in public or reproduced in an engraving—defined only by an inquiring mind, that is, by the "pursuit [that] makes a great part of the pleasure" of the possessing, as laid out in *The Analysis of Beauty*.

Locke's example of the Indian who has "killed" the deer to make it his property leads directly into an image of the chase: "And even amongst us the Hare that any one is Hunting, is thought his who pursues her during the Chase" (*Second Treatise*, 5.30, p. 331). This, of course, recalls the passage in Locke's "To the Reader" in his *Essay concerning Human Understanding* about the way in which the mind's "searches after truth are a sort of hawking and hunting, wherein the very pursuit makes a great part of the pleasure" (p. 7) and leads to Hogarth's central concern in his *Analysis of Beauty* with the "pleasure of the chase." The notion of the art object as a property combines with Hogarth's particular principle of artistic play or labor.

The alternative case to Pope's then, an extension of the Swiftean position, is that of Hogarth, who denies—or, in the discourse of iconoclasm, breaks—the discourse of property by thematizing and problematizing it, and thus producing a more active form of disinterestedness.

Hogarth's work emphasizes the antinomies that emerge from the common post-Lockean assumptions about property, eventuating in their most picturesque forms in the work of William Blake (who also carries the thematizing of *making* to its extreme in *The Marriage of Heaven and Hell*):

Property versus the Human: This was the view that the individual should have priority in one way or another over property—certainly cannot, as Locke assures us, be him or herself regarded as property.

Property versus Liberty: The individual is defined by liberty, a state of being nonproperty. At the same time liberty is permitted and determined by the individual's property owning.

Property versus Ability: This antinomy is expressed most vigorously in Burke's discussion of sluggish property and lively energetic (and so dangerous) ability in his *Reflections on the Revolution in France* (1791). It probably originated, however, in Locke's opposition of *labor* to Filmer's hereditary inherited right to property.

Finally, there is the opposition of *Property versus Aesthetics*, and so the idea that aesthetic experience excludes interestedness and possession, embodied in the notion of property. The political critique was formulated and verbalized in the 1750s by Rousseau, who distinguished in his *Discourse on the Origin of Inequality* between mere possession and genuine property, between fact and law, between moral and legal relationships. For Rousseau property was the root of all our later misfortunes. The skeptical view expressed by Hogarth and the artists influenced by him comes closer to Rousseau's than to Locke's position. Hogarth thematized these oppositions, and in particular that of human identity *and* liberty compromised by property.[15] Instead of disinterestedness Hogarth employs the element of play, codified in *The Analysis of Beauty:* I mean the play of morality against art, of nature against art (even beauty against rhetoric), and so, in the present context, of possession against art—art as labor, both the artist's and the spectator's reading of it (possessing it).

Hogarth's example served different ends in the next generation. He showed one group of artists the way to recontextualize as a mode of cultural aggrandizement quite the contrary of his own. Reynolds's Commodore Keppel as Apollo, Sarah Siddons as Michelangelo's Sybil, and Master Crew as Hans Holbein's Henry VIII, but above all West's General Wolfe as Christ in a Pietà, became positive images of British imperialism. This procedure is an example of the domestication that took over as well with subsequent interpretations of Hogarth's own work, which was "moralized" by Trusler, rendered Shandean by Lichtenberg and anecdotal by Nichols. On the other hand, Johann Zoffany in conversation pictures and Gainsborough in landscape carried on at least the problematizing aspect of Hogarth's program. They did it by means of a *human* gesture, whether of a human figure within the picture or of the artist's hand: an animated sculpture, an obtrusive bird added where it is not expected. I shall cite the examples of the portrait and the landscape painting.

To frame our Lockean action, we might look ahead to Adam Smith's *Wealth of Nations* in 1776: Smith replaces "to make" by "to truck, barter, and exchange one thing for another," heralding (or rather validating) the rise of the merchant and stockjobber. This happens, as Smith explains, when one man's labor becomes more satisfactorily the "division of labor," making it impossible for one man—a *homo faber*—to totalize or grasp the totality of the object he is making: to control, as Hogarth attempted to do, its total production and distribution.[16] Indeed, Smith defines man as neither maker nor user but the merchant who contrives (introducing a favorite canine metaphor) "to make a fair and deliberate exchange of one bone for another."[17] Thus the joy of the making itself, or even its utilization, has been replaced by the exchange of what you make for what you need. Every man "becomes in some measure a merchant," he writes, projecting a society that becomes "a commercial society" (p. 37).

Labor now comes to mean more narrowly physical labor—not making but contributing to a common, divided labor, carrying out one's own part of the labor only and mechanically at that. Thus from labor defining property Smith takes us to a new formulation: "Labour . . . is the real measure of the exchangeable value of all commodities." Owning or possessing is replaced by the incessant changing of hands of an object. And in terms of an art object, the buying and selling take precedence in interest over the creation *or* the making or even the owner's enjoyment of possession. At the same time, the "power" of possession is replaced by "the power of purchasing: a certain command over all the labour, or over all the produce of labour which is then in the market." And the power or value of labor comes to be determined not by the amount or quality of labor but by "the higgling and bargaining of the market" (pp. 47–49).

I do not mean to suggest that the joy of making or collecting or owning disappeared; only that Smith formulated a situation that Hogarth, for example, had exemplified and projected negatively in his graphic works of the 1750s.

PORTRAIT AND LANDSCAPE:
ZOFFANY AND GAINSBOROUGH

The portrait began, of course, as an icon, an image to be worshiped, with magical properties. After the movement of iconoclasm in England portraits represented three types: monarchs, heroes in the sense of role models, and family members or close friends. The function was therefore political, moral, and commemorative. The political function was that portraits of the monarch took on the iconophilic function of the images of Christ and Mary and the Apostles. In the moral function portraits of ancient philosophers, warriors, and poets served as models for emulation or (as with the Roman emperors) admonition. The category of commemorative portraits covers everything else from relatives to close friends, from forebears to wives and mistresses.

The preference in England for the portrait over the allegorical or historical painting derived from the need for an image of memory (an unabused image). The English layman found his spokesman in Samuel Johnson. To Boswell's example of the little girl who sees a picture of Justice with her scales and explains, "See, there's a woman selling sweetmeats," Johnson replied emphatically: "I had rather see the portrait of a dog that I know than all the allegorical paintings they can show me in the world."[18] He means *even* the portrait of a dog—but preferably the portrait of a human friend, something in the world and (in Calvin's words) "seen by one's own eye," rather than "phantoms" or abstractions, but also actual friends whose absence can be filled by these remembrances.

The image is acquired in order to bring back something that is absent—lost through death or the changes of aging—and so serves as a control or method of redemption in both the religious and financial sense. For a portrait is also a means of annexing "friend" to the category of possession. It was obvious that an image (like paper credit) can outlast what it represents; it has a survival power denied its referent.

At this point the aesthetics of mourning and possession join in the fact of absence: absence covered, in the first instance, by a tomb, and in the second compensated for by the attempt to *possess* what has been lost, make it one's property.

Possession and iconoclasm share the element of property and not only in the sense that one collects while the other breaks it. On the contrary, iconoclasm in England was historically a procedure for acquiring property: on the highest level in the appropriation of the monastic properties, and more modestly in the remaking of idols into articles of everyday use.

In some cases there is a clear sense of property in a portrait, as when Charles II collected not only the person of Nell Gwynne but also paintings of her to hang in his closet which are clothed, unclothed, or costumed to appear a princess, shepherdess, or (more ironically) a Magdalen. It is easy to imagine for whom she appears eternally unclothed, but the disguise as a Magdalen could have been for the sake of the sitter (her self-image), some friend, or the artist himself—in other words, a way of making her *and* the picture respectable—as well as for the witty monarch.

A related question is why there are so few nudes (the example par excellence of painting-as-property) in English art before Thomas Rowlandson and William Etty at the end of the eighteenth century. Aside from Sir Peter Lely's *Nell Gwynne,* I am aware of only one nude figure in Hogarth's *Pool of Bethesda* and the conventional nudes who appear here and there in mythological decorations. But as a genre, parallel to the portrait, the nude does not exist in English art until the Romantic period. Presumably the absence relates once again to the positively Swiftean distrust of images and their potential for idolatry, which extended even to the ways of "possessing" which were popular on the continent. (The exception, Charles II, was, after all, a crypto-Catholic.)

On the other side, an important name in English portraiture between 1720 and 1749 was the drapery painter Joseph Vanaken. He painted the fashionably attired body, in fact, all but the head—that is, all of the possessions that established and supported identity but were distinguishable from the center of identity, the face itself, and that covered the naked body. The separability was an interesting fact, dictated of course by conventions of studio work, but showing how important the splendor and realism of the dresses and surroundings were to the identity of the sitter. Hogarth is supposed to have made a drawing at the time of Vanaken's death showing all the portrait painters of London disconsolately following his coffin.

It may have been partly iconoclasm and partly skepticism as to whether a man's whole character could be captured in a life-size (or larger-than-life) full-length Anthony Van Dyck portrait that led to the diminutive conversation picture that opened up native British portraiture in the 1720s and 1730s.[19] In this form the artist (and in particular Hogarth, its most daring exponent) sought, more realistically, to show the man or woman embodied or imbedded in his/her milieu. That milieu consisted of possessions and collections of paintings and sculpture. The people were shown among these possessions in actions of the most conventional and passive sort. But the possessions, miniaturized along with their owner, as Hogarth showed in his paintings and prints of the 1730s and 1740s (most completely and definitively in *Marriage A-la-mode*), possessed the possessor in the sense of defining him, shaping his character, even forcing him into patterns of behavior which are cruel, aggressive, destructive, and self-defeating.[20]

Rowlandson adapted the principles of Hogarth's Sculpture Garden in many drawings and watercolors of sculpture galleries, gardens, and showrooms, based on simple contrasts of beauty and the ugly, grotesque, or picturesque. But basically the art of the sculpture (itself animated erotically) is played against the grotesque rotundity of the male connoisseur-collectors and the living vitality of a young woman (fig. 34).

Zoffany painted a more complex version, developing Hogarth's idea that the art objects as possessions defined their owner. If Hogarth recontextualized the classical canon, satirizing its owners but also repossessing it himself by establishing its meaning as his own, Zoffany then repeated Hogarth's representations of these art objects, emphasizing their existence as property, and making his central question: *Whose* meaning, the patron's or the artist's? Whereas Hogarth's theme was the folly of the collector-possessor and, implicitly, the artist's repossession, Zoffany's theme is the agon of artist and collector, and he seems to show more anxiety—or aggression—than Hogarth about the alienability of his art as property.

He painted a copy of the Tribuna in the Uffizi Gallery in Florence for Queen Charlotte, who wanted to remember and, in some sense, possess the masterpieces in that gallery of paintings and sculptures.

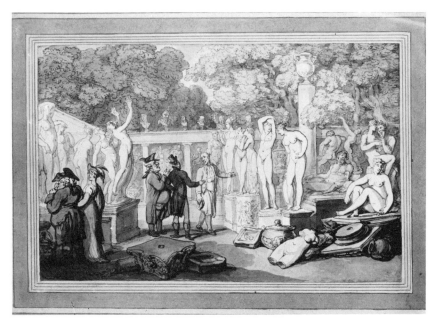

34. Thomas Rowlandson, A Statuary Yard *(1780s), drawing.*

The Venus de Medici itself, for example, was there, as well as Titian's *Venus of Urbino,* many Raphaels, and antique sarcophagi. The gallery was to be copied by Zoffany, the most accurate of delineators in the German manner—to be copied, possessed, and hung in the palace. I have written at length about this painting elsewhere,[21] and only note here that Zoffany turned this melange of public reference, this gallery of canonical objects in their gallery setting (not, as in Hogarth's irony, in a sale room) meant for Queen Charlotte, into a private and personal meaning of his own, which was specifically memorial, primarily about personal loss and death.[22]

This is a simple case of the painter's appropriating the possessions he has been commissioned to paint—appropriating, in effect, the painting itself. He treats the human figures within the Tribuna in the same way, playing jokes by his juxtapositions of them with statues and each other. In the generality of his conversation pictures—or at least whenever the extravagance of the commission allowed, when the objects were bizarre enough or the patron eccentric enough—he kept from being himself possessed by playing jokes on his patron. If, as sitter, Charles Towneley is a homosexual bachelor, Zoffany shows him with his art collection around him as an extended family, and throws in a cuckold joke in the juxtaposition of his prize piece, the Isis (which he called his "wife"), with his homosexual circle.[23] Sometimes he simply puts himself in the picture, or his dog (as Hogarth had used his dog as an artist surrogate).

What, for example, does Zoffany signify in *William Ferguson Introduced as Heir to Raith* (1769, private collection) by formally balancing an empty and tilting chair on the left of this natural landscape (the friends are grouped under a tree) with his own figure on the right side of the group? The notion may derive from Hogarth's *Lord Hervey and His Friends* (1738), but the empty, tilting chair in some way reinforces the gloomy indifference of Zoffany to this scene of celebration. The Zoffany-specialist Mary Webster's only explanation for such details is that it is in the intimate nature of conversation pictures to be undecipherable except by the family—an explanation which hardly explains the figure of the painter Zoffany, neither member nor friend of the family.[24] I am reminded, when I read Webster's justifications of such details, of the Monty Python routine in which John Cleese as the Pope chides Michelangelo (sic) for the artistic license he has taken in his *Last Supper*—twenty-eight disciples and three Christs just for the sake of the composition.

Zoffany's iconography falls roughly into three categories: the family grouped around a tree in the country house park (the tree usually an oak, symbolizing the continuity of family and estate); the *pater familias* in the midst of his possessions and the collector in the midst of his collection; and a group tied together by a common interest, as of a life-class at the Royal Academy. I have discussed the first two groups in *Emblem and Expression,* and so I shall take my example from the third group.

The Sharp Family (fig. 35) was painted in 1779–81.[25] The Sharps were so musical a family that they wrote their names "Frances #," "Granville #," and so on. The structure of their conversation picture then, rather than being a family around a tree with a stately home in the distance, is an orchestra. The members of the family are crowded along with their musical instruments on their specially built barge, equipped with sleeping compartments and an awning for warm weather. William, at the apex of the triangle and captain of the vessel, owned a fleet of ships, one of which shows its Union Jack on the other side of the Thames, where his balconied house can also be seen. And so he is posed as ship's captain, and the scene is both an orchestral performance and naval engagement, or rather victory. It is a celebratory group, with allusions to heroic victories at sea.

The base of the triangle (a favorite Zoffany structure for a group)

35. Johann Zoffany, The Sharp Family *(1779–81), painting.*

is indicated by the eldest brother John at the right and James at the
left. Contained within the triangle is the other brother, Granville, the
nonself-supporting member of the family. A bachelor, Granville
lived in William's house across the river and was known for his support of the abolition of slavery and other radical causes. During the
American Revolution he had given up his job as clerk in the Ord-
nance Department at the Tower of London rather than supply the
British troops who were fighting the colonists—and so "had no paid
employment and lived with members of his family."[26] He is also at
the center of the family because he organized these outings. The
wives are placed nearest their husbands: John's is to his immediate
right; William's just in front of him, her head over his heart; James's
is farthest away, with two figures intervening.

But what are we to make of the curious detail of Granville's right hand (arm extended) holding a double flageolet behind brother James's head? Anyone familiar (as Zoffany would have been) with Hogarth's *Evening* (1738) could not look at this without thinking of a cuckold's horns. There is no reason at all to think that anything was amiss in James Sharp's marriage: his wife, the next woman up the triangle from him, looks down at him lovingly. It seems however, that the family that signed itself # was also given to self-mythologizing. The barge was appropriately named the Apollo, and Mr. and Mrs. James Sharp were known as Vulcan and Venus. The penchant for self-mythologizing may have led Zoffany to present the orchestra performance mock-heroically as a naval triumph. But he also shows "Venus" graphically separated from her husband "Vulcan," forming part of a small triangle (its apex William) within the larger one; she is holding hands with William's wife while William in his military uniform of surgeon to the king has the role of "Mars." The role is strictly assigned by Zoffany; I know of no such designation within the family. But the detail of the "horns," determined by the roles of "Venus" and "Vulcan," and therefore the story of Vulcan/Venus/Mars, is another example of Zoffany's playful control as artist, already stamped on the picture in the intent presence of his dog, Roma. (It is possible, of course, that Zoffany is characterizing Granville, whose pursuit of radical causes made the family uneasy, as a Lord of Misrule who has assigned the role of Mars.)

Zoffany is the *metteur en scène* of each group he paints. But he learned to see art objects through the eyes of Hogarth, especially the *Analysis*, Plate 1, with its suggestion of a romantic triangle involving the cuckolding of Hercules. The approach he takes shifts the focus from the gallery spectator, whose experience will be aesthetic in the Burkean sense of disinterested, to the intensely interested feelings of the painter and his patron (and/or the subject, him or herself). Given the assumption that the title to property is the labor, what Locke projects in his *Second Treatise* is a conflict between the natural title of the *worker* and the legal title of the *owner* or the patron with reference to the artist, to the picture itself, but also to the possessions represented within the picture. Much practical and intellectual play was given by Hogarth and his followers to the relationship between the fruits of the labor played off against the physical object on which the labor has been expended.

If one response to luxury was to show it as a clutter overwhelming its owners, disrupting the social relations of the family, the other was to black it out. Wright of Derby illuminates *his* conversation picture room with an object that clearly transcends the category of property (though the bird in the air pump, with its destined cage visible, could imply a sense of property). And at the same time this bright object casts all the possessions around and on the walls of the room into darkness. Wright's candlelit mode serves to elide the real world of property—possibly in order to repress awareness of it, but more likely in order to avoid its distraction, to draw our attention away from this centrifugal clutter to the kind of thing that can stimulate sympathy and unite radically different people in some strange almost supernatural way. Whereas, as the conversations of the Hogarth-Zoffany type show, property inevitably draws people apart.

LANDSCAPE is the crucial, perhaps the enabling, genre in the discourse of property. The landscape is clearly owned, as is the representation of it, by someone who is not the artist. And yet especially in the fluid shapes of landscape it is easy to trace what Ann Bermingham has called the "physicality of the landscape painter's encounter with his object," and sense the "material proximity" of the artist, as distinct, for example, from "the mediating presence of literary narrative" which is added for (or at the behest of) the critic-connoisseur or patron-spectator.[27] The question is whether there is a category of landscape that is *non*-property. Landscape allows us to isolate the discourse of property as only one of a number of appropriate discourses that can reveal a landscape: a discourse of "possession" in the sense of love or desire (the landscape is experienced or enjoyed), for example, or in the passive sense of the spectators' being gripped by the landscape.

Let us suppose another kind of control of the landscape, prior to possession, in the atavistic spectator of prospect-refuge theory who experiences with the eyes of an animal seeking a place from which to see without being seen; this figure can be either a predator or a prey, perhaps both simultaneously. In so far as the spectator is a Hobbesian predator he is, of course, on the way to becoming a proprietor; and the meekest prey carries within it the bared teeth of a predator-proprietor.[28]

Or, here is another possibility: let us suppose a landscape through which we see something beyond itself—an imaginary, ideal place that specifically transcends the notion of property, as in Samuel Palmer's Shoreham landscapes. By creating something better than we can "possess" the artist both transcends property and allows the spectator who is unable to define himself or herself in terms of real property to feel the possession of ideal property. But representing something as transcending the immediate landscape is, of course, to allegorize it; as, in the case of incomprehensible waste, calling it "sublime" serves to domesticate the incomprehensibility, or make it acceptable, and in that sense allegorize or possess it.

It was often said that the spectator was taught to feel humility before the sublime scene, as in the case of the tiny human figures whose presence on the fringe of a Friedrich or Turner prospect emphasizes the landscape's resistance to possession. But, as Frances Ferguson has noted, it is precisely the humble, the propertyless who can possess a piece of property of their own by being a tourist or by calling it "sublime": by reclaiming the Lockean "waste" that has not been worked—cannot be worked—and so cannot belong to someone else.[29] And yet, at the same time, this landscape, while in one sense "property," is in a more important sense transcendent of categories such as property. As Ferguson has also noted,

> On the one hand, the Lockean account of property made property valuable in relation to the individual; but it also, and perhaps more importantly, made waste places . . . in a sense more important than property itself.[30]

And so we return to the "waste" land with which Locke begins: "land that is left wholly to nature, that hath no improvement of pasturage, tillage, or planting, is called, as indeed it is, waste." This waste stands at the center of eighteenth-century aesthetics as well as politics. It can be left waste, that is, "Nature." Or it can be worked, made farmland, and so become property. But it can also be decorated, made into a garden—whether emblematic or expressive or *ferme ornée*—or, called "sublime," it can become the possession of the propertyless, including the artist.

For if the unworked waste is reclaimed by the spectator of the picturesque or sublime, the same opportunities existed for the artist-maker. He could attempt to duplicate the sense of sublimity, humility, or possession desired by the spectator; or he could lay personal claim to it. As for the spectator, the result would be some combination of possession and transcendence outside the category of property.

For example, there was a great potential for Hogarthian "play" in the juxtaposition of aesthetic and socio-political categories such as "the aesthetics of the painted landscape" *versus* "the economics of the enclosed one," or the rise of "rustic landscape painting" *versus* the "accelerated enclosure of the English countryside" (these are Ann Bermingham's terms).[31] Beyond these dichotomies, there was the "pattern of actual loss" in the enclosures as against the act of "imaginative recovery" in landscape painting.

Enclosure itself, dividing into fields and hedging, was equivalent to—or seen as a precondition for—the working of "waste" land in Locke's sense. So to working the land we must add dividing and demarcating it, ruling it off as well as making a particular kind of landscape characterized by horizontal divisions. If we distinguish, as Bermingham does, the different historical stages of enclosure, we discern different aesthetic forms as well, from the rough and overgrown (picturesque) to the ordered and recently "inclosed" (the rational ordering, whether by geometrical or, with Capability Brown, by serpentine lines).[32] And each offered different possibilities for the artist's reclamation of the landscape on his canvas.

In such ways the landscape painter establishes his own right to his representation of a landscape that belongs to someone else, or to no one, or to a spectator or purchaser of the painting. Gainsborough, emerging as he does in mid-eighteenth century England, out of the ambience of Hogarth's *Analysis of Beauty,* the St. Martin's Lane Academy, and the rococo decorations of the French immigrant artists, uses various means to keep his paintings his own—and in particular those paintings most dear to him, his landscapes.[33] He carries on at least the problematizing aspect of Hogarth's dealings with property. Both artists do it by means of a human gesture, whether of a human figure within the picture or of the artist's hand in the making of the picture: an animated sculpture, a formal parallel between human and tree or animal, an obtrusive detail added where it is not expected; but most obviously—especially in landscape painting—by the signs of brushwork, which then return, within the discourse of property itself as "labor" and so as the artist's Lockean justification for possessing the object. In Gainsborough's case the brushwork also serves to make the landscape unidentifiable as *some*one's. It helps to disfigure and disguise the landscape as topography, that is, to distinguish the art object from the subject of representation as different kinds of property or as property *versus* nonproperty; saying: *this* peculiar narrative, this paint on canvas is the art object, the product of labor, and not the object (or subject) of representation. Indeed, Gainsborough reclaims many of his later portraits by turning them into the personal mode of his landscape shapes with the same indeterminacy as the masses of foliage in their backgrounds, often encroaching on, or absorbing, the sitter.

From the beginning of his career Gainsborough reclaims (in the sense of placing his personal mark on) his landscape shapes. As early as the topographical painting of St. Mary's Church, Hadleigh (of c. 1748),[34] he injects into its foreground a quotation from Hogarth's second plate of *Industry and Idleness* of 1747—the idle apprentice gambling on a slab tombstone in a churchyard. But the most intriguing example of this marking of a painting was the landscape-conversation of Mr. and Mrs. Robert Andrews (1748–49, London, National Gallery), showing the squire and his lady with their estate, Auberies, which stretches over the right half of the scene.

Gainsborough represents the landscape as topography, that is, as someone's property, parallel to—in this case a part of—the conversation picture portrait group. Since Mr. and Mrs. Andrews were married in November 1848, the painting may have been a marriage portrait. Sheaves of stooked corn, seen in the foreground, could be a symbol of fertility. But the roundish unfinished shape in Mrs. Andrews's lap, defined only by a feather, seems to indicate that Gainsborough intended to paint a bird—and had second thoughts or was prevented. Was it a game bird to be related to the husband's gun—something he had shot and presented to his wife, thus a symbol (related to the slang, bird = maiden) of his possession of *her*? What is evident on close examination is that where the bird's head should be the lines suggest the head of a penis.[35] The facts that the bird was undertaken and then left unfinished —and the picture remained with the artist—are equally significant and self-assertive of the painter.

As Edgar Wind has noted, Gainsborough's aim was to represent in his sitters (and, I would add, in his painting) precisely that play or leisure time that denies the civic humanist emphasis on office and the significant (heroic) moment. In this sense, he has gone as far beyond Hogarth as beyond Reynolds. Hogarth still required the debris of heroism (tainted by the Great Man) as well as what he came to call (and Gainsborough called) Nature; and Gainsborough came at this form of antiheroism by way of Hogarth's opposition of the heroic and the modern, in particular the opposition of exercise (copying of the antique) and play in *The Analysis of Beauty*. Hogarth advocated not rote copying, or imitation of the Reynolds variety for the purpose of elevation, but playfulness. The latter was a term that included the sense, on which Gainsborough placed his emphasis, of everyday living outside roles.

THE question of who owns the landscape is predicated on the question of who stands before the canvas? We can compare two Gainsborough canvases of a year apart, *Wooded Landscape with Country Waggon, Milkmaid and Drover* (private collection, England) of 1766 and the great painting of the following year, usually known as *The Harvest Wagon* (fig. 36). Both were exhibited in London at the Society of Artists in their respective years, but while the first was bought at once by Sir William St. Quintin, the second remained in Gainsborough's studio and was eventually in 1774 given to his carter, Walter Wiltshire, either as a gift or in exchange for a horse.

The difference in this case does not lie in anecdote. Both are centered on an incident. In the 1766 painting Gainsborough shows a boy and girl embracing at a stile. That the boy has abandoned his labor is clear from the fact that his horses are continuing to pull his cart; only his barking dog shows alarm at this consequence of his dereliction of duty. Whether labor or duty is the issue, some such minor narrative is projected—and one that (characteristically for Gainsborough) shows a withdrawal from an official role (laborer at the lower end of the range, but prime minister at the upper). Most often this departure is into a situation of love.

Gainsborough's juxtaposition of lovers and cattle, sometimes atop a hill, begins as early as 1755–57 (Hayes, nos. 59, 62, 64, 65) and reflects a wry contrast of young love and an old, either polarded or dead tree (out of Jacob van Ruisdael's landscapes). By 1780 (perhaps now from Gainsborough's reading of Gray's *Elegy*) the lovers are in a churchyard reading an epitaph on a gravestone, a more literal-minded *vanitas* image (to be contrasted also with the boys cheerfully gambling on a gravestone in the *View of St. Mary's Church, Hadleigh*, of 1748).

As early as 1748–50 Gainsborough painted a pair of rustic lovers balanced by a black and a white cow. By 1762–63 the lovers are again appearing with a pair of cows (79) and in 1766 (87), a major work, two lovers at a stile are paired with two horses, one light and one dark (corresponding to the lovers' dress) drawing a cart up a road into the distance. In 1771–73 (103) lovers are juxtaposed with a line of cattle being driven down a path, and in no. 109 the beau is separated from his lover by the inconvenient cattle (see also 108, 113).

To verify the sense of these examples, all we have to do is recall

Two Shepherd Boys with Dogs Fighting of 1783 (Kenwood), where the humans and animals are unquestionably paralleled as to hair color and allegiance, for it to become fairly clear that the parallels in the landscapes are not fortuitous. In short, a basic strategy of the early Dutch-inspired landscapes seems to be the removal of a laborer from his "office," his private life being designated as that of a lover, and the juxtaposition of a pair of lovers with some equivocal symbol, a dead bird or tree, or with a bovine pair or a lemminglike procession of cattle.

It is useful to know, as Marcia Pointon has shown, that Richard Graves's poem *On Gainsborough's Landskips with Portraits; full length Figures less than life, drawn in Pairs as walking thro' woods, etc.* (in Shenstone's *Miscellany 1759–63*) connects such "pairs" as Mr. and Mrs. Andrews and his other couples-in-landscapes with Adam and Eve in a lost paradise which through Gainsborough's brush becomes "a Paradise regain'd." Pointon argues that scenes of this sort are literary, illustrative of the retirement theme or melancholy contemplation, the result of reading Gray's *Elegy* and other graveyard poetry.[36] In short, Gainsborough's brush, in his lifetime, was referred to as a means of redeeming fallen Adams and Eves. There may be a sense in which his lovers, often shown standing before or near a blasted tree, could be taken for Adam and Eve in a landscape. But given the context of Hogarth's *Analysis*, Plate 1, and before that Hogarth's conversation pictures of the 1730s, they would seem more playful than conducive to melancholy meditation.

This sort of evocation was caught by Joseph Burke when he noted that the "fancy picture," *Cottage Girl with Dog and Pitcher* (1785), "evokes the Christ Child as the Good Shepherd," and *The Woodman* (1787) recalls

> the saint or hermit in a wilderness while depicting old age at the mercy of wild nature. Visionary devotion has been translated into the tramp's fear before the lightning; his hands are clasped not in prayer but on his stick; in place of St. Jerome's placid lion, a Synders-like dog shrinks back with snarling defiance.

As if startled by the temerity of his suggestion, however, Burke retreats: "The evocation of religious art is probably unconscious and due simply to Gainsborough's study of religious paintings by Murillo and similar masters."[37] But he has put his finger on the kind of "translation" that takes place when one style or configuration is used

36. Thomas Gainsborough, The Harvest Wagon *(1767), painting.*

to represent a very different subject. In the ambience of the St. Martin's Lane artists the evocation may still be a travesty in the manner of Gay's *Shepherd's Week* or Hogarth's *Analysis*, Plate 1; the woodman and his dog are to a St. Jerome and his lion as Gay's butcher's son is to Cupid, son of Mars and Venus.

A kind of self-assertion is undeniably evident in Gainsborough's generally acknowledged borrowings—for example, of Peter Paul Rubens's *Descent from the Cross,* of which he had made a copy himself, into *The Harvest Wagon*—one of the pair of paintings with which we began this excursus (figs. 36, 37).[38] The mock form involves not only painting the rustics in the elegant and fluent style of Rubens but evoking, in a sense that Hogarth would have understood, in these "peasants" striving upward toward a drink of wine from the "leathern Bottle, long in Harvest try'd" (bequeathed in Gay's version by Blouzelinda to her lover Grubbinol), a low popular version of the figures reaching up for Christ's Body and Blood in the eucharistic Descent from the Cross. The effect is not deflation but the suggestive engen-

37. Gainsborough, Copy of Rubens' Deposition, *painting.*

dering of equivalence and contemporary myth. Gainsborough not only is suggesting that these carousing peasants are participating in some primitive fertility ritual in a landscape bathed in the lushest yellows and greens, but is appropriating the subject (indeed, both subjects) in a process that establishes—we could say, in the discourse of property—his own, the artist's transcendent reclamation of the scene, of that counterreformation iconography, as his possession of his representation. And he does so by problematizing the landscape and figures, and thereby aestheticizing them, that is, removing his figures and his painting from the discourse of property he shared with the purchaser, if not the spectator, of the painting.

Thus, comparing *Wooded Landscape with Country Waggon, Milkmaid and Drover* with *The Harvest Wagon,* we notice that in the latter instead of a narrative theme Gainsborough represents a drinking scene and allusions to high art—to history painting, not only to Rubens's *Descent from the Cross* but to Raphael's *Expulsion of Heliodorus* and the classical sculpture known as the *Dioscuri.*

Significant as is this change in Gainsborough's landscape painting, I suspect that what sold the first landscape and caused the second to remain on his hands was the different degrees of finish in the two paintings. The 1766 painting was finished, virtually every leaf articulated, not so much in the manner of Ruisdael as of the French, perhaps François Boucher ("the trees are too blue and hard," a contemporary reviewer accurately wrote).[39] By contrast, the great *Harvest Wagon* looks unfinished; it resembles a large drawing rather than a painting; the brushwork draws attention to itself rather than being subordinated to the representation, and suggests the appropriative function of the brushwork in less extreme cases.

Gainsborough is thus asserting *his* ownership, for example vis-à-vis a patron like St. Quintin for whom he has made the earlier painting an acceptable property. There is no way in which St. Quintin or one of Gainsborough's known patrons can be projected in front of this canvas—only the artist himself, or perhaps some unlettered anticonnoisseur like Walter Wiltshire.

We see by following the chronology of the landscape paintings that shortly after 1750, after the early London and Sudbury years, Gainsborough abandoned a careful observation of place in order to rely on "mannerisms of the rococo" or a "tendency towards generalization."[40] We could rephrase this to say that Gainsborough elides the topographical differences of the landscape in order to remove its sense of property. As Bermingham has noticed, he also does this by representing terrain in which the enclosure lines have been blurred and overgrown (whereas Constable, a generation later, under different circumstances, emphasizes these divisions of property).[41]

Both the allusions to Rubens and the lack of finish are signs that

Gainsborough's landscapes are as much about the art of painting as about the Sudbury or Bath countryside. He was a painter whose phases can better be named after the painters he imitated than the places he inhabited. The Dutch landscapists, especially Johannes Wijnants, were followed by Rubens and Van Dyck, as he moved from one palette and one way of handling paint to another.

The early and pervasive model was Jacob van Ruisdael. Although a Gainsborough could never be mistaken for a Ruisdael landscape (as it might be, at different times, for a Wijnants or a Rubens), the two artists saw landscape in a fundamentally similar way. Ruisdael elided historical elements in his landscapes, instead rearranging his topographical elements for picturesque emphasis or melodramatic reinforcement, sometimes adding symbolic ruins or tombstones. A pervasive theatricality was Ruisdael's replacement for history. But their solutions were diametrically opposed. Ruisdael's most personal and deeply felt landscapes were focused on a single giant tree or a forest and on the tactility and mass of foliage; Gainsborough used trees as the fringe surrounding an empty declivity.

Of the prodigious number of landscape types developed by Ruisdael, Gainsborough employed only one, the least informative or definitive, the most decorative or rhetorical. This is the landscape mode described by Wolfgang Stechow in his *Dutch Landscape Painting* as "an arrangement of details to fit a preconceived pattern," a "distribution of light and shade . . . dictated by compositional convenience," as opposed to "a 'find' in nature," a composition which "seems to obey the laws of natural lighting, is less symmetrical and serves to bring out the individual qualities of the foliage."[42] It is from the authority of this extreme, and minor, Ruisdael type that Gainsborough's landscapes after 1750 derive.

John Hayes, author of the authoritative catalogue of Gainsborough's landscape paintings, recognizes that this "repertory of motifs, . . . forms and rhythms" became a personal vocabulary for Gainsborough—that they "sprang from the depths of his being and gradually came to reflect his feelings about the world around him" better than could "the most penetrating naturalism." It is easy enough to say that Gainsborough combines the rococo style he learned from the St. Martin's Lane Academy and the aesthetics of the picturesque, as he joins French elegance and English empiricism. It seems to me, however, that these simple stylized forms serve as a way for the artist to comment on and control, even subordinate, his sitter in the portraits and the particularity of place in the landscape to formal solutions carried out by his personal landscape shapes. It is not, as used to be thought, that Gainsborough escaped from portraiture into landscape but that he employed landscape with its malleable shapes as a way of controlling human experience. And I think his characteristic shapes functioned similarly in the pure landscapes.

Present in the Dutch landscapes of his youth, and in a more painterly and emphatic way in Rubens's landscapes, was a confluence of serpentine lines in a lazy Y or gamma. In one of Hayes's sensitive formal analyses he describes the rococo serpentine structure of a landscape in St. Louis (no. 52), where the "powerful serpentine line . . . begins in the foreground, sweeps over the hillock, . . . passes down and beyond the bank into the middle distance and thence, through the agency of the winding river, into the very depths of the composition." This is, of course, the way the eye ordinarily functions in a Claude Lorrain landscape. In this particular Gainsborough landscape, though Hayes should have mentioned the remarkable discontinuity of this particular serpentine line, the eye tends to follow the broken lines into the scene because the figures on the road are traveling in that direction. What Hayes does not mention is that in the vast majority of Gainsborough's landscapes the figures conform to the landscape lines, moving away from the horizon and toward the viewer, down into either the middle distance or the foreground of the composition and off the canvas. With all of the landscapes before us in Hayes's catalogue, we can see that statistically this form predominates, becoming more emphatic in the later paintings, until in the landscapes with a single shepherd and his flock the downward sweep defines mountain gorges (fig. 38).[43]

Instead of leading into the landscape, the winding track usually draws the eye down and out of the bottom, or into a pool or a crevasse of some sort near the bottom. Gainsborough's early copy (drawing) of Ruisdael's *La Forêt*, described by Hayes (citing Mary Woodall) as "a faithful repetition," in fact cuts off the bottom of Ruisdael's composition, leaving it open where Ruisdael closed it. The line is rococo, certainly, and the faces and figures when discernible are pretty, but the fact that they are all gravitating downward is surely a distinctive feature. And the effect of the various stages of style is to give different meaning to the movement: whether a light, airy merging or metamorphosis of human into nature, the metamorphosis summed up in the story of Diana and Actaeon, or a darker, more intense, hectic, "romantic" composition that melodramatizes the situation.

38. Gainsborough, Classical Landscape *(1780s), painting.*

By emptying the landscape of its demarcations, its connotations of property, of work, even of history painting in the traditional sense in order to make it subject for art—that is, to make it his own, to transcend "property"—Gainsborough reclaims the landscape. Gainsborough's landscape represents a desire for some prelinguistic area, prior to history, prior to property rights, literature, or any formulation. At the same time, however it also raises the question—that will be most clearly seen in the case of Constable—of whether the vortex itself is not simply another allegory, though a personal one.

REYNOLDS'S *MRS. ABINGTON AS MISS PRUE*

The portrait projects a three-way struggle: the artist and the sitter and the patron who commissioned the portrait—who, of course, in the case of the portrait is often also the sitter. Once beyond the simple likeness, the image becomes a play with the expansion of the sitter in his own eyes struggling against the artist's use of the image to elevate or express himself, sometimes at the sitter's expense. If the sitter, his works, his life, and his times make up one side of the portrait equation, the painter as "artist" and as man, as he relates to—perhaps tries to control or exploit—his subject is the Other: from the artist's dominating the sitter by keeping him/her immobile in one position for hours of posing—for days and weeks of sittings—to the artist's transformation of the sitter's likeness, into the artist's personal image of the sitter, or a self-portrait, or a caricature, or a pretext for another kind of painting altogether. There is, of course, a prevailing sense in which a painter acts out a drama of aggression on his powerful or famous subjects. This was presumably Lady Churchill's feeling about Graham Sutherland's portrait of Winston Churchill. Her destruction of the portrait was an example of the occasional triumphant (or tragic) case where the sitter has the last word. But more often a Reynolds makes his sitter Commodore Keppel echo the Apollo Belvedere not only to elevate Keppel but to distinguish himself as portrait painter.

The degree of incarnation or disincarnation may be an appropriate way to talk about portrait painting in iconoclastic England. In the pure icon Jesus *is* Jesus; then, slipping from identity to similitude, Henry VIII is Jesus (surrounded by Joseph and Mary and the saints) but with a difference, or Lenin is painted as Jesus. And as Jesus is simulated by a king, the king is simulated by a nobleman and the nobleman by a merchant—the incarnational relationship becomes more remote, more secondary, more imitative. Eventually (1) Hogarth the satirist portrays a harlot *as if* she were the Virgin Mary, a Rake *as if* he were Christ, and (2) Reynolds paints Keppel as if he were the sculpture considered the ideal of male beauty. The only true subject for the iconic portrait, if the artist is self-conscious, is himself.

Reynolds paints himself as Rembrandt (portraitist, Dutch tradition, humble subjects and style) posing with the bust of Michelangelo (history painter, highest tradition, Italian Renaissance). The first is considered at this time to be not quite first rate, the second absolutely first rate. Reynolds shows himself *as* the first but with the attribute of the second; with the reality of the first, the aspiration of the second. Style and allusion transform the plain Joshua Reynolds of 1773 in this way (London, Royal Academy).

A child, Master Crewe, he paints *as* Henry VIII, painted by Holbein, legs apart—as Hogarth wrote in his *Analysis of Beauty*, a form designating male power: this is Henry VIII the tyrant, wife slayer, and lecher, in some sense a grown hyped-up version of little Master Crewe (private collection). In the case of Crewe, and also of Theophila Palmer shown reading Richardson's *Clarissa* (fig. 40), the process reduces pretension: a stripping down of Clarissa into Theophila reading *about* her is like Henry VIII reduced to Master Crewe or indeed Rembrandt or Michelangelo to Reynolds. One could say that Henry VIII (or Clarissa) is him/herself unmasked—the reverse of the masked child—by the merger with the child. Or, if we look up from Crewe or Palmer, we see the dreams and illusions implicit in costume or reading matter. The process might be regarded as the iconoclasm of the great figure; or as a hankering upward of the small, as in the more dignified Reynolds portraits. But the success, at least in the children's portraits, may derive from the iconoclastic tradition, of which its transformation is so gentle and feminized a version.

With Reynolds's *Mrs. Abington as Miss Prue* (fig. 39), the portrait on which we shall focus, the wit comes with the reversal of Abington and Prue, which raises Abington, the adult playing the role of the ingenue Prue. *Raising*, of course, draws attention to a competition between the painter and the poet. The implicit comparison between the portrait by a painter and the "character" written by a poet stands near the center of Reynolds's career. If the portrait is only a likeness—a "face painting" as it was called in the eighteenth century—the painter need fear no competition from the poet. But the moment the face is said to have "character"—as when Rembrandt casts shadows to highlight certain features, eyes or mouth—the artist may be seen moving toward the model of the poet and vying with him to produce qualities that transcend mere resemblance.

A version of these transcendent qualities was summed up by Reynolds: "Thus if a portrait-painter is desirous to raise and improve his subject, he has no other means than by approaching it to a general idea." He goes on to say that the portrait painter "leaves out all the minute breaks and peculiarities in the face, and changes the dress from a temporary fashion to one more permanent, which has annexed to it no ideas of meanness from its being familiar to us." On the other hand, Reynolds acknowledges, "It is very difficult to ennoble the character of a countenance but at the expense of the likeness, which is what is most generally required by such as sit to the painter."[44] And in a letter to James Boswell, who had asked him to put into words a character of the late Samuel Johnson, whom he had known for thirty years and painted repeatedly, Reynolds wrote: "The habits of my profession unluckily extend to the consideration of so much only of character as lies on the surface, as is expressed in the

39. Sir Joshua Reynolds, Mrs. Abington as Miss Prue *(1771), painting.*

lineaments of the countenance." Only in writing, he tells Boswell, can one "attempt to go deeper and investigate the peculiar colouring of his mind, as distinguished from all other minds."[45]

Here is a candid outline of the problems faced by the portrait painter as opposed to the writer of "character" (say the moralist, from Theophrastus to Samuel Butler, or the historian, from Thucydides to Halifax, Clarendon, and Bishop Burnet) or the writer of biography like Boswell himself.[46] If he is to be more than a face painter—if he is to aspire to the more elevated art of the historian—he must generalize his sitter. But if he generalizes he risks sacrificing the resemblance, and in any case, he finds himself hard pressed to introduce the "character" that lies beneath the sitter's surface, "the peculiar colouring of his mind" (as Reynolds puts it).

There are two issues at stake, however, in Reynolds's statements: one is the elevation of the sitter (and probably also thereby the artist) by approximating portraiture to history painting, and the other is the delineation of "the peculiar colouring of the mind." The one is satisfied by the imitation of elevated, heroic forms taken from the graphic tradition of history painting; the other, the "colouring of the mind," is by no means so easily satisfied. Much of the time Reynolds was satisfied in his portraits with the former. But at his most impressive he represents "character."

The portrait of the actress Frances Abington (1737–1815) as Miss Prue in Congreve's *Love for Love* carried the title *Portrait of a Lady. Three Quarters* when Reynolds exhibited it at the Royal Academy in 1771. This is a conventional title (its pendant, *Theophila Palmer Reading* [fig. 40], was called *A girl reading*), but since it is clearly not a "Lady" but a girl (and its pendant *is* a "girl"), at once questions arise. It is a "Lady" *as if* she were a girl, as in the "Young Johnson" or "Young St. John"; and, as spectators were bound to recognize, it was a famous actress *playing* a girl—a particular actress and a particular girl in a particular play.

The portrait of an actress, to begin with, offers a solution to the problem of general and particular: her profession carries with it an authority for her being simultaneously both (as it offers an excuse for an overly forward and vulgar pose). When in Oliver Goldsmith's *Vicar of Wakefield* the painter represents the housewife Mrs. Primrose as Venus he produces a hybrid monster; only slightly less outré was the Restoration portraitist who represented one of Charles II's mistresses as Mary Magdalen. When merchants' wives commissioned portraitists to paint *them* as Magdalens too, it became clear that the image represented less personal elevation than social climbing for the sitter and, for the artist, irreverent wit. Actresses, however, are professional Magdalens, raising themselves only by the roles they play into a world of imagination, literature, and art.

When Reynolds painted Sarah Siddons as the Tragic Muse he was showing her, as a fine actress, becoming the role, which (because Reynolds, with his own assumptions about the general and about

40. Reynolds, Theophila Palmer Reading *(1771), painting.*

elevation in art, painted her) becomes also an allegorical equivalent of her genius: she is so great a tragic actress that she *is* in some sense the Tragic Muse. In the same way, he portrayed Garrick as Hercules choosing not between Virtue and Vice but between the muses of Comedy and Tragedy—in a situation of a man being wooed by two women—because Garrick was so versatile an actor that he was equally good at comedy and tragedy. Reynolds had previously, in 1768, painted Frances Abington as the Comic Muse (Siddons as the Tragic Muse came much later in 1784), but this—the Siddons–Garrick solution—is not the solution he takes in 1771 for his exhibition picture of Abington (see fig. 41).

Mrs. Abington, for one thing, is shown in a particular play, William Congreve's *Love for Love;* she is neither the Comic Muse nor exactly herself but one of the roles for which she was famous. She was most celebrated for playing a kind of role—"country girls, romps, hoydens, and chamber maids" as the *DNB* puts it. Ophelia and Desdemona were the upper reaches of her range, and off to the side, a somewhat different type, Portia. Miss Prue was a recent role, one Abington first played to great applause at Garrick's Drury Lane Theatre in a revival of *Love for Love* in December 1769—and again in June 1770: Reynolds is in a sense celebrating that recent triumph.

We may even experience a disappointment of expectation approaching this portrait from Reynolds's *Discourses* (including the one he delivered in December 1770 where he says "that Nature herself is not to be too closely copied") and from the heroic full-lengths. In contrast to the elevated Reynolds portrait or the usual Reynolds society portrait, this one is signalized by the reversed chair—a convention that we might trace back not to Reynolds but to Hogarth's conversation pictures, where chairs sometimes are turned around or overturned.[47] And, worse, the young woman employs the strange gesture of thumb to mouth and the stare. The thumb to mouth recalls Reynolds's remark in one of the *Discourses* against Bernini's David with slingshot, grimacing. But David was a tragic figure; she is comic, in a comedy, not elevated, and so decorum is not violated.

There is, I should add parenthetically, an important emphasis in that term *exhibition* picture. By choosing to hang a picture amid a group of pictures for the annual Royal Academy exhibition Reynolds was making a didactic, a programmatic, an exhibitionist statement about his art and also—the case with Reynolds as with his predecessor Hogarth—about the course English art ought to follow. I think he was making in this case a statement about *character* rather than *elevation* in portraiture.

The principle of "character" Reynolds is employing in this portrait had its source and authority in Aristotle's *Poetics* (25.10 ff.), where we read:

> The poet being an imitator just like the painter or other maker of likenesses, he must necessarily in all instances represent things in one or

41. Reynolds, Mrs. Abington as the Comic Muse *(1768; rev. 1773), painting.*

other of three aspects, either as they were or are, or as they are said or thought to be or to have been, or as they ought to be.

Reynolds's usual way was to represent his sitters "as they *ought* to be." Just before Reynolds's time Hogarth in painting and Henry Fielding in fiction were representing characters "as they are *said* or *thought* to be," either by themselves or by others, that is, by gossip or reputation or rumor. But at the same time they were juxtaposing the other categories, "as they are" with "as they ought to be," and thus modifying the notion of "hero" as well as of "portrait" in terms of what I have called the immediacy and contingency of the modern rather than the stereotypes of ancient models.

When Fielding, for example, wants to characterize Joseph Andrews he does so in relation to various types or models or mock-heroic analogies, that is, to characters he is not but *thinks* himself to be (or is thought to be by other characters)—or that Fielding, writing the history of the novel as he writes his novel, exposes by moving from one generic expectation to another. Joseph sees himself as an emulator of his sister Pamela (i.e., the literary Pamela of Richardson's novel), and when Lady Booby tries to entice him into her bed he sees himself as the biblical Joseph; more generally he is seen by Lady Booby and her women friends as a young Priapus. In society, Fielding is saying, a person is defined by sets of manners that are self-imposed or imposed by others; the rest emerges in Joseph's actions of love and charity which do *not* fit these categories but are defined *against* them. Tom Jones is defined by the false "character" of a n'er-do-well he is assigned by neighbors and by his enemies Blifil, Thwackum, and Square—or the quite erroneous identification of him as Bonnie Prince Charlie during the Rebellion of '45.[48]

This is the kind of double exposure that a portrait painter could best utilize when painting an actor or actress. In Hogarth's *Strolling Actresses Dressing in a Barn* (fig. 5) the discrepancy was between the individual actresses and the roles assigned them. By contrast, in Reynolds's portrait of Abington as Prue the distinction between actress and role, between the pretty young woman and the trappings of the goddess Diana, is much modulated. With Abington not the discrepancy but the merger is manifest: actress and role are closely, interestingly related, and this is at the heart of Reynolds's characterization of Abington, as it is of his art of portraiture. As in *Garrick between the Comic and Tragic Muse* Reynolds's fancy is producing a compliment—how Herculean is Garrick as an actor!—whereas Hogarth's judgment produces a witty discrepancy between the strolling actress and the role of Diana, for which she is unsuited. The difference between the Hogarth and the Reynolds modes is summed up by this example.

But Reynolds does allow one question: which qualities in the portrait can be attributed to Abington and which to "Miss Prue"? Is this the woman or the actress or the role of Congreve's Miss Prue? The genius of the actress may lie in the ability of a woman of thirty-four (her age at this time) to play a girl of seventeen—or the youthful appearance of the thirty-four-year-old actress. In a real sense the title "*Mrs.* Abington as *Miss* Prue" expresses the oxymoron of Reynolds's conception. What we notice is the adolescent pose, the informality of the turned-about chair, the thumb to the mouth, and the faraway (perhaps adolescent) gaze.

First, here are the biographical facts: Abington was city-bred, progressing from real-life roles of flower girl, street singer, servant, cookmaid, and possibly prostitute to actress and with success to a celebrity figure of fashion and sophistication in London society.[49] Second, we have the text of Congreve's play, in which Miss Prue was an innocent from the country (one of many anticipations of Hogarth's Harlot), brought to London and exposed to the ultrasophistication of the fop Mr. Tattle, with whom she at once fell in love. (The name *Prue* of course indicates the quality of prudence—another case of a definition-by-negatives, of a social commonplace that does not fit: she is obviously *im*prudent, though she comes to learn a certain kind of prudence.)

Her "country" sensuality is summed up in her response to her stepmother:

> Mr. Tattle is all over sweet, his peruke is sweet, and his gloves are sweet, and his handkerchief is sweet, pure sweet, sweeter than roses. Smell him, mother, madam, I mean. He gave me this ring for a kiss.[50]

But at the same time her innocence, as in her words to this same Tattle, shines through:

> Well, and how will you make love to me? Come, I long to have you begin. Must I make love too? You must tell me how.   [p. 57]

Prue succumbs to Tattle and is immediately discarded, but she is left with the double lesson that she is now infatuated with a man and that one must tell lies in order to survive in London.

"Why, must I tell a lie then?" she asks Tattle, her instructor and seducer. "Yes," replies Tattle, if you would be well-bred. All well-bred persons lie. Besides, you are a woman; you must never speak what you think. Your words must contradict your thoughts, but your actions may contradict your words. So, when I ask you if you can love me, you must say no, but you must love me too.   [p. 57]

The point is that Prue is a young country girl whom Tattle teaches that a prudent society lady says "No" when she means "Yes." Nevertheless, when she is courted by the other ingenu of the play, the sailor Ben, she responds with complete frankness, rejecting him and calling him a "stinking tar-barrel" (p. 74). In this situation, as an actress the worldly-wise Frances Abington is playing a simple girl who is taught to act but cannot feign: she does love Tattle and doesn't Ben.

The scene represented by Reynolds has been identified as Scene 7 of Act 3, the one in which Miss Prue says "No" to Ben—and which involves some byplay with chairs.[51] If we look more closely at this scene we see that the chairs are used either to increase or to ward off intimacy. Ben asks Prue to sit down and then offers to pull up his own chair—and "thus, an you please to sit, I'll sit by you." "You need not sit so near one," she replies; "if you have anything to say, I can hear you farther off; I an't deaf." Ben then moves his chair and (according to the stage direction) *"sits farther off."* The business with the chairs serves in the play as a visual metaphor for the game of courtship and its consequence, in terms as social as the card game in Pope's *Rape of the Lock.* Less genteel metaphors, visual but unmaterialized, are projected verbally by Ben when he tells Prue that "I may steer into your harbor," or that "we may chance to swing in a hammock together." But the chairs present the crucial aspect of exclusion or denial: Prue moves her chair away from Ben's.

What Reynolds develops in his portrait which is not suggested in Congreve's text (but which may have been part of the stage business at Drury Lane) is the turning of the chair's back. Combined with the gesture of her thumb it may express her rejection of the poor seaman. But the thumb to mouth could be either a biting of her thumb at Ben, defiance or impudence as in Shakespeare's "I will bite my thumb at them, which is disgrace to them if they bear it" (*Romeo and Juliet,* I.i.42–51; it is as if she thumbed her nose, a gesture recalling the vulgar arm gesture of Reynolds's *Cupid as a Link Boy*); or it could be a sign of pensivity. This is the scene—parallel to the one where Tattle instructs Prue in social hypocrisy—in which she uses natural frankness to reject a frank suitor after having learned the ways of deceit in order to give herself to a deceitful sophisticated city fop.

This is a central scene and the chair is a central symbol. But the impression the portrait gives is of Prue's being alone, and although Reynolds may be illustrating the chair scene, with Ben implicitly in the position of the spectator, one of the most interesting things about Prue's expression is that she is completely self-engrossed, showing no awareness whatever of a second person. This does not of course rule out poor Ben's presence. But I suspect that Reynolds is conflating the memory of the chair scene with two other moments. One is the moment following her final scene with her father Foresight and beyond the actual limits of the play. The other involves the sitter's chair in Reynolds's studio.

By the end of the play, with Tattle not only far beyond her reach but himself trapped into a marriage with Mrs. Frail, Prue can conclude to her father—in words of power and beauty:

> for now my mind is set upon a man, I will have a man some way or other. O! methinks I'm sick when I think of a man, and if I can't have one, I would go to sleep all my life, for when I'm awake, it makes me wish and long, and I don't know for what—and I'd rather be always sleeping, than sick with thinking.

She adds resolutely:

> . . . I'll have a husband, and if you won't get me one I'll get one for myself; I'll marry our Robin, the butler. He says he loves me, and he's handsome man, and shall be my husband; I warrant he'll be my husband and thank me too, for he told me so.   [pp. 124–25]

Her father thereupon gives the order to have her locked up: I am suggesting that his order has been carried out and that Prue is sitting alone in her room, the chair now a barrier not only between her and Ben but also her father, and the spectator.

We should return to Reynolds's diffidence about character in portraiture. In painting a Samuel Johnson, he remarked, it is not so easy as in writing to "attempt to go deeper and investigate the peculiar colouring of his mind." He offers an "attempt" in the simple, unadorned portrait of Giuseppi Baretti engrossed in a book (or, even better, the early *Boy Reading*). This model he displayed in his portrait of Abington and underlined at the 1771 Royal Academy exhibition by pairing it with another portrait. The other intimate portrait he showed was of his young niece Theophila Palmer reading a book (fig. 40, called simply *A girl reading*, no. 158). The same size (both 74 by 62 centimeters), the pair remained together until the 1970s: both are of self-absorbed young women. Theophila, as it happens, is reading a book that is identified on its spine as Richardson's *Clarissa,* another story of love and betrayal, though accompanied here by rape and death—very much the sort of thing that is on Prue's mind by the end of *Love for Love.*

We shall return later to the matter of love and betrayal, but first I want to pursue the matter of the sitter's absorption. A third painting exhibited in 1771, a "fancy picture" called *Resignation* (no. 159), was a half-length profile of an old, apparently imaginary man engrossed in thought. In all three of these paintings Reynolds is depicting a state that had not been—or was seldom—represented in English art, one that has been fully dealt with in French art of the eighteenth century by Michael Fried.[52] Fried would presumably call Abington's state absorption—a term that designates the painter's desire to free his painting of the portrait sitter's self-display and self-consciousness before a viewer. The best case, of course, along the line of the sleeping or blind men painted by Chardin and Greuze, was a person engrossed in some typical profession, employment, or pastime: for example, the bibliophile Baretti reading a book. (Though the Baretti might appear to be about nearsightedness rather than absorption.)

But to portray the profession of acting is to portray someone absorbed in a theatrical role, and better yet in a role that itself involves self-absorption, as in the case of Miss Prue at the final curtain of *Love for Love.* The pendant portrait of a little girl engrossed in the adventures of a grown-up lover, Clarissa Harlowe, bears a chiastic relationship to the portrait of a grown-up, thirty-four-year-old woman playing the young, comic-Clarissa role of Miss Prue.

With Reynolds, however, we have to return to his own words about the representation of mind, for the appropriate term here is not so much absorption as "reflection," a Johnsonian term that appears, for example, thirty times in the first twenty-nine *Ramblers.*[53] Before Johnson it was one of the crucial terms of British empiricism, the other being sensation. In Locke's words:

> These two, I say, viz. external material things, as the objects of SENSATION, and the operation of our own minds within, as the objects of REFLECTION, are the only originals from whence all our ideas take their beginnings.[54]

All human knowledge, all "colouring of . . . mind," Locke says, is derived either from sensation, man's response to the outside world, or from reflection, "the action of the mind upon itself" (to use Johnson's definition in his *Dictionary*). As Locke also says: "When the mind turns its view inwards upon itself, and contemplates its own actions, *thinking* is the first that occurs" (2.19.1, p. 298). As Robert Griffin explains:

> Therefore the mind has the power to reflect before it has the idea of "thinking," and only reaches that idea in self-reflection. Accordingly, Locke derives all of the mind's ideas of its own modes, such as retention, contemplation, discursive reasoning, and judging, from reflection. The priority of the reflective power identifies it with "mind" itself.[55]

"Mind" and "reflection" are virtually synonymous for a painter like Reynolds. But to be more precise, Johnson defines "reflection" in the *Dictionary* as "thought thrown back upon the past, or the absent, or itself." In this definition I would stress "the past" and "the absent" as important complements to "itself." In *Rambler* No. 203 Johnson recalls the episode in the *Aeneid* where Aeneas comforts his shipwrecked comrades with the words that "perhaps one day it will help to have remembered even these things" (1.203). Aeneas's words sum up, of course, the situation Reynolds is illustrating in his portrait of Abington: as Prue she is recollecting a difficult experience, the admonitory lesson, the loss of Tattle. And in Johnson's words about Aeneas in *Rambler* No. 203: "There are few higher gratifications than that of reflection upon surmounted evils, when they were not incurred nor protracted by our fault, and neither reproach us with cowardice, nor guilt." In these terms Prue at the end of *Love for Love* embodies all the requirements and is the ideal subject for the representation of reflection—and therefore of mind.

Fried has acknowledged the basic difference between the French focus in the eighteenth century on absorption and the English interest in the diversity or variety (or relativity) of responses. But within English art there was also a historical transition that corresponded roughly to the French reaction against rococo art, evident in the movement from the Hogarthian amplitude of *Strolling Actresses Dressing in a Barn* to the single focus of Reynolds's *Mrs. Abington as Miss Prue*. Reynolds retained the Hutchesonian emphasis on the unity side of the unity-variety ratio. In doing this he was following the art treatises (as were the opponents of the rococo in France) which stress singleness of effect as a higher aim of art than dispersal or discrepancy, amplitude or difficulty, the mode practiced by Hogarth and his followers.

The literary analogy is important here. When a particular aesthetic criterion is predominant in a historical period, the art that best fulfills this aesthetic criterion will become the model for the other arts. With the rise of the Longinian aesthetic in the eighteenth century, the intense isolated moment, because it was supposedly sublime, assured priority over the accumulation or amplitude of moments (of details) which we associate with verbal art. In prose and poetry the author looked to painting, which did catch the intense moment, and in painting the artist turned from Hogarth's amplitude (or in his literary contemporaries Pope's or Fielding's) to the simple unities of Reynolds.

And yet in Prue's case—as in her pendant Theophila Palmer's case—we know what she is reflecting on. Reynolds paints a picture that is manifestly both theatrical and reflective because Prue-Abington *is* aware of a spectator whom she is cutting off, whether he be Ben, her father, the theater audience, the spectators at the Royal Academy show, or the painter Reynolds. The important characteristic that is both English and Reynoldsian is that Prue is not somnolent or self-enclosed in so passive a way as the figures advocated by Diderot and painted by Greuze. She is not merely focusing on her own thoughts; she is not merely blocking out Ben. She is seeing Tattle or the more general Man or even Robin; she is specifically contemplating her newly found knowledge of the world and its ways, but with our (spectators') knowledge that she has only learned from her sensations that she wants a man and, moreover, that she must adapt to the ways of the world in order to get him and hold him—and not merely be exploited by him. In short, she is thinking about, or reflecting on, what is absent. The thumb to mouth now can be read to imply not only reflection but retrospection and regression. The action of thumb-sucking gives the sense, in the play context, that frustration (at the hands of a father, a lover) has led in Prue to oral forms of regression.[56]

Frances Barton, as Abington was named to begin with, was not an innocent from the country, any more than she was seventeen years old, but she had married her Tattle. She had come to terms with a London of Tattles and Scandals by becoming street-wise and by suffering a disastrous marriage with her music teacher, James Abington, from which she only extricated herself by paying him an annuity to stay away from her. Accordingly in his sitter Reynolds portrays both Prue as ingenue and Frances Barton Abington as former ingenue now playing an ingenue—now herself an experienced woman of the world, a center of fashion, but in life, formerly, Frances Barton both innocent and outside society. Now, in this portrait, she is inside but shown portraying the yet-outsider, the earlier Frances, who perhaps still exists inside. (This is, of course, a very Hogarthian situation to which Reynolds finds himself drawn.)

But if there was a general sense in which Reynolds could have defined Frances Abington negatively and positively in terms of Miss Prue, there was also a sense in which he would have seen in this actress both as artist and as individual a parallel between the sitter and the painter. His own self-portrait painted in the style of Rembrandt showed him with the ideal of Michelangelo's history painting but not the illusion that he is himself more than a Rembrandtesque portrait painter, much farther down what he considered the ladder of painterly importance. Like Reynolds, Abington excelled in the secondary parts, the Ophelias and Miss Prues, not the great Siddons heroines and protagonists: not even Angelica of the main plot of *Love for Love* but Prue (a very brief though vivid role) of the subplot—let alone a heroic, tragic Clarissa, alluded to in the pendant of Theophila Palmer.

More significant, the intimacy of the portrait is combined by Reynolds with a strongly marked emphasis on artifice, for which the chair sets the pattern. The composition draws attention to itself (certainly in a way it does not in the pendant): the virtual coincidence of the chairback, Prue's crossed arms, and even her face and the picture plane constitute one feature; the abstract pattern produced by the arms and chairback is another. These elements draw attention to the painting as artifice, or the painter's artifice, in a way parallel to the artifice of the sitter, who is herself employing artifice in so many different senses—the thirty-four-year-old actress playing the teenage Prue who has herself, in the play, learned the lesson of artifice. Reynolds emphasizes his own and his sitter's artifice not by introducing heroic echoes and poses, as in so many of his portraits, but by emphasizing the formal pattern of his painting's surface.

If, therefore, reflection is one term that governs this portrait, artifice is another: which is only to show the relation between the artifice of the artist and the reflection of his creation, only to show one reason why an actor or actress is an optimal subject for a portrait painter. Actress and painter have in common the control of external appearances to express character. If in this case we may sense a deeper affinity than usual, say in the peripheral roles assigned to and accepted by this actress and this painter (the painter who preaches history painting but practices portrait painting, including portraits of young actresses and demimondaines such as Kitty Fisher and Nelly O'Brien), it only explains something of the power we feel in the portrait.

A few more biographical facts might now be appropriately mentioned. Although there was a difference of twenty years in their ages, the careers of the painter and the actress were in a general way parallel. Abington's debut in London was in 1755, Reynolds's only two years earlier in 1753; she was thereafter kept from the roles she wanted by the reigning actresses of her time and so went to Dublin, where she enjoyed great success and five years later returned to Drury Lane, now a star. Prior to 1753 Reynolds had left the London of Hogarth and Allan Ramsay to paint in Italy, the standing model for Western art, after which he returned to immediate and lasting success. These are only very rough parallels, but I mean them to suggest something of the affinity Reynolds may have seen or wished to see between himself and this actress. The evidence for a sentimental relationship between Reynolds and Abington consists of the known facts that he painted more portraits of her than of any other actress and that—strange for a man as purse-conscious as Reynolds—he bought a block of twelve seats for Abington's benefit in April 1772. At any rate, some sort of personal subtext can reasonably be inferred for this portrait. Once again there seems to be a kind of chiastic relationship in the portrait, between on the one hand the young Abington and the aging Reynolds and on the other the aging Abington and the adolescent Prue, emphasized, as I have said, by Reynolds's niece, the *very* young Theophila Palmer, in the pendant.

There is also the coincidence we have already seen that both sitters, Abington and Palmer, are engrossed in the particular subject of love. Depending on how Reynolds may have regarded Richardson's novel, whether as tragedy or titillation, one thing is plain: both pictures are about "Love for Love"—are in fact activated by the idea of *this* love for *that*. In *Love for Love*, real is substituted for showy love by the hero Valentine; real love for (his) real love by the heroine Angelica; and false love for false love among the merely social characters such as Tattle and Frail and the childlike presocial characters such as Prue and Ben. In *Clarissa*, the two kinds of love—lust and Christian charity, eros and agape—are traded between the protagonists Clarissa and Lovelace.

Another piece of evidence is the clear thread that connects the mythological paintings Reynolds included in the exhibition of 1771— with each other and with the two portraits of Abington–Prue and Theophila Palmer.[57] They are all stories of love and of age versus youth, with the youth embodying (or imbibing) passion to the detriment or dismay of his/her elders. *Venus Chiding Cupid for Casting Accounts* (now at Kenwood) was another experiment at a higher level in gamin art; the second mythological subject was *Ino and the Infant Bacchus,* showing Ino, Semele's sister (according to Ovid's story) watching over the infant Bacchus. In this case she is a stepmother who is later driven mad by the vindictive Juno, who had already destroyed Semele, Bacchus's mother. In both subjects an authority figure, an older person, is shown protecting or chiding a child associated in both cases with disseminating love, passion, lunacy, and inebriation in the world. These older people are also engrossed or absorbed in the situation of the child. Ino regards Bacchus much as Theophila does her book. So we have hanging together on the wall of the Royal Academy in 1771 a series of ingenues—reminiscent of those later grown-ups Reynolds painted shrunk back into infancy (St. John the Baptist, Samuel Johnson, for example): Cupid, Bacchus, Miss Prue, and the young niece Theophila, all concerned in stories of love, seduction, rape, and passionate transformation of an Ovidian sort. The elder on stage is either a Venus chiding her Cupid, or an Ino nursing her Bacchus—or offstage angry victims of Cupid's darts and Bacchus's power of inebriation.

The strongest evidence, the visual structure of *Mrs. Abington as Miss Prue* itself, remains to be considered. We have discussed it so far as formal pattern, emphasizing the presence, indeed the role of the artist, and a kind of parallel to the profession of the actress in her ingenue role. Reynolds limits the portrait to her face and hands, the double center of expressiveness. The hand to her mouth, the thumb to her lips, is a childish, naïve gesture, a "country" gesture, but also one that places the hands intervening between her and the viewer. The chair, of course, is the chief visual metaphor, but reinforcing the chairback are Prue's crossed arms. The black rectangles of her wristbands are striking too. They add to the pattern of the crossed arms on the chairback: all of which serves not just as pattern but as a kind of barrier or protection between Prue–Abington and the spectator. But the wristbands are also, in the context of the play, badges of mourning for the lost lover Tattle—and at the same time resemble shackles which confine her to her room ("lock her up," says her father Foresight) and prevent her from finding her man, perhaps shackle her to Tattle or any man. She is in some sense shackled to the chair, imprisoned by her father or by her love.

One wonders how far such a painting asks (in the fashion of a

Hogarth) to be verbalized.[58] The title "Love for Love" in a way activates the vocabulary. The black wristbands are—we may verbalize
them—manaclelike. But we also, looking at that chair, keep coming
up with the word "back": the *back* of the chair; she sits not forward
but *back*ward on the chair; she is, while still facing us, "turning her
back" on Ben—or on her father—or even Tattle—or on the audience—or on Reynolds the painter. "Turning her back" while still facing them: that is the point, and biting her thumb at them all, as Prue
and as Abington.

The picture is of course about the relationship of Prue's *back*ward-
ness and her country *back*ground—posed against the black and
stormy *back*ground or *back*drop,[59] and about her *back*wards means of
gaining access to love and society—to Tattle—to Reynolds's studio—
to Reynolds himself.[60]

The little dog, whose face is as flat-pressed against the surface as
Abington–Prue's, a parallel meditation (both with emphatic mouths),
may have been Prue's (and have played a part in the production of
Love for Love) or may have been Abington's own. In the context of the
play the dog has a definite iconographical significance. A dog, when
he appeared in a portrait with a couple tended to signify fidelity; but
when he was with a lone woman, or women, often in a bordello—or
alone with a woman in her boudoir as in Fragonard's young woman
holding a furry dog aloft in the air between her legs—the dog was
clearly a displacement of a lover, a substitute for an absent or vanished lover, in this case Tattle or the projected Man. He is in her lap,
like Belinda's Shock or Nelly O'Brien's Christological dog in the portrait in which she poses as a secular, a London Madonna (London,
Wallace Collection).[61]

The general effect of all this detail and formal pattern—of the
chairback, the crossed arms, the dog, and the face—is a pressing forward and yet a holding back, or being held back by barriers. These
forms serve as barriers or protection between Prue and Tattle or
Robin the butler—or between her and the viewer. But despite her
apparent reticence, the frontality, the closeness of the picture plane,
and the chair and pose nevertheless push her out at the viewer.

This picture, with its strange intimacy, raises the question of the
spectator: whether it is, as in the immediate context of the play, either Ben or only the memory of Tattle; or whether it is the spectators
at the play or at the Royal Academy; or, by no means least, whether it
is the painter, who embodies aspects of all of these. Given the intimacy, the closeness of figure pressed against the picture plane, the

sense is of the sitter's being in the painter's studio, in the painter's chair, facing her portraitist—the ultimate figure opposite Miss Prue. The chair is turned to separate Abington and the artist, as actress to painter and as person to person.

Is this Reynolds's way of showing her "putting something between" herself and him, saying that she will not respond to his professional or personal entreaties? Or, comically, that she is "trapped" by her love of him, as for—the ironic self-deprecation of Reynolds's self-portraits again—Tattle? Or merely that she must have someone, even poor old Sir Joshua? Is Reynolds, one wonders, in his own terms, Tattle or is he Ben? Or Ben to someone else's Tattle? Perhaps, with his scarred lip, his pockmarked face, his deafness, and his carefully self-deflating self-portraits and public persona, he could think of himself as Ben, the male equivalent of Prue in the play, but nevertheless rejected by her in her fashionable Tattle-like pretensions.

I have become fanciful and speculative, but I do not wish to retract the central relationship of sitter and artist—which corresponds in a portrait like this one to the imaginary, the fictive relationships of Prue and Tattle and the rest. There is a long sequence in the center of Act 1 when Tattle and his friend Scandal bandy about the metaphor of painting the woman you love, as a mode of seduction, or as a way to keep her in your closet, or as a satire on her follies.[62] This passage about painting, character, and the power of art to control in one way or another the sexual object could have been a subtext for Reynolds's portrait in the larger context of the 1771 Royal Academy exhibition as well as in its smaller context of the relationship of artist and sitter, artist and actress.

Once beyond the simple likeness, the portrait image plays with the expansion of the sitter in his own eyes as it struggles against the artist's use of the image to elevate or express himself—at the sitter's expense. In reference to *Mrs. Abington as Miss Prue*, we can say that the Tattle or Ben who challenges the sitter within the plot of Congreve's play is a metaphorical equivalent for the artist who stands in the space this side of Abington–Prue and plays out an agon of representation that includes not an inanimate rock or tree but a living referent with whom he has a greater or lesser closeness of affiliation.

If Hogarth thematized the agon between painter and patron, Reynolds has shown us the overt rivalry in his portraits between the painter and the poet and the less obvious but equally potent relationship in *Mrs. Abington as Miss Prue* between the painter and his sitter.

STUBBS'S *HAMBLETONIAN*

A canvas seven by twelve feet nearly filled by a huge horse and two dwarfed humans with a racetrack and horizon glimpsed through the horse's nervous legs: George Stubbs's *Hambletonian, Rubbing Down* (fig. 42), painted in 1800 in the artist's seventy-fifth year, asks to be seen from the anachronistic perspective of Goya's floating horses and bulls in the *Disparates* of 1816–20.[63] But even in the 1790s when Goya first began to disrupt the hierarchical structure of post-Renaissance painting, isolating and magnifying subordinate elements out of all proportion, he justified his departure by joining his grotesque forms to a subject equally upsetting, the European and Spanish upheavals related to the French Revolution. Goya was the painter who first painted the ugly and evil in equivalent forms, without any attempt to assimilate them to the tradition of the beautiful. He introduced the genre of the nightmare, where rules of proportion no longer apply. Unlike those dream animals, Stubbs's *Hambletonian* remains anchored to the realistic conventions of the upper-class English genre of the horse picture, conventions that Stubbs himself had brought to perfection over the preceding forty years.

42. *George Stubbs*, Hambletonian, Rubbing Down *(1808), painting.*

Hambletonian has to be seen in the context of Stubbs's whole career, from the earliest provincial portraits of country squires and their hunts, and the *Anatomy of the Horse* in the 1750s and 1760s, to the innumerable portraits of horses in precisely delineated social and natural settings and the final image of *Freeman, the Earl of Clarendon's Gamekeeper* (1800). But there were also the curious drawings and etchings for Stubbs's *Comparative Anatomical Exposition of the Structure of the Human Body with That of a Tiger and a Common Fowl* (left unfinished at his death in 1806), which recall the illustrations at the very beginning of his career of the human uterus in parturition in John Burton's *Complete New System of Midwifery* (1751). The human and the animal are inextricable in Stubbs's oeuvre. Besides the animal pictures (there are almost as many dogs as horses), he painted many conversation pictures, human-centered groups usually including horses, with equal attention paid to human and animal likeness. Besides these, he also experimented in the 1760s—at the peak of his inventiveness—with the Burkean sublime, producing a series of wild animals in remote, wild settings engaged, or about to engage, in mortal combat. Understanding *Hambletonian* is partly a matter of which of these modes we see as the determining one for Stubbs—the conversational portrait, the sublime encounter, or the anatomical diagram.

Stubbs's undeniable appeal to the English of all classes and to many Americans as well, however, derives from his unique control of the animal genre. He presents with incomparable elegance and "truth"— or accuracy—both sides of the English mystery, the John Bullish love of horses and dogs as friends to man and also the aristocratic myth in which the thoroughbred horse is the outward sign of the English aristocrat's descent from William the Conqueror. Each horse, dog, trainer, groom, and stable boy, and sometimes also their master, is placed and related spatially to the others as precisely as each bone and body part in Stubbs's still authoritative *Anatomy of the Horse*. The relationship is, of course, homocentric and hierarchical, emphasized by Stubbs's placement of them in the context of the great country estates—with prominent British oaks, stables, kennels, and occasionally the country house itself—or in that of the race track where the horses and their masters compete and prove their respective orders of precedence.

Stubbs's scene sums up pictorially the world of the aristocratic or would-be aristocratic owners, their breed lines, genealogy, and property. Even now many of the owners and admirers of horses will know that Hambletonian's sire was King Fergus, son of Eclipse, and his dam a daughter of Highflyer, all descended from one of the three great sires (the Byerley Turk, the Darley Arabian, and the Godolphin Arabian). They will know, long before remembering the allusions of a historical or mythological painting, that Hambletonian was foaled in 1792, purchased in 1796 by Sir Henry Vane Tempest after he won the St. Leger, and subsequently defeated Joseph Cookson's horse Diamond on 15 March 1799 in one of the most famous of all Newmarket races, the subject of Stubbs's painting.

Paul Mellon, when asked in an interview at the pubic unveiling in 1977 of his great collection of British art what was the most rewarding moment of his career, replied that it was the day his horse won the Derby. But it is also true that Stubbs served as the fulcrum on which Mellon was turned by the late Basil Taylor from collecting horse pictures to collecting the masterpieces of British art. For Stubbs transforms a myth of English animals and aristocracy into something more. To a remarkable degree the aesthetic and the descriptive orders unite in these paintings: a formalism based on the Golden Section (the classical ideal of proportion) and the love of sheer paint texture joins with the almost biological classification of animal and human types in their habitats.

The world of Stubbs's paintings includes as well the mythic English countryside, which stretches idyllic and peaceful beyond the figures and houses. This is not the romanticized and stylized landscape of Gainsborough nor the academicized history-painting landscape of Richard Wilson but rather a habitat as carefully defined as the uterus of the *Complete New System of Midwifery*. A middle-distance plane of trees, a single blurred and random element in the otherwise carefully ordered composition, serves as an enveloping form, but one that widens and extends the context of the humans and animals to the distant and larger world to which both are subordinated.

In the masterpiece of the genre, *Gimcrack* (c. 1765, fig. 43), the representational and the diagrammatic, the iconic and the indexical, unite along a horizontal scale. From left to right, the victorious horse poses, his head held in place by his trainer or groom, while the stable boy kneels between his legs arranging straw. The three figures are enclosed by the large foreground profile of the rubbing-down house. A noticeable interval from the right, near the picture's center designated by one of the spectator stands along the racetrack, stands the jockey—alone, distanced from the horse he has ridden, his riding crop making a diagonal that recalls the slope of the roofs of the two buildings, the horse's hind leg and tail, and the extended rear legs of

43. Stubbs, Gimcrack *(c. 1765), painting.*

the racing horses beyond him. His face, the most striking detail in the painting, is delicate and his eyes, though looking toward the horse, are unfocused—registering memory rather than perception. While the horse is looking in the opposite direction from the jockey, out of the picture to the left, the eyes of both groom and stable boy are on the jockey. And to the right and beyond the jockey, set off by the little racetrack house, stretched along the horizon, dreamlike, is a re-play of the race Gimcrack has just won, with Gimcrack in exactly the position in which he crossed the finish line. The jockey is poised be-tween the actual world of the horse and his keepers and the distant memory of the race. The track itself is punctuated by the white fence, a line of pickets which resembles a scale of gradations, intervals, and ratios, carried on in the verticals of the rubbing-down house and the straight back of the jockey. The horizon line seems a scale on which are charted differences in genus, species, and class, both biological and social, as well as in time, memory, and existence.

In his composition Stubbs is the Linnaean classifier (according to the features common to a class rather than the particular plant, ani-mal, or human), but in his detail he follows Buffon into the complete description of each individual creature. At the same time, he conveys something of the sense of multiple time schemes he would have seen in Renaissance altarpieces; something of the timeless quiet of a religious painting also distinguishes *Gimcrack*. Indeed, biological classification in eighteenth-century England still rested uneasily on philosophico-theological distinctions such as the crucial one between man and horse: "Man feels, a Plant does not: But a Horse also feels," and therefore the ultimate distinction which separates horse from man lies in man's possession of reason (*animal rationale*).[64]

This was, of course, the source of Swift's paradox in Gulliver's fourth voyage where he placed reason in a horse's body and unreason in a man's. The slight frisson I feel looking at paintings of Gulliver (the prototype of the country squire who prefers his horses to his family) and the Houyhnhnms by Stubbs's contemporary Sawrey Gilpin shows me how little difference there is when Stubbs replaces Gulliver-Houyhnhnm or Yahoo-Houyhnhnm by the jockey John Pratt and the horse Gimcrack on the Newmarket racetrack. Such simple matters as the difference between a man and a horse standing diagrammatically side by side and the man *riding* the horse (unthinkable in Houyhnhnmland) are less simple once Gulliver's fourth voyage has become part of the English consciousness, even after it has been relegated to the safety of the nursery and the horses have been romanticized.

Stubbs is thus representing a primary subject socially, aesthetically, and perhaps morally, the horse being the creature which mediated for the aristocratic Englishman between man and nature, serving as hinge of the state of nature and the state of society. It is absolutely necessary for Stubbs to repudiate the rhetoric of the Rubens–Snyders–Oudry tradition of painting, or the Reynolds–Gainsborough tradition, which blurs the difference, either anthropomorphizing the animals, plants, and trees, or sympathetically merging the humans with a *genius loci*. The works of Reynolds, Gainsborough, Barry, and Mortimer, the Royal Academicians who were trying to connect English painting to Italy and France, stand in striking contrast to Stubbs. The broad generalizing brushstrokes of the academicians (including the relatively deviant Gainsborough) were intended as a graphic equivalent of poetic diction or the high style, distancing and transforming into fantasy—into memories of Venetian and Bolognese paintings or Van Dyck's Carolean portraits—the same English men and horses Stubbs fixes in relation to their milieu with precise and differentiating brushstrokes.

Given the contemporary pressures of the Royal Academy and the followers of the Burkean sublime, it is not surprising that Stubbs experimented in the 1760s with animal "histories" such as Phaeton's falling chariot with its plunging horses, or Hercules capturing the Cretan Bull, or the centaur Nessus and Dejanira. Far more impressive were the heightened images of animals pitted directly against each other in remote "sublime" landscapes. The masterpiece of Stubbs's hyped-up paintings, however, was the *Cheetah and Stag with Two Indians* (1768): here the cheetah is swathed in a gorgeous harness and being held in readiness by two voluminously robed Indians for the moment when they will release it to attack the stag who stands at a little distance. The patron's commission was to depict an encounter that took place in Windsor Great Park, though the landscape looks vaguely Indian.

This painting combines the unmediated encounter of the horse-lion pictures with the clothed and caparisoned figures of the conversation pictures, but in the size and scale of a history painting (six by nine feet). It would appear that the sublime paintings of encounter began with the interpersonal relationships of the conversation picture, the popular middle-class genre of the 1720s and 1730s which was renewed about the time Stubbs launched his career in the 1750s. Here social classification was stressed in the depiction of clothes, interiors, and interpersonal spacing, and the central relationship was often the encounter between a host and his guests or between different groups of guests mediated by the host. In the subtlety with which Stubbs depicts the distance and tension between the lion and horse, or the cheetah and stag, he produces an image that is arguably at the other end of the spectrum of the conversation picture.

But if the paintings of classification (man-horse-dog-estate-house-forest-landscape on a continuum) are augmented by paintings of encounter, in Stubbs's terms the encounter is only another form of classification. The origin of the horse and lion paintings is the Pergamene sculpture Stubbs saw in Rome of lion and horse locked in unequal combat.[65] But after he initially copied the lion fastened by his teeth to the horse's neck, he adapted the motif to his own scheme of things, moving the natural predator into the background and absorbing him in the enveloping dark screen of foliage. It is against the obscurity and integration of the lion into the landscape that he shows the clearly defined figure of the (in most cases white) horse. He emphasizes not the sheer mortal combat but the horse's relationship to its environment, and the wild horse remains the transitional figure between nature, red in tooth and claw, and the world that Stubbs and his patrons knew—that of the obedient thoroughbreds Gimcrack, Turf, and Eclipse.

IN the presence of *Hambletonian, Rubbing Down* the first question is its great size as compared to Stubbs's other paintings of that time, and indeed of the previous forty years. It is possible, though unlikely, that the size was part of the commission. But even if Sir Henry Vane Tempest did stipulate so large a painting, he would not have asked for the unparalleled size of the horse in relation to the picture space. The remarkable aspect of *Hambletonian* is less the size of the horse than the complete reversal of the usual hierarchical relationship in the racing and other horse pictures. When a horse is put in the foreground and so dwarfs the humans and even the distant landscape, the picture carries a message different from *Gimcrack* and the usual horse picture.

If the family tree of Hambletonian was and still is known to many viewers of Stubbs's canvas, the events of the famous match scheduled by Vane Tempest at Newmarket on 15 March 1799 were also familiar. From an early lead, Hambletonian ran neck and neck with Diamond; both jockeys mercilessly whipped and spurred their horses, "but particularly Hambletonian; he was shockingly goaded"; Hambletonian, with blood running down his flanks, "by an extraordinary stride or two, some say the very last stride, won the match by a little more than *half a neck*."[66]

That neck—but not the stride—is emphatically displayed straining toward the right side of Stubbs's picture; indeed the whole body is stretched under such tension as to substantiate Robert Hughes's sense of a "floating . . . dream image" and the basic insight of Basil Taylor, still Stubbs's most sensitive critic: "It is the image of a creature enduring the aftermath of a terrible, almost sacrificial, triumph of which it has been the hero" (i.e., it, rather than any human participant).[67]

What are the sources of this image? Although Stubbs claimed to have learned nothing from the art seen on his trip to Italy, his horse and lion paintings, as I have noted earlier, took off from the Pergamene sculpture of a horse-lion combat he saw in Rome. The only paintings in Stubbs's oeuvre that compare in size to *Hambletonian* were the huge horse-lion and horse-stag pictures, eight by ten feet, painted in the 1760s for the Marquess of Rockingham (now in the Yale Center for British Art). In the first of these (fig. 44), the earliest version of the lion-horse sculpture, the subject is the great suffering figure of the horse, taking up the same proportion of the picture space as Hambletonian, in much the same pose (even to the gaping mouth) except for its head which is turned back toward its tormentor.

Perhaps we can suggest that if from the direction of the horse pic-

44. Stubbs, A Lion Attacking a Horse *(1762), painting.*

tures Stubbs is overturning expectations and introducing the scale, proportions, and pathos of the horse-lion pictures, then from the direction of the horse-lion pictures he is transforming the conventional horse picture, with all its usual accoutrements of stable boy, trainer, and rubbing-down house, into a sublime spectacle, by simply omitting the lion from the suffering horse's back.

The art-historical prototype that suggests itself for Stubbs's *Hambletonian* composition—one Stubbs can be assumed to have seen—was Caravaggio's *Conversion of St. Paul* in Sta. Maria del Popolo in Rome. In an extraordinary gesture, Caravaggio places the horse at the center, filling and dominating the picture space, and the saint on the ground at the lower periphery. "Nothing more incongruous," Bernard Berenson wrote of this painting, "than the importance given to horse over rider, to dumb beast over saint. . . . No trace of a miraculous occurrence of supreme import."[68] Size, scale, and effect reappear in Stubbs's Rockingham version of the horse and lion and in *Hambletonian.* The huge horse can be regarded either, as Sir Lawrence Gowing believes, as Caravaggio's demonstration of "the grotesque incongruities of the actual,"[69] or as a conflation of the stories of Saul's conversion in Acts (which mentions no steed) with Balaam's in Numbers 22. As an animal in more immediate touch with the divine intention than its human rider, the horse serves as witness to, and mediator for, Saul-Paul's conversion. The other human figure, who holds the horse's bridle, fills the same secondary function as the trainer standing to the right of Hambletonian.

St. Paul's horse finds a parallel in the equally closeup and dominant body of St. Peter on the cross in Caravaggio's pendant in Sta. Maria del Popolo. And as St. Peter makes immediate eye contact with the viewer, it is St. Paul's horse that seems to turn his gaze in our direction, taking in the plight of his stricken rider. The composition can also be compared with the *Entombment of Christ* which Caravaggio painted at about the same time, which could have been seen by Stubbs in the Chiesa Nuova (Sta. Maria in Vallicella): the body of Christ, though not so large in relation to the total space, fills the same area on the frontal plane as the horse and St. Peter. If all three of these paintings are conflated we get some sense of the importance of Hambletonian vis-à-vis the humans, its extended and displayed body, and the sacrificial nature of its ordeal.

The relationship of St. Paul's horse to the prone body of Saul-Paul recalls a contemporary story that links *Hambletonian* to the third of the large paintings made by Stubbs for Rockingham. This was *Whistlejacket* (1762, eight by nine feet), equally large but with a rearing horse considerably smaller in proportion to the picture space than in the horse and lion painting. To both *Whistlejacket* and *Hambletonian* there was attached a Zeuxis–Parrhasius story of the artist's power to deceive the spectator. The illusion in both stories depends on the horse's size and proximity to the picture plane. But the difference is instructive: in one story, Stubbs's painted Whistlejacket deceived the actual horse Whistlejacket, who reared up and pawed at it. In the other story, told by Stubbs's common-law wife Mary Spencer, Hambletonian deceived a man at the exhibition who had stooped down near the canvas, become absorbed in another small picture, and then stood up—to the alarming sense that he was about to be kicked by this horse with its raised rear hoof.[70] The spectator, in short, bears a peculiarly intense relationship to the horse in *Hambletonian*.

Another contemporary response to the picture was evoked by the Royal Academy exhibition. The *Morning Herald* thought "the figure of the horse is calculated to give but a very slender idea of the swiftness of his speed; but the attendants are painted in a very masterly manner."[71] This comment draws attention both to a disappointment of expectations (Hambletonian's performance in the race is not shown) and to the striking human figures.

The stable boy rubbing down Hambletonian is bent down by the horse's neck, as under a yoke, his right hand on its back in a steadying gesture. The trainer, holding the horse's bridle, stands on the same plane as the animal, his expression as remarkable in its way as the expression of Gimcrack's jockey. Our sense of him, with his oversized top hat, is probably confused by our memories of Lewis Carroll's Mad Hatter. But the facts remain that his proportions alongside the horse make him appear dwarfish or stunted, and the wearing of the hat in this postcrisis moment, as well as the equally bulky overcoat, suggests a mock-heroic contrast between the sleek unencumbered body of the horse and this grotesquely swathed little man. The pupils of his eyes look to the right; his face is turned toward the horse, but his eyes seek out—not the horse, as with Gimcrack's jockey—but the spectator. The most general impression is concern, resignation, reproach, perhaps compassion—very different from the eager-to-please face of the stable boy peering out from under the horse's neck at the same spectator.

The horse itself is in motion, its legs cantering, its elongated body expressive of an almost convulsive straining both to pull ahead and to the rear, as if the separate images of Gimcrack during and after the race had been joined in one terrific tension embodying both. (Mary Spencer described him, though perhaps only to support her story, as both "cringing and threatening to kick.") In this context, both men are trying to calm and restrain the horse, while also holding him in profile for this moment of inspection (for which the coat and top hat would seem to be worn). But contrasted to the solid braced legs of the stable boy is the upright, restful, and somewhat aloof pose of the trainer. Some of his strangeness may come from the memory, in this alien context, of the figures to the side of the central mystery in an *Ecce Homo* composition.

The most immediate contemporary response to the painting was Vane Tempest's refusal to pay Stubbs his fee, followed by a lawsuit in which artists testified on both sides. He had commissioned Stubbs to paint pendants, the second of which, depicting Hambletonian winning the race, survives only in a copy by James Ward. Stubbs apparently completed only the view of Hambletonian *after* the race. I presume, since no transcript of the lawsuit survives, that Vane Tempest's complaint indicated displeasure with the reversal of the ordinary man and horse relationship in such pictures and the omission of any signs of the victory—of the jockey, who had "cut with the whip, and severely goaded with the spur," or the owner himself, or at least the Vane Tempest colors.

In many horse pictures the subject, the horse, painted in profile—to show its best points—takes the form of a minor secular icon, parallel in its way to the family images in the portrait gallery of the country house. Sometimes the horses hung in a subsidiary gallery, more a smoking room, but at others they hung in the primary gallery of family portraits, one line of thoroughbreds supporting the other. The horse, portrayed alone, was probably as good an example as we shall find in this period (after Swift's Celia) of the icon that is in fact a fetish. To imply that Stubbs, as well as the horse's owner, regarded a mere horse as something like an icon is, however, to be quite unhistorical. But it does suggest certain possibilities: that the horse in a conversation picture next to a man, loses its independent iconicity and becomes a supporter to the picture's secular icon; or that Stubbs as an artist may have regarded the horse, in lone horse pictures, as a marginalizing of the human, as a modification of the portrait genre (just as in the lion-horse paintings he is modifying, or modernizing, the ordinarily human-oriented genre of history painting); or that this centralizing of the horse for artistic purposes exists in a tension with the owner/patron's primary wish, which is to represent his horse only as a piece of property.

These possibilities, in any case, project a kind of picture in which the man dominates the picture space when it is the horse that deserves the position of honor. And *Hambletonian* seems to be the picture that rights that situation by marginalizing the human figures.

Vane Tempest may also have been disturbed by the unusual relationship Stubbs established in this picture between the owner of the horse (and the patron of the artist) and the horse: the owner is the implied viewer standing before the picture and being presented with his horse. He is the object of both the stable boy's and the trainer's eyes, the one showing subservience and the other undisguised concern and/or reproach. In the aftermath of the race the response of the owner of the horse is set against the responses of those who feed and care for the creature. The unequivocal relation of the owner/patron to the picture and its figures is felt by every viewer of the painting as he/she tries to find a place in relation to this other assumed spectator (as one does also in, say, Velazquez's *Las Meninas* or Goya's *Family of Charles VI* or, further back, in an *Ecce Homo*).

The question we are approaching has to do with Stubbs's relation to his patron and the degree of his artistic control over the subject the patron has commissioned him to paint. For there is no doubt that the great majority of his paintings were commissioned by patrons with particular requirements, which he obviously met well enough to enjoy a long and successful career. And it also seems clear that the patron's requirements are best summed up as the accurate representation of property.[72] Of Stubbs then it must be asked whether his representation of his patrons' possessions in the horse and conversation pictures is merely the naïve description of a provincial and/or subservient copyist, or whether he expresses a comment—aesthetic, satiric, or at least detached, originating perhaps in the objectivity of the anatomist, but also expressed within *Hambletonian* in the gaze of the top-hatted trainer.

The difficulties of establishing precedence between painter and patron, and of assigning priority to the idea of "property," is evident in what we know of the painting of *Whistlejacket*. Here the absence of a rider on the rearing horse, which ordinarily (as in its prototype, Titian's equestrian *Charles V*) carried an emperor, might be regarded as a subversive gesture. Being riderless implies something about the absent man as well as about the beautiful, autonomous horse. The stories connected with the painting support this interpretation, but the rider—he was supposedly to have been George III—was omitted at the behest of the Marquess of Rockingham, the patron, who had broken with the king while the picture was being painted.[73]

On the other hand, if because of the patron's wishes the rider was omitted, and possibly the landscape background too (the rearing horse stands out against a blank, primed canvas), one conclusion is that artist and patron, on the matter of the independent importance of the horse, see eye to eye. Both omissions (as also in the blank background in some of the horse "friezes") focus attention on the animal. Patron and artist, both horse lovers, agree to break away from the old academic categories of history, portrait, and landscape in which the horse was a subordinate element. And when Stubbs does raise the horse in stature, his innovation, which would have met with the approval of such a patron, is to replace the old generic categories and hierarchies of "art" with the new category of the sublime, as a term originating in nature not art.

In part then, we can answer the patron-artist issue by saying that in Stubbs's case his subject allowed him to enjoy a rapport with his patrons denied other artists of his time. Both patron and artist were antitraditionalist and forward looking at least in terms of the genre in which Stubbs distinguished himself. (The contemporary common-place referred to him, as earlier to Hogarth, as "the best painter *in his way*"—which meant in his subordinate genre.)

The chief argument in favor of Stubbs's control is, as we have seen, that he distinguishes in his paintings the realms of art and nature, implicitly grounding the hierarchy he portrays in terms of human art and power rather than a natural order. The horse symbolizes the natural order; all the artifacts and ordering, from bridles onward, symbolize the human. It is Reynolds and Gainsborough who meta-morphically blur the differences, either by raising nature to the level of art or by suggesting the illusion of humans happily merging with their natural settings. It is misleading to valorize Reynolds's art, as John Barrell does, as a noble attempt to generalize particular posses-sions (those vulgar objects Stubbs paints) into general ideas "in which no one could have exclusive property." For Reynolds's paintings merely offer what appears to be an image beyond property, "art" it-self, as in fact a piece of property to be hung with the other portraits in the country house gallery.[74]

For Stubbs we must start with his tendency, plain from the begin-ning but increasingly emphatic in his later years, to line up the people, animals, and carriages along a row parallel to the picture plane, as if on a shelf. To some extent this procedure carried over from his sci-entific work, where the horse was posed in profile so as best to display its anatomical configuration. By adding other elements—humans of varying degree—Stubbs simply supplemented along the same plane or along parallel planes until he had the complexly intricate world of his major conversation pictures. One result of the displaylike com-position is to make it unmistakable that the owner/patron is intended as the spectator. The size and scale project the picture into a smallish room where it can be seen from only a few feet away by the owner and his friends.

When Stubbs represents the owner/patron within the painting, in the middle world of the men and horses, he sets him in a position of awareness of both picture space and spectator space, in much the way he places the trainer in *Hambletonian*. One of a pair of pendants he painted for John Musters in the 1770s shows Musters in profile look-ing at his wife (both are riding on horseback along a ridge above their country house) whose face is turned toward the spectator (fig. 45). Musters is regarding her both from within and beyond the canvas (whence he can also see himself regarding her). The dominance of

45. Stubbs, John and Sophia Musters Riding at Colwick Hall *(1777),*
painting.

the owner/patron is summed up by the fact that when Mrs. Musters
proved unfaithful, Musters had Stubbs obliterate her from the horse's
back. This may recall Lord Rockingham's deciding not to sully Whistlejacket's back with the figure of George III. But Musters's gesture is
quite different: the absence or presence of Mrs. Musters denotes her
as Musters's property. The implication is that the power to add or
subtract from the picture is the owner/patron's, not the artist's, though
the artist may tacitly retain a mental reservation. Stubbs painted out
Mrs. Musters in such a way that she could easily be recovered again
(as indeed she has been).

The extreme version of the patron's power over the artist was seen
(an example I mentioned earlier) in the destruction of Graham
Sutherland's portrait of Churchill by Lady Churchill. Stubbs, I would
argue, experienced and envisaged the owner/patron in that role. In
Hambletonian he omits any sign of the artist within the hierarchic
structure of the painting (unlike paintings ranging from Raphael's
Disputa and Velazquez's *Las Meninas* to the comic histories of Hogarth

and the landscapes of Richard Wilson). No artist is even implied on the spectator's side of the canvas, as in the emphatic painterly style of a Reynolds or Gainsborough. He steps back, paints with all the signs of objectivity called for by the genre, which patently transfers the responsibility for the care and arrangement of the objects represented onto their owner. This tends to associate the artist with the servants within the painting, those who hold the bridle and display the horse. With the extravagantly deferential gesture of the ironic servant touching hand to cap, he presents the painting just as the master asked for it. "Never submit to lift a Finger in any Business but that for which you were particularly hired," Swift wrote in his *Instructions to Servants*.[75]

In some paintings of the 1790s the dutiful lineup of figures and objects across the picture plane approaches parody. The horse's elaborate harness—the owner's colors, bridle, saddle, and stirrups—is placed parallel to the servants' uniforms, which increasingly resemble harnesses. In the pair of paintings made for the Prince of Wales of his new phaeton and his regimental soldiers (1793, fig. 46), the strange swaddled shapes of horses and men, and particularly the three toylike

46. *Stubbs,* Soldiers of the 10th Light Dragoons *(1793), painting.*

soldiers, seem hardly animate. In *The Prince of Wales' Phaeton* (Royal Collection) the sense of tied-up possessions is compounded by the introduction of one disruptive element, a very alive, free, unharnessed, leaping dog.

THESE later works inevitably recall the English iconoclastic tradition that regarded art in all its subtlest and grossest manifestations as an imposition upon natural creatures and instincts, often on the poor and helpless by the rich and powerful, emphasized by the counter-presence of some small destructive creature like a dog or a child. The ultimate sense of "property" for Hogarth was the pair of manacled dogs juxtaposed with the young affianced couple in the first scene of *Marriage A-la-mode*. In this case each object in the room, including the dogs, has the earl's coronet stamped on it. For Blake it was London's "chartered streets" and the child who cries out: "Struggling in my father's hands; / Striving against my swadling bands / Bound and weary . . ." Hierarchical authority is connected with the physical restraint of clothing tightly wrapped like fetters.

The theme of constricting art also fits into the Protestant tradition of conversion (another reason Caravaggio's *St. Paul* may have impressed its image on Stubbs), which was taken to mean the discovery not of a new self so much as the authentic self that has been suppressed by the powerful pressures of social structures. For the conversion to take place, these had to be removed or at least seen through. Even the ethos of the anatomist included in the idea of dissection both the cutting through of appearances and the "anatomizing" of criminals following their execution.

The crucial case is Stubbs's paintings of reapers of the 1780s, in which the harvest landscapes are punctuated by the smallish figures of laborers in the foreground. It is not the suggestion of a psychological relation between the figures that draws our attention, as it might in a conversation picture, but the self-absorption of each separate figure, lined up precisely as the horses and dogs were in "friezes," here against the metonymic displacement of bound sheaves. They are a review of possessions held in line by the overseer on his horse (being on horseback is significant in the hierarchy of the painting), who is further heightened and enlarged by the embracing and expanding shape of the tree above him.

Barrell, with these paintings in mind, has accused Stubbs of being the painter for a ruling class, whose copies are at best (in the manner he associates with Reynolds) "representative of the idea of property, rather than its actuality," and he contrasts him unfavorably with Gainsborough. Stubbs cannot fulfill the need of "a great credibility in the image of rural life," according to Barrell, because "in his paintings of humans, if not of horses, he seems to aspire always to the formal, the monumental—for an image of life as contained and shaped by form, and not appearing to create that form itself."[76] This is an accurate statement of the visual evidence, but Barrell has the interpretation backwards. While Gainsborough's forms are more artificial than Stubbs's, they enliven and romanticize the figures. Stubbs's emphatic forms immobilize them, rendering them patently objects, with the large label of property always and almost satirically manifest.

The clean, dress-up clothing worn by Stubbs's workers is not ragged enough for Barrell, who believes the tatters Gainsborough paints on his peasants are both realistic and provocative. But within their stagy tatters, Gainsborough's rural nymphs and putti are merely picturesque; they are both stylized and idealized, censored and made presentable for the city dwellers who bought his country paintings. Gainsborough's rural scenes were painted "on spec," and so necessarily for a more general and sentimental clientele than Stubbs's hard-nosed horse breeders. Stubbs's reapers, posed in their holiday best, are dressed for the occasion by their paternalistic master—as the horses are arranged for their portraits in all their best harness and colors. And reapers and horses are being seen—inspected—by the patron-owner in the position of Hambletonian's owner. The strength of Stubbs's figures lies in the fact that they manage to maintain their individuality while also fitting into a structure obviously imposed from above. His reapers have the dignity of the German workers in August Sanders's photographs, frozen and individualized, without any of the stylization of Gainsborough which prettifies and causes them to lose their particularity as humans.

It might be argued that while Stubbs as artist and man asserts a political statement, he also contains it. Let us look at some of the details of the version of *The Reapers* in the Yale Center for British Art (fig. 47).[77] The church spire is at the physical center of the picture, on the skyline. Does it preside over and sanction the labor that takes place below it? Or is Stubbs distancing the steeple and what it stands for, on the model of Hogarth's church steeple in *Gin Lane*—remote from the needs of the poor? (Certainly he knew and understood *Gin Lane*.) For the patron, the steeple presides as paternal authority, but with how much irony on Stubbs's part? Two reapers bend over as they must to pick up the sheaves. This forces them into a gesture that

47. Stubbs, The Reapers *(1795), enamel on Wedgwood biscuit.*

resembles either an obeisance, a sort of bowing to the overseer, or a movement somewhere on the way from the upright stance of men down to that of the horse.

There are two figures that stand out, the overseer and one laborer. Like the church steeple, the tree rising above the overseer (who is already elevated by his horse) can be read in either of two ways: it merely enhances him, emphasizing his power over these laborers; or it naturalizes his power and authority, suggesting that they are part of the natural order. One male laborer, the only one who appears almost full-face, stands out from the others: his face reflects pride (probably not defiance), certainly some sense of individuality—and offers a contrast with the other prominent figure, the overseer, whose face and glance are almost hidden, in fact directed toward the workmen immediately beneath him. Or his face can be read as attentive to the overseer's directions.

There is a dog, as ambiguous as the humans: he can be the laborer's, lying at his feet and reinforcing his stance vis-à-vis the overseer; or he can be the overseer's, guarding the laborers as he would a herd of sheep.

Stubbs could have associated himself with the overseer or with the laborers. But it is the latter who are building the sheaves into a pyramidal and solid structure that is as architectonic as Stubbs's composition of the picture (further fixed and made permanent in this case by the process of enameling). The stability, careful definition, and enclosure of the workers' situation and of the painting coincide and reinforce each other, suggesting that the workers' labor is analogous to Stubbs's, the overseer's to the patron's. Stubbs consciously assumes the role of worker-craftsman: he allows the surface of the enamel, the grain of the wood, or the weave of the canvas to show beneath his paint; he emphasizes the flat surface of his panels as he does the flat lineup of the represented objects; and he anatomizes a horse, executes his own engravings and enamel paintings, and collaborates with other craftsmen on work for the Wedgwood Pottery.

Very different from Wright's illusionistic surface, Stubbs's painterly surface enacts a tension between illusion and making. The tension he seeks is between the realistic representation of the figures and the stylized arrangement in which they have been placed, like so many sheaves, by Stubbs the craftsman for the owner of the property: he represents two different kinds of ordering, one that of the possessor, the other that of the subordinate but ironic artist.

He signs his name beneath the overseer's horse, in the stubble. Given the verbal tradition of English art (from Hogarth's verbalizations within the *Harlot* to Turner's visualization of his own name Turner and Mallord as vortices and ducks),[78] it is not far-fetched to say that Stubbs is punning on his own name: stubble being the "stumps or lower ends of grain-stalks left in the ground after reaping" (*OED*), as in Swift's couplet in *The Progress of Poetry:* "The farmer's goose, who in the stubble, / Has fed without restraint, or trouble." If so, it is a self-deprecating reference, recalling the verb. A "stubber" is one who cuts off branches or cuts stumps near the ground; the word clearly defines his sense of artist as one who reduces, simplifies, and gets down to essentials.[79]

The unique power of Stubbs's best paintings derives from the implicit presence of the owner/patron as addressee and the drama his presence engenders.[80] But Stubbs is also the one painter of the time (as opposed to the slick upper-class stylists Reynolds and Gainsborough) who seeks to paint an actuality from the point of view of the possessed rather than the possessor. If he places the owner/patron in the position of power before his finished canvas, it is also in a position like that of the judges and lawyers, the patrons who commissioned the painting, whom Hogarth assumed as spectators of his problematic image of corrupt judges and lawyers in *Paul before Felix*.[81] Hogarth painted a picture that could be read in an admonitory way by the judges and lawyers, because it was in fact painted from the point of view of the prisoner before the bench, St. Paul before the corrupt judge Felix. My suspicion is that Stubbs regarded himself as, in distinction to the owner/patron, another of the humble possessions he was commissioned to paint. While in the case of *The Reapers,* he could associate with one of the laborers, there was also much to be said for an association with a champion racehorse.

As to the horse, we see that it not only is the pivotal mediating creature in a hierarchy, the element that relates man to the natural world, but also appears as part of a catalogue of possessions belonging to the spectator. The central irony of Stubbs's paintings lies in the juxtaposition of these natural and man- or owner-oriented functions.

In *Hambletonian* we see that the sense in the earlier paintings of the literal copy bordering on parody, or of possession writ large, is replaced by something more radical. The assumption of hanging the picture in a large room, a great hall or saloon, for example, has been taken it seems from the early lion, horse, and stag pictures and imposed on the patron, who is forced to see *Hambletonian* in association with large scenes of devouring, though the predator is omitted. The possession, by being displayed still in the realistic convention of horse pictures, but on a scale and with an expression of the savaged horse, places the patron—or his jockey—in the position of the responsible party. The possession, by being displayed at full size, flat across the picture plane as a one-to-one copy, not only dominates but engrosses the other nameable things in the picture including the owner/patron outside the picture regarding it. Vane Tempest is being threatened by it, as the owner was not by *Whistlejacket.* Or, more precisely, the possession overwhelms the possessor, turning the tables and becoming his possessor.

In the same way, the horse, by its sheer size and scale and place in the foreground, is also replacing, or wiping out, the natural landscape. The remote, absolutely still world of the racetrack, the spectator stands along it, and the white picket fence exist in a space defined by the continuous outlines of the horse: a race once took place there, in that framed area, now over and unrepeatable, subsumed under the horse who ran it. On the other hand, the anxious movement of the horse is bisected by the long restful line of the horizon. The glimpse of the human and natural signs of the landscape is seen literally through the interstices of the horse's figure, which articulates the space and gives it meaning.

Hambletonian is a text comparable in significance to Stubbs's *Comparative Anatomical Exposition* in which a comical (to say the least, humbling) man and chicken are paired and played off against the beautiful, lithe, threatening tiger, who moves across its space with the same confidence as the horse. It lacks only the two attendant figures who serve as commentary. We see an artist who has spent his career painting possessions—small and discrete—subordinated to an owner's plan, rebelling and reversing the human-centered hierarchy.

CONSTABLE'S *WHITE HORSE*

Constable is a landscape painter who documentably attempted to reclaim a particular property, one defined as Constable family property and as a landscape in which he lived out his youth and young manhood, in particular the years of his courtship with Maria Bicknell.[82] He painted the area over and over, focusing on Constable family buildings (views both of and from); when he painted other areas (Salisbury, Hampstead Heath, or Brighton), they were assimilated in one way or another to the Stour Valley. His happiness when he overheard someone on a coach, as they entered the Stour Valley, refer to it as "Constable's Country" was at a recovery of some amalgam of youthful memories and real property.[83]

Constable's recovery, redemption, or (given the facts of his case) possession of this landscape fell into three phases. The first was descriptive. This aspect of Constable's painting has recently been traced by Ann Bermingham to his drawing lessons by the "progressive method" of instruction that had replaced the Gilpinesque formulae for landscape.[84] This source explains, for example, Constable's abandonment of the Claude landscape structure of the open central perspective to the horizon, which Turner continued to follow to the end of his days. But it also sheds light upon Constable's argument about the need for "a natural painture" and the densely descriptive quality of his early landscapes.

The second phase expressed itself in the six-foot paintings he began to exhibit at the Royal Academy in 1719: from *The White Horse* (fig. 48) to *Stratford Mill, The Hay Wain, The Leaping Horse* (fig. 49), to

48. John Constable, The White Horse *(1819), painting.*

Hadleigh Castle and *Salisbury Cathedral from the Meadows.* With the basic assumption that he must give up the sense of his own property (or someone else's, *Wivenhoe Park* or *Malvern Hill,* for example), Constable transmuted his essentially topographical, almost maplike paintings into a characteristic form, which I have described at length in *Literary Landscape.*[85] This structure is focused on a particular scene that singles out one Stour Valley setting, a configuration of woods, a vicarage, and an open space that had been the setting for his courtship of Maria Bicknell (unsuccessful, followed by several years of separation). We might say, in the terms we have been exploring in this chapter, that, almost as if he were recreating Wright's *Corinthian Maid,* Constable was representing the empty space left by his memory of Maria.

Thus, in the six-foot paintings, by employing certain obsessive forms related to experiences of his youth, he made a memorial of his painting, while at the same time eliding the sense of personal property. Indeed, the origin of landscape, he argues in one of his lectures on landscape painting, was in the elision of a center of what we might call interestedness, or self-interestedness shared by painter and viewer. Landscape originated, he argues, in history painting—of a religious subject, a martyrdom (his example is Titian's *Martyrdom of St. Peter Martyr*), an Agony in the Garden, a Crucifixion, or an Entombment.[86] Landscape is a setting for a religious painting, a martyrdom in which the landscape's pathetic fallacy survives the removal of the martyr and his murderers. The figures have been removed, leaving only the responding or corresponding landscape, rendered disinterested and at the same time more impressive by the absence. The Constable houses and mills have also been moved off to the periphery. The effect of the six-footers depends to some extent on the central empty area, empty of martyrs, of narrative incident, of property (and of Maria Bicknell)—with only the surrounding response of nature (in *Stratford Mill* the trees positively lean as if in a strong wind).

This structure is most plainly seen in Constable's third phase, which involves heightening, increased emphasis, and hyperbole. The foreground is now a complexly tactile area of debris, with a heavily wooded area running part way across the middle distance, beyond which (to the right) the viewer's eye moves out, as if for relief, to a sunlit stretch of meadow or water. In *Salisbury Cathedral from the Meadows* (private collection, on loan to the National Gallery, London) the picturesque muddle in the foreground has to be visually circumvented in order to reach the point of sunlit rest, on the other side of the small vicaragelike building (hugely reinforced by the cathedral looming to its left), here further emphasized by the rainbow that comes down at just this spot.

The watershed between his early landscapes, in which he tried to get in as much information as possible, and the six-foot canvases he exhibited at the Royal Academy in the 1720s, was *The White Horse,* the first of the six-footers (1819, fig. 48).[87] In this landscape, still studded with farm buildings, Constable employs two foci of interest rather than the single eye path of the later paintings, and the viewer cannot settle on a single gestalt. There are two foci of water surface, separated by the dark reflection of a tree; and there is the water below and the sky above; and there is, over to the left, the white horse.

The two dominant features are the water and the sky. One might say this picture is about the water and its relationship to the sky; the reflections of the one play off against the clouds of the other. The water exists as part of the canal system along the Constable property. It is mercantile water in that produce is ordinarily conveyed along it—but not in this picture. The canal as canal, with the horse being transported across it, is marginalized; the empty, unused part of the water is central. (Only some cattle drink at the furthest edge.) Yet the water also hardly exists for itself; taken *hors de combat,* it is there only to reflect the trees and cloud-filled sky, the complex patterns above it. Rather than the water, the picture is about reflection, this seeming mirror (related to the Romantic poet-painter's concern with "reflection" in both senses of the word), and reflection's transcendence in the clouds overhead.[88] One is a myth of representation, the other of representation transcended.

The effect recalls the Ovidian transformation in Pope's *Windsor Forest* of warfare into poetry in terms of the nymph Lodona transformed into the gently moving River Loddon, which now reflects a "watry Landskip of the pendant Woods," in which "Floating Forests paint the Waves with Green" (see above, p. 56). But how different this watery metamorphosis of the landscape is from the reflections often found in Richard Wilson's landscapes of the 1750s–1760s: Wilson used these bodies of water to contribute to a theme about painting which included a landscape, the water's distorted reflection of it, and a small depiction of the artist and his painting within the landscape. But Wilson's lakes merely reflected a castle or a mountain upside down and wriggly. Constable's water breaks up, displaces, and reformulates the trees and clouds in a way analogous to—or allegorically the equivalent of—the way his own hand has transformed the trees or the weeds and foliage in the foreground of the painting.

There is no doubt that this is a *painting* of a landscape, despite the powerfully illusionistic constituent at a certain distance. This, in other words, is the six-footer which, summing up Constable's past achievement, is *about* and *shows* the transformation of landscape into art. And so it is the one that relates the artist's brushwork to the equivalent of the natural image in the reflecting water, the center of the scene, which like the artist absorbs all the other elements of the scene, the trees, clouds, buildings, and livestock, and turns them into a painterly image that is about the painting of landscape, and that dramatizes while announcing the great Constable contribution to landscape painting, what he called in his lectures on landscape a "history of the weather" or a naturalized history painting or—as I said at the beginning—one from which the history has been emptied.

The white horse, at the left of the scene in the middle distance, not at the center which is the water, is outside the real subject of the painting. It serves as a comment, gloss, or motto (as to an emblem), saying: This landscape *could* have been about the white horse—as *The Leaping Horse* (fig. 49) is later about the leaping horse, or its leaping

49. Constable, The Leaping Horse *(1827), painting.*

toward the remote sunlit area of water and meadow—but is not and need not be. The white horse, the figure and the title, is not the subject of the painting but rather a symbol of whiteness and blankness, a kind of tabula rasa like the water—and like the canvas itself—on which the artist performs his (as the water performs its) transformations of the sky and trees. It is the whiteness, the sense of a primed but blank canvas, that Constable plays upon in the white horse—a symbol, not of escape or liberation but simply of the artist's craft and labor.

I cannot agree with Michael Rosenthal's interpretation: "The barge was emblematic of trade, and the wry contrast of its movement with the depopulated quiescence pervading the rest of the landscape enhances the idea that trade never ceases."[89] And yet the horse's "story" has to be explained. Constable paints the horse that draws the barge but places him *in* the barge; he takes the horse out of labor, shows it being transported across the canal from one stretch of labor to another but momentarily at rest. It is enclosed in a man-constructed boat, and only the men are laboring; they are transporting the workhorse; and all three, horse, boat, and men, are enclosed within a self-man-constructed boat—and that within a conspicuously man-constructed painting. This is a strange image of labor, showing the labor required in order to get the horse into a position where it can labor. Constable seems to be suggesting that the image—as emblematic as the leaping horse—is about secondary labor, which includes the labor of representation. The artist is like these men who labor to get the horse to a place where he can pull the barge. The barge is coming toward us, the spectators, who stand on the tow track ready to receive horse, whiteness, and the work of the artist. The most remarkable thing about this image of the boat and horse is its stillness, perhaps due to the horse's being turned at ninety degrees to the bow of the boat.

There is a sense in which the six-foot canvases after *The White Horse* gradually retreat from the bold statement of that painting, which sums up the nonsubject landscapes that (on a smaller scale) preceded it and corresponds to Constable's demand for a "natural painture" of the changing weather, not of history or myth. From the white horse to the leaping horse he turns from the subject of his art to the lively experience of his viewers (and of himself) *re*living an experience. But in terms of *The White Horse* he demonstrates his retreat from representation (and the artist's awareness of himself as artist) into conventional symbolization.

The White Horse is the picture in which Constable summed up everything he knew and felt up to that point about landscape painting. For example, the silvery whiteness of the white horse and water and sky—the silvery light that pervades the landscape—sums up all of his talk (and writing) about the silvery, fresh, airy quality he wanted his landscapes to have. In *The Leaping Horse* and subsequent landscapes dominated by deep browns, greens, and yellows, he turned this whiteness into a superimposed "whitewash" (as it was called by unsympathetic critics) interposed between the landscape and the viewer. These scrapes of white over dried pigment literalized a freshness no longer inherent in the landscape itself but added as Constable also added leaping horse, a castle ruin, or a cenotaph.

Constable might have wished to connect the compensatory gesture of adding more symbolism, pigment, and atmosphere with his own definition of landscape as a passionate history with the history omitted. As history is elided, it is replaced (and too directly recalled) by whitewash, dark clouds, and ominous architecture. In other words, the subject of the history's absence is replaced by a substitutive allegory, though one that (in that sense following from *The White Horse*) draws the spectator's attention to the painter and his brush.

There is also, however, a sense in which *The White Horse* sets the agenda for the following six-footers. Focusing as I have on the distant sunlit meadow, I am brought by *The White Horse* to the realization that the succeeding paintings, *Stratford Mill* and *The Hay Wain*, are primarily about the central body of water, and so in that sense are continuous with *The White Horse*. They are therefore about a central area of reflection, but also an area of labor or play, of barge-drawing or fishing. In *Stratford Mill* the barge is still peripheral to the river that fills the center, and peripherality is emphasized by the fishermen on its banks, who introduce the second sense of "reflection": fishing, they are meditating on the riverbank.[90] In *The Hay Wain*, however, the cart moves into the center of the water and becomes itself a reflected object.

What goes on in the water is, I take it (coming as we have from *The White Horse*), analogous to the question of the way the empty canvas is filled by the painter. It can be untouched, all itself, free to reflect and absorb and project natural forms; thus filled by sheer reflection of the sky and trees on its banks. Or it can be invaded to some degree by the peripheral barges and white horses. In the climactic *Salisbury Cathedral from the Meadows* the horse-drawn wagon, in the midst of the pond, is being led off by another white horse. But by this time (beginning with *The Leaping Horse*) the water has become occluded, almost opaque with "whitewash" (standing for it is not quite clear what), merging with the rotting wood and plant life in the foreground, part of a foreground obstruction that emphasizes by contrast the distant sunlit *locus amoenus*.

Constable distances his six-foot landscapes from what apparently interested him most, the "property" in both senses of real and memorial, by turning to art. We have seen one sense in which he thematizes the painting of landscape in *The White Horse*. But the structure I have referred to as a personal configuration derives, in terms of the landscape tradition, from Jacob van Ruisdael's dark, occluded fields with one distant spot (often with a church spire) transfigured by a shaft of sunlight. In his lectures on landscape painting Constable singles out this particular landscape type and attributes it to Ruisdael.[91]

Almost every type of landscape developed by Constable finds an equivalent in Ruisdael; indeed, the major shifts in Constable's landscape types and in his attitude toward landscape correspond to Ruisdael's. Ruisdael initiated, and Constable follows, the idea of building a landscape around a water mill or a canal lock, of exploring the possibilities of sand roads and cuts (whether in Holland or on Hampstead Heath), and above all of placing deep within the landscape a sunlit meadow without a clear path or road leading to it. But even more interesting than the exploration of the same landscape models (which Ruisdael must be given credit if not for inventing at least for exploring and raising into a paradigmatic state) there is the change from this sort of representational landscape to a symbolic landscape consisting of ruins and tombs with a planar and extremely frontal, almost stagelike, monumental composition. If *The Jewish Cemetery* was the pivotal Ruisdael painting between the closely observed (or densely descriptive) and the symbolized landscape, Constable's *Cornfield* serves the same function for him. Moreover, Constable's lectures on landscape express themselves most forcefully in the example of Ruisdael, with those two crucial landscape types: the history of the weather and the allegorical landscape—the latter with and without its allegory.

In the model Ruisdael landscape, Constable says, he "has . . . told a story" of the weather; but in a contrasting and less successful landscape, probably one of the *Jewish Cemetery* paintings, "he attempted to tell that which is out of the reach of art: In this Allegory of the Life of Man . . . there are ruins to indicate old age, a stream to signify the course of life, and rocks and precipices to shadow forth its dangers."[92] These two types correspond to the two stages of Constable's six-foot landscapes, before and after *The White Horse*.

The second type closely evokes his *Cornfield*, exhibited at the Royal Academy in 1826. He painted the scene, a specific view into the Stour Valley, where one can still stand and see many of the same trees, in both modes, first representational and then allegorical. In the first (Reading Gallery) we can see what the scene presumably looked like at noon in the 1820s ("Noon" is an alternative title); it is empty of human life. In the second painting (London, National Gallery) Constable has filled the central space with figures, marking the spatial progression into the landscape by the signposts of a youth drinking out of a stream, a middle-aged farmer in the middle distance with a plow and a wheat field ready to harvest, and on the horizon a church tower (which was not in the earlier painting either, and indeed is not visible from that spot on the ground)—all of which corresponds to some such topos as the Ages of Man, the church tower being an emblem of faith or hope in the afterlife.

Constable tells us that he decided for the Royal Academy show of 1826 to add "more eye-salve than I usually give them" (that is, the spectators of the exhibition), something tarted up in the way landscape had to be tarted up in order to be taken seriously.[93] It seems important that this superimposed imagery or allegory be public: Constable intended to impose significance on a natural scene which, he would at first have argued, carries its own significance; then, in the context of the six-footers, he would have seen the significance as remaining or reflected in the response of the landscape surrounding the emptied space; and now he feels that he must introduce external signs for emphasis, in a sense restoring the "history" he had advised should be removed. But also, I think, he feels that a meaning that was largely private needs to be made ostentatiously public.

The impetus derives, I suspect, from Ruisdael's monumental landscapes, intensified with dramatic lighting, rainbows, striking contrasts, and added symbols—leading up to the *Jewish Cemetery* paintings and symbolic landscapes of ruins and tombs with a planar and frontal composition. But to see how Constable's premelodramatized landscapes, and in particular *The White Horse,* function we should recall Ruisdael's most famous painting, *The Windmill at Wijk* (Amsterdam, Rijksmuseum). The windmill, though to right of center, is the focal point, a palpable structure that is both picturesque in the technical eighteenth-century sense and symbolic—it seems to represent something more than itself. It prevents us by its centrality and palpability from seeking paths around or past it; it also draws our attention away from the sheet of water below and the clouds above it. The *Windmill* is, in fact, one of those heavily horizontal prospects Ruisdael loved to paint out of which rises one strong vertical feature. In the early cityscapes the horizontal lines of the horizon and the houses are contradicted by the one vertical of a rising church tower. In the most strikingly melodramatic of Ruisdael's seascapes the horizontal line of the sea, and the horizontality of the composition, are broken with the cross (and even the simulated arms) of a tall beacon that warns the ships. We are standing on a promontory at the end of which the dock and the crosslike beacon stand, looking out on a raging sea, lit by a single patch of sun or moonlight. And in the typical (and often repeated) landscape panorama, dark and occluded, in which a single patch of sunlight is intensely picked out on a distant field or meadow, in this spot of sunlight a very Christological windmill stands out reinforced by a nearby church spire: a spire that Constable retains in *The Cornfield* but usually, as in *The Leaping Horse,* moves far to the periphery.

Ruisdael's *Windmill at Wijk,* in this context, evokes a landscape not so much *without* a Crucifixion as with a displaced version of it, reinforced by the actual cross on a ship's mast to the left. This is the landscape *appropriate to* a Crucifixion, representing the ninth hour, but instead of the cross something else appears centrally silhouetted against the dark sky. The cross-blades of the windmill become a secularized or a naturalized analogue of the cross, or rather of the combined syndrome of Crucifixion, Atonement, and Incarnation. For the windmill has its source of strength in the sky, to which its arms are outstretched in the sacrificial posture, but is rooted in the earth, in the production or the grinding of meal and the service of man. Everything in the painting seems to be tending downward and to the right into the discarded millstones in the right foreground. The windmill is a symbol of a man-made structure that has transformed wind/spirit into grain/flesh.[94]

The symbolism of *The Windmill at Wijk* is on a continuum with the overt allegory of the *Jewish Cemetery* paintings, where it takes the form of the bare, broken dead tree contrasted with the tree in flower at the right; the ruins and tombs *versus* the rainbow, contrasting decay and the promise of resurrection. Some of the nonallegorical paintings carry the same message, and the same view of landscape as tragic but embodying also a hope of redemption. Ruisdael's oak tree paintings are about the huge shape in the middle, or as it relates to (for example) another on the left and one further back, less emphatic, on the right. It is the same sort of protagonist as the windmill, in some cases the dominant center of a naturalized crucifixion triad. Protagonist is the word I wish to emphasize: for a tree, like a windmill, can be a protagonist of a landscape.[95]

Only later in his career does Ruisdael remove the trees and deal with the hollowed-out center of the forest, making the trees to some extent serve the function of the Claude coulisse. Constable, however, except in a few experiments with water mills, removes the central feature from his later work or moves it to the periphery. In the six-footers we have been examining, he leaves the middle space open; this empty but intense central area is of water and green grass, sometimes indistinguishable. Only when he feels he must emphasize, publicize, and elevate that area does he fill it with Reynolds's cenotaph or Westminster Bridge (or, though less central, Hadleigh Castle).

There are various ways to formulate what we have seen. For example, Constable elevates his six-footers for the Royal Academy—painted to demonstrate his mastery; or, we might say, he elevates the stigmatic matter of Constable property—by replacing the particularity of the property with the "art," the generalization of the greatest Dutch landscapes. Or perhaps by doing this Constable in fact lays claim to property owned by the Constable family, or *possessed* by John

Constable's memory. He also lays claim to a painterly landscape that is Dutch and of the seventeenth century, which mediates between him and the Constable property. He signalizes his personal claim to the real property by means of his utilization of the aesthetic property. He even comes to flaunt the latter by borrowing Ruisdael's symbolic gestures. But then he puts his own mark on the Ruisdael landscape, making *it* his own. Primarily by moving the central feature, including Ruisdael's tree or forest (even the church spire), to the side and into the far distance, he empties the focal center of the landscape—not as Claude had done by opening the prospect to the horizon but by hollowing out an area that he has designated in *The White Horse* as the area of representation and transcendence.

But it is probably more apropos to say that Constable first replaces the conventional history landscape of Claude and Richard Wilson with Ruisdael's naturalization of history (or the sacred) in the narrative of the tree or the windmill and then subordinates the tree or windmill, emptying the landscape of its central feature in an iconoclastic way. This empty area is only featureless in the sense that it lacks anthropomorphic trees or houses; its openness gives Constable not, as with Gainsborough, merely a mysterious hole in which one can lose oneself, but a carefully delineated body of water or grass that either literally or metaphorically illuminates the circumambient landscape in the luminous manner of Wright's glowing ingot.

If we wish to see Ruisdael's way of dealing with history as a natural equivalent of Hogarth's urban version (his "modern moral subjects"), we can then discern between Hogarth and Constable two phases of eighteenth-century English art. If the Hogarthian painter displaces the gods, history, and figures of the Renaissance tradition to contemporary and unidealized Londoners, the post-Hogarthian painter creates by omission of these elements, weaving a plot around absence. One was of presence, *about* presence at least: a satiric, moral, rhetorical, persuasive, emblematic, and anecdotal image—quite conscious and delimited—concerned with presence, the present, the here and now, which makes an aesthetic of that contemporaneity. And the other was of absence: the absence of the Hogarthian elements, but also commemorative, memorial, and about the dead and past—about the *un*presentable. Most obviously, there was Gainsborough's landscape, emptied of history, topography, "content," which in a discourse of property may refer to the artist's ownership; but in a discourse of landscape proper is an emptying in order to suggest a liminal area or the invisible presence of a *genius loci*.

A thesis about English landscape painting (which means also its

Dutch precursors) can be stated thus: landscape has been habitually used as a frame for human action—as a way of thinking about or feeling about others or oneself—and this humanism includes in its eighteenth-century English form above all the self-interest of property. When landscape is naturalized, the figures removed, one of three things happens. The figuration is displaced onto some aspect of the landscape, as in Ruisdael's great gnarled trees or his windmill. Or the landscape remains animated by the absent figures or experience, as in Constable's six-footers. Or the landscape comes to be about a central absence—as in the large central empty space of *The White Horse,* all reflection and texture, nothing tangible—or as again in Turner's landscapes, where the figures, though present, are by their peripherality rendered ironic at the fringe of a great vortical emptiness. Turner's *Regulus* (Tate Gallery) has this central emptiness/ fullness, whether we read it as the death and destruction of Carthage or as the fullness of God's (Rome's) power, or as the sun, and/or the artist's power of representation.

What we see here is a process of omission: omission and displacement of the human, literary, moral, and religious as subject, and as justification or pretext for the landscape. It is at this stage that landscape begins to be about property—whether the topographical or decorative property, of the owner of the real land or the idealized Campagna or Mt. Snowden or the Stour Valley. And when it becomes *about* property, as it often does in eighteenth-century England, the artist's departure is Constable's—who not only painted the property of landed gentry but his own. And that departure is to make it about itself, about the representing and painting of it, as in *The White Horse*—which is not to say that the symbolism in Constable's later works does not also refer to the problem of painting as well as to public issues. In this way I should wish to imply something about the preeminence of this English landscape, in particular as a way for the artist to assert his own right to his painting.

We see that for the painter the adjustment of the role of spectator/ owner in relation to a landscape seen as property points to the underlying subject of loss. Sheer painterly metamorphosis—or later symbolic additions—is the artist's way of recovering what is otherwise his patron's, but also of recovering a landscape that is no longer his own— in various senses of loss, whether ownership, enclosure, encroaching urbanization, or sheer temporality. In *The White Horse* control and possession take the form of the painter's remaking, the signs of his labor—whereas in the later six-foot paintings, the painter's need to memorialize tends to supersede the physical remaking.

This happens when Constable adds Ruisdael's landscape forms, his symbolic appurtenances, castles and rainbows, which melodramatize the scene. These shift his emphasis to a thematizing of the emptying into the subject of loss and mourning, nostalgia and memory: first for a home and then, in the last paintings, for lost georgic (heroic, political, property) ideals.

By emptying the historical landscape of its history, Constable turns it into an autonomous landscape: we must sense that something *was* there, *has* happened. Or, as in the great *Stour Valley* scene in Edinburgh, he may retain the turbulence of the foreground in order to frame a contrastingly quiet, peaceful distant prospect—the *locus amoenus* he seems to require as part of his staffage. But in *The White Horse*, for that moment, the emptying is complete: there is not even a memory of an absence, but only the idea of "landscape" expressed by an artist just as he is about to engage in a series of landscape explorations that will carry "landscape" into its dramatization of emptying and refilling.

Notes

CHAPTER 1 THE AESTHETICS OF ICONOCLASM

1. Named so by Alexander Gottlieb Baumgarten in *Meditationes Philosophicae de Nonnullis ad Poema Pertinentibus* (1735).

2. For this line of political theory, see the works of J. G. A. Pocock, esp. *The Machiavellian Moment: Florentine Political Thought and the Atlantic Republican Tradition* (Princeton, 1975), pp. 462–505; and *Virtue, Commerce, and History* (Cambridge, 1985), pp. 215–74. For an adaptation of Pocock's "civic humanism" to aesthetic theory, see John Barrell, *The Political Theory of Painting from Reynolds to Hazlitt* (New Haven, 1986); cf. my review, *The New Republic*, 10 and 17 Aug. 1987, 39–42.

3. Shaftesbury, *Characteristics*, ed. J. M. Robertson (London, 1900), 2. 268–69.

4. Michael Fried has pointed out to me the significant "frame" that Shaftesbury (if it was *his* conscious choice) had Gribelin inscribe around the picture, designating it "picture" and establishing the distance he required.

5. In *Beer Street* (1751), where Hogarth places Turnbull's *Treatise* among volumes destined for the usual uses of waste paper.

6. Harold Bloom, *The Anxiety of Influence* (New York, 1973); Thomas Weiskel, *The Romantic Sublime* (Baltimore, 1976); Neil Hertz, *The End of the Line* (New York, 1985), esp. chaps. 1 and 3; and Frances Ferguson's various essays on the sublime which are collected in her forthcoming book, *Solitude and the Sublime: The Aesthetics of Individualism.*

7. Mr. Spectator called this phenomenon not iconoclasm but politeness (as he called *his* satire comedy and the Tories' lampoon); see *Spectator* No. 58 (ed. Donald F. Bond [Oxford, 1965]).

8. See Ronald Paulson, *Representations of Revolution* (New Haven, 1983).

9. Shaftesbury, "Soliloquy or Advice to an Author" (1710), in *Characteristics*, 1.136.

10. For a general survey of English georgic in the eighteenth century, see John Chalker, *The English Georgic: A Study in the Development of a Form* (London, 1969); for the example of Defoe, pp. 12–13. I am particularly indebted, however, to Ralph Cohen's seminal essay on the influence of the georgic genre in the eighteenth century: "The Augustan Mode in English Poetry," *ECS*, 1 (1967), 3–32.

11. "Schreber," in *The Standard Edition of the Complete Psychological Works of Sigmund Freud*, trans. James Strachey, 12 (London, 1950), 71.

12. Jung, *Collected Works*, trans. R. F. C. Hull, 3 (Princeton, 1972), 189.

13. *Second Treatise*, 5.27, in John Locke, *Two Treatises on Government*, ed. Peter Laslett (New York, 1960), p. 329.

14. See Paulson, *Satire and the Novel* (New Haven, 1967); but more generally, José Ortega y Gasset, *Meditations on Quixote*, trans. Julian Marias (New York, 1961), pp. 138–40; and Mikhail Bakhtin, *The Dialogic Imagination*, trans. Caryl Emerson and Michael Holquist (Austin, 1981). The novel, says Bakhtin, predicates "a rigorous critique of the literariness and poeticalness inherent in *other* genres and also in the *predecessors* of the contemporary novel"; and here he crosses Ortega's path, for whom romance and poetry are the Other. But Ortega the conservative sees the novelistic process as a way of conserving the "poetic" in life; Bakhtin sees it as a way "to reverse the fundamental concepts of literariness and poeticalness dominant at the time" and of "making of it the dominant genre in contemporary literature . . . in the vanguard of all modern literary development" (pp. 10–11).

15. McKeon, *The Origins of the English Novel, 1600–1740* (Baltimore, 1987); for his critique of Bakhtin, see pp. 11–14.

16. Iconoclasm has been widely discussed in recent years. The essential historical work is John Phillips, *The Reformation of Images: Destruction of Art in England, 1535–1660* (Berkeley and Los Angeles, 1973). Recent suggestive theoretical discussions include: Kenneth Gross, *Spenserian Poetics: Idolatry, Iconoclasm, and Magic* (Ithaca, 1985); Ann Kibbey, *The Interpretation of Material Shapes in Puritanism: A Study of Rhetoric, Prejudice, and Violence* (Cambridge, 1986); and W. J. T. Mitchell, *Iconology: Image, Text, Ideology* (Chicago, 1985), chap. 6. I was particularly stimulated by Keith Thomas's lecture on the historical phenomenon of English iconoclasm at Yale University in the spring of 1983. See also Margaret Aston, *England's Iconoclasts* (Oxford, 1988) and Ernest B. Gilman, *Iconoclasm and Poetry in the English Reformation* (Chicago, 1986).

A version of this section was first delivered before the annual ASECS meeting in Boston in April 1984 and a symposium on visual-verbal issues at Dartmouth in the fall of 1984. It was published as "English Iconoclasm in the Eighteenth Century" in *Space, Time, Image, Sign: Essays on Literature and the Visual Arts*, ed. James A. W. Heffernan (New York, 1987), pp. 41–56. Gilman's response (pp. 56–62) fills in some sixteenth and seventeenth-century English background.

17. From a diary of a Jacobin Club meeting, quoted in Albert Mathiez, *Les origines des cultes révolutionnaires* (Paris, 1904), p. 112. See Stanley Idzerda,

"Iconoclasm during the French Revolution," *American Historical Review*, 60 (1954), 13–14, and my *Representations of Revolution*, pp. 15–16.

18. Lynn Hunt, *Politics, Culture, and Class in the French Revolution* (Berkeley and Los Angeles, 1984), pp. 90, 99.

19. Phillips, pp. 117, 118.

20. See Havelock, *Preface to Plato* (Cambridge, Mass., 1963), p. 100.

21. Frances A. Yates, "Broken Images," in *Collected Essays*, 3 (London, 1984), 40–48.

22. Perkins, *The Workes* (London, 1626, 1631 ed.), 2.331; cited, Phillips, p. 174.

23. The words are Cynthia Ozick's, quoted in Edmund White, "Images of a Mind Working," *New York Review of Books*, 11 Sept. 1983, p. 3.

24. Phillips, p. 174, citing Perkins, *The Workes*, 2.222–23.

25. See Gross, pp. 33–41.

26. Hogarth, *The Analysis of Beauty*, ed. Joseph Burke (Oxford, 1955), p. 82.

27. *Don Juan*, 2.940–44, in *The Complete Poetical Works*, ed. Jerome J. McGann, 5 (Oxford, 1987).

28. John Calvin, *Institutes of the Christian Religion*, 1.11.12, trans. Henry Beveridge (London, 1953), 1.100.

29. See Keith Thomas, *Religion and the Decline of Magic* (New York, 1971), p. 75, and Phyllis Crew, *Calvinist Preaching and Iconoclasm in the Netherlands, 1544–1569* (Cambridge, 1978), chap. 1; and Kibbey, pp. 48, 49–50. Kibbey refers (p. 48) to the strategy as "satiric reinterpretation," but I prefer her other term, "sacramental realism" (p. 49).

30. It is easy to see the relationship between this iconoclastic process and metonymy as Kenneth Burke described it ("Four Master Tropes," in *A Grammar of Motives* [New York, 1945], pp. 503–17); and, according to Kibbey, as Calvin projected it in his sense of iconoclasm (pp. 54–58).

31. See E. P. Thompson, e.g., "The Moral Economy of the English Crowd in the Eighteenth Century," *Past and Present*, No. 50 (1971), 76–136; "Rough Music: 'Le charivari anglais,'" in *Annales*, e.c.s., 27 (1972), 285–312.

32. Kibbey, pp. 48 ff.

33. See Mitchell, *Iconology*, pp. 164–65.

34. To Bolingbroke, 21 March 1729/30, *The Correspondence of Jonathan Swift*, ed. Harold Williams, 3 (Oxford, 1963), 383.

35. Ehrenpreis, *Swift: The Man, His Works, and the Age*, 3 (Cambridge, Mass., 1983), 332; for the other interpretation, see Carole Fabricant, *Swift's Landscape* (Baltimore, 1982), pp. 14–15.

36. Gen. 49.5–7; *Prose Works of Jonathan Swift*, ed. Herbert Davis, 9 (Oxford, 1948), 225. The sermon is on pp. 219–31.

37. Frances Yates's words, "Broken Images," p. 46.

38. Nussbaum, *The Brink of All We Hate: English Satires on Women, 1660–1750* (Lexington, 1984), pp. 106–07. On cosmetics and how "the lover was cured" by being shown his mistress's toilette, see also *Spectator* No. 41 (17 Apr. 1711).

39. Ovid, *The Art of Love,* tr. Rolfe Humphries (Bloomington, 1958), pp. 191–92.

40. Dale Underwood, *Etherege and the Seventeenth Century Comedy of Manners* (New Haven, 1957), p. 39.

41. Tertullian, in *The Ante-Nicene Fathers,* ed. Alexander Roberts, James Donaldson, and A. Cleveland Coxe (New York, 1907), 3.72; Cyprian, "On the Dress of Virgins," in ibid., 5.434.

42. Ibid., 4.20–21.

43. Letter 54, "To Furia on the Duty of Remaining a Widow," in *Select Letters of St. Jerome,* trans. F. A. Wright (New York and London, Loeb Library, 1933), p. 241.

44. Nussbaum, pp. 112–13.

45. Ll. 293–98. My text for Swift's poetry is Pat Rogers's *Jonathan Swift: The Complete Poems* (New Haven, 1983).

46. *Discoveries,* in *Ben Jonson,* ed. C. H. Herford, Percy and Evelyn Simpson, 8 (Oxford, 1947), 623. It is a metaphor Jonson employs frequently. Sir William Davenant's preface "to his much honor'd friend, M. Hobbes," begins by assuring his addressee that "you shall passe through this new Building with more ease to your disquisition," for he "will acquaint you, what care I tooke of my materialls, ere I began to worke" (*Gondibert,* ed. David F. Gladish [Oxford, 1971], p. 3). The architectural metaphor recurs when Davenant means to signal major shifts in the topics he is discussing, for example, "I have now given you the accompt of such provisions as I made for this new Building . . ." (p. 15); "'Tis now fitt, after I have given you so long a survay of the Building, to render you some accompt of the Builder . . ." (p. 20).

47. Fabricant, in *Swift's Landscape.*

48. Cited by Geoffrey Galt Harpham in *The Ascetic Imperative in Culture and Criticism* (Chicago, 1987), pp. xiv, 6–8.

49. *The Complete English Gentleman* (written 1728–29), ed. Karl D. Bülbring (London, 1890), pp. 16–17.

50. *Prose Works of Jonathan Swift,* 9:34–35.

51. Both Swift and Pope write obsessively about themselves. There are many sources for their foregrounding of the poet—Milton comes to mind, and in a way perhaps closer to Swift, the Earl of Rochester. But I suspect that the passage in *A Tale of a Tub* in which the Grub Street Hack, in the voice of Dryden, describes his sad career and sadder physical state, though parodic, nevertheless set the terms for Swift's own obsessive use of himself as the central symbol of his poetry. Revisions of Dryden—the Dryden of the late poetry, especially the confessional part of *The Hind and the Panther,* and the prose surrounding the *Aeneis*—permeate the text of the *Tale.*

52. For a list of the interpretations of the *Verses,* see David Vieth, "The Mystery of Personal Identity: Swift's Verses on His Own Death," in *The Author in His Work,* ed. Louis L. Martz and Aubrey Williams (New Haven, 1978), pp. 245–62; Barry Slepian's essay was "The Ironic Intention of Swift's Verses on His Own Death," *Review of English Studies* n.s., 14 (1963), 249–56.

53. See Paulson, "Swift, Stella, and Permanence," *ELH,* 27 (1960), 298–314, and in *The Fictions of Satire* (Baltimore, 1967), pp. 189–210.

54. "Essay on the Georgics," in *Works of John Dryden,* ed. Walter Scott, 14 (1808), 14–25.

55. My examples are Joshua Scodel's; see "Lapidary Texts: The English Poetic Epitaph from Jonson to Pope," diss., Yale University, 1985.

56. Mark 16.1–8, Matthew 28.1–8, Luke 24.1–11. Scodel makes this point and cites the epitaph *In cultum reliquiarum* by Thomas Bastard, which includes the lines: "But to tye holy worshipp to dead bones, / To bowe religion to the wicket trust / Of crosses, reliques, ashes, sticks, and stones, / To throwe downe living men to honour dust."

57. See Scodel, "'Your Distance Keep!' Pope's Epitaphic Stance," *ELH,* 55 (1988), 615–42.

CHAPTER 2   THE AESTHETICS OF GEORGIC RENEWAL

1. My text is the *Twickenham Edition of the Poems of Alexander Pope,* 11 vols. (New Haven, 1940–69).

2. I am, of course, indebted to Earl Wasserman's "Critical Reading," in *Pope's Epistle to Bathurst* (Baltimore, 1960), pp. 11–55, with which in general I agree.

3. Howard Erskine-Hill fills in the historical and biographical context of this passage in *The Social Milieu of Alexander Pope* (New Haven, 1975), pp. 27–33.

4. The line is clarified by Swift's lines (164–71) in *Cadenus and Vanessa* (1713):

> From whence that Decency of Mind,
> So lovely in the Female Kind,
> Where not one careless Thought intrudes,
> Less modest than the Speech of Prudes;
> Where never Blush was call'd in Aid,
> That spurious Virtue in a Maid,
> A Virtue but at second-hand;
> They blush because they understand.

5. *Guardian,* ed. J. C. Stephens (Lexington, 1982), No. 23, p. 109.

6. *Spectator* Nos. 29, 83, 249, 555, etc. (ed. Donald F. Bond [Oxford, 1965]).

7. See, e.g., Peter V. Marinelli, *Pastoral* (London, 1971), p. 12. The remainder of this chapter takes off from my article, "Satire, and Poetry, and Pope," in Ronald Paulson and Leland H. Carlson, *English Satire* (Los Angeles, 1972), pp. 55–106.

8. I am indebted in my discussion of Pope's pastorals to Martin C. Battestin, "The Transforming Power of Nature and Art in Pope's Pastorals," *ECS,* 2 (1969), 183–204; rpt. in his book, *The Providence of Wit* (Oxford, 1974), pp. 58–78.

9. We could compare Pope's transformation of pastoral with Virgil's in his *Eclogues:* Virgil appears (in 1 and 9, and also 10) to be writing both pastoral

and critique of pastoral, already moving into the more historically determined and characteristic mode of georgic.

10. I am quoting Battestin, *Providence of Wit*, p. 70.

11. *Eclogues*, 1, ll. 59–62; trans. E. V. Rieu (Penguin, Harmondsworth, 1954), p. 25.

12. Swift to Pope, 29 Sept. 1725, in *The Correspondence of Jonathan Swift*, 3 (Oxford, 1963), 103.

13. See, e.g., Ronald Syme, *The Roman Revolution* (Oxford, 1939; ed. 1971), pp. 467–68; Richard Lanham, *Motives of Eloquence* (New Haven, 1976), pp. 48–64.

14. For a somewhat different view of metamorphosis in Pope, see Ralph Cohen, "Transformation in *The Rape of the Lock*," *ECS*, 2 (1969), 205–24.

15. The text says that she calls Father Thames and Diana for help; they cannot help her (she has strayed beyond Diana's precincts). But, it is implied, Diana *can* save her by this transformation.

16. For this conventional analogy, embodied most pertinently by Dryden in poems running from *To Dr. Charlton* to *Mac Flecknoe* and *Absalom and Achitophel*, see Wasserman, *The Subtler Language* (Baltimore, 1959).

17. See Addison's "Essay on the Georgics."

18. Nicolson, *Mountain Gloom and Mountain Glory* (New York, 1959), p. 30.

19. Pope draws upon Polyphemus's lament in Theocritus's eleventh idyll, upon which he also drew for the "Summer" pastoral (both of which were also dedicated to physicians).

20. In one of his *Spectator* papers, Steele had introduced the subject of an Ugly Club, the group that meets to celebrate its members' deformities, including a prominent "Pair of Shoulders." The point, Steele advises, is to be like Paul Scarron, "as merry upon himself, as others are apt to be." Steele also introduces a Merry Club for large mouths, celebrating his own "deformity." (See *Spectator* No. 17 [20 Mar. 1711] and others following, especially No. 32, which mentions Alexander the Great, as Pope does in *Arbuthnot;* Pope also refers to Scarron.)

21. See Maynard Mack, *Alexander Pope: A Life* (New Haven, 1985).

22. *Guardian* No. 40, pp. 160–65.

23. See Wasserman, "The Limits of Allusion in *The Rape of the Lock*," *Journal of English and Germanic Philology*, 65 (1966), 415–44.

24. The Baron's speech about his conquering steel is a less direct version of Clarissa's passage about time: it is after all Time that will "strike to Dust th' Imperial Tow'rs of Troy," and his scissors evokes the Three Sisters as his term "steel" covers a scythe as well as a scissors or sword.

25. Erskine-Hill, "Alexander Pope: The Political Poet in His Time," *ECS*, 15 (1981–82), 130–31. For the prominence of Jacobitism, see, e.g., J. C. D. Clark, *Revolution and Rebellion: State and Society in England in the Seventeenth and Eighteenth Centuries* (Cambridge, 1986), passim., and bibliography, pp. 174–77.

26. The immediate reference, in the context of the *Epistle to Bathurst*, for example, is to usury and economic corruption (a subject of the civic human-

ist propagandists). For this, the paper-credit aspect of these satiric figures, see p. 250.

27. Peter Stallybrass and Allon White, in their study of transgressive materials in English literature, have argued that *The Dunciad* is simply a popular carnivalesque conflation of monarch and hack, of Shakespearean theater and Bartholomew Fair puppet shows, of high and low cultures. This is an interesting supposition, but it depends on looking at *The Dunciad* from a distant Bakhtinian perspective, which might signify if Pope were Rabelais, or even possibly, in some moods, Swift. But Pope's strategy involves different assumptions: first, that this king, George II, is *allowing* himself to be conflated with the dregs of Bartholomew Fair; second, that those dregs are aspiring to, in effect appropriating, the mantle of classical learning, poetry, and art, with all of its high values—and, if it were known, so is George II himself. And so the dregs *and* George II (and Cibber) are the materials, one shabby amalgam or pinchbeck, which Pope utilizes, transmuting them all into his beautiful poetry. See Stallybrass and White, *The Politics & Poetics of Transgression* (Ithaca, 1986), p. 110.

28. Pope to Ralph Allen, 8 Feb. 1741/2; *Correspondence*, ed. George Sherburn (Oxford, 1957), 4.387.

29. A carefully qualified fame, as it happens: see the images of adultery, erotic assignations, and fragmented marriage associated with Belinda's metamorphosed lock (and Wasserman's analysis in "Limits of Allusion").

30. Murray Krieger, "Eloisa to Abelard: The Escape from Body or the Embrace of Body," *ECS*, 3 (1969–70), 30.

31. In passing, we should mention Pope's translation of Chaucer's *Prologue of the Wife of Bath* (1713), which is also concerned with a sensuous woman's attempt to reconcile her real urge toward the love of men with the Church's teachings and the laws about marriage; she enacts the Popean drama in her own figure, a comic Eloisa who has had her lovers and now needs only to justify her conduct.

32. Each of these poems poses the question, explicitly or implicitly, "Is it a crime [or sin] to love too well?" The "Unfortunate Lady" has "loved too well" in the sense that she has rejected the world of repression and the way of "those sullen pris'ners in the body's cage," and has, like Sappho (and, another hero admired by Pope, Cato), committed suicide. Her response has taken her to the extreme of self-murder, and so (in terms of orthodoxy) to damnation.

33. *Cleopatra* (pub. 1717) anticipates the case in the *Epilogue to the Satires* of Virtue being led in a Roman triumph behind the chariot of Vice. Cleopatra's loving too well means preferring Antony to the values of Augustan Rome and, like the "Unfortunate Lady," committing suicide rather than walking in Octavian's triumphal procession. She is, however, speaking herself instead of being discussed as a subject by the poet. And yet the poem is again about the artist who effects the metamorphosis. Octavius, cheated of his prize, has had a statue made of her as a surrogate to ride in the triumphal procession and be set up in the Roman Forum. He has falsified her by omitting her tears: no

one can now tell that she is weeping, and that these tears are not for herself but for Antony. She is thus both confined and misunderstood in this statue as Eloisa was in her cell and the dead and forgotten Lady in her unmarked grave. Once again the poet is required: here he appears in the form of Pope Leo X, the great patron, the Man of Magnificence (whom Pope will later seek to parallel with the poet in *Burlington*), who has her statue transformed into a fountain, releasing her tears which are her true fame, proving her not cold marble but a warm, still-loving woman. It is the poet's role to re-create the poetic truth out of the statue, turning the triumphal simulacrum into a nourishing fountain (which materializes her tears), by putting the story into words. This is almost literally an epitaph, of the ancient sort in which the dead speaks to the living, asking for their prayers and admonishing them with his/her example. Quite a different image from the carved bowl of the "Spring" pastoral, it marks a natural development from the idea of metamorphosis in *The Rape of the Lock*. In both cases, an artifact of ill fame, falsified, has been remetamorphosed into something truth telling and meaningful, as Syrinx the reed is transformed by Pan into an instrument of art.

34. See Earl Wasserman, "Pope's Ode for Musick," *ELH*, 28 (1961), 163–86.

35. That is,

> . . . a Boggy *Systis*, neither sea,
> Nor good dry Land: nigh founder'd on he fares,
> Treading the crude consistence, half on foot,
> Half flying; behoves him now both Oar and Sail . . .
> With head, hands, wings, or feet pursues his way,
> And swims or sinks, or wades, or creps, or flies.   [2.939–50]

The words recall not only the dunces diving and swimming but the verbs of sinking, wading, creeping, and so on define the regression into chaos in *The Dunciad* as a whole. And Satan's journey, of course, ends when he comes upon the "universal hubbub wild" of ll. 951 ff., which describes the chaos picked up by Pope as the starting point for his mock epic.

36. Maynard Mack argues, in his biography of Pope, that the "friendship" about which Pope writes so much (in his letters but also in his Horatian epistles) is not just epistolary convention but the one stable fact of his personality. Even the broken friendships (Addison, Lady Mary) were as significant for an understanding of his character as the lasting ones. The most interesting inference Mack draws is that friendship was the one moral conviction that led Pope into acts (often untenable and self-defeating) of courage, heroism, and folly—as with his defenses of Atterbury, Bolingbroke, and Swift, and even Lady Mary, which could not have been explained by his beliefs alone, whether religious or political. Pope's satires did follow, as Mack acknowledges, from revenge and as reactions to prior attacks on himself—but also on his friends, whom he regarded as an essential part of his own identity. (See Mack, *Alexander Pope*.)

37. David Piper, *The Image of the Poet* (Oxford, 1982), p. 58.

38. W. K. Wimsatt, *The Portraits of Alexander Pope* (New Haven, 1965).

39. Maynard Mack, "Wit and Poetry and Pope," *Pope and His Contemporaries,* ed. J. L. Clifford and Louis Landa (Oxford, 1949), pp. 37–39; Aubrey Williams, *Pope's Dunciad* (London, 1949); and Thomas R. Edwards, *This Dark Estate: A Reading of Pope* (Berkeley and Los Angeles, 1963), chap. 5. Alvin B. Kernan ("*The Dunciad* and the Plot of Satire," *Studies in English Literature,* 2 [1962], 255–66) shows that beyond the parallels of the Lord Mayor's procession, the action of Virgil's *Aeneid,* the movement (outlined in Book 3) of the forces of darkness and dullness moving from east to west, parodying the traditional progress of learning as well as following the course of the sun, there is the action of the verbs describing Dulness: pour, spread, sluice, creep, drawl on, stretch, spawn, crawl, meander, eke out, flounder on, slip, roll, extend, waddle, involve, gush, swell, loiter, decay, slide, waft, lumber, blot, o'erflow, trickle—in other words, mimicking the movement from creation backward to chaos.

40. *Twickenham Pope,* 5 (2d ed., 1953), 202.

41. *Peri Bathous,* chap. 14. First Scriblerus explains "the Method of turning a vicious Man into a Hero." The first rule is the "*Golden Rule of Transformation,* which consists in converting Vices into their *bordering Virtues,*" and the second is the "*Rule of Contraries,*" by which the more a man lacks a virtue the more it is bestowed upon him. "The Reverse of these Precepts," Scriblerus concludes, "will serve for *Satire,* wherein we are ever to remark, that whoso loseth his Place, or becomes out of Favour with the Government, hath forfeited his Share in *Publick Praise and Honour.*"

42. The action-response pattern still obtains if we may believe the story of Pope's final charade of planting a false sheet from the projected 1743 *Dunciad* on Cibber in order to elicit a real attack on Pope, so that Pope could then respond by putting Cibber (who had not previously attacked him) into the 1743 version (*Twickenham Pope,* 5.xxxiv).

43. Cf. David Morris, *Alexander Pope: The Genius of Sense* (Cambridge, Mass., 1984), pp. 214–40 ("The Muse of Pain").

44. See above, the first section of Chapter 1.

45. This sequence may be thought to correspond in a general way to Mack's scenario for the Popean persona: the ingenu is transformed by contact with the world first into a *vir bonus* who can see and ironically comment and finally, when the stimulus is too outrageous, into a heroic chastiser of evil. (See "The Muse of Satire," *Yale Review,* 41 [1951], 80–92.)

46. Maynard Mack, *The Garden and the City* (Toronto, 1969), p. 177.

47. See G. K. Hunter, "The 'Romanticism' of Pope's Horace," *Essays in Criticism,* 10 (1960), 390–414.

48. For a very interesting essay on Pope's *Bathurst* in terms of an intertwining of different "discourses," see John Barrell and Harriet Guest, "On the Use of Contraction: Economics and Morality in the Eighteenth-Century Long Poem," in *The New 18th Century: Theory, Politics, English Literature,* ed. Felicity Nussbaum and Laura Brown (New York, 1987), pp. 121–43.

49. *Twickenham Pope,* 6.376.

CHAPTER 3   THE AESTHETICS OF REVOLUTION/RESTORATION

1. Kelsall, *Byron's Politics* (Brighton, 1987), pp. 29, 149, 161.

2. *How Superior Powers Ought to be Obeyed* (1558, reproduced Facsimile Society, New York, 1931), p. 139.

3. I am indebted to Laura Brown for her discussion of the political aspects of these plays in her *English Dramatic Form 1660–1760* (New Haven, 1981), chap. 1.

4. Winn, *John Dryden and His World* (New Haven, 1987), esp. pp. 178–89.

5. The remarks on Rochester are drawn from Paulson, "Rochester: The Body Politic and the Body Private," in *The Author in His Work*, ed. Louis L. Martz (New Haven, 1978), pp. 103–21.

6. Gilbert Burnet, *Some Passages of the Life and Death of Rochester* (1680), in *Rochester: The Critical Heritage*, ed. David Farley-Hills (London, 1972), p. 54.

7. *The Remains of Thomas Hearne*, ed. John Bliss, rev. John Buchanan-Brown (Carbondale, 1966), p. 122.

8. See my iatrohydraulic essay in *Popular and Polite Art* (South Bend, Ind., 1979) for the application to Fielding's novels. Cf. also Freud's Wolf-Man, Standard Edition, 17 (1955), 74–75. Swift's imagery of evacuation includes the purge of physical and moral filth in "A Description of a City Shower."

9. See Carole Fabricant, "Rochester's World of Imperfect Enjoyment," *Journal of English and German Philology*, 73 (1974), 338–50.

10. My text is David Vieth's edition of *Complete Poems* (New Haven, 1968), where he calls the poem *A Satyr on Charles II*.

11. I prefer the 1680 edition's "boy" to Vieth's "Man."

12. This supposition was first suggested to me by my student William Walker.

13. ?1680, in *The Letters of John Wilmot Earl of Rochester*, ed. Jeremy Treglown (Chicago, 1980), pp. 241–42.

14. John Dennis, "Defence of Sir Fopling Flutter" (1721), in *The Critical Works of John Dennis*, ed. E. N. Hooker (Baltimore, 1943), 2.248.

15. ?Spring 1676 (emphasis added), in *Letters*, p. 117.

16. *The Famous Pathologist, or the Noble Mountebank*, ed. V. de Sola Pinto (*Nottingham University Miscellany*, 1 [Nottingham, 1961]), p. 34.

17. Burnet, *History of His Own Time* (1753), 1.370–72.

18. The subject of Rochester's masquerades and their meaning has been well treated by Anne Righter, "John Wilmot, Earl of Rochester," *Proceedings of the British Academy*, 53 (1967), 47–69; Dustin Griffin, *Satires against Man* (Berkeley & Los Angeles, 1973); and Carole Fabricant, "John Wilmot, Earl of Rochester: A Study of the Artist as Role-Player," diss., Johns Hopkins University, 1972, esp. chap. 3, pp. 153–225.

19. The sequence of subjects: fame, his skill as a swimmer, boxer, cricketer, and the power of his eyes—all lead, in the "Detached Thoughts," into the very long sequence of anecdotes about orators and their relative skills, which then continues scattered among anecdotes of actors. Sheridan, as orator, wit, Whig, and so on, is especially emphasized.

20. *Byron's Letters and Journals,* ed. Leslie A. Marchand (Cambridge, Mass., 1973–82), 9.23; on gaming and Scrope Davies, see no. 77, pp. 38–39.

21. No. 6, p. 15. For Byron–Sheridan, see Paulson, *Representations of Revolution,* p. 279; and on Sheridan, pp. 142–50.

22. In particular see the essays answering William Lisle Bowles's attack on Pope. For the matter of stigmas, see Erving Goffman, *Stigma: Notes on the Management of Spoiled Identity* (New York, 1963; 1986 ed.).

23. *Works of Lord Byron,* ed. R. E. Prothero (London, 1898–1901), 5.565.

24. See Jerome Christensen on this subject: "Setting Byron Straight: Class, Sexuality, and the Poet," in Elaine Scarry, ed., *Literature and the Body: Essays on Populations and Persons* (Baltimore, 1988), pp. 125–59. On the subject of Byron's homosexuality, see Louis Crompton, *Byron and Greek Love: Homophobia in 19th-Century England* (Berkeley and Los Angeles, 1985).

25. Mackintosh, *Vindiciae Gallicae;* discussed in Kelsall, *Byron's Politics,* p. 23. We know that Byron knew Mackintosh in his conservative old age and revered the memory of his heroic words in the 1790s.

26. I have discussed this in *Representations of Revolution,* pp. 275–80. My text for *Don Juan* is *The Complete Poetical Works,* 5 (Oxford, 1987).

27. Kelsall, *Byron's Politics,* pp. 176–77. On the political dimension of *Don Juan* I have found Jerome McGann's works useful, in particular his chapter in *The Beauty of Inflections: Literary Investigations in Historical Method and Theory* (New York, 1985), pp. 115–17, 258–93.

28. His Britain had been appropriated by the Romans, as the Norman ecclesiastical property had been by Henry VIII, and as (Byron points out in 10.35–36) the Saxon property had been by the Norman William the Conqueror.

29. Byron lacked interest in visual art, though he looked at it and was able to attach names to objects, as in his description of the Norman Abbey gallery. But looking at a picture, a Teniers, for example, only summons up pleasureful memories of eating and drinking (see 13.72).

30. Mackintosh, p. 82. See Paulson, *Representations of Revolution,* p. 163.

31. See in the essay on Bowles, for example: "The Georgics are indisputably . . . even a finer poem than the Aeneid."

32. The reference to Death the Devourer, followed by the "rigid guts of reapers" (9.13, 15), echoes the passage in the first canto, "And flesh (which Death mows down to hay) is grass" (1. 220), which is also the first of the many passages about mutability. These are tied together by, among other things, the triad of heart-liver-stomach—the bodily center of the poem. For Time the mower, see also 14.53.

33. Cf. 11.36–38, on lies: "And, after all, what is a lie? 'Tis but / The truth in masquerade; and I defy / Historians—heroes—lawyers—priests, to put / A fact without some leaven of a lie" (36). But the sequel establishes the irony of the statement: That the "very shadow of true Truth" would raise havoc, close up annals," and so on (37). And so: "Praised be all liars and all lies!"– spoken in the same tone as Pope's *Epilogue to the Satires,* Dialogue 2.

Byron's Popean sense of "Truth" (expressed in the Bowles essay as well as in *Don Juan*) is summed up in his manuscript essay on Pope:

> I take him on his strong ground as an *ethical* poet: . . . the highest of all poetry, because it does that in *verse*, which the greatest of men have wished to accomplish in prose. If the essence of poetry must be a *lie*, throw it to the dogs, or banish it from your republic, as Plato would have done. He who can reconcile poetry with truth and wisdom, is the only true "*poet*" in its real sense, "the *maker*," "the *creator*,"—why must this mean the "liar," the "feigner," the "tale-teller?" A man may make and create better things than these?

The search for "truth" in the sense of true Fame was an important element of Pope's poetry, one that Byron makes much of when he seeks the sanction of Pope's poetry for his own.

34. "Thought" No. 51, *Byron's Letters and Journals*, 9:29.

35. The text of *The Prelude* is from *The Poetical Works of William Wordsworth*, ed. Thomas Hutchinson and Ernest de Selincourt, rev. ed. (Oxford, 1959). All other Wordsworth poems quoted in this section are taken from *William Wordsworth: The Poems*, ed. John O. Hayden, 2 vols. (New Haven, 1981).

36. *Works of Lord Byron*, 5. 551.

37. Marjorie Levinson, "Insight and Oversight: A Reading of 'Tintern Abbey,'" in *Wordsworth's Great Period Poems: Four Essays* (Cambridge, 1987); Jerome McGann, *The Romantic Ideology* (Chicago, 1983), pp. 81–92.

38. See David Simpson, *Wordsworth's Historical Imagination: The Poetry of Displacement* (New York, 1987), pp. 113–21—an account that came to my attention after I had written this chapter.

39. Note, by the way, that the emphasis on love (e.g., 14.162ff.) in conjunction with imagination, has a georgic source too, viz. *Georgic* 3 on love.

CHAPTER 4   THE AESTHETICS OF MODERNITY

1. For a full analysis, see Paulson, *Hogarth's Graphic Works*, 3d ed. (London, 1989), cat. no. 140.

2. The one manifestation of divinity in a Hogarth print—a lightning bolt descending on White's gambling house in *A Rake's Progress* 3—might suggest that he is excluding not divine providence but only the image of the divinity itself—that is, that he is a traditional Protestant iconoclast. We would then have to decide whether the jagged bolt of lightning is intended as a stylized act of God or a natural phenomenon. But obviously Hogarth could not show a figure of God without taking his "modern moral subject" into another, an idolatrous genre. The lightning bolt is another iconoclastic act (against White's) by Hogarth the artist.

3. Parker, "A Declaration of Certain Principal Articles of Religion" (1559), Article 10, in Edward Cardwell, *Documentary Annals of the Reformed Church of England (1546–1716)* (Oxford, 1844), 1.263–67; Edmund Gibson, *Codex Juris Ecclesiastici Anglicani* (Oxford, 1761), p. 321.

4. See Hogarth, *The Analysis of Beauty*, p. 50. My text of the *Analysis* is edited by Joseph Burke (Oxford, 1955).

5. Calvin, *Institutes*, 1.11.12 (Beveridge ed., 1.100).

6. For the matter of renaming in the Renaissance, see Robert Martin Adams, *The Roman Stamp* (Berkeley and Los Angeles, 1974). For the *Analysis* plates, see Paulson, *Hogarth's Graphic Works*, cat. nos. 195–96.

7. For thorough descriptions of the canonical sculptures, see Francis Haskell and Nicholas Penny, *Taste and the Antique* (New Haven, 1981).

8. David Dabydeen sees an allusion in the Rake to Walpole (*Hogarth, Walpole and Commercial Britain* [London, 1987], pp. 132–35). For comparisons of Walpole to Roman tyrants, see the *Craftsman* Nos. 94, 100, 222, 220, 259, 268, etc.

9. This was suggested to me by Michael Fried.

10. The figure of the dancing master is, moreover, complemented by the drawing in the book displayed at the lower right: figure 20 is identified by Hogarth in the text (p. 49) as an absurdity, a dancing master representing Jupiter—and this, in terms of the illustration, sets up Jupiter–Ganymede associations with the pair in the Sculpture yard.

11. Hercules, in fact, appears three times, since the Belvedere Torso was usually identified as Hercules. The first, the Farnese Hercules, was extensively restored (as is perhaps suggested by the appearance of the separate head-and-shoulders, while the other, the Torso, was remarkable among antique sculptures as the one piece that was not restored presumably because Michelangelo (as Hogarth notes) "is said to have discover'd a certain principle in the trunk" (p. 5), which was a source of Hogarth's own formalist principle of the serpentine line. Hogarth shows the Torso in *Time Smoking a Picture* as grotesquely restored, with an unfitting arm and another statue's head, which Time seems to have lopped off with his scythe.

12. *Polymetis* (1747), p. 67. The subject of classical iconography was revaluated by Spence's tour of antique sculptures in a garden in his *Polymetis*, published just five years before the *Analysis*. As his primary illustrations Spence chose the Venus de Medici, Apollo Belvedere, and Farnese Hercules—limiting his examples to deities, as he explained, with the single exception of Hercules. Hogarth's scene is a rewriting of Spence's.

13. The story that Hogarth argues in the *Analysis* (p. 90 and n.) has it that the Apollo Belvedere was found by Augustus and removed from the site of Apollo's oracle at Delphi (Haskell and Penny, p. 148).

14. To adopt Norman Bryson's terms, iconography of the Greek gods was a code of strict denotation, one that now in the 1750s, stimulated perhaps by the ideological needs of demystification, could be broken by a counter code of what we might call connotation. Iconography, as witness Ripa's *Iconologia*, was embodied in a lexicon which, put up against the connotative codes of fashion, dress, and physiognomy, simply collapses. (See Bryson, *Word and Image: French Painting of the Ancien Régime* [Cambridge, 1981], pp. 15–18.)

15. We could make connections between Hogarth's Sculpture Yard and the views of Rome by his younger contemporary Piranesi, who was representing Rome's monuments as they were now in the second half of the eighteenth century, with contemporary Romans functioning in the same way as Hogarth's contemporary Englishmen. In some cases these contemporaries are shown relieving themselves on the Roman architecture; in others, as in the representation of Trajan's Column, a gentleman in frock coat is shown in the pose of a Roman flamen in adoration—joining the two periods in an act of emulation as precise as that of Hogarth's dancing master. Piranesi depicts Rome as a moldering corpse but at the same time re-creates its grandeur in the sublime ruin: so demonstrating the same Hogathian or iconoclastic progression from destruction to recreation, the destruction itself renamed, reseen, and revalued. (See Adams, *Roman Stamp*, p. 191.)

16. The classical/Latin stories and texts were regularly and consistently expurgated in the classroom and in most unlearned editions. The sexual and politically subversive passages were censored. The level Hogarth is exposing is, in this sense, merely a submerged subtext that he allows to emerge in this contemporary context: that is, the *literary* texts from which the sculptures derive, delineating the sexuality of the Apollo–Venus–Hercules group and the homosexuality of the Antinous–dancing master. One detects the precocious schoolboy here, the Hogarth whose father taught Latin, imposed it on him, and at the same time attempted (though with a failure that led to bankruptcy and imprisonment in the debtors' prison) to operate a coffee house whose patrons spoke only Latin. This is the same Latin scholar who filled the *Harlot's Progress* subscription ticket with Latin double entendres, both visual and verbal. (See Paulson, *Hogarth: His Life, Art, and Times,* New Haven, 1971, *1,* 260–61.)

17. Haskell and Penny, who quote these remarks of Raguenet, pass them off as "absurd" (Raguenet, *Monumens de Rome* [Rome, 1700], pp. 321–26; Haskell and Penny, p. 30). But then Haskell and Penny are not concerned with what these sculptures may have meant, in themselves or to spectators, besides associations of ancient history and ideal beauty.

18. See Edgar Wind, *Hume and the Heroic Portrait,* ed. Jaynie Anderson (Oxford, 1986), pp. 8–10, 22.

19. For the view that one should take account of the whole character of the individual when deciding whether to say his action is good or bad, see Shaftesbury, "An Inquiry concerning Virtue or Merit," *Characteristics,* bk. 1, pt. 2, sec. 3, ed. Robertson, 1.247–50; and Fielding in *Tom Jones* and Lillo in the last act of *The London Merchant.*

20. Campbell, "'When Men Women Turn': Gender Reversals in Fielding's Plays," in *The New 18th Century,* ed. Felicity Nussbaum and Laura Brown (New York, 1987), pp. 62–83. See also Campbell's Yale University doctoral dissertation, "'Natural Masques': Gender and Identity in Fielding's Early Works" (1988).

21. It is telling, however, that Shaftesbury thought of Hercules's action as

a "judgment," Hogarth thought of it as a choice: that is, Shaftesbury looked at the story from the point of the view of the aristocratic J.P., Hogarth from that of the Adam or Eve faced with the problem of choice.

22. The thesis was first laid out in Paulson, *Hogarth: His Life, Art, and Times*, then developed in *Emblem and Expression* (London, 1975) and *Book and Painting* (Knoxville, 1982).

23. As is seen by the inscription on the tag on the goose's neck: she has brought it for her "loving cousin in Thames Street," who has *not* shown up to protect her.

24. For the details, see Paulson, *Hogarth*, 1.244–51.

25. Even Walpole, represented in imitation Roman busts and housed in an imitation Roman temple, was humanized in many satires by having the lover revealed beneath the official mask (as in Macheath's two wives, or Tom Thumb's two loves in Fielding's *Tom Thumb*, or Robin's love problems in his *Grub-street Opera*). The sexualization of the public figure was, of course, a feature of the *chronique scandaleuse*, but with Walpole an almost piquant sense of humanization emerges in Fielding's satires—or in Pope's *Epilogue to the Satires*.

26. Vertue, *Notebooks*, 3 (Walpole Society, Oxford, 1934), 58 (written in 1732).

27. Pope's Belinda, I should recall parenthetically, was of course a "little" hero, a feminized hero, a her*oine*, a mock-Eve, part of the reduction of large to small in *The Rape of the Lock*.

28. So also it is not enough for Hercules to be a woman; the woman must be a harlot. There is another aspect of the Harlot, part of her negative aspect, which should be mentioned. The figure also derives from the prostitute of the South Sea satires, who was connected with the quick rise of whores to ladies via speculation. The great ladies who were whores and the whores who were clearly *not* great ladies were related to the ordinary thief who dies on the gallows and the respectable thief, like Walpole or the South Sea director, who dies in his bed. See Dabydeen, *Hogarth, Walpole and Commercial Britain*, pp. 30–34, 86.

29. Her rebelliousness is one of the additions Dryden made to the story in his version in his *Fables*, Hogarth's source. Another is that Guiscardo and Sigismunda are *married* and that her only sin is marrying beneath her and thus defying her father.

30. See Paulson, *Book and Painting*, pp. 104–15.

31. I am indebted for this interpretation to Leslie Moore's analysis of Richardson in the fourth chapter of her book, *The Creation of Milton* (Palo Alto, 1989).

32. See Erskine-Hill, *The Social Milieu of Alexander Pope*, pp. 243–58.

33. This can be compared with the other way of representing the scene, as for example in Louis Chéron's illustration, as a parody Trinity, with Father flanked by Son and Holy Ghost.

34. Hogarth's is the first illustration of the Satan-Sin-Death Scene which

groups Sin in the middle position, between Satan and Death; it was followed by Barry, Fuseli, Blake, and others. (See Paulson, *Book and Painting,* pp. 104–15).

35. The woman in *The Sleeping Congregation* is also clearly a displacement for a Virgin Mary or some female saint.

36. See Maynard Mack, *The Garden and the City,* pp. 63–64; cf. Peter Martin, *Pursuing Innocent Pleasures: The Gardening World of Alexander Pope* (Hamden, 1985). For grottos as refuges from oppression, see Oakley. *To Sir John Chetwode, Baronet,* in *Poems on Several Occasions* (Manchester, 1733), p. 109.

37. Hutcheson, *Inquiry Concerning Beauty,* 2d ed., p. 17.

38. Locke, "Epistle to the Reader," *Essay concerning Human Understanding,* ed. A. C. Fraser (Dover ed., New York, 1959), pp. 7–8.

39. *Essay,* 2.2, pp. 245 and 121. Hogarth must have carried in his mind such passages as the following: "Men then come to be furnished with fewer or more simple ideas from without, according as the objects they converse with afford greater or less variety; and from the operations of their minds within, according as they more or less reflect on them" (2.1.7, p. 126).

40. Pp. 41–42. See also his introduction, at the very outset, of "Curiosity" (pp. 3 and 10), and the prints, p. 21.

41. What he says applies particularly to the emergent novel of his time (of the period between the publication of his modern moral subjects in the 1730s and *The Analysis of Beauty* in 1753). He does not mention the epic, which like history painting has no surprises to offer since the end is already known.

42. See Leslie Moore, "Moments of Delay: A Student's Guide to *Paradise Lost*," in *Approaches to Teaching Milton's "Paradise Lost",* ed. Galbraith M. Crump (New York, 1986), pp. 84–86.

43. *Spectator,* ed. Donald F. Bond, 3. 541.

44. For Hogarth's anticipation of the picturesque, see my *Representations of Revolution,* pp. 130–33.

45. Hogarth, p. 101. See Lessing, *Laocoon* (1766), chap. 22; trans. Edward Allen McCormick (Baltimore, 1962), p. 120. The passage Lessing quotes compares the Antinous and Apollo, the first calling forth "admiration," the second "surprise." One can read those words, in conjunction with the illustrative plate, in more than one sense.

46. But the sleeping woman in *The Sleeping Congregation* is also like the actress-Diana in that she cannot sustain the role imposed on her in church: she falls asleep. And she too attracts her Peeping Tom.

47. On the other hand, it could be said (perhaps more historically) that Hogarth is only making an aesthetics out of Gay's solution to the Pope–Phillips controversy over the pastoral in *Shepherd's Week, Trivia,* and *The Beggar's Opera.*

48. In *The Enraged Musician* Hogarth was remembering, almost illustrating, a passage in Addison's *Spectator* No. 29: "Musick is not design'd to please only Chromatick Ears, but all that are capable of distinguishing harsh from

disagreeable Notes. A Man of an ordinary Ear is a Judge whether a Passion is express'd in proper Sounds, and whether the melody of those Sounds be more or less pleasing" (Bond ed., 1.123).

49. Whose name carries him back to the Rake's choice in *Rake* 3 (see above, p. 159).

50. See Addison's *Spectator* No. 315, and Paulson, *Hogarth,* 1.261. This shared responsibility of the reader was one of the strong links Sterne made with *The Analysis of Beauty* in his *Tristram Shandy* of 1759 ff.

CHAPTER 5   THE AESTHETICS OF MOURNING

1. Ronald Paulson, "Zoffany and Wright of Derby: Context of Art in the Late Eighteenth Century," *ECS,* 3 (1969), 278–95; revised in *Emblem and Expression,* pp. 184–203. This chapter is based on my essay, "The Aesthetics of Mourning," in Ralph Cohen, ed., *Eighteenth-Century British Art and Aesthetics* (Berkeley and Los Angeles, 1985), pp. 148–81.

2. See Nicolson, *Joseph Wright of Derby, Painter of Light* (London, 1969), esp. pp. 50–51, 111–12, and 120–21. Of course, the phenomenon of the excessive light in the ingot could be explained—as both Nicolson and I do explain it, in a slightly different, though complementary way—as the influence of a kind of painting Wright was imitating: the candlelit tradition (Honthorst, La Tour) in which a Christ Child is overilluminated by a nearby candle simulating his own holy luminescence. We differ over the vestigial role of the Christ Child.

3. Ibid., p. 121.

4. Cummings, "Joseph Wright at the National Gallery," *Art Quarterly,* 34 (1971), 476. See also F. D. Klingender, *Art and the Industrial Revolution* (London, 1947; rev. ed., 1968), pp. 60–61 (where he makes the point that Cummings elaborates).

5. Wright's Account Book, quoted by Nicolson, p. 51.

6. Cummings, "Boothby, Rousseau, and the Romantic Malady," *Burlington Magazine,* 110 (1968), 659–66.

7. Ibid., p. 660.

8. Wright's Account Book, quoted by Nicolson, p. 54.

9. See Joshua Scodel, "Lapidary Texts: The English Poetic Epitaph from Jonson to Pope," diss., (Yale University, 1985); and above, Chapter 1, last section.

10. For more detail, see Paulson, *Emblem and Expression,* p. 190.

11. Burke, *Philosophical Enquiry,* ed. J. T. Boulton (London, 1967), p. 51.

12. Hogarth, *Analysis of Beauty,* p. 35.

13. See *Hogarth's Graphic Works,* cat. no. 215.

14. See Paulson, *Book and Painting,* pp. 104–15.

15. Burke's sublime was based on the experience of feeling powerless in relation to something external to oneself. This was something that would have gone against the whole strain of Hogarth's career, but would have seemed to have a specially personal application in 1762–64 when his friends were turning against him, his health was deteriorating, and his own aesthetic

theory was more often than not held up to ridicule by the faction that was campaigning for a national academy of art.

16. Significantly, Burke also, like Hogarth, raises wit over judgment: "by making resemblances we produce new images, we unite, we create, we enlarge our stock; but in making distinctions we offer no food at all to the imagination" (p. 18).

17. Richard Wendorf has made the point about Pope as Collins's career model in *William Collins and Eighteenth-Century English Poetry* (Minneapolis, 1981).

18. The odes have usually been taken as a working model (for Bate, Bloom, Sherwin, and Weiskel) of the poet struggling with the "burden of the Past" or the "anxiety of influence," that is, the oedipal situation. See W. J. Bate, *The Burden of the Past and the English Poet* (Cambridge, Mass., 1970); Harold Bloom, *The Anxiety of Influence* (New York, 1973); Paul S. Sherwin, *Precious Bane: Collins and the Miltonic Legacy* (Austin, 1977); Thomas Weiskel, *The Romantic Sublime* (Baltimore, 1975). I have shown elsewhere that Burke's discussion of "Obscurity" in terms of the implied oedipal confrontation probably derives from a conflation of Hogarth's painting, *Satan, Sin, and Death*, and Collins's implied scenario (combining memories of the Satan-Sin-Death confrontation with the Oedipus–Jocasta) in his *Ode to Fear* (Paulson, *Book and Painting*, pp. 109–10).

19. See Geoffrey Hartman, *Beyond Formalism* (New Haven, 1970), pp. 311–36.

20. On obscurity, picked up without the Popean satire, by Young in his *Night Thoughts* and Collins in his *Odes*, see John Sitter, "Mother, Memory, Muse and Poetry after Pope," *ELH*, 44 (1977), 312.

21. Although, as Frances Ferguson has said, Burke "Stipulates that a human observer be the passive instrument of the external object," he leaves it not very clear how any but the most overwhelming "object" can fulfill the requirement. His argument requires that "the *mind* is so entirely *filled* with its object, that it cannot entertain any other nor by consequence reason on that object which employs it" ("Legislating the Sublime," in Cohen, ed., *Eighteenth-Century British Art*, p. 132).

22. Hume, *An Enquiry concerning the Principles of Morals* (1777 ed.), App. 1.242, ed. P. H. Nidditch (Oxford, 1975), pp. 291–92.

23. See *Analysis*, p. 50.

24. See Irwin Panofsky, "Et in Arcadia Ego: Poussin and the Elegiac Tradition," in *Meaning in the Visual Arts* (New York, 1955), pp. 295–320. Versions of Poussin's painting are at Chatsworth and the Louvre; Giovanni Battista Cipriani's painting of the subject, with the full tomb shown, is reproduced by Panofsky; Reynolds's version, *Mrs. Bouverie and Mrs. Crewe* (1769), is in Crewe Hall in England. In Richard Wilson's version, "*Ego fui in Arcadia*" (1755), as Panofsky says, "the shepherds and the funerary monument—here a slightly mutilated *stele*—are reduced to a *staffage* accentuating the muted serenity of the Roman Campagna at sundown" (p. 319).

25. "Thoughts," no. 15, in *Byron's Letters and Journals*, 9 (1979), 31.

26. Bindman, "Roubiliac in Westminster Abbey," *The Oxford Art Journal,* Nov. 1981, pp. 10–16.

27. Penny, *Church Monuments in Romantic England* (New Haven, 1977), p. 66. For Guelfi's monument to Craggs, see Penny, p. 64.

28. The statue is in the Conservatori Museum, Rome. See Gisela Richter, *A Handbook of Greek Art* (London, 1959), pl. 199; cited, Joseph Burke, *English Art, 1714–1800* (Oxford, 1976), pp. 106–07. See Emily Vermeule, *Aspects of Death in Early Greek Art and Poetry* (Berkeley and Los Angeles, 1979), pp. 145–47, 154–55: "*Pothos* is generally a feeling of longing in the nighttime for someone who is not there, a lover gone overseas, or the absent dead" (p. 154).

29. See Margaret Whinney, *British Sculpture* (Harmondsworth, 1964), p. 81.

30. See Paulson, *Emblem and Expression,* pp. 108–09, pl. 141.

31. Quoted, Bindman, "Roubiliac," p. 14.

32. The Nightingale monument is just off the south aisle in an alcove where chairs are now piled, making it difficult to see or get close to the sculpture.

33. Penny, *Church Monuments,* pp. 21, 116, pls. 10, 87.

34. The monument is in the Dartrey Mausoleum, County Monaghan; see Penny, *Church Monuments,* pl. 33, pp. 47–48.

35. Penny, *Church Monuments,* pp. 44 and 210n13.

36. As a comparison of the great nineteenth-century cemeteries in Milan and Paris with those in London shows, however, while the continental version derived from the cityscape, the English cemetery grew out of the English landscape garden. By the 1750s the sense of iconoclasm had extended to the reaction of Capability Brown to the emblematic garden: he suppressed the statues, the iconography itself, leaving only the empty rolling fields. The sculptures subsequently moved from the gardens into the cemeteries of the 1830s and 1840s.

Brown's reform was a part of the tradition of iconoclasm as well as of the movement from emblematic to expressive structure of feeling rather than meaning. And Brown's reforms, which still formalized the landscape by shaping it into serpentine lines, were iconoclasted by the picturesque theorists, who erased his formal structures and returned the landscape to the gradualism of picturesque nature itself. Nature impinged on, defined, indeed overcame and replaced art in the form of the sculptures, stopping art before it could become icon, often literally overrunning it and altering its form. In this sense the picturesque functioned in nature as Hogarth's notion of beauty had functioned in relation to human society and art.

37. Ariès, *The Hour of Our Death,* trans. Helen Weaver (New York, 1981), p. 219.

38. I owe these to the researches into New England gravestone inscriptions of Debra Fried.

39. Ariès, p. 218.

CHAPTER 6   THE AESTHETICS OF POSSESSION

1. William Blackstone, *Commentaries*, bk. 2, chap. 1 (London, 1765–69), 2.2.

2. John Berger, *Ways of Seeing* (London, 1972); Raymond Williams, *The Country & the City* (London, 1973); John Barrell, *The Idea of Landscape and the Sense of Place, 1730–1840: An Approach to the Poetry of John Clare* (Cambridge, 1972) and *The Dark Side of the Landscape: The Rural Poor in English Painting, 1730–1840* (Cambridge, 1980); Carole Fabricant, *Swift's Landscape* (Baltimore, 1982); Frances Ferguson, "The Rhetoric of Entitlement and the Politics of the Sublime," in *Solitude and the Sublime: The Aesthetics of Individualism* (forthcoming).

3. *Commentaries*, bk. 3, chap. 10; 3.190.

4. See Alan Ryan, *Property and Political Theory* (Oxford, 1984), p. 14. See also C. B. Macpherson, *The Political Theory of Possessive Individualism* (Oxford, 1962); H. T. Dickinson, *Liberty and Property* (London, 1977); Paschal Larkin, *Property in the Eighteenth Century* (Cork, 1930); and James Tully, *A Discourse on Property* (Cambridge, 1980).

5. Locke, *Second Treatise*, ed. Laslett, 5.25, p. 327. See Richard Ashcraft's convincing argument that Locke was defending "property"—in both the narrow sense of goods and estates and the broader sense of "lives, liberties and external possessions"—against the power of the monarch and so Filmer's patriarchy (not, as some Marxist critics have believed, against the propertyless laboring classes). See Ashcraft, *Revolutionary Politics and Locke's "Two Treatises of Government"* (Princeton, 1986) and *Locke's "Two Treatises of Government"* (London, 1986).

6. See *Essay concerning Human Understanding*, 2.11.2, p. 245: "When the understanding is once stored with these simple ideas, it has the power to repeat, compare, and unite them, even to an almost infinite variety, and so can make at pleasure new complex ideas. But it is not in the power of the most exalted wit, or enlarged understanding, by any quickness or variety of thought, to *invent* or *frame* one new simple idea in the mind, not taken in by the ways before mentioned."

7. *Second Treatise*, 2.6, ll. 10–14, p. 311.

8. Ryan, p. 32.

9. Ibid., p. 19.

10. D. C. Feeney, "Mining an Epic," *TLS*, 3 July 1987, p. 722.

11. But Locke's vocabulary in the *Essay* for describing the way the mind receives sensations—and therefore ideas, their only source—also emphasizes such words as *acquire, appropriate, subdue, take,* and *have dominion over;* the sensations "make the deepest and most lasting impressions" (p. 195), *imprint, impress upon,* and other words recalling Aristotle's image of a seal impressed on soft wax; the mind is said to *combine* and *compound* these ideas (e.g., p. 205), and to *furnish, lodge,* and *store* them. The memory is "a storehouse of our ideas" (compared with St. Augustine's cathedral): "It was necessary to have a repository, to lay up those ideas which, at another time, it

might have *use* of" (2.10.4, p. 195, my emphasis). In short, these words denote acquiring property, adding to it, and storing it.

12. Ll. 7–12. I am indebted for this approach to *Epistle* II.ii. to Lyn Peterson's essay written for my graduate seminar in Pope at Yale in 1984.

13. See Aubrey L. Williams, "Pope and Horace: *The Second Epistle of the Second Book,*" in *Restoration and Eighteenth-Century Literature,* ed. Carroll Camden (Chicago, 1963), pp. 309–21.

14. Except, of course, for portraits—and also, I should add, given his habit of having it both ways, for the commissions he sought (especially in the 1750s) from such noblemen as Charlemont and Grosvenor.

15. Frances Ferguson, in "The Rhetoric of Entitlement," in *Solitude and the Sublime,* has shown that Mary Wollstonecraft articulated this position in *Vindication of the Rights of Man;* and we could also cite Blake.

16. *An Inquiry into the Nature and Causes of the Wealth of Nations,* 1.5, ed., R. H. Campbell and A. S. Skinner (Oxford, 1976), p. 25.

17. Ibid., p. 26. For the canine metaphor, see also p. 30.

18. Boswell, *Life of Samuel Johnson,* ed. A. B. Hill (New York, 1889), 4.370.

19. I do not mean that the conversation picture was indigenous to England (it came from France and the Netherlands), nor that the miniature portraits of the Elizabethan age were not worthy art objects: only that Hogarth and his followers used the conversation picture to lay claims to what they propagandized as native British art.

20. One can, for example, imagine Hogarth, beginning as a portrait painter of people who wanted themselves painted as shepherdesses and Magdalens—who made themselves so by costume, pose, and surroundings—painting a Harlot as if she were a Virgin Mary.

21. See Paulson, *Emblem and Expression,* pp. 138–58.

22. Take the example of the Medici Vase (see Haskell and Penny, *Taste and the Antique,* p. 316).

23. See *Emblem and Expression,* pp. 138–58, and more recently, George Rousseau's essay on the Towneley circle: "The Sorrows of Priapus: Anticlericalism, Homosocial Desire, and Richard Payne Knight," in *Sexual Underworlds of the Enlightenment,* ed. George Rousseau and Roy Porter (Chapel Hill, 1988), pp. 101–53.

24. Webster, *Johan Zoffany, 1733–1810* (London, National Portrait Gallery Catalogue, 1976), p. 48. For Webster's dismissal of my analyses, see p. 19. Cf. William L. Pressly, "Genius Unveiled: The Self-Portraits of Johan Zoffany," *Art Bulletin,* 69 (1987), 88–101.

25. These comments first appeared in Paulson, "James Ensor, Johann Zoffany, etc.," *Georgia Review,* 21 (1977), 508–10.

26. Sharp diary, 26 July 1775, box 56, Hardwicke MSS., Gloucestershire Public Record Office; Prince Hoare, *Memoirs of Granville Sharp* (1820), pp. 128–29.

27. I am using Ann Bermingham's words, "Reading Constable," *Art History,* 10 (1987), 41, 44.

28. See Jay Appleton, *The Experience of Landscape* (New York, 1975).

29. Ferguson, "An Introduction to the Sublime," in *Solitude and the Sublime.*

30. Ibid. See also: "For if the existence of other persons is essential for commerce, from the perspective of sublime aesthetics it is an evil whose necessity should only be obscured from view. Thus, people made journeys specifically to view sublime scenery, as if to gain a sense of their uniqueness from looking at what seemed to be unique."

31. Bermingham, *Landscape and Ideology: The English Rustic Tradition, 1740–1860* (San Francisco and Los Angeles, 1986), pp. 1–3, 11–13.

32. Ibid.

33. Hogarth's relevance is established by John Hayes (*The Landscape Paintings of Thomas Gainsborough* [London, 1982]), who makes a great deal of the possibility that Hogarth was involved in Gainsborough's commission to execute the roundel for the Foundling Hospital in 1748. (By the third repetition of the story Hayes has Gainsborough "seemingly encouraged by Hogarth" to paint this landscape. There is, I should add, no direct evidence on this point.) There is also the fact (see below, n. 34) that Gainsborough used the Hogarth figures gambling on a gravestone in *Industry and Idleness,* Plate 2, in *View of St. Mary's Church, Hadleigh* (no. 29). But most important is the connection among Gainsborough, Gravelot, Hayman, Hogarth, the rococo, and the St. Martin's Lane Academy, as well as Hogarth's *Analysis of Beauty,* which, though published after Gainsborough's return to Sudbury, Hayes assumes he had heard Hogarth "constantly discuss in conversation." Hayes even believes that "the strikingly perspectival composition" of *The Charterhouse,* the Foundling Hospital roundel, derives from Hogarth's prints (I suppose an interior like *Harlot,* Plate 4). Whereas it seems to me that the single long diagonal of the exterior wall in the roundel has a more reasonable source in some of Canaletto's topographical compositions accessible to Gainsborough in London in 1747 or 1748.

34. My references, except in a few cases to paintings in well-known collections, will be to Hayes's excellent catalogue, *The Landscape Paintings of Thomas Gainsborough:* in this case, Plate 28. Gainsborough's reference to Hogarth's *Industry and Idleness,* Plate 2, was first pointed out by me to Sidney Sabin, its then owner, and to Hayes.

35. I simply ask the skeptical reader to examine the detail in the National Gallery for him/herself (and recall that Zoffany specialists still refuse to see a condom hanging on the wall in the Parma self-portrait). For accounts of this puzzling picture, see John Hayes, *Gainsborough* (London, 1975), p. 203, and Bermingham, *Landscape and Ideology,* pp. 28–33; for Zoffany, see Paulson, *Emblem and Expression,* p. 146.

36. Pointon, "Gainsborough and the Landscape of Retirement," *Art History,* 2 (1979), 452–58.

37. Burke, *English Art, 1714–1800* (Oxford, 1976), pp. 218–19.

38. Cf. Barrell's analysis of this painting in terms of the realistic depiction of laborers (*Dark Side of the Landscape,* pp. 59–62).

39. Quoted, Barley Roscoe, *Gainsborough in Bath* (Bath, 1988), p. 35.

40. Hayes, *Landscape Paintings,* p. 75. This section appeared in a different form in a review of John Hayes's *Landscape Paintings,* in the *TLS,* 25 Mar. 1983, 283–84.

41. Bermingham, *Landscape and Ideology,* pp. 39–41.

42. Stechow, *Dutch Landscape Painting of the Seventeenth Century* (London, 1966), p. 66.

43. Thus confirming my thesis in *Emblem and Expression,* pp. 218–31.

44. Reynolds, *Discourses,* ed. R. R. Wark (New Haven, 1975), p. 72.

45. Reynolds, *Portraits,* ed. F. W. Hillis (New York, 1952), p. 66.

46. See Richard Wendorf, "Ut Pictura Biographia: Biography and Portrait Painting as Sister Arts," in *Articulate Images: The Sister Arts from Hogarth to Tennyson,* ed. Richard Wendorf (Minneapolis, 1983), pp. 98–124.

47. Chairs in such drinking scenes as *A Midnight Modern Conversation* are overturned, but in such polite conversation pictures as *The Cholmondeley Family* the turned-around chair combines with the wrinkled carpet to signalize the liminal area between the polite adults and the natural uproariously playing children.

48. See Paulson, *Popular and Polite Art,* pp. 190–208.

49. For biographical information on Mrs. Abington, see the entries in Philip H. Highfill, Jr., et al. eds., *A Biographical Dictionary of Actors, Actresses, . . .* (Carbondale, 1982) and the *DNB.*

50. *Love for Love,* ed. Emmett L. Avery (Lincoln, Neb., 1966), p. 54.

51. See Malcolm Cormack's note in *Art News,* 82 (1983), 114; *Love for Love,* p. 72. A more substantial essay by Joseph F. Musser, Jr., "Sir Joshua Reynolds's 'Mrs. Abington as "Miss Prue,"'" *South Atlantic Quarterly,* 83 (1984), 176–92, was a product of an NEH Summer Seminar I directed in 1979 at Yale University, where I presented the materials of this section. They were first presented at a NEH Summer Seminar at Johns Hopkins University in 1975.

52. Fried, *Absorption and Theatricality* (San Francisco and Los Angeles, 1980).

53. Robert Griffin, "Samuel Johnson and the Art of Reflection," diss., (Yale University, 1985), p. 6.

54. *Essay concerning Human Understanding,* 2.1.4; ed., Fraser, 1.124.

55. Griffin, p. 35. Reynolds explicitly declared that Johnson taught him the art of thinking (Reynolds, *Portraits,* p. 66).

56. I am indebted for this suggestion to Ellen Spitz, one of the fellows in my NEH Summer Institute of 1988.

57. It is not possible to know whether they were hung together—probably not, since hanging was usually by size. Even in the catalogue entry, though they are listed together, they are not in order; even the two pendant portraits are separated.

58. Broken heart shapes are figured on her chairback. (In *Harlot* 2 Hogarth denoted a cuckold by having the wallpaper behind his head reveal, by an optical illusion, cuckold horns.) The heart-shaped pattern is incom-

plete—open— and perhaps no more than suggestive of a voluptuous female shape, connecting with the sensuousness (as well as naïveté) of Prue's gesture of thumb to lips.

59. Behind the head is a divided background, perhaps a stage set. There is no sign of a window sill: either it is a painted stage set (or french windows) or the painter is asserting the presence of sheer paint in this part of the picture. One-half is black wall or curtain, the other shows a storm brewing, moving toward the front. The dark cloud is opposite Prue's head, a darkness equivalent to, and metonymically related to, her reflections. Here it seems to say that while on the outside Abington–Prue looks one way, inside all is turmoil and storm, her thoughts presumably of Tattle and Robin the butler. But the split background may serve as a visual metaphor for the duality of Abington's appearance (her role) as well as of Prue's state of mind.

60. There is no relevant use of the word "back" in Congreve's play, only the implicit one that Reynolds may have derived from Prue's play with her chair vis-à-vis Ben in the seventh scene of Act 3. Only one verbal use (3.1 by Scandal) refers to Mrs. Foresight's "back"; the others mean *back* as *return* or as *back way* (rear door). See David Mann, *A Concordance to the Plays of William Congreve* (Ithaca, 1973), p. 57.

61. See Paulson, "The English Dog," in *Popular and Polite Art,* pp. 49–63; and, for Nelly O'Brien, *Emblem and Expression,* p. 88.

62. As Valentine says: "For as Tattle has pictures of all that have granted him favors, he has the pictures of all that have refused him, if satires, descriptions, characters, and lampoons are pictures" (p. 34). Scandal describes *his* collection:

> Yes, mine are most in black and white. And yet there are some set out in their true colors, both men and women. I can show you pride, folly, affectation, wantonness, inconstancy, covetousness, dissimulation, malice, and ignorance, all in one piece. Then I can show you lying, foppery, vanity, cowardice, bragging, lechery, impotence, and ugliness in another piece; and yet one of these is a celebrated beauty, and t'other a professed beau.

He goes on to say that he has "some hieroglyphics too," that is, emblematic portraits of "a lawyer with a hundred hands, two heads, and but one face," and "a divine with two faces, and one head," and so on.

63. Cf. Robert Hughes in *Time,* 19 Nov. 1984, p. 133: "That immense, glossy brown form of the horse, floating across one's whole field of vision, has the compulsive power of a dream image." This section, originally appearing in *Raritan,* 4 (1985), 22–43, took off from the Stubbs exhibition at the Tate Gallery in 1984–85. The catalogue, from which I take my contemporary quotations, is Judy Egerton, *George Stubbs, 1724–1806* (London, 1984).

64. R. S. Crane, "The Houyhnhnms, the Yahoos, and the History of Ideas," in *The Idea of the Humanities and Other Essays Critical and Historical* (Chicago, 1967), 2.261–82.

65. See Basil Taylor, "George Stubbs: 'The Lion and Horse' Theme," *Bur-

lington Magazine, 57 (1965), 81–86. The Pergamene group, given its fame and appearance in illustrations, was certainly intended by Stubbs as an allusion. (See Haskell and Penny, *Taste and the Antique,* p. 250.)

66. Egerton, *George Stubbs,* p. 182.

67. Hughes, p. 133; Taylor, *Stubbs* (New York and London, 1971), p. 30.

68. Berenson, quoted, Lawrence Gowing, *TLS,* 23 Mar. 1984, p. 313.

69. Gowing, p. 313.

70. See Egerton, *George Stubbs,* pp. 60, 182.

71. Quoted, ibid., p. 182.

72. Cf. John Barrell, *TLS,* 9 Nov. 1984, p. 1285; for John Berger, see, e.g., *Ways of Seeing* (London, 1972).

73. Egerton, p. 60.

74. Barrell, *TLS,* p. 1285. Barrell has developed the idea in *The Political Theory of Painting from Reynolds to Hazlitt: 'The Body of the Public'* (New Haven, 1986). Barrell thinks that Reynolds transcends the discourse of property by raising his representations into universals—a Keppel to an Apollo Belvedere, a Siddons to a Tragic Muse. But of course this is only to turn one kind of commodity into another: a human into an art object, whose market price is raised by the elevation of the representation.

75. Swift, *Prose Works,* ed. Herbert Davis, 13 (Oxford, 1959), 9.

76. Barrell, *The Dark Side of the Landscape,* p. 30; see pp. 25–31; and the *TLS* review.

77. This analysis emerged from my discussion with Jules Prown, David Solkin, and other participants in the NEH Summer Institute held at Yale University in the summer of 1985.

78. Cf. my discussion of Turner's name in *Literary Landscape* (New Haven, 1982), pp. 98–101.

79. The Yale painting, which I have discussed, is, to be sure, a contracted version of the other paintings of *The Reapers.* By removing the central pair, and especially the woman, Stubbs has concentrated the relationship between the now chief laborer and overseer, and at the same time—hardly even by intention, since it is effected by the removal of the other figures and stays in exactly the same place—centered the church spire.

In the full (oil-on-canvas) version of *The Reapers* in the Tate (very plainly painted on a wood panel), the chief man now, though probably looking toward the overseer, could be regarding the central woman. She, in the exact center horizontally, breaks the row of apparently bowing reapers, intervening between the two main figures (antagonists), laborer and overseer. In the engraving the central female laborer is enlarged, softened, and sentimentalized. In this version Stubbs's signature overlaps stubble *and* a bound sheaf, as if to say that he begins with stubble, what is left after the reaping, but produces his own bound sheaf.

80. The painting itself pleased the patron, to judge by the evidence of the number of copies (of this and the pendant) in oil, and the general public as well since it was reproduced in both ceramics and engravings.

81. See Paulson, *Book and Painting,* pp. 91–96.

82. See Paulson, *Literary Landscape*, pp. 126–32.

83. On Constable and property, see Michael Rosenthal, *Constable: The Painter and His Landscape* (New Haven, 1983) and Bermingham, *Landscape and Ideology*, chap. 3. This is of course to adopt property as a discourse more appropriate to Constable than to Turner, for example: Turner, we could say, who added history to his landscape to legitimate it as history painting, also did so in order to *possess* it. But that seems to me to miss the point about Turner, whose discourse is focused on moral and/or metaphysical matters (much closer in their way to Hogarth's comic histories).

84. Bermingham, in lectures delivered for the 1988 NEH Summer Institute in Word-Image at The Johns Hopkins University.

85. *Literary Landscape*, pp. 126–32.

86. *John Constable's Discourses*, ed. R. B. Beckett (Ipswich, 1970), pp. 40–41, 46–47.

87. I did not write about *The White Horse* in *Literary Landscape* because it was being restored and I had no opportunity to examine the original, which in this case was crucial; this section first appeared as a part of "From White Horse to Leaping Horse: The Landscapes of Constable and Ruisdael" in *Bennington Review*, 14 (1982), 66–76.

88. See James Heffernan, *The Re-Creation of Landscape* (Hanover, 1984), pp. 201–24.

89. Rosenthal, *Constable*, p. 120.

90. We could extend this discussion to the Hampstead paintings, the most frequently painted scene being Branch Hill Pond, with humans on its banks, sometimes venturing in to swim. It is a sand pit, and sand is being dug out of its margins. Labor is very much on the margin of the body of water.

91. *Discourses*, p. 63; Paulson, *Literary Landscape*, p. 126.

92. *Discourses*, p. 64.

93. *Correspondence*, 6.216–17.

94. An essay by H. Kauffmann ("Jacob van Ruisdael: 'Die Mühle von Wijk bei Duurstede,'" *Festschrift für Otto von Simson zum 65. Geburtstag*, ed. L. Grisebach and K. Renger [Frankfurt a.M., 1977], pp. 379–97) links the windmill to emblems of wind turning the arms of a windmill with such mottoes as "The letter killeth, but the spirit giveth life" or "They are moved by the spirit." If nothing else, this scholarship suggests something of our feeling about the windmill—that to say it is a windmill is not sufficient.

95. It is also possible to note of *The Windmill at Wijk* that the windmill as subject appears not in a purely, unmediatedly natural space but rather in a commercial space. Into the Dutch collector's chamber is injected the ideas of possession, business, and labor—even the commerce of shipping the product of the mill to other, perhaps foreign ports. There is a representation of commerce, but there is also a transcendence of commerce and labor, in its own way as striking as Wright's in the *Air Pump:* the Dutch analogy would be with Jan Vermeer's magic room, a woman in sunlight, and an Annunciation or even a Danaë implicit.

Index

Addison, Joseph, 1, 4, 30, 78, 193, 197–98, 346n48; essay on the georgic, 40, 50, 52–53, 59, 77; "Pleasures of the Imagination," 2, 9, 188
Ariès, Philippe, 239, 240, 244
Aristotle, 248; *Poetics*, 283, 285
Ashcroft, Richard, 350n5

Bacon, John: Monument for Herman Katencamp, 239; Monument for Richard Solly, 237
Bakhtin, Mikhail, 12–13, 86–87
Barrell, John, 246, 309, 312–13
Barry, James, 3, 301
Baudelaire, Charles, 199
Beckett, Samuel, 23–24
Bentley, Richard, 77
Bentley, Richard, Jr., illustration for Gray's *Elegy*, 20, 21, 121, 156, 218
Berenson, Bernard, 304
Berger, John, 246
Bermingham, Ann, 266, 268, 274, 317
Bindman, David, 230–31
Blackstone, Sir William, *Commentaries*, 246, 247
Blake, William, 312
Boswell, James, 279–81
Boucher, François, 274
Bowles, William Lisle, 121, 135, 341n22

Boyle, Robert, 155
Brown, Lancelot (called Capability), 155, 268, 349n36
Bryson, Norman, 343n14
Buckingham, second duke of (George Villiers), 98–99; *The Rehearsal*, 98
Burke, Edmund, 4, 13, 124, 197–98, 200, 348n18; *Philosophical Enquiry . . .* , 212, 213–16, 218–19, 228, 244, 298; *Reflections on the Revolution in France*, 111, 257
Burke, Joseph, 272
Burnet, Gilbert, 100, 106
Burton, John, *Complete New System of Midwifery*, 298, 299
Burton, Robert, *The Anatomy of Melancholy*, 100, 207
Butler, Samuel, *Hudibras*, 155, 169
Byron, Lord (George Gordon), 5, 94–95, 107–11, 135, 141, 230; *Cain*, 125; *Childe Harold*, 95, 111, 125; *Corsair, The*, 125; "Detached Thoughts," 108, 112, 340n19; *Don Juan*, 18, 94, 95–96, 108–9, 111–34, 138, 142; *Manfred*, 125; *Marino Faliero*, 111, 125; *On Leaving Newstead Abbey*, 115, 118–19; *Two Foscari, The*, 125; *Vision of Judgment, The*, 116, 121–22

Calvin, John, 18, 19, 153–54, 155, 168, 259
Campbell, Jill, 169
Caravaggio: *Conversion of St. Paul,* 304–5, 312; *Entombment of Christ,* 305
Carew, Thomas: *To My Friend G. N. from Wrest,* 116; *To Saxham,* 116
Caryll, John, 12, 61, 78
Cervantes, Miguel de, *Don Quixote,* 86, 126
Chaucer, Geoffrey, Pope's translation of, 337n31
Cibber, Colley, 29, 34, 57, 68, 110, 339n42
Cipriani, Giovanni Battista, 348n24
Claude Lorrain, 276, 317, 327
Collins, William, 4, 219; *Ode on the Popular Superstitions of the Highlands,* 217–18; *Ode to Fear,* 348n18; *Odes,* 216; *Persian Eclogues,* 216
Congreve, William, *Love for Love,* 281, 283, 286–89, 290, 292, 293–96
Constable, John, 3, 11, 274; *Cornfield, The,* 324, 325; *Hadleigh Castle,* 318; *Hay Wain, The,* 317, 323; *Leaping Horse, The,* 317, 320–21, 322, 323, 325; *Salisbury Cathedral from the Meadows,* 318, 319, 323; *Stour Valley,* 329; *Stratford Mill,* 317, 319, 323; *White Horse, The,* 317, 318, 319–24, 327, 328, 329
Copley, John Singleton: *Death of Lord Chatham,* 228; *Death of Major Pierson,* 228
Cotton, Charles: *Epitaph for His Uncle Robert Port,* 46; *Scarronides,* 155
Cowley, Abraham, 199
Craftsman, The, 158, 170, 171
Cummings, Frederick, 205–8
Curll, Edmund, 63, 76, 96
Cyprian, 26

Davenant, Sir William, 334n46
David, Jacques-Louis, 15, 229
Davies of Hereford, John, *An Epitaph upon . . . Sir Thomas Gorge,* 43
Defoe, Daniel, 35; *Robinson Crusoe,* 8–9, 10–11, 132, 155
Dennis, John, 61, 63, 81, 91
Diderot, Denis, 291; *Encyclopédie,* 224
Dioscuri, 274
Domenichino, *Martyrdom of St. Agnes,* 151–52
Dryden, John, 104, 114, 156, 334n51, 345n29; *Absalom and Achitophel,* 79; *Conquest of Granada, The,* 97–98; *Indian Queen, The,* 97; *Mac Flecknoe,* 79, 91; translation of Virgil, 50
Dürer, Albrecht, 165; *Annunciation, The,* 179, 180; *Visitation, The,* 179

Edwards, Thomas, 80
Ehrenpreis, Irvin, 22
Erskine-Hill, Howard, 66
Etherege, Sir George, *The Man of Mode,* 99, 104–6

Fabricant, Carole, 28
Ferguson, Frances, 267, 348n21
Fielding, Henry, 9, 33, 77, 155, 169, 192; *Jonathan Wild,* 87, 170; *Joseph Andrews,* 87, 285; *Tom Jones,* 10, 87, 100, 239, 285; *Tom Thumb,* 179, 345n25
Filmer, Robert, 247, 257
Fortescue, William, 88, 249
Fragonard, Jean-Baptiste, 295
Fried, Michael, 289, 290, 331n4
Friendly Vindication of Mr. Dryden, The, 99
Frost, Robert, 23

Gainsborough, Thomas, 3, 11, 258, 268–69, 274–77, 299, 301, 309, 311, 315, 327; *Classical Landscape,* 276–77; *Cottage Girl . . . ,* 272;

Deposition by Rubens, copy, 272–74; *Harvest Wagon, The*, 270, 271, 272, 274; portrait of Garrick, 233; *Two Shepherd Boys*, 271; *View of St. Mary's Church, Hadleigh*, 269, 270, 352n33; *Wooded Landscape . . .* , 270, 274; *Woodsman, The*, 272

Gardiner, Stephen, 16

Garth, Sir Samuel, 54

Gay, John, 155, 346n47; *Beggar's Opera, The*, 175–77, 187; *Polly*, 177–79, 185; *Shepherd's Week*, 40, 272

Gilpin, Sawrey, 301, 317

Goldsmith, Oliver, *The Vicar of Wakefield*, 281

Goodman, Christopher, 96

Gowing, Sir Lawrence, 304

Goya y Lucientes, Francisco de: *Disparates*, 297; *Family of Charles VI*, 307

Graves, Richard, *On Gainsborough's Landskips . . .* , 271

Gray, Thomas, 4, 219; *Bard, The*, 82–83, 214; *Descent of Odin, The*, 83; *Elegy Written in a Country Churchyard*, 20, 21, 40–46, 208, 218, 270, 272; *Progress of Poesy, The*, 83

Greuze, Jean-Baptiste, 222, 289, 291

Gribelin, Simon, 3

Griffin, Robert, 290

Guardian, The, 55, 62–63

Hamilton, Gavin, *Death of Hector*, 227, 229

Havelock, Eric A., 16

Haydon, Benjamin Robert, 3

Hayes, John, 275, 276, 352n33

Hervey, Lord, 61, 64, 87, 91; *Verses Address'd to the Imitator of Horace* (with Lady Montague), 252–53, 254

Hesiod: *Hymn to the Muses*, 16; *Works and Days*, 40

Hoare, Henry, 175

Hogarth, William, 1, 3, 4, 11, 33, 35, 77, 124, 169, 244, 254–55, 261, 267–68, 278, 285; *Analysis of Beauty, The*, 4–5, 8, 18, 133, 159, 166, 167–68, 184, 192–202, 220, 244, 256–59, 269 (plates from, 39, 156, 157, 160–65, 190, 212, 214, 223, 224, 238, 255–56, 265, 272); *Battle of the Pictures, The*, 215; *Beggar's Opera* paintings, 175–79, 180–81, 185, 189, 190, 235; *Boys Peeping at Nature*, 155, 181, 189, 195, 197, 224; *Cholmondeley Family, The*, 353n47; *Credulity, Superstition, and Fanaticism*, 152; *Distrest Poet, The*, 154, 186; *Election*, 215; *Enraged Musician, The*, 154, 184, 187–88, 215; *Evening*, 265; *Gin Lane*, 149, 152, 313; *Great Seal of England, The*, 171–72; *Harlot's Progress, A*, 151, 152, 164, 172, 174–78, 179, 181, 185, 190, 192, 195, 286, 344n16, 353n58; *Industry and Idleness*, 184, 186, 193, 201, 269, 352n33; *Lady's Last Shake, The*, 201; *Lord Hervey and His Friends*, 263; *Marriage A-la-mode*, 151, 165, 167, 183, 195, 201, 261, 312; *Midnight Modern Conversation, A*, 353n47; *Paul before Felix*, 201, 316; *Pool of Bethesda, The*, 184, 260; *Rake's Progress, A*, 159, 167, 170, 182–83, 190, 191, 342n2; *Satan, Sin, and Death*, 188–90, 218–19, 235, 348n18; *Scene from 'The Tempest,'* 184, 185, 189–90; *Sleeping Congregation, The*, 20, 149–53, 191; *South Sea Scheme*, 152; *Southwark Fair*, 187; *Stages of Cruelty*, 201; *Strolling Actresses Dressing in a Barn*, 165–67, 186–87, 198, 199, 285, 290, 346n35, 346n46; *Tailpiece, or The Bathos*, 196, 213–15, 219; *Time Smoking a Picture*, 245, 343n11; *Times*, 215

Homer, 16, 57, 229; *Iliad,* 49, 66; *Odyssey,* Pope's translation, 63, 77–78, 80, 83

Horace, 49, 57, 100–101, 119, 169, 251–54

Howard, Sir Robert, 97

Hughes, Robert, 303

Hume, David, 22; *Essays, Moral and Political,* 219, 229; *History of England,* 168

Hutcheson, Francis, *Inquiry concerning Beauty . . . ,* 192–93, 197, 200, 202, 212, 229, 290

Jerome, St., 26–27, 35

Johnson, Samuel, 42, 156, 259; *Dictionary,* 14, 18, 290; *Rambler,* 289, 290; *Rasselas,* 144

Jonson, Ben, 28; *Charles Cavendish to His Posteritie,* 42–43, 45, 211, 239–40; *To Penshurst,* 116; *Volpone,* 104, 106

Juvenal, *Satire* 6, 25

Kant, Immanuel, 4, 5, 13

Kauffmann, Angelica, *Cleopatra Decorating the Tomb of Mark Antony,* 227, 228

Keats, John, 111, 124, 125

Kelsall, Malcolm, 95, 116

Kernan, Alvin, 80, 339n39

Kibbey, Ann, 339n29

Krieger, Murray, 69–70

Laud, Archbishop, 17, 34

Lely, Sir Peter, *Nell Gwynne,* 260

Lesage, Alain-René, 110

Lessing, Gotthold Ephraim, *Laocoon,* 198, 346n45

Lewis, M. G., *The Monk,* 133

Lillo, George, 169

Locke, John, 20–22, 193–94; *Essay concerning Human Understanding,* 248, 256, 289–90; *Second Treatise on Government,* 5, 7, 11, 247–49, 254, 255, 256–57, 265, 267, 268

Mack, Maynard, 63, 80, 338n36, 339n45

McKenzie, Henry, 220, 222

McKeon, Michael, 13, 32

Mackintosh, James, *Vindiciae Gallicae,* 110–11, 123–24

Marvell, Andrew, *Upon Appleton House,* 116

Mattheis, Paulo de, *The Judgment of Hercules,* 3, 172, 173, 175

Milton, John, 107, 109, 123, 180, 334n51; *Paradise Lost,* 49, 53, 56, 79, 85–86, 90, 169, 188–91, 195–96, 199, 215

Montague, Lady Mary Wortley, 57, 61, 63, 72, 87, 110; *Verses Address'd to the Imitator of Horace* (with Lord Hervey), 252–53, 254

Montfaucon, Bernard de, *Antiquités,* 233

Moore, Leslie, 188

Nicolson, Benedict, 204–6

Nicolson, Marjorie, 61

Nussbaum, Felicity, 25, 27

Ortega y Gasset, José, 332n14

Ovid, 154; *Acis and Galathea,* 61–62, 70; *Amores,* 103; *Metamorphoses,* 56–59, 71; *Remedies for Love,* 25; *Sappho to Phaon,* 62, 72

Paine, Thomas, *Common Sense,* 121

Palmer, Samuel, 266

Panofsky, Irwin, 348n24

Parker, Matthew, 152

Parsons, Robert, 106

Penney, Nicolas, 231

Perkins, William, 17

Philips, Ambrose, 52, 53, 55, 63, 216

Phillips, John, 16

Piper, David, 78, 79

Piranesi, Giambattista, 344n15

Pointon, Marcia, 271–72

Pope, Alexander, 4, 5–6, 8, 30, 32, 35, 39, 46, 94, 95–96,

99, 107–10, 119, 121, 123, 124, 127, 156, 170, 191, 248, 334n51, 342n33; *Cleopatra,* 74, 337–38n33; *Dunciad, The,* 37, 42, 48–49, 60, 68, 75, 76–77, 78–87, 88, 90–93, 122, 124, 135, 143, 154, 191–92, 200, 214, 216–17, 250–51; *Elegy to the Memory of an Unfortunate Lady,* 73; *Eloisa to Abelard,* 69–73, 74–75; *Epilogue to the Satires,* 69, 72, 82 (Dialogue 1, 56, 84, 89–90, 158, 252, 337n33, 345n25; Dialogue 2, 65, 88–89, 250, 341n33); *Epistle to Augustus,* 68, 111; *Epistle to Bathhurst,* 50–51, 90, 250, 251; *Epistle to Burlington,* 49–51, 74, 88, 156; *Epistle to Dr. Arbuthnot,* 38, 54, 76, 87–88, 230, 250, 252; *Epistle* II.ii of Horace, imitation, 251, 252, 254; *Essay on Criticism, An,* 63, 77; *Essay on Man, An,* 78, 92; *Key to the Lock, The,* 66, 91; *Messiah,* 55, 92; *Ode for Musick,* 60, 74–75; *Pastorals,* 53, 75 (*Spring,* 54, 338n33; *Summer,* 53, 54, 61, 63, 70, 72, 90, 336n19; *Autumn,* 54; *Winter,* 54, 70, 216); *Peri Bathous,* 80–81; *Rape of the Lock, The,* 24, 28, 31, 49, 51–52, 58–59, 61–63, 64–67, 69, 70, 72, 73, 81, 88, 91, 137, 169, 196, 287, 338n33, 345n27; *Satire* II.ii of Horace, imitation, 87, 89, 251–52, 253; *Temple of Fame, The,* 67–69, 73, 92; *Windsor Forest,* 11, 52, 53, 55, 57–58, 66, 320; *See also* Chaucer; Homer; Shakespeare
Pothos (Scopas), 233, 237
Poussin, Nicolas, 229; *Death of Germanicus,* 227; *Et in Arcadia Ego,* 20, 227

Raguenet, Abbé, *Monumens de Rome,* 164–65, 224

Ramsay, Allan, *Chief of McCloud,* 162
Randolph, Thomas, *Epitaph upon His Honoured Friend,* 45
Raphael: cartoons, 169; *Disputa,* 310; *Expulsion of Heliodorus,* 274
Rembrandt van Rijn, 278
Reynolds, Sir Joshua, 3, 11, 199, 227, 277–79, 301, 309, 311, 315, 326; *Boy Reading,* 288; *Commodore Keppel,* 162, 258, 278; *Cupid as a Link Boy,* 287; *Discourses on Art,* 283; *Garrick between the Comic and Tragic Muse,* 282–83, 285; *Ino and the Infant Bacchus,* 294; *Mrs. Abington as the Comic Muse,* 282–83, 284; *Mrs. Abington as Miss Prue,* 279–96; *Mrs. Siddons as the Tragic Muse,* 226, 258, 281–83; *Resignation,* 289; *Theophila Palmer Reading,* 279, 281, 282, 288–89, 291–94; *Venus Chiding Cupid . . . ,* 294
Richardson, Jonathan, 3, 212; *Explanatory Notes . . . on Milton's 'Paradise Lost,'* 188–91, 199
Richardson, Samuel, 87; *Clarissa,* 169, 180, 181, 222, 279, 289, 292, 293; *Pamela,* 9, 169, 239, 285
Rochester, Lord (John Wilmot), 96, 98–99, 106–7, 114; *Allusion to Horace, An,* 100–101, 104; *Artemesia to Chloe,* 102; *Disabled Debauchee, The,* 103; *Imperfect Enjoyment, The,* 99, 103–4, 105; *Ramble in St. James's Park, A,* 99, 104, 105; *Satyr against Reason and Mankind,* 102; *Scepter Lampoon,* 101–2; *Timon,* 102; *Very Heroical Epistle . . . ,* 105
Rosenthal, Michael, 321
Roubiliac, Louis-François, 220, 231, 233; Monument to John, Duke of Argyle, 235; Monument to George Lynn, 242, 245; Monument to Hargrave, 213, 214, 233, 243; Monument to Lady

Roubiliac, Louis-François (*continued*)
Nightingale, 233, 234, 235;
Monument to Richard Boyle,
242, 245
Rousseau, Jean-Jacques, 4; *Discourse
on the Origin of Inequality*, 257; *La
nouvelle Héloïse*, 207, 208
Rowlandson, Thomas, 260, 261;
Dance of Death, 125, 128; *Statuary
Yard, A*, 261, 262
Rubens, Peter Paul, 275, 276; *De-
scent from the Cross*, 272, 273, 274
Ruisdael, Jacob van, 270, 274, 275,
323–24, 328, 329; *La Forêt*, 276;
Jewish Cemetery, The, 324, 325, 326;
Windmill at Wijk, The, 325–26
Ryan, Alan, 248
Rysback, Michael, 157, 158, 213,
231, 233, 235

Sanders, August, 313
Scarron, Paul, *Virgile travesti*, 155
Scheemakers, Peter, Monument to
Shakespeare, 231–33
Scodel, Joshua, 45, 46
Scott, Sir Walter, 111
Shaftesbury, third earl of (Anthony
Ashley Cooper), 192, 197, 199,
200, 202, 212, 229, 248; *Charac-
teristics . . .* , 2–3, 4, 5, 8, 344 n 19;
*Notion of the . . . Judgment of Her-
cules, The*, 3, 168, 172–75
Shakespeare, William, 79, 151,
231– 33; Pope's edition, 77–78,
80, 83; *Romeo and Juliet*, 287;
Tempest, The, 184, 185
Shelley, Percy Bysshe, 124
Sheridan, Richard Brinsley, 108
Simpson, David, 141
Slepian, Barry, 39
Smith, Adam, 249; *Wealth of Na-
tions*, 258–59
Smollett, Tobias, *Travels through
France and Italy*, 221
Southey, Robert, 99, 109, 110, 112,
122, 123, 124, 125; *Wat Tyler*, 134

Spectator, The, 2, 34, 35, 52, 96, 188,
197, 331 n 7, 346 n 48
Spence, Joseph, 161, 163; *Polymetis*,
165, 343 n 12
Stallybrass, Peter, 337 n 27
Stechow, Wolfgang, 275
Steele, Richard, 52, 336 n 20; *Chris-
tian Hero, The*, 169, 184
Sterne, Laurence, 33, 110; *Sentimen-
tal Journey, A*, 219, 221; *Tristram
Shandy*, 10, 12, 109, 125–26, 133,
219–22, 347 n 50
Stubbs, George, 11; *Anatomy of the
Horse*, 297; *Cheetah and Stag . . .* ,
302; *Comparative Anatomical Expo-
sition*, 298, 317; *Freeman . . .* , 298;
Gimcrack, 299–301, 306; *Hamble-
tonian*, 297–99, 303–11, 316–17;
John and Sophia Musters . . . , 309;
Lion Attacking a Horse, A, 303–4;
Prince of Wales' Phaeton, The, 312;
Reapers, The, 312–16; *Soldiers of
the 10th Light Dragoons*, 311–12;
Whistlejacket, 305, 310, 316
Sutherland, Graham, portrait of
Winston Churchill, 278, 309
Swift, Jonathan, 4, 8, 10, 20, 22–23,
33, 35, 56, 69, 74, 95, 99, 105,
108, 191, 248, 251; *Battle of the
Books, The*, 29, 31; *Baucis and Phi-
lemon*, 154–55; *Beautiful Young
Nymph Going to Bed, A*, 26, 27, 28,
151; *Day of Judgement, The*, 37;
Description of a City Shower, A, 28;
Description of the Morning, A, 36;
Epistle I.vii of Horace, imitation,
36–37; *Gulliver's Travels*, 155,
301; *Instructions to Servants*, 311;
Lady's Dressing Room, The, 27–28,
32; *Progress of Beauty, The*, 26, 28,
151; *Progress of Poetry, The*, 37,
315; *Strephon and Chloe*, 27, 28, 32;
Tale of a Tub, A, 2, 10, 28, 29, 30,
36, 37, 38, 44, 86, 100, 344 n 51;
*Upon the Martyrdom of King Charles
I*, 23–24; *Vanbrugh's House . . . ,*

28–32; *Verses on the Death of Dr. Swift,* 24–25, 35–40, 42–46, 83

Taylor, Basil, 299, 303
Tertullian, 25–26, 35
Theobald, Lewis, *Shakespeare Restored,* 78, 81, 91
Thornhill, Sir James, 175, 184, 185
Tickell, Thomas, 52, 53, 63, 216, 217
Titian: *Charles V,* 308; *Martyrdom of St. Peter Martyr,* 319; *Venus of Urbino,* 262
Turnbull, George, 1; *Treatise upon Ancient Painting,* 3
Turner, J. M.W., 3, 315, 317, 356n83; *Regulus,* 328

Underwood, Dale, 25

Valle, Filippo della, *Livia, Wife of Augustus* (or *Pudicity*), 158
Van Dyck, Anthony, 261, 275, 301
Vanaken, Joseph, 260–61
Vanbrugh, John, 29, 30, 31; *The Relapse,* 29
Velazquez, Diego, *Las Meninas,* 307, 310
Virgil: *Aeneid,* 56, 80, 290; *Eclogues,* 53, 55, 335n9 (fourth ["Pollio"], 49, 55, 60, 80); *Georgic(s),* 11, 40, 50, 51, 56, 249 (first, 28, 128; third, 59; fourth, 8, 40, 59, 84, 129)

Warton, Thomas, the Elder, *Verses on Henry the Eighth's Seizing . . . ,* 218
Watt, Ian, 13
Webster, Mary, 263
Wesley, John, 233
West, Benjamin, 3; *Death of General Wolfe,* 227–29, 258
White, Allon, 337n27

Wijnants, Johannes, 275
Williams, Aubrey, 80
Williams, Raymond, 246
Wilmot, John, second earl of Rochester. *See* Rochester, Lord
Wilson, Richard, 299, 311, 320, 327, 348n24
Wilton, Joseph, 220; Monument to Lady Anne Dawson, 237
Wimsatt, W. K., 78
Wind, Edgar, 230, 269
Winn, James, 99
Woodall, Mary, 276
Wordsworth, William, 4, 5, 109, 112, 122, 124; *Excursion, The,* 7, 135, 136, 142; *Lines . . . above Tintern Abbey,* 134, 136–41, 146; *Lyrical Ballads,* 6–7, 135, 142, 144–46; *Nutting,* 144–45; *Peter Bell,* 135; *Prelude, The,* 7, 123, 126, 136, 137, 138, 141–46; *Thorn, The,* 144, 145
Wright of Derby, Joseph, 219–20, 226–29, 235, 265–66, 314; *Academy by Lamplight, An,* 224–26; *Blacksmith's Forge, The,* 20, 121, 203–6, 227, 327; *Brooke Boothby,* 206–8, 211, 226, 237; *Corinthian Maid,* 318; *Experiment with an Air Pump, An,* 222–24; *Miravan Opening the Tomb of His Ancestors,* 45, 208–12, 237–38; paintings to illustrate Sterne, 219–22
Wycherley, William: *Country Wife, The,* 54, 99, 104–5, 106; *Plain Dealer, The,* 54

Young, Edward, *Conjectures on Original Composition,* 48

Zoffany, Johann, 224, 258, 261–63; *Sharp Family, The,* 263–65; *William Ferguson . . . ,* 263